# Accounting for Managers

## A Business Decision Guide

## Third Edition

Steven M. Bragg

Published by AccountingTools, Inc., Centennial, Colorado.



For more information about AccountingTools® products, visit our Web site at www.accountingtools.com.

ISBN-13: 978-1-64221-022-4

Printed in the United States of America

# Table of Contents

# Preface

Managers are constantly confronted with situations in which they need to make decisions based on information originating in the accounting department. In *Accounting for Managers: A Business Decision Guide*, we explore the accounting information available to managers, and how the information can be employed to improve operational and financial results. The topics covered include the interpretation of financial statements, responsibility centers, relevant accounting standards, decision making issues in specific departments, and a variety of analysis tools. As examples of the topics covered, *Accounting for Managers* provides answers to the following questions:

- How does accounting information roll up into the financial statements?
- What is the purpose of each of the financial statements?
- What are the limitations of ratio analysis?
- How can transfer prices impact the profits of a subsidiary?
- How can the accounting for inventory impact profits?
- Which pricing formulations depend on product cost?
- What methods are available for reducing compensation costs?
- How do I conduct a discounted cash flow analysis?
- Which accounting issues should be investigated during due diligence?
- What methods are available for improving the profitability of new products?
- How do I decide whether to outsource production?
- Which variances from the budget are worth tracking?

*Accounting for Managers: A Business Decision Guide* is intended for managers in any functional area of a business, as well as for those students wanting to learn about management techniques. The book also provides references to the author's popular Accounting Best Practices podcast, which provides additional coverage of many accounting and management topics. As such, it may serve as a reference tool for years to come.

Centennial, Colorado
January 2019

# About the Author

**Steven Bragg, CPA,** has been the chief financial officer or controller of four companies, as well as a consulting manager at Ernst & Young. He received a master's degree in finance from Bentley College, an MBA from Babson College, and a Bachelor's degree in Economics from the University of Maine. He has been a two-time president of the Colorado Mountain Club, and is an avid alpine skier, mountain biker, and certified master diver. Mr. Bragg resides in Centennial, Colorado. He has written the following books and courses:

7 Habits of Effective CEOs
7 Habits of Effective CFOs
7 Habits of Effective Controllers
Accountant Ethics [for multiple states]
Accountants' Guidebook
Accounting Changes and Error Corrections
Accounting Controls Guidebook
Accounting for Casinos and Gaming
Accounting for Derivatives and Hedges
Accounting for Earnings per Share
Accounting for Income Taxes
Accounting for Intangible Assets
Accounting for Inventory
Accounting for Investments
Accounting for Leases
Accounting for Managers
Accounting for Mining
Accounting for Retirement Benefits
Accounting for Stock-Based Compensation
Accounting for Vineyards and Wineries
Accounting Information Systems
Accounting Procedures Guidebook
Activity-Based Costing
Activity-Based Management
Agricultural Accounting
Behavioral Ethics
Bookkeeping Guidebook
Budgeting
Business Combinations and Consolidations
Business Insurance Fundamentals
Business Ratios
Business Valuation
Capital Budgeting
CFO Guidebook
Change Management
Closing the Books
Coaching and Mentoring
Conflict Management
Constraint Management
Construction Accounting
Corporate Bankruptcy
Corporate Cash Management
Corporate Finance
Cost Accounting (college textbook)
Cost Accounting Fundamentals
Cost Management Guidebook
Credit & Collection Guidebook
Crowdfunding
Developing and Managing Teams
Effective Collections
Effective Employee Training
Employee Onboarding
Enterprise Risk Management
Entertainment Industry Accounting
Fair Value Accounting
Financial Analysis
Financial Forecasting and Modeling
Fixed Asset Accounting
Foreign Currency Accounting
Franchise Accounting
Fraud Examination
Fraud Schemes
GAAP Guidebook
Governmental Accounting
Health Care Accounting
Hospitality Accounting
How to Audit Cash
How to Audit Equity
How to Audit Fixed Assets
How to Audit for Fraud

(continued)

How to Audit Inventory
How to Audit Liabilities
How to Audit Receivables
How to Audit Revenue
How to Conduct a Compilation
How to Conduct a Review
How to Run a Meeting
Human Resources Guidebook
IFRS Guidebook
Interpretation of Financial Statements
Inventory Management
Investor Relations Guidebook
Law Firm Accounting
Lean Accounting Guidebook
Mergers & Acquisitions
Money Laundering
Negotiation
New Controller Guidebook
New Manager Guidebook
Nonprofit Accounting
Oil & Gas Accounting
Optimal Accounting for Cash
Optimal Accounting for Payables
Partnership Accounting
Payables Management
Payroll Management
Performance Appraisals
Project Accounting
Project Management
Property Management Accounting
Public Company Accounting
Purchasing Guidebook
Real Estate Accounting
Records Management
Recruiting and Hiring
Revenue Management
Revenue Recognition
Sales and Use Tax Accounting
Succession Planning
The Balance Sheet
The Income Statement
The MBA Guidebook
The Soft Close
The Statement of Cash Flows
The Year-End Close
Treasurer's Guidebook
Working Capital Management

# On-Line Resources by Steven Bragg

Steven maintains the accountingtools.com web site, which contains continuing professional education courses, the Accounting Best Practices podcast, and thousands of articles on accounting subjects.

*Accounting for Managers* is also available as a continuing professional education (CPE) course. You can purchase the course (and many other courses) and take an on-line exam at:

www.accountingtools.com/cpe

# Chapter 1
# The Need for Accounting Information

## Introduction

The manager of a business is required to operate it in such a manner that the entity reliably produces a profit, year after year. Doing so calls for proper strategic positioning, the correct use of resources, and the hiring of a talented group of employees. It also requires a feedback loop to tell the manager how he or she is performing, which is also known as the financial statements. The financial statements are produced by the accounting department, which is responsible for recording all business transactions and converting this information into reports that can be used to operate the organization (known as accountancy). In this chapter, we describe the accountancy concept, financial and managerial accounting, the types of management decisions that require accounting information, and how the remainder of this book is structured.

## The Accountancy Concept

Accountancy is the practice of recording, classifying, and reporting on financial transactions for a business. These tasks are expanded upon as follows:

- *Recordation*. The recording of accounting transactions usually involves several key business transactions that are handled on a repetitive basis, which include the issuance of customer invoices, paying supplier invoices, recording cash receipts from customers, and paying employees. There are also a number of accounting transactions that are non-repetitive in nature, and so require the use of journal entries to record them in the accounting records. Journal entries are explained in the next chapter.
- *Classification*. The results of these recordation activities are accumulated into a set of accounting records, of which the summary document is the general ledger. The general ledger consists of a number of accounts, each of which stores information about a particular type of transaction, such as product sales, accounts receivable, debt, and so on. Certain high-volume transactions, such as customer billings, may be stored in a sub-ledger, with only its totals rolling into the general ledger. The information in the general ledger is used to derive financial statements, and may also be the source of information used for internal management reports.
- *Reporting*. The reporting aspects of accountancy are considerable, and so have been divided into smaller areas of specialization, which are:
    - *Financial accounting*. This area is the province of the general ledger accountant, controller, and chief financial officer, and is concerned

with the accumulation of business transactions into financial statements. These documents are presented based on sets of rules known as accounting frameworks, of which the best known are Generally Accepted Accounting Principles (GAAP) and International Financial Reporting Standards (IFRS).

  - *Management accounting*. This area is the province of the cost accountant and financial analyst, who investigate ways to improve the profitability of a business and present their results to management. Their reports may be derived from the main system of accounts, but may also include separate data accumulation systems. Management accounting is not governed by any accounting framework – the structure of the reports issued to management can be tailored to the needs of the business.

The financial and managerial accounting concepts are addressed at greater length in the next section.

The accountancy function is managed by the corporate controller, which is the position that most managers will interact with on accounting matters. The controller is responsible for the following activities:

- *Transactions*. This involves the proper processing of all types of business transactions, which includes supplier invoices, billings to customers, payroll, and cash receipts and disbursements. It also requires the use of a system of controls to ensure that transactions are processed properly, and a record keeping system in which transactions are recorded and archived.
- *Reporting*. This involves the preparation of the standard set of monthly financial statements, as well as a variety of management reports.
- *Planning*. This involves coordinating the creation of the annual budget, as well as the investigation and reporting of any subsequent variances between it and actual results.
- *Compliance*. This involves compliance with a variety of tax reporting requirements, government reports, debt covenants, and accounting standards.

There may also be a chief financial officer. This position has different responsibilities from those of the controller, which include the following:

- *Planning*. This involves the formulation of the strategic direction of the business and the tactical plans, budgeting systems, and performance metrics required to achieve that direction.
- *Operations*. This involves the direct oversight of a number of departments, as well as coordinating the operations of those departments with other areas of the business. It can also include the selection, purchase, and subsequent integration of acquired businesses.

- *Financial information*. This involves the compilation of financial information into financial statements, and the presentation of this information to various internal and external recipients.
- *Risk management*. This involves understanding the current and potential risks to which the business is subjected and taking steps to mitigate those risks.
- *Financing*. This involves monitoring projected cash balances and arranging for either additional financing or investment options, depending on the amount of expected cash balances.

The manager needs to understand the differences in the roles of the controller and CFO in order to determine which person to approach with accounting questions. In most cases, the controller will be the best source of information about financial and managerial reporting issues.

## Financial and Managerial Accounting

In general, *financial accounting* refers to the aggregation of accounting information into financial statements, while *managerial accounting* refers to the internal processes used to account for and improve upon business transactions. There are a number of differences between financial and managerial accounting, which fall into the following categories:

- *Aggregation*. Financial accounting reports on the results of an entire business. Managerial accounting almost always reports at a more detailed level, such as profits by product, product line, customer, and geographic region.
- *Efficiency*. Financial accounting reports on the profitability (and therefore the efficiency) of a business, whereas managerial accounting reports on specifically what is causing problems and how to fix these issues.
- *Proven information*. Financial accounting requires that records be kept with great precision, which is needed to prove that the financial statements are correct. Managerial accounting frequently deals with estimates, rather than proven and verifiable facts.
- *Reporting focus*. Financial accounting is oriented toward the creation of financial statements, which are distributed both within and outside of a company. Managerial accounting is more concerned with operational reports, which are only distributed within a company.
- *Standards*. Financial accounting must comply with various accounting standards, whereas managerial accounting does not have to comply with any standards when it compiles information for internal consumption.
- *Systems*. Financial accounting pays no attention to the overall system that a company has for generating a profit, only its outcome. Conversely, managerial accounting is interested in the location of bottleneck operations, and the various ways to enhance profits by resolving bottleneck issues.

- *Time period.* Financial accounting is concerned with the financial results that a business has already achieved, so it has a historical orientation. Managerial accounting may address budgets and forecasts, and so has a somewhat greater orientation toward the future.
- *Timing.* Financial accounting requires that financial statements be issued following the end of a reporting period. Managerial accounting may issue reports much more frequently, since the information it provides is of most relevance if managers can see it right away.
- *Valuation.* Financial accounting addresses the proper valuation of assets and liabilities, and so is involved with impairments, revaluations, and so forth. Managerial accounting is not concerned with the value of these items, only their productivity.

From the perspective of the manager, the financial accounting area provides the financial statements that yield a general overview of a company's results and financial condition. Since these documents are only an overview, managers must then turn to managerial accounting reports to obtain more detailed information about how to manage operations.

## Decisions Requiring Accounting Information

This section provides a sampling of the multitude of management decisions that require the use of accounting information. All of these decisions are discussed later in *Accounting for Managers*:

- *How well am I managing company assets?* To answer this question, use the asset turnover measurements described in the Interpreting Financial Statements chapter. The results can be compared to historical turnover rates or industry standards to see how well the company is performing on a comparative basis.
- *Do I have enough cash to support sales?* A business may run out of cash because it does not have sufficient working capital to support increased customer demand. This can come as quite a surprise, and requires continual monitoring to avoid. The sales to working capital ratio, found in the Interpreting Financial Statements chapter, can be used to evaluate the cash level.
- *Am I collecting the right information for departmental reporting?* It is difficult to have an effective departmental reporting structure unless business transactions are being stored in a certain format. The correct chart of accounts structure needed for this task is described in the Evaluation of Responsibility Centers chapter.
- *Will a contingent event appear in the financial statements?* A company may face the prospect of a large expense, though it has not yet occurred. There are specific rules for when these expenses must be included in the financial statements, which are described in the Overview of Selected Accounting Standards chapter.

- *How far can sales decline before I lose money?* The margin of safety measures the amount by which sales can drop before a company reaches its breakeven point, as described in the Sales and Marketing Decisions chapter.
- *When is someone classified as an employee or a contractor?* A company must withhold payroll taxes and match certain taxes if a person is an employee, but does not have to do so if the person can be classified as a contractor. This issue is dealt with in the Human Resources Decisions chapter.
- *When should I fund a research project?* There is no perfect funding level for research and development activities, but the expected commercial value concept can be used to quantify possible outcomes of such funding. The measure is located in the Investment Decisions chapter.
- *Which acquisition structure reduces taxes?* When an acquisition is being negotiated, the seller may want to defer the recognition of income in order to put off paying income taxes. This can be achieved with a variety of acquisition structures, which are outlined in the Acquisition Decisions chapter.
- *How can I match overhead to specific activities?* It is not possible to precisely match overhead costs with certain activities, but it is possible to bring the two into close alignment through an activity-based costing project. How to do so is described in the Cost Accounting Tools and Concepts chapter.
- *How can I design products that always earn a profit?* The product design staff in most companies creates new products without close attention to whether their built-in costs will allow a profit to be earned. The target costing concept integrates close attention to costs into the design process, as outlined in the Target Costing chapter.
- *Should I sell at a lower price?* A customer asks for a lower price in exchange for a large order. Should the deal be accepted? Constraint analysis is a modeling tool that can be used to determine the net result of the lower price point, as noted in the Constraint Analysis chapter.
- *Which variances should I follow?* A manager can be snowed under by variance analysis reports. The benefit of each variance is described in the Budgetary Control chapter. In most cases, only a few variances need to be tracked; the others do not yield actionable information.

This section only provided the accounting-supported answer to a single question from each chapter in *Accounting for Managers* (with a few exceptions). In the following chapters, each of these management decisions are expanded upon, while a number of related topics are also addressed.

## The Structure of this Book

*Accounting for Managers* begins in Chapter 2 with an overview of how accounting information is compiled and then translated into financial statements. The structure of each financial statement is discussed in Chapter 3, along with permissible alternative formats. This preliminary information is needed as the basis for a lengthy discussion of how one can extract information from the financial statements, as noted in Chapter 4. We then move to a discussion in Chapter 5 of an alternative format for the financial statements, where the traditional reports are reconfigured for use by responsibility centers. Finally, the discussion of financial statements concludes in Chapter 6 with a summarization of those accounting standards that can impact general management activities.

The cluster of chapters just described spans the financial accounting topic, which centers on the creation and use of the financial statements. Every manager must have a working knowledge of these financial accounting topics, since any review of their performance will likely be based, at least in part, on the financial statements.

Chapters 7 through 10 deal with management decisions in specific functional areas, such as sales and marketing and human resources. We also cover specific types of decisions that do not fall within a functional area in the Investment Decisions chapter. There is separate treatment of the acquisitions topic, which covers a multitude of decision points. The focus of these chapters is on managerial accounting, with the intent of enhancing operations and making better decisions in very specific areas. Sample topics are cost-volume-profit analysis, price formulation, payroll processing, unemployment insurance, compensation cost reductions, whether to invest in fixed assets, due diligence issues, and acquisition legal structures.

The remaining five chapters continue with the managerial accounting theme, but now focus on decision tools, rather than functional or decision areas. We describe direct costing and activity-based costing in Chapter 11, with an emphasis on specific situations in which each tool can improve management decisions. Chapter 12 turns to the concept of target costing, which is used in the design of products to ensure that targeted price points and costs are built into the design considerations. In Chapter 13, we address the important topic of constraint analysis, in which proper management of a bottleneck operation is used to enhance the profitability of an entire organization. And in the final two chapters, we cover the detailed construction of a company-wide budget and how a system of control can be established that is based on that budget. Depending upon the management structure of a business, budgetary control may be the key tool used to monitor operations and financial results.

In short, we use the first third of *Accounting for Managers* to cover all aspects of financial accounting that pertain to the manager, and then shift to managerial accounting topics in the remaining chapters. This weighting of chapters reflects the importance of managerial accounting information in the proper management of an organization.

## Summary

The management of a business depends to a great extent upon accounting information. In this chapter, we have established the broad range of decision areas that depend on accounting information, and noted the areas of this book in which a discussion of the pertinent topics can be found.

Many managers are aware that they must have a rough knowledge of the financial statements, and so may already be cognizant of the basic structure of these statements and the uses to which they can be put. In the following pages, we provide more detailed information about financial statements, and then go on to address the more practical aspects of managerial accounting. The result is a well-rounded knowledge base for any manager that avoids the minutiae of accounting operations, while focusing on those aspects of accounting that best support the manager's role.

# Chapter 2
# Introduction to Accounting

## Introduction

Before a manager can understand the uses to which the accounting function can be put, it is first necessary to understand the basic underpinnings of accounting, as well as the general flow of accounting transactions. In this chapter, we describe the concept of an accounting framework and accounting principles, on which all accounting activities are based. We then give an overview of how accounting transactions are recorded and aggregated into financial statements, which involves the use of double entry accounting, ledgers, and journal entries. We conclude with a discussion of the accrual and cash bases of accounting.

**Related Podcast Episode:** Episode 181 of the Accounting Best Practices Podcast discusses accounting in a startup company. It is available at: **accountingtools.com/podcasts** or **iTunes**

## Accounting Frameworks

The accounting profession operates under a set of guidelines for how business transactions are to be recorded and reported. There are a multitude of transactions that an organization might enter into, so the corresponding guidelines are also quite large. These guidelines can be subject to interpretation, so there are standard-setting bodies that maintain and support the guidelines with official pronouncements.

Not every organization operates under the same set of guidelines. There may be different guidelines for different types of entities, and slight differences in guidelines by country. Each of these unique guidelines is referred to as an accounting framework. Once an organization adopts a certain accounting framework, it continues to record transactions and report financial results in accordance with the rules of that framework on a long-term basis. Doing so provides the users of its financial reports with a considerable amount of reporting continuity. Also, because an accounting framework provides a consistent set of rules, anyone reading the financial statements of multiple companies that employ the same framework has a reasonable basis for comparison.

The most commonly-used accounting framework in the United States is GAAP, which is short for Generally Accepted Accounting Principles. GAAP is the most comprehensive accounting framework in the world, with an extensive set of detailed rules covering a massive range of accounting topics. GAAP also provides rules for how to handle accounting transactions in specific industries, such as mining, airlines, and health care.

GAAP is derived from the pronouncements of a series of government-sponsored accounting entities, of which the Financial Accounting Standards Board is the latest. The Securities and Exchange Commission also issues accounting pronouncements through its Staff Accounting Bulletins and other announcements that are applicable only to publicly-held companies, and which are considered to be part of GAAP.

International Financial Reporting Standards, or IFRS, is the accounting framework used in most other countries. GAAP is much more rules-based than IFRS, which focuses more on general principles than GAAP. This focus makes the IFRS body of work much smaller, cleaner, and easier to understand than GAAP.

There are several working groups that are gradually reducing the differences between the GAAP and IFRS accounting frameworks, so eventually there should be minor differences in the reported results of a business if it switches between the two frameworks.

The accounting information in this book is based on the GAAP framework. At the higher level of discussion used in this book, there are few notable differences between GAAP and IFRS.

## Accounting Principles

There are a number of accounting principles upon which the accounting frameworks are based. These principles have been derived from common usage, as well as from the documentary efforts of several standard-setting organizations. The principles are:

- *Accrual principle*. The concept that accounting transactions should be recorded in the accounting periods when they actually occur, rather than in the periods when there are cash flows associated with them. This is the foundation of the accrual basis of accounting (as described in a later section). It is important for the construction of financial statements that show what actually happened in an accounting period, rather than being artificially delayed or accelerated by the associated cash flows. For example, if a company ignores the accrual principle, it records an expense only after paying for it, which might incorporate a lengthy delay caused by the payment terms for the associated supplier invoice.
- *Conservatism principle*. The concept that one should record expenses and liabilities as soon as possible, but record revenues and assets only when certain that they will occur. This introduces a conservative slant to the financial statements that may yield lower reported profits, since revenue and asset recognition may be delayed for some time. This principle tends to encourage the recordation of losses earlier, rather than later. The concept can be taken too far, where a business persistently misstates its results to be worse than is realistically the case.
- *Consistency principle*. The concept that, once a business adopts an accounting principle or method, the company should continue to use it until a demonstrably better principle or method comes along. Not following the consistency principle means that a business could continually jump between

different accounting treatments of its transactions that make its long-term financial results extremely difficult to discern.

- *Cost principle.* The concept that a business should only record its assets, liabilities, and equity investments at their original purchase costs. This principle is becoming less valid, as a host of accounting standards are heading in the direction of adjusting to the current fair value of many items.
- *Economic entity principle.* The concept that the transactions of a business should be kept separate from those of its owners and other businesses. This prevents intermingling of assets and liabilities among multiple entities.
- *Full disclosure principle.* The concept that one should include in or alongside the financial statements of a business all of the information that may impact a reader's understanding of those financial statements. The accounting standards have greatly amplified upon this concept in specifying an enormous number of informational disclosures.
- *Going concern principle.* The concept that a business will remain in operation for the foreseeable future. This means that a business would be justified in deferring the recognition of some expenses, such as depreciation, until later periods. Otherwise, the company would have to recognize all expenses at once and not defer any of them.
- *Matching principle.* The concept that, when revenue is recorded, all related expenses should be recorded at the same time. Thus, a business charges inventory to the cost of goods sold at the same time that it records revenue from the sale of those inventory items. This is a cornerstone of the accrual basis of accounting.
- *Materiality principle.* The concept that one should record a transaction in the accounting records if not doing so might have altered the decision making process of someone reading the company's financial statements. This is quite a vague concept that is difficult to quantify, which has led some of the more picayune accountants to record even the smallest transactions.
- *Monetary unit principle.* The concept that a business should only record transactions that can be stated in terms of a unit of currency. Thus, it is easy enough to record the purchase of a fixed asset, since it was bought for a specific price, whereas the value of the quality control system of a business is not recorded. This concept keeps a business from engaging in an excessive level of estimation in deriving the value of its assets and liabilities.
- *Reliability principle.* The concept that only those transactions that can be proven should be recorded. For example, a supplier invoice is solid evidence that an expense has been recorded. This concept is of prime interest to auditors, who are constantly in search of the evidence supporting transactions.
- *Revenue recognition principle.* The concept that one should only recognize revenue when a business has substantially completed the earnings process. So many people have skirted around the fringes of this concept to commit reporting fraud that a variety of standard-setting bodies have developed a

massive amount of information about what constitutes proper revenue recognition.

- *Time period principle*. The concept that a business should report the results of its operations over a standard period of time. This may qualify as the most glaringly obvious of all accounting principles, but is intended to create a standard set of comparable periods, which is useful for trend analysis.

It may not initially appear that accounting principles are of much use on a day-to-day basis. However, when there is a question about the proper treatment of a business transaction, it is sometimes useful to resolve the question by viewing the guidance in the relevant accounting framework in light of these accounting principles. Doing so may indicate that one solution more closely adheres to the general intent of the framework, and so is a better solution.

## The Accounting Cycle

The accounting cycle is a sequential set of activities used to identify and record an entity's individual transactions. These transactions are then aggregated at the end of each reporting period into financial statements. The accounting cycle is essentially the core recordation activity that an accounting department engages in, and is the basis upon which the financial statements are constructed. The following discussion breaks the accounting cycle into the treatment of individual transactions and then closing the books at the end of the accounting period. The accounting cycle for individual transactions is:

1. Identify the event causing an accounting transaction, such as buying materials, paying wages to employees, or selling goods to customers.
2. Prepare the business document associated with the accounting transaction, such as a supplier invoice, customer invoice, or cash receipt.
3. Identify which accounts are affected by the business document.
4. Record in the appropriate accounts in the accounting database the amounts noted on the business document. This may involve recording transactions in a specific journal, such as the cash receipts journal or cash disbursements journal, which are later posted to the general ledger. Some transactions may be posted directly to the general ledger.

The preceding accounting cycle steps were associated with individual transactions. The following accounting cycle steps are only used at the end of the reporting period, and are associated with the aggregate amounts of the preceding transactions:

5. Prepare a preliminary trial balance, which itemizes the debit and credit totals for each account.
6. Add accrued items, record estimated reserves, and correct errors in the preliminary trial balance with adjusting entries. Examples are the recordation of an expense for supplier invoices that have not yet arrived, and accruing for unpaid wages earned.

7. Prepare an adjusted trial balance, which incorporates the preliminary trial balance and all adjusting entries. It may require several iterations before this report accurately reflects the results of operations of the business.
8. Prepare financial statements from the adjusted trial balance.
9. Close the books for the reporting period.

In the following sections, we expand upon a number of the concepts just noted in the accounting cycle, including accounting transactions, ledgers, journal entries, and the trial balance.

## Accounting Transactions

An accounting transaction is a business event having a monetary impact on the financial statements of a business. It is recorded in the accounting records of an organization. Examples of accounting transactions are:

- Sale in cash to a customer
- Sale on credit to a customer
- Receive cash in payment of an invoice owed by a customer
- Purchase fixed assets from a supplier
- Record the depreciation of a fixed asset over time
- Purchase consumable supplies from a supplier
- Investment in another business
- Investment in marketable securities
- Borrow funds from a lender
- Issue a dividend to investors
- Sales of assets to a third party

A *transaction cycle* is an interlocking set of business transactions. Most transactions can be aggregated into a relatively small number of transaction cycles related to the sale of goods, payments to suppliers, payments to employees, and payments to lenders. These cycles are as follows:

- *Sales cycle.* A company receives an order from a customer, examines the order for creditworthiness, ships goods or provides services to the customer, issues an invoice, and collects payment.
- *Purchasing cycle.* A company issues a purchase order to a supplier for goods, receives the goods, records an account payable, and pays the supplier. There are several ancillary activities, such as the use of petty cash or procurement cards for smaller purchases.
- *Payroll cycle.* A company records the time of its employees, verifies hours and overtime worked, calculates gross pay, deducts taxes and other withholdings, and issues paychecks to employees. Other related activities include the payment of withheld income taxes to the government, as well as the issuance of annual wage statements to employees.

- *Financing cycle.* A company issues debt instruments to lenders, followed by a series of interest payments and repayments of debt. Also, a company issues stock to investors in exchange for periodic dividend payments and other payouts if the entity is dissolved. These clusters of transactions are more diverse than the preceding transaction cycles, but may involve substantially more money.

Accounting transactions are either directly or indirectly recorded with a journal entry. The indirect variety occurs when someone uses a module in the accounting software to record a transaction, and the module automatically creates the journal entry on behalf of the employee. For example, the billing module in the accounting software will record revenue and a receivable whenever an invoice is issued.

## Source Documents

Source documents are the physical basis upon which business transactions are recorded. They usually contain the following information:

- A description of the transaction
- The date of the transaction
- A specific amount of money
- An authorizing signature (in some cases)

Examples of source documents, and their related business transactions that appear in the financial records, are:

- *Bank statement.* This contains a number of adjustments to a company's book balance of cash on hand that the company should reference to bring its records into alignment with those of a bank.
- *Cash register tape.* This can be used as evidence of cash sales, which supports the recordation of a sale transaction.
- *Credit card receipt.* This can be used as evidence for a disbursement of funds from petty cash.
- *Lockbox check images.* These images support the recordation of cash receipts from customers.
- *Packing slip.* This describes the items shipped to a customer, and so supports the recordation of a sale transaction.
- *Sales order.* This document, when coupled with a bill of lading and/or packing list, can be used to invoice a customer, which in turn generates a sale transaction.
- *Supplier invoice.* This document supports the issuance of a cash, check, or electronic payment to a supplier. A supplier invoice also supports the recordation of an expense, inventory item, or fixed asset.

- *Time card.* This supports the issuance of a paycheck or electronic payment to an employee. If employee hours are being billed to customers, the time card also supports the creation of customer invoices.

## Double Entry Accounting

Double entry accounting is a record keeping system under which every transaction is recorded in at least two accounts. There is no limit on the number of accounts used in a transaction, but the minimum is two accounts. There are two columns in each account, with debit entries on the left and credit entries on the right. In double entry accounting, the total of all debit entries must match the total of all credit entries. When this happens, a transaction is said to be *in balance*. If the totals do not agree, the transaction is said to be *out of balance*. An out of balance transaction must be corrected before financial statements can be created.

The definitions of a debit and credit are:

- A debit is an accounting entry that either increases an asset or expense account, or decreases a liability or equity account. It is positioned to the left in an accounting entry.
- A credit is an accounting entry that either increases a liability or equity account, or decreases an asset or expense account. It is positioned to the right in an accounting entry.

An account is a separate, detailed record associated with a specific asset, liability, equity, revenue, expense, gain, or loss. Examples of accounts are noted in the following table.

**Characteristics of Sample Accounts**

| Account Name | Account Type | Normal Account Balance |
|---|---|---|
| Cash | Asset | Debit |
| Accounts receivable | Asset | Debit |
| Inventory | Asset | Debit |
| Fixed assets | Asset | Debit |
| Accounts payable | Liability | Credit |
| Accrued liabilities | Liability | Credit |
| Notes payable | Liability | Credit |
| Common stock | Equity | Credit |
| Retained earnings | Equity | Credit |
| Revenue - products | Revenue | Credit |
| Revenue - services | Revenue | Credit |
| Cost of goods sold | Expense | Debit |
| Compensation expense | Expense | Debit |
| Utilities expense | Expense | Debit |
| Travel and entertainment | Expense | Debit |
| Gain on sale of asset | Gain | Credit |
| Loss on sale of asset | Loss | Debit |

The key point with double entry accounting is that a single transaction always triggers a recordation in *at least* two accounts, as assets and liabilities gradually flow through a business and are converted into revenues, expenses, gains, and losses.

## The Ledger Concept

A *ledger* is a book or database in which double-entry accounting transactions are stored or summarized. A *subsidiary ledger* is a ledger designed for the storage of specific types of accounting transactions. The information in a subsidiary ledger is summarized and posted to an account in the *general ledger*, which in turn is used to construct the financial statements of a company. The account in the general ledger where this summarized information is stored is called a *control account*. Most accounts in the general ledger are not control accounts; instead, transactions are recorded directly into them.

A subsidiary ledger can be set up for virtually any general ledger account. However, they are usually only created for areas in which there are high transaction volumes, which limits their use to a few areas. Examples of subsidiary ledgers are:

- Accounts receivable ledger
- Fixed assets ledger
- Inventory ledger
- Purchases ledger

In order to research accounting information when a subsidiary ledger is used, drill down from the general ledger to the appropriate subsidiary ledger, where the detailed information is stored. Consequently, if there is a preference to conduct as much research as possible within the general ledger, use fewer subsidiary ledgers.

As an example of the information in a subsidiary ledger, the inventory ledger may contain transactions pertaining to receipts into stock, movements of stock to the production floor, conversions into finished goods, scrap and rework reporting, and sales of goods to customers.

**Tip:** Subsidiary ledgers are used when there is a large amount of transaction information that would clutter up the general ledger. This situation typically arises in companies with significant sales volume. Thus, there may be no need for a subsidiary ledger in a small company.

The following chart shows how the various data entry modules within an accounting system are used to create transactions which are recorded in either the general ledger or various subsidiary ledgers, and which are eventually aggregated to create the financial statements.

## Transaction Flow in the Accounting System

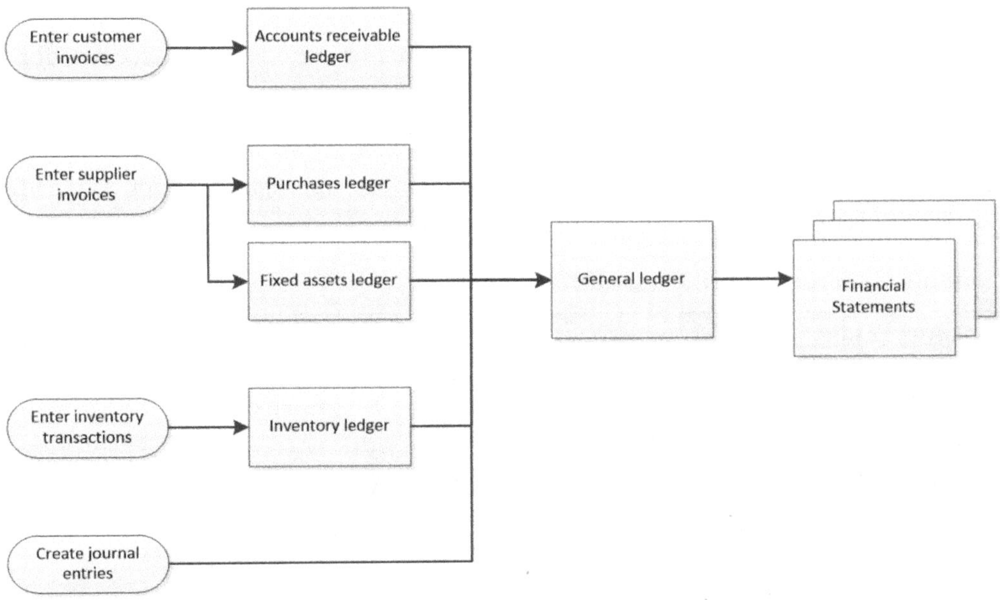

## The General Ledger

The general ledger is the master set of accounts in which are summarized all transactions occurring within a business during a specific period of time. The general ledger contains all of the accounts currently in use, and is sorted by account number. Either individual transactions or summary-level postings from subsidiary ledgers are listed within each account number, and are sorted by transaction date. Each entry in the general ledger includes a reference number that states the source of the information. The source may be a subsidiary ledger, a journal entry, or a transaction entered directly into the general ledger.

The format of the general ledger varies somewhat, depending on the accounting software being used, but the basic set of information presented for an account within the general ledger is:

- *Transaction number.* The software assigns a unique number to each transaction, so that it can be more easily located in the accounting database if the transaction number is available.
- *Transaction date.* This is the date on which the transaction was entered into the accounting database.
- *Description.* This is a brief description that summarizes the reason for the entry.

- *Source.* Information may be forwarded to the general ledger from a variety of sources, so the report states the source, in case the source is needed to research the reason for the entry.
- *Debit and credit.* States the amount debited or credited to the account for a specific transaction.

The following sample of a general ledger report shows a format that could be used to present information for several transactions that are aggregated under a specific account number.

**Sample General Ledger Presentation**

| Trans. No. | Trans. Date | Description | Source | Debit | Credit |
|---|---|---|---|---|---|
| **Acct. 10400** | | **Acct: Accounts Receivable** | **Beginning balance** | | **$127,500.00** |
| 10473 | 3/22/xx | Customer invoice | ARL | 93.99 | |
| 10474 | 3/23/xx | Customer invoice | ARL | 47.80 | |
| 10475 | 3/24/xx | Credit memo | ARL | | 43.17 |
| 10476 | 3/25/xx | Customer invoice | ARL | 65.25 | |
| 18903 | 3/26/xx | Cash receipt | CRJ | | 1,105.20 |
| | | | **Ending balance** | | **$126,558.67** |

It is extremely easy to locate information pertinent to an accounting inquiry in the general ledger, which makes it the primary source of accounting information. For example:

- A manager reviews the balance sheet and notices that the amount of debt appears too high. The accounting staff looks up the debt account in the general ledger and sees that a loan was added at the end of the month.
- A manager reviews the income statement and sees that the bad debt expense for his division is very high. The accounting staff looks up the expense in the general ledger, drills down to the source journal entry, and sees that a new bad debt projection was the cause of the increase in bad debt expense.

As the examples show, the source of an inquiry is frequently the financial statements; when conducting an investigation, the accounting staff begins with the general ledger, and may drill down to source documents from there to ascertain the reason(s) for an issue.

We will now proceed to brief discussions of the accounts receivable ledger and purchase ledger, which are representative of the types of subsidiary ledgers that can be used to compile information within the accounting system.

## Accounts Receivable Ledger

The accounts receivable ledger is a subsidiary ledger in which is recorded all credit sales made by a business. It is useful for segregating into one location a record of all amounts invoiced to customers, as well as all credit memos issued to them, and all payments made against invoices by them. The ending balance of the accounts receivable ledger equals the aggregate amount of unpaid accounts receivable.

A typical transaction entered into the accounts receivable ledger will record an account receivable, followed at a later date by a payment transaction from a customer that eliminates the account receivable.

If the accounting staff were to maintain a manual record of the accounts receivable ledger, it could contain substantially more information than is allowed by an accounting software package. The data fields in a manually-prepared ledger might include the following information for each transaction:

- Invoice date
- Invoice number
- Customer name
- Identifying code for item sold
- Sales tax invoiced
- Total amount billed
- Payment flag (states whether paid or not)

The primary document recorded in the accounts receivable ledger is the customer invoice. Also, if a credit is granted back to a customer for such items as returned goods or items damaged in transit, a credit memo could also be recorded in the ledger.

The information in the accounts receivable ledger is aggregated periodically and posted to a control account in the general ledger. This account is used to keep from cluttering up the general ledger with the massive amount of information that is typically stored in the accounts receivable ledger. Immediately after posting, the balance in the control account should match the balance in the accounts receivable ledger. Since no detailed transactions are stored in the control account, anyone wanting to research customer invoice and credit memo transactions will have to drill down from the control account to the accounts receivable ledger to find them.

Before closing the books and generating financial statements at the end of an accounting period, the accounting staff must complete all entries in the accounts receivable ledger, close the ledger for that period, and post the totals from the accounts receivable ledger to the general ledger.

## Purchase Ledger

The purchase ledger is a subsidiary ledger in which is recorded all purchases made by a business. It is useful for segregating into one location a record of the amounts the company is spending with its suppliers. The purchase ledger shows which purchases have been paid for and which ones remain outstanding. A typical transaction entered into the purchase ledger will record an account payable, followed at a later date by a payment transaction that eliminates the accounts payable. Thus, there is likely to be an outstanding account payable balance in the ledger at any time.

If one were to maintain a manual record of the purchase ledger, it could contain substantially more information than is allowed by an accounting software package. The data fields in a manually-prepared purchase ledger might include the following information for each transaction:

- Purchase date
- Supplier code (or name)
- Supplier invoice number
- Purchase order number (if used)
- Identifying code for item purchased
- Amount paid
- Sales tax paid
- Payment flag (states whether paid or not)

The primary document recorded in the purchase ledger is the supplier invoice. Also, if suppliers grant a credit back to the business for such items as returned goods or items damaged in transit, the accounting staff might also record credit memos issued by suppliers in the purchase ledger.

The information in the purchase ledger is aggregated periodically and posted to a control account in the general ledger. The purchase ledger control account is used to keep from cluttering up the general ledger with the massive amount of information that is typically stored in the purchase ledger. Immediately after posting, the balance in the control account should match the balance in the purchase ledger. Since no detailed transactions are stored in the control account, anyone wanting to research purchase transactions will have to drill down from the control account to the purchase ledger to find them.

Before closing the books and generating financial statements at the end of an accounting period, the accounting staff must complete all entries in the purchase ledger, close the ledger for that period, and post the totals from the purchase ledger to the general ledger.

## Journal Entries

A journal entry is a formalized method for recording a business transaction. It is recorded in the accounting records of a business, usually in the general ledger, but sometimes in a subsidiary ledger that is then summarized and rolled forward into the general ledger.

Journal entries are used in a double entry accounting system, where the intent is to record every business transaction in at least two places. For example, when a company sells goods for cash, this increases both the revenue account and the cash account. Or, if merchandise is acquired on account, this increases both the accounts payable account and the inventory account.

The structure of a journal entry is:

- A header line may include a journal entry number and entry date.
- The first column includes the account number and account name into which the entry is recorded. This field is indented if it is for the account being credited.
- The second column contains the debit amount to be entered.
- The third column contains the credit amount to be entered.
- A footer line may also include a brief description of the reason for the entry.

Thus, the basic journal entry format is:

| | Debit | Credit |
|---|---|---|
| Account name / number | $xx,xxx | |
|     Account name / number | | $xx,xxx |

The structural rules of a journal entry are that there must be a minimum of two line items in the entry, and that the total amount entered in the debit column equals the total amount entered in the credit column.

A journal entry is usually printed and stored in a binder of accounting transactions, with backup materials attached that justify the entry. This information may be accessed by the company's auditors as part of their annual audit activities.

There are several types of journal entries, including:

- *Adjusting entry*. An adjusting entry is used at month-end to alter the financial statements to bring them into compliance with the relevant accounting framework. For example, a company could accrue unpaid wages at month-end in order to recognize the wages expense in the current period.
- *Compound entry*. This is a journal entry that includes more than two lines of entries. It is frequently used to record complex transactions, or several transactions at once. For example, the journal entry to record a payroll usually contains many lines, since it involves the recordation of numerous tax liabilities and payroll deductions.
- *Reversing entry*. This is an adjusting entry that is reversed as of the beginning of the following period, usually because an expense was accrued in the preceding period, and is no longer needed. Thus, a wage accrual in the preceding period is reversed in the next period, to be replaced by an actual payroll expenditure.

In general, journal entries are not used to record high-volume transactions, such as customer billings or supplier invoices. These transactions are handled through specialized software modules that present a standard on-line form to be filled out. Once the form is complete, the software automatically creates the accounting record.

## Major Journal Entries

The following journal entry examples are intended to provide an outline of the general structure of the more common entries encountered. It is impossible to provide a complete set of journal entries that address every variation on every situation, since there are thousands of possible entries.

In each of the following journal entries, we state the topic, the relevant debit and credit, and additional comments as needed.

Revenue journal entries:

- *Sales entry*. Debit accounts receivable and credit sales. If a sale is for cash, the debit is to the cash account instead of the accounts receivable account.
- *Allowance for doubtful accounts entry*. Debit bad debt expense and credit the allowance for doubtful accounts. When actual bad debts are identified, debit the allowance account and credit the accounts receivable account, thereby clearing out the associated invoice.

Expense journal entries:

- *Accounts payable entry*. Debit the asset or expense account to which a purchase relates and credit the accounts payable account. When an account payable is paid, debit accounts payable and credit the cash account.
- *Payroll entry*. Debit the wages expense and payroll tax expense accounts, and credit the cash account. There may be additional credits to account for deductions from benefit expense accounts, if employees have permitted deductions for benefits to be taken from their pay.
- *Accrued expense entry*. Debit the applicable expense and credit the accrued expenses liability account. This entry is usually reversed automatically in the following period.
- *Depreciation entry*. Debit depreciation expense and credit accumulated depreciation. These accounts may be categorized by type of fixed asset.

Asset entries:

- *Cash reconciliation entry*. This entry can take many forms, but there is usually a debit to the bank fees account to recognize changes made by the bank, with a credit to the cash account. There may also be a debit to office supplies expense for any check supplies purchased and paid for through the bank account.
- *Prepaid expense adjustment entry*. When recognizing prepaid expenses as expenses, debit the applicable expense account and credit the prepaid expense asset account.
- *Obsolete inventory entry*. Debit the cost of goods sold and credit the reserve for obsolete inventory. When inventory is actually disposed of, debit the reserve and credit inventory.

- *Fixed asset addition entry.* Debit the applicable fixed asset account and credit accounts payable.
- *Fixed asset derecognition entry.* Debit accumulated depreciation and credit the applicable fixed asset account. There may also be a gain or loss on the asset derecognition.

Liability entries:

See the preceding accounts payable and accrued expense entries.

Equity entries:

- *Dividend declaration.* Debit the retained earnings account and credit the dividends payable account. Once dividends are paid, this is a debit to the dividends payable account and a credit to the cash account.
- *Stock repurchase.* Debit the treasury stock account and credit the cash account.

These journal entry examples are only intended to provide an overview of the general types and formats of accounting entries. There are many variations on the entries presented here that are used to deal with a broad range of business transactions.

## The Accruals Concept

An accrual is a journal entry that is used to recognize revenues and expenses that have been earned or consumed, respectively, and for which the related source documents have not yet been received or generated. Accruals are needed to ensure that all revenue and expense elements are recognized within the correct reporting period, irrespective of the timing of related cash flows. Without accruals, the amount of revenue, expense, and profit or loss in a period will not necessarily reflect the actual level of economic activity within a business. Accruals are a key part of the closing process used to create financial statements under the accrual basis of accounting; without accruals, financial statements would be considerably less accurate.

It is most efficient to initially record most accruals as reversing entries. This is a useful feature when a business is expecting to issue an invoice to a customer or receive an invoice from a supplier in the following period. For example, a company controller may know that a supplier invoice for $20,000 will arrive a few days after the end of a month, but she wants to close the books as soon as possible. Accordingly, she records a $20,000 reversing entry to recognize the expense in the current month. In the next month, the accrual reverses, creating a negative $20,000 expense that is offset by the arrival and recordation of the supplier invoice.

Examples of accruals that a business might record are:

- *Expense accrual for interest.* A local lender issues a loan to a business, and sends the borrower an invoice each month, detailing the amount of interest owed. The borrower can record the interest expense in advance of invoice receipt by recording accrued interest.
- *Expense accrual for wages.* An employer pays its employees once a month for the hours they have worked through the 26$^{th}$ day of the month. The employer can accrue all additional wages earned from the 27$^{th}$ through the last day of the month, to ensure that the full amount of the wage expense is recognized.
- *Sales accrual.* A services business has a number of employees working on a major project for the federal government, which it will bill when the project has been completed. In the meantime, the company can accrue revenue for the amount of work completed to date, even though the work has not yet been billed.

If a business records its transactions under the cash basis of accounting, it does not use accruals. Instead, the organization records transactions only when it either pays out or receives cash.

## The Realization Concept

The realization principle is the concept that revenue can only be recognized once the underlying goods or services associated with the revenue have been delivered or rendered, respectively. Thus, revenue can only be recognized after it has been earned. The best way to understand the realization concept is through the following examples:

- *Advance payment for goods.* A customer pays $1,000 in advance for a custom-designed product. The seller does not realize the $1,000 of revenue until its work on the product is complete. Consequently, the $1,000 is initially recorded as a liability, which is then shifted to revenue only after the product has shipped.
- *Advance payment for services.* A customer pays $6,000 in advance for a full year of software support. The software provider does not realize the $6,000 of revenue until it has performed work on the product. This can be defined as the passage of time, so the software provider could initially record the entire $6,000 as a liability and then shift $500 of it per month to revenue.
- *Delayed payments.* A seller ships goods to a customer on credit, and bills the customer $2,000 for the goods. The seller has realized the entire $2,000 as soon as the shipment has been completed, since there are no additional earning activities to complete. The delayed payment is a financing issue that is unrelated to the realization of revenues.
- *Multiple deliveries.* A seller enters into a sale contract under which it sells an airplane to an airline, plus one year of engine maintenance and initial

> pilot training, for $25 million. In this case, the seller must allocate the price among the three components of the sale, and realizes revenue as each one is completed. Thus, it probably realizes all of the revenue associated with the airplane upon delivery, while realization of the training and maintenance components will be delayed until earned.

The realization concept is most often violated when a company wants to accelerate the recognition of revenue, and so books revenues in advance of all related earning activities being completed.

## The Trial Balance

The trial balance is a report run at the end of an accounting period, listing the ending balance in each account. The report is primarily used to ensure that the total of all debits equals the total of all credits, which means that there are no unbalanced journal entries in the accounting system that would make it impossible to generate accurate financial statements. The trial balance can also be used to manually compile financial statements, though given the predominant use of computerized accounting systems that create these statements automatically, the report is rarely used for this purpose.

When a trial balance is first printed, it is called the *unadjusted trial balance.* Then, when the accounting staff corrects any errors found and makes adjustments to bring the financial statements into compliance with the relevant accounting framework, the report is called the *adjusted trial balance.*

Each line item in a trial balance only contains the ending balance in an account. All accounts having an ending balance are listed in the trial balance. The following sample trial balance combines all debit and credit totals into the second column, so that the summary balance for the total is (and should be) zero. Adjusting entries are added in the next column, yielding an adjusted trial balance in the far right column.

**Sample Adjusted Trial Balance**

Snuggable Pillow Company
Trial Balance
August 31, 20XX

| Account Name | Unadjusted Trial Balance | Adjusting Entries | Adjusted Trial Balance |
|---|---|---|---|
| Cash | $60,000 | | $60,000 |
| Accounts receivable | 180,000 | $50,000 | 230,000 |
| Inventory | 300,000 | | 300,000 |
| Fixed assets | 210,000 | | 210,000 |
| Accounts payable | -90,000 | | -90,000 |
| Accrued liabilities | -50,000 | -25,000 | -75,000 |
| Notes payable | -420,000 | | -420,000 |
| Equity | -350,000 | | -350,000 |
| Revenue | -400,000 | -50,000 | -450,000 |
| Cost of goods sold | 290,000 | | 290,000 |
| Salaries | 200,000 | 25,000 | 225,000 |
| Payroll taxes | 20,000 | | 20,000 |
| Rent | 35,000 | | 35,000 |
| Other expenses | 15,000 | | 15,000 |
| Total | $0 | $0 | $0 |

## Accrual Basis of Accounting

The accrual basis of accounting is the concept of recording revenues when earned and expenses as incurred. This concept differs from the cash basis of accounting, under which revenues are recorded when cash is received, and expenses are recorded when cash is paid. For example, a company operating under the accrual basis of accounting will record a sale as soon as it issues an invoice to a customer, while a cash basis company would instead wait to be paid before it records the sale. Similarly, an accrual basis company will record an expense as incurred, while a cash basis company would instead wait to pay its supplier before recording the expense.

The accrual basis of accounting is advocated under both the GAAP and IFRS accounting frameworks. Both of these frameworks provide guidance regarding how to account for revenue and expense transactions in the absence of the cash receipts or payments that would trigger the recordation of a transaction under the cash basis of accounting.

The accrual basis tends to provide more even recognition of revenues and expenses over time than the cash basis, and so is considered by investors to be the most valid accounting system for ascertaining the results of operations, financial position, and cash flows of a business. In particular, it supports the matching principle, under which revenues and all related expenses are to be recorded within the same reporting period; by doing so, it should be possible to see the full extent of the profits and losses associated with specific business transactions within a single reporting period.

The accrual basis requires the use of estimated reserves in certain areas. For example, a company should recognize an expense for estimated bad debts that have not yet been incurred. By doing so, all expenses related to a revenue transaction are recorded at the same time as the revenue, which results in an income statement that fully reflects the results of operations. Similarly, the estimated amounts of product returns, sales allowances, and obsolete inventory may be recorded in reserve accounts. These estimates may not be entirely accurate, and so can lead to materially inaccurate financial statements. Consequently, care must be used when estimating reserves.

A small business may elect to avoid using the accrual basis of accounting, since it requires a certain amount of accounting expertise. Also, a small business owner may choose to manipulate the timing of cash inflows and outflows to create a smaller amount of taxable income under the cash basis of accounting, which can result in the deferral of income tax payments.

A significant failing of the accrual basis is that it can indicate the presence of profits, even though the associated cash inflows have not yet occurred. The result can be a supposedly profitable entity that is starved for cash, and which may therefore go bankrupt despite its reported level of profitability.

## Cash Basis of Accounting

The cash basis of accounting is the practice of only recording revenue when cash is received from a customer, and recording expenses only when cash has been paid out. The cash basis is commonly used by individuals and small businesses, especially those with no inventory. A start-up company will frequently begin keeping its books under the cash basis, and then switch to the accrual basis of accounting (see the preceding section) when it has grown to a sufficient size. The cash basis of accounting has the following advantages:

- *Taxation*. The method is commonly used to record financial results for tax purposes, since a business can accelerate some payments in order to reduce its taxable profits, thereby deferring its tax liability.
- *Ease of use*. A person requires a reduced knowledge of accounting to keep records under the cash basis.

However, the cash basis of accounting also suffers from the following problems:

- *Accuracy*. The cash basis yields less accurate results than the accrual basis of accounting, since the timing of cash flows does not necessarily reflect the proper timing of changes in the financial condition of a business. For example, if a contract with a customer does not allow a business to issue an invoice until the end of a project, the company will be unable to report any revenue until the invoice has been issued and cash received.

- *Manipulation*. A business can alter its reported results by not cashing received checks or altering the payment timing for its liabilities.
- *Lending*. Lenders do not feel that the cash basis generates overly accurate financial statements, and so may refuse to lend money to a business reporting under the cash basis.
- *Audited financial statements*. Auditors will not approve financial statements that were compiled under the cash basis, so a company will need to convert to the accrual basis if it wants to have audited financial statements.
- *Management reporting*. Since the results of cash basis financial statements can be inaccurate, management reports should not be issued that are based upon it.

In short, the numerous problems with the cash basis of accounting usually cause businesses to abandon it after they move beyond their initial startup phases.

## Summary

The main focus of this chapter was to reveal how business transactions are recorded into the accounting database. The level of detail given was intended to provide the manager with a basic understanding of the process, rather than the more detailed knowledge needed to actually operate such a system.

With this knowledge in hand, the next step for the manager is to see how accounting information is transformed into the financial statements, which is one of the main work products of the accounting department. The contents and presentation formats of the financial statements are described in the following Financial Statements chapter.

# Chapter 3
# The Financial Statements

## Introduction

The financial records of a business are summarized into a set of financial statements at the end of each reporting period. These statements reveal the results, financial position, cash flows, and retained earnings of the organization. In this chapter, we describe the nature of each of the financial statements and different presentation formats. We also include overviews of financial statement footnotes, as well as describe consolidated, interim, and pro forma financial statements. We finish with a brief discussion of the nature of the audits, reviews, and compilations with which financial statements may be associated.

**Related Podcast Episode:** Episode 203 of the Accounting Best Practices Podcast discusses the presentation of financial statements. It is available at: **accountingtools.com/podcasts** or **iTunes**

## The Income Statement

In most organizations, the income statement is considered the most important of the financial statements, and may even be the only one of the financial statements that is produced (though we do not recommend doing so). Given its importance, we spend extra time in this section addressing different income statement formats.

### Income Statement Overview

The income statement is an integral part of an entity's financial statements, and contains the results of its operations during an accounting period, showing revenues and expenses, and the resulting profit or loss.

There are two ways to present the income statement. One method is to present all items of revenue and expense for the reporting period in a statement of comprehensive income. Alternatively, this information can be split into an income statement and a statement of other comprehensive income. Other comprehensive income contains all changes that are not permitted in the main part of the income statement. These items include unrealized gains and losses on available-for-sale securities, cash flow hedge gains and losses, foreign currency translation adjustments, and pension plan gains or losses. Smaller companies tend to ignore the distinction and simply aggregate the information into a document that they call the income statement; this is sufficient for internal reporting, but auditors will require the expanded version before they will certify the financial statements (see the later Financial Statement Audits, Reviews, and Compilations section).

There are no specific requirements for the line items to include in the income statement, but the following items are typically used, based on general practice:

- Revenue
- Tax expense
- Post-tax profit or loss for discontinued operations and their disposal
- Profit or loss
- Other comprehensive income, subdivided into each component thereof
- Total comprehensive income

A key additional item is to present an analysis of the expenses in profit or loss, using a classification based on their nature or functional area; the goal is to maximize the relevance and reliability of the presented information. A presentation of income statement expenses by their nature looks similar to the following exhibit.

**Sample Presentation by Nature of Items**

| | | |
|---|---|---|
| Revenue | | $xxx |
| | | |
| Expenses | | |
| Direct materials | $xxx | |
| Direct labor | xxx | |
| Salaries expense | xxx | |
| Payroll taxes | xxx | |
| Employee benefits | xxx | |
| Depreciation expense | xxx | |
| Telephone expense | xxx | |
| Other expenses | xxx | |
| Total expenses | | $xxx |
| | | |
| Profit before tax | | $xxx |

Alternatively, if the company presents expenses by their functional area, the format looks similar to the following exhibit, where most expenses are aggregated at the department level.

**Sample Presentation by Function of Items**

| | |
|---|---|
| Revenue | $xxx |
| Cost of goods sold | xxx |
| Gross profit | xxx |
| | |
| Administrative expenses | $xxx |
| Distribution expenses | xxx |
| Research and development expenses | xxx |
| Sales and marketing expenses | xxx |
| Other expenses | xxx |
| Total expenses | $xxx |
| | |
| Profit before tax | $xxx |

Of the two methods, presenting expenses by their nature is easier, since it requires no allocation of expenses between functional areas. Conversely, the functional area presentation may be more relevant to users of the information, who can more easily see where resources are being consumed.

Additional headings, subtotals, and line items should be added to the items noted above if doing so will increase the user's understanding of the entity's financial performance.

An example follows of an income statement that presents expenses by their nature, rather than by their function.

**EXAMPLE**

Milagro Corporation presents its results in two separate statements by their nature, resulting in the following format, beginning with the income statement:

Milagro Corporation
Income Statement
For the years ended December 31

| (000s) | 20x2 | 20x1 |
|---|---|---|
| Revenue | $900,000 | $850,000 |
| | | |
| Expenses | | |
| Direct materials | $270,000 | $255,000 |
| Direct labor | 90,000 | 85,000 |
| Salaries | 300,000 | 275,000 |
| Payroll taxes | 27,000 | 25,000 |
| Depreciation expense | 45,000 | 41,000 |
| Telephone expense | 30,000 | 20,000 |
| Other expenses | 23,000 | 22,000 |
| Finance costs | 29,000 | 23,000 |
| Other income | -25,000 | -20,000 |
| Profit before tax | $111,000 | $124,000 |
| Income tax expense | 38,000 | 43,000 |
| Profit from continuing operations | $73,000 | $81,000 |
| Loss from discontinued operations | 42,000 | 0 |
| Profit | $31,000 | $81,000 |

Milagro Corporation then continues with the following statement of comprehensive income:

Milagro Corporation
Statement of Comprehensive Income
For the years ended December 31

| (000s) | 20x2 | 20x1 |
|---|---|---|
| Profit | $31,000 | $81,000 |
| | | |
| Other comprehensive income | | |
| Exchange differences on translating foreign operations | $5,000 | $9,000 |
| Available-for-sale financial assets | 10,000 | -2,000 |
| Actuarial losses on defined benefit pension plan | -2,000 | -12,000 |
| Other comprehensive income, net of tax | $13,000 | -$5,000 |
| | | |
| Total comprehensive income | $18,000 | $76,000 |

## The Single-Step Income Statement

The simplest format in which one can construct an income statement is the single-step income statement. In this format, present a single subtotal for all revenue line items, and a single subtotal for all expense line items, with a net gain or loss appearing at the bottom of the report. A sample single-step income statement follows.

**Sample Single-Step Income Statement**

| Revenues | $1,000,000 |
|---|---|
| | |
| Expenses: | |
| Cost of goods sold | 350,000 |
| Advertising | 30,000 |
| Depreciation | 20,000 |
| Rent | 40,000 |
| Payroll taxes | 28,000 |
| Salaries and wages | 400,000 |
| Supplies | 32,000 |
| Travel and entertainment | 50,000 |
| Total expenses | 950,000 |
| Net income | $50,000 |

The single-step format is not heavily used, because it forces the reader of an income statement to separately summarize information for subsets of information within the income statement. For a more readable format, try the following multi-step approach.

### The Multi-Step Income Statement

The multi-step income statement involves the use of multiple sub-totals within the income statement, which makes it easier for readers to aggregate selected types of information within the report. The usual subtotals are for the gross margin, operating expenses, and other income, which allow readers to determine how much the company earns just from its manufacturing activities (the gross margin), what it spends on supporting operations (the operating expense total) and which components of its results do not relate to its core activities (the other income total). A sample format for a multi-step income statement follows.

**Sample Multi-Step Income Statement**

| | |
|---|---|
| Revenues | $1,000,000 |
| Cost of goods sold | 350,000 |
| Gross margin | $650,000 |
| | |
| Operating expenses | |
| Advertising | 30,000 |
| Depreciation | 20,000 |
| Rent | 40,000 |
| Payroll taxes | 28,000 |
| Salaries and wages | 380,000 |
| Supplies | 32,000 |
| Travel and entertainment | 50,000 |
| Total operating expenses | $580,000 |
| | |
| Other income | |
| Interest income | -5,000 |
| Interest expense | 25,000 |
| Total other income | $20,000 |
| | |
| Net income | $50,000 |

### The Condensed Income Statement

A condensed income statement is simply an income statement with many of the usual line items condensed down into a few lines. Typically, this means that all revenue line items are aggregated into a single line item, while the cost of goods sold appears as one line item, and all operating expenses appear in another line item. A typical format for a condensed income statement appears in the following exhibit.

**Sample Condensed Income Statement**

| | |
|---|---|
| Revenues | $1,000,000 |
| Cost of goods sold | 350,000 |
| Sales, general, and administrative expenses | 580,000 |
| Financing income and expenses | 20,000 |
| Net income | $50,000 |

A condensed income statement is typically issued to those external parties who are less interested in the precise sources of a company's revenues or what expenses it incurs, and more concerned with its overall performance. Thus, bankers and investors may be interested in receiving a condensed income statement.

### The Contribution Margin Income Statement

A contribution margin income statement is an income statement in which all variable expenses are deducted from sales to arrive at a contribution margin, from which all fixed expenses are then subtracted to arrive at the net profit or loss for the period. This income statement format is a superior form of presentation, because the contribution margin clearly shows the amount available to cover fixed costs and generate a profit (or loss).

In essence, if there are no sales, a contribution margin income statement will have a zero contribution margin, with fixed costs clustered beneath the contribution margin line item. As sales increase, the contribution margin will increase in conjunction with sales, while fixed costs remain approximately the same.

A contribution margin income statement varies from a normal income statement in the following three ways:

- Fixed production costs are aggregated lower in the income statement, after the contribution margin;
- Variable selling and administrative expenses are grouped with variable production costs, so that they are a part of the calculation of the contribution margin; and
- The gross margin is replaced in the statement by the contribution margin.

The format of a contribution margin income statement appears in the following exhibit.

**Sample Contribution Margin Income Statement**

| | |
|---|---|
| + | Revenues |
| - | Variable production expenses (such as materials, supplies, and variable overhead) |
| - | Variable selling and administrative expenses |
| = | Contribution margin |
| | |
| - | Fixed production expenses (including most overhead) |
| - | Fixed selling and administrative expenses |
| = | Net profit or loss |

In many cases, direct labor is categorized as a fixed expense in the contribution margin income statement format, rather than a variable expense, because this cost does not always change in direct proportion to the amount of revenue generated. Instead, management needs to keep a certain minimum staffing in the production area, which does not vary even if there are lower production volumes.

The key difference between gross margin and contribution margin is that fixed production costs are included in the cost of goods sold to calculate the gross margin, whereas they are not included in the same calculation for the contribution margin. This means that the contribution margin income statement is sorted based on the variability of the underlying cost information, rather than by the functional areas or expense categories found in a normal income statement.

It is useful to create an income statement in the contribution margin format when you want to determine that proportion of expenses that truly varies directly with revenues. In many businesses, the contribution margin will be substantially higher than the gross margin, because such a large proportion of production costs are fixed and few of its selling and administrative expenses are variable.

## The Multi-Period Income Statement

A variation on any of the preceding income statement formats is to present them over multiple periods, preferably over a trailing 12-month period. By doing so, readers of the income statement can see trends in the information, as well as spot changes in the trends that may require investigation. This is an excellent way to present the income statement, and is highly recommended. The following exhibit shows the layout of a multi-period income statement over a four-quarter period.

**Sample Multi-Period Income Statement**

| | Quarter 1 | Quarter 2 | Quarter 3 | Quarter 4 |
|---|---|---|---|---|
| Revenues | $1,000,000 | $1,100,000 | $1,050,000 | $1,200,000 |
| Cost of goods sold | 350,000 | 385,000 | 368,000 | **480,000** |
| Gross margin | $650,000 | $715,000 | $682,000 | $720,000 |
| | | | | |
| Operating expenses | | | | |
| Advertising | 30,000 | **0** | **60,000** | 30,000 |
| Depreciation | 20,000 | 21,000 | 22,000 | 24,000 |
| Rent | 40,000 | 40,000 | **50,000** | 50,000 |
| Payroll taxes | 28,000 | 28,000 | 28,000 | 26,000 |
| Salaries and wages | 380,000 | 385,000 | 385,000 | 370,000 |
| Supplies | 32,000 | 30,000 | 31,000 | 33,000 |
| Travel and entertainment | 50,000 | 45,000 | 40,000 | 60,000 |
| Total operating expenses | $580,000 | $549,000 | $616,000 | $593,000 |
| | | | | |
| Other income | | | | |
| Interest income | -5,000 | -5,000 | -3,000 | -1,000 |
| Interest expense | 25,000 | 25,000 | 30,000 | **39,000** |
| Total other income | $20,000 | $20,000 | $27,000 | $38,000 |
| | | | | |
| Net income | $50,000 | $146,000 | $39,000 | $89,000 |

The report shown in the sample reveals several issues that might not have been visible if the report had only spanned a single period. These issues are:

- *Cost of goods sold.* This cost is consistently 35% of sales until Quarter 4, when it jumps to 40%.
- *Advertising.* There was no advertising cost in Quarter 2 and double the amount of the normal $30,000 quarterly expense in Quarter 3. The cause could be a missing supplier invoice in Quarter 2 that was received and recorded in Quarter 3.
- *Rent.* The rent increased by $10,000 in Quarter 3, which may indicate a scheduled increase in the rent agreement.
- *Interest expense.* The interest expense jumps in Quarter 3 and does so again in Quarter 4, while interest income declined over the same periods. This indicates a large increase in debt.

In short, the multi-period income statement is an excellent tool for spotting anomalies in the presented information from period to period.

## The Balance Sheet

In most organizations, the balance sheet is considered the second most important of the financial statements, after the income statement. A common financial reporting package contains the income statement and balance sheet, along with supporting materials. This does not comprise a complete set of financial statements, but is considered sufficient for internal reporting purposes in many organizations. In this section, we explore several possible formats for the balance sheet.

### Overview of the Balance Sheet

A balance sheet (also known as a statement of financial position) presents information about an entity's assets, liabilities, and shareholders' equity, where the compiled result must match this formula:

Total assets = Total liabilities + Equity

The balance sheet reports the aggregate effect of transactions as of a specific date. The balance sheet is used to assess an entity's liquidity and ability to pay its debts.

There is no specific requirement for the line items to be included in the balance sheet. The following line items, at a minimum, are normally included in it:

Current Assets:

- Cash and cash equivalents
- Trade and other receivables
- Investments
- Inventories
- Assets held for sale

Non-Current Assets:

- Property, plant, and equipment
- Intangible assets
- Goodwill

Current Liabilities:

- Trade and other payables
- Accrued expenses
- Current tax liabilities
- Current portion of loans payable
- Other financial liabilities
- Liabilities held for sale

Non-Current Liabilities:

- Loans payable
- Deferred tax liabilities
- Other non-current liabilities

Equity:

- Capital stock
- Additional paid-in capital
- Retained earnings

The following exhibit contains an example of a balance sheet which presents information as of the end of two fiscal years.

Milagro Corporation
Balance Sheet
As of December 31, 20X2 and 20X1

| (000s) | 12/31/20X2 | 12/31/20X1 |
|---|---|---|
| **ASSETS** | | |
| **Current assets** | | |
| Cash and cash equivalents | $270,000 | $215,000 |
| Trade receivables | 147,000 | 139,000 |
| Inventories | 139,000 | 128,000 |
| Other current assets | 15,000 | 27,000 |
| **Total current assets** | $571,000 | $509,000 |
| | | |
| **Non-current assets** | | |
| Property, plant, and equipment | 551,000 | 529,000 |
| Goodwill | 82,000 | 82,000 |
| Other intangible assets | 143,000 | 143,000 |
| **Total non-current assets** | $776,000 | $754,000 |
| | | |
| **Total assets** | $1,347,000 | $1,263,000 |
| | | |
| **LIABILITIES AND EQUITY** | | |
| **Current liabilities** | | |
| Trade and other payables | $217,000 | $198,000 |
| Short-term borrowings | 133,000 | 202,000 |
| Current portion of long-term borrowings | 5,000 | 5,000 |
| Current tax payable | 26,000 | 23,000 |
| Accrued expenses | 9,000 | 13,000 |
| **Total current liabilities** | $390,000 | $441,000 |

| (000s) | 12/31/20X2 | 12/31/20X1 |
|---|---|---|
| | | |
| **Non-current liabilities** | | |
| Long-term debt | 85,000 | 65,000 |
| Deferred taxes | 19,000 | 17,000 |
| **Total non-current liabilities** | $104,000 | $82,000 |
| | | |
| **Total liabilities** | $494,000 | $523,000 |
| | | |
| **Shareholders' equity** | | |
| Capital | 100,000 | 100,000 |
| Additional paid-in capital | 15,000 | 15,000 |
| Retained earnings | 738,000 | 625,000 |
| **Total equity** | $853,000 | $740,000 |
| | | |
| **Total liabilities and equity** | $1,347,000 | $1,263,000 |

An asset should be classified on the balance sheet as current when an entity expects to sell or consume it during its normal operating cycle or within 12 months after the reporting period. If the operating cycle is longer than 12 months, use the longer period to judge whether an asset can be classified as current. Classify all other assets as non-current. Classify all of the following as current assets:

- *Cash.* This is cash available for current operations, as well as any short-term, highly liquid investments that are readily convertible to known amounts of cash and which are so near their maturities that they present an insignificant risk of value changes. Do not include cash whose withdrawal is restricted, to be used for other than current operations, or segregated for the liquidation of long-term debts; such items should be classified as longer-term.
- *Accounts receivable.* This includes trade accounts, notes, and acceptances that are receivable. Also, include receivables from officers, employees, affiliates, and others if they are collectible within a year. Do not include any receivables that are not expected to be collected within 12 months; such items should be classified as longer-term.
- *Marketable securities.* This includes those securities representing the investment of cash available for current operations, including trading securities.
- *Inventory.* This includes merchandise, raw materials, work-in-process, finished goods, operating supplies, and maintenance parts.
- *Prepaid expenses.* This includes prepayments for insurance, interest, rent, taxes, unused royalties, advertising services, and operating supplies.

A liability should be classified as current when the entity expects to settle it during the normal operating cycle or within 12 months after the reporting period, or if the liability is scheduled for settlement within 12 months. Classify all other liabilities as non-current. Classify all of the following as current liabilities:

- *Payables*. This is all accounts payable incurred in the acquisition of materials and supplies that are used to produce goods or services.
- *Prepayments*. This is amounts collected in advance of the delivery of goods or services by the entity to the customer. Do not include a long-term prepayment in this category.
- *Accruals*. This is accrued expenses for items directly related to the operating cycle, such as accruals for compensation, rentals, royalties, and various taxes.
- *Short-term debts*. This is debts maturing within the next 12 months.

Current liabilities include accruals for amounts that can only be determined approximately, such as bonuses, and where the payee to whom payment will be made cannot initially be designated, such as a warranty accrual.

### The Common Size Balance Sheet

A common size balance sheet presents not only the standard information contained in a balance sheet, but also a column that notes the same information as a percentage of the total assets (for asset line items) or as a percentage of total liabilities and shareholders' equity (for liability or shareholders' equity line items).

It is extremely useful to construct a common size balance sheet that itemizes the results as of the end of multiple time periods, so that one can construct trend lines to ascertain changes over longer time periods. The common size balance sheet is also useful for comparing the proportions of assets, liabilities, and equity between different companies, particularly as part of an industry or acquisition analysis.

For example, if a manager were comparing the common size balance sheet of the company to that of a potential acquiree, and the acquiree had 40% of its assets invested in accounts receivable versus 20% by the manager's company, this may indicate that aggressive collection activities might reduce the acquiree's receivables if the company were to acquire it.

The common size balance sheet is not required under any accounting frameworks. However, being a useful document for analysis purposes, it is commonly distributed within a company for review by management.

There is no mandatory format for a common size balance sheet, though percentages are nearly always placed to the right of the normal numerical results. If a balance sheet contains results as of the end of many periods, one may even dispense with numerical results entirely, in favor of just presenting the common size percentages.

**EXAMPLE**

Milagro Corporation creates a common size balance sheet that contains the balance sheet as of the end of its fiscal year for each of the past two years, with common size percentages to the right:

Milagro Corporation
Common Size Balance Sheet
As of 12/31/20x02 and 12/31/20x1

| | ($) 12/31/20x2 | ($) 12/31/20x1 | (%) 12/31/20x2 | (%) 12/31/20x1 |
|---|---|---|---|---|
| **Current assets** | | | | |
| Cash | $1,200 | $900 | 7.6% | 7.1% |
| Accounts receivable | 4,800 | 3,600 | 30.4% | 28.3% |
| Inventory | 3,600 | 2,700 | 22.8% | 21.3% |
| **Total current assets** | $9,600 | $7,200 | 60.8% | 56.7% |
| | | | | |
| Total fixed assets | 6,200 | 5,500 | 39.2% | 43.3% |
| **Total assets** | $15,800 | $12,700 | 100.0% | 100.0% |
| | | | | |
| **Current liabilities** | | | | |
| Accounts payable | $2,400 | $41,800 | 15.2% | 14.2% |
| Accrued expenses | 480 | 360 | 3.0% | 2.8% |
| Short-term debt | 800 | 600 | 5.1% | 4.7% |
| **Total current liabilities** | $3,680 | $2,760 | 23.3% | 21.7% |
| | | | | |
| Long-term debt | 9,020 | 7,740 | 57.1% | 60.9% |
| **Total liabilities** | $12,700 | $10,500 | 80.4% | 82.7% |
| | | | | |
| Shareholders' equity | 3,100 | 2,200 | 19.6% | 17.3% |
| **Total liabilities and equity** | $15,800 | $12,700 | 100.0% | 100.0% |

## The Comparative Balance Sheet

A comparative balance sheet presents side-by-side information about an entity's assets, liabilities, and shareholders' equity as of multiple points in time. For example, a comparative balance sheet could present the balance sheet as of the end of each year for the past three years. Another variation is to present the balance sheet as of the end of each month for the past 12 months on a rolling basis. In both cases, the intent is to provide the reader with a series of snapshots of a company's financial condition over a period of time, which is useful for developing trend line analyses.

The comparative balance sheet is not required for a privately-held company, but the Securities and Exchange Commission (SEC) does require it in numerous circumstances for the reports issued by publicly-held companies, particularly the annual Form 10-K and the quarterly Form 10-Q. The usual SEC requirement is to report a comparative balance sheet for the past two years, with additional requirements for quarterly reporting.

There is no standard format for a comparative balance sheet. It is somewhat more common to report the balance sheet as of the least recent period furthest to the right, though the reverse is the case when a company is reporting balance sheets in a trailing twelve months format.

The following exhibit contains a sample of a comparative balance sheet that contains the balance sheet as of the end of a company's fiscal year for each of the past three years.

**Sample Comparative Balance Sheet**

| | as of 12/31/20X3 | as of 12/31/20X2 | as of 12/31/20X1 |
|---|---|---|---|
| **Current assets** | | | |
| Cash | $1,200,000 | $900,000 | $750,000 |
| Accounts receivable | 4,800,000 | 3,600,000 | 3,000,000 |
| Inventory | 3,600,000 | 2,700,000 | 2,300,000 |
| **Total current assets** | $9,600,000 | $7,200,000 | $6,050,000 |
| | | | |
| Total fixed assets | 6,200,000 | 5,500,000 | 5,000,000 |
| **Total assets** | $15,800,000 | $12,700,000 | $11,050,000 |
| | | | |
| **Current liabilities** | | | |
| Accounts payable | $2,400,000 | $1,800,000 | $1,500,000 |
| Accrued expenses | 480,000 | 360,000 | 300,000 |
| Short-term debt | 800,000 | 600,000 | 400,000 |
| **Total current liabilities** | $3,680,000 | $2,760,000 | $2,200,000 |
| | | | |
| Long-term debt | 9,020,000 | 7,740,000 | 7,350,000 |
| **Total liabilities** | $12,700,000 | $10,500,000 | $9,550,000 |
| | | | |
| Shareholders' equity | 3,100,000 | 2,200,000 | 1,500,000 |
| **Total liabilities and equity** | $15,800,000 | $12,700,000 | $11,050,000 |

The sample comparative balance sheet reveals that the company has increased the size of its current assets over the past few years, but has also recently invested in a large amount of additional fixed assets that have likely been the cause of a significant boost in its long-term debt.

## The Statement of Cash Flows

The statement of cash flows is the least used of the primary financial statements, and may not be issued at all for internal financial reporting purposes. The recipients of financial statements seem to be mostly concerned with the profit information on the income statement, and to a lesser degree with the financial position information on the balance sheet. Nonetheless, the cash flows on the statement of cash flows can provide valuable information, especially when combined with the other elements of the financial statements. This section addresses the two formats used for the statement of cash flows.

### Overview of the Statement of Cash Flows

The statement of cash flows contains information about the flows of cash into and out of a company; in particular, it shows the extent of those company activities that generate and use cash. The primary activities are:

- *Operating activities*. These are an entity's primary revenue-producing activities. Examples of operating activities are cash receipts from the sale of goods, as well as from royalties and commissions, amounts received or paid to settle lawsuits, fines, payments to employees and suppliers, cash payments to lenders for interest, contributions to charity, and the settlement of asset retirement obligations.
- *Investing activities*. These involve the acquisition and disposal of long-term assets. Examples of investing activities are cash receipts from the sale of property, the sale of the debt or equity instruments of other entities, the repayment of loans made to other entities, and proceeds from insurance settlements related to damaged fixed assets. Examples of cash payments that are investment activities include the acquisition of fixed assets, as well as the purchase of the debt or equity of other entities.
- *Financing activities*. These are the activities resulting in alterations to the amount of contributed equity and the entity's borrowings. Examples of financing activities include cash receipts from the sale of the entity's own equity instruments or from issuing debt, proceeds from derivative instruments, and cash payments to buy back shares, pay dividends, and pay off outstanding debt.

The statement of cash flows also incorporates the concept of cash and cash equivalents. A cash equivalent is a short-term, very liquid investment that is easily convertible into a known amount of cash, and which is so near its maturity that it presents an insignificant risk of a change in value because of changes in interest rates.

The statement of cash flows can be presented using either the *direct method* or the *indirect method*. These methods are described next.

**The Direct Method**

The direct method of displaying the statement of cash flows presents the specific cash flows associated with items that affect cash flow. Items that typically do so include:

- Cash collected from customers
- Interest and dividends received
- Cash paid to employees
- Cash paid to suppliers
- Interest paid
- Income taxes paid

The format of the direct method appears in the following example.

---

**EXAMPLE**

Milagro Corporation constructs the following statement of cash flows using the direct method:

Milagro Corporation
Statement of Cash Flows
For the year ended 12/31/20X1

| | | |
|---|---|---|
| **Cash flows from operating activities** | | |
| Cash receipts from customers | $45,800,000 | |
| Cash paid to suppliers | -29,800,000 | |
| Cash paid to employees | -11,200,000 | |
| Cash generated from operations | 4,800,000 | |
| | | |
| Interest paid | -310,000 | |
| Income taxes paid | -1,700,000 | |
| Net cash from operating activities | | $2,790,000 |
| | | |
| **Cash flows from investing activities** | | |
| Purchase of fixed assets | -580,000 | |
| Proceeds from sale of equipment | 110,000 | |
| Net cash used in investing activities | | -470,000 |

| | | |
|---|---|---|
| **Cash flows from financing activities** | | |
| Proceeds from issuance of common stock | 1,000,000 | |
| Proceeds from issuance of long-term debt | 500,000 | |
| Principal payments under capital lease obligation | -10,000 | |
| Dividends paid | -450,000 | |
| Net cash used in financing activities | | 1,040,000 |
| | | |
| Net increase in cash and cash equivalents | | 3,360,000 |
| Cash and cash equivalents at beginning of period | | 1,640,000 |
| Cash and cash equivalents at end of period | | $5,000,000 |

**Reconciliation of net income to net cash provided by operating activities:**

| | | |
|---|---|---|
| Net income | | $2,665,000 |
| Adjustments to reconcile net income to net cash provided by operating activities: | | |
| Depreciation and amortization | $125,000 | |
| Provision for losses on accounts receivable | 15,000 | |
| Gain on sale of equipment | -155,000 | |
| Increase in interest and income taxes payable | 32,000 | |
| Increase in deferred taxes | 90,000 | |
| Increase in other liabilities | 18,000 | |
| Total adjustments | | 125,000 |
| Net cash provided by operating activities | | $2,790,000 |

---

The standard-setting bodies encourage the use of the direct method, but it is rarely used, for the excellent reason that the information in it is difficult to assemble; companies simply do not collect and store information in the manner required for this format. Instead, they use the indirect method, which is described next.

### The Indirect Method

Under the indirect method of presenting the statement of cash flows, the presentation begins with net income or loss, with subsequent additions to or deductions from that amount for non-cash revenue and expense items, resulting in net income provided by operating activities. The format of the indirect method appears in the following example.

**EXAMPLE**

Milagro Corporation constructs the following statement of cash flows using the indirect method:

Milagro Corporation
Statement of Cash Flows
For the year ended 12/31/20X1

| | | |
|---|---|---|
| **Cash flows from operating activities** | | |
| Net income | | $3,000,000 |
| Adjustments for: | | |
| Depreciation and amortization | $125,000 | |
| Provision for losses on accounts receivable | 20,000 | |
| Gain on sale of facility | -65,000 | |
| | | 80,000 |
| Increase in trade receivables | -250,000 | |
| Decrease in inventories | 325,000 | |
| Decrease in trade payables | -50,000 | |
| | | 25,000 |
| Cash generated from operations | | 3,105,000 |
| | | |
| **Cash flows from investing activities** | | |
| Purchase of fixed assets | -500,000 | |
| Proceeds from sale of equipment | 35,000 | |
| Net cash used in investing activities | | -465,000 |
| | | |
| **Cash flows from financing activities** | | |
| Proceeds from issuance of common stock | 150,000 | |
| Proceeds from issuance of long-term debt | 175,000 | |
| Dividends paid | -45,000 | |
| Net cash used in financing activities | | 280,000 |
| | | |
| Net increase in cash and cash equivalents | | 2,920,000 |
| Cash and cash equivalents at beginning of period | | 2,080,000 |
| Cash and cash equivalents at end of period | | $5,000,000 |

The indirect method is very popular, because the information required for it is relatively easily assembled from the accounts that a business normally maintains.

## The Statement of Retained Earnings

The statement of retained earnings, also known as the statement of shareholders' equity, is essentially a reconciliation of the beginning and ending balances in a company's equity during an accounting period. It is not considered an essential part of the monthly financial statements, and so is the least likely of all the financial statements to be issued. However, it is a common part of the annual financial statements. This section discusses the format of the statement.

### Overview of the Statement of Retained Earnings

The statement of retained earnings reconciles changes in the retained earnings account during a reporting period. The statement starts with the beginning balance in the retained earnings account and then adds or subtracts such items as profits and dividend payments to arrive at the ending retained earnings balance. The general calculation structure of the statement is:

Beginning retained earnings + Net income – Dividends +/- Other changes

= Ending retained earnings

The statement of retained earnings is most commonly presented as a separate statement, but can also be added to another financial statement. The following example shows a simplified format for the statement.

---

**EXAMPLE**

Milagro Corporation's accountant assembles the following statement of retained earnings to accompany his issuance of the financial statements of the company:

Milagro Corporation
Statement of Retained Earnings
For the year ended 12/31/20X1

| | |
|---|---:|
| Retained earnings at December 31, 20X0 | $150,000 |
| Net income for the year ended December 31, 20X1 | 40,000 |
| Dividends paid to shareholders | -25,000 |
| Retained earnings at December 31, 20X1 | $165,000 |

---

It is also possible to provide a greatly expanded version of the statement of retained earnings that discloses the various elements of retained earnings. For example, it could separately identify the par value of common stock, additional paid-in capital, retained earnings, and treasury stock, with all of these elements then rolling up into the total just noted in the last example. The following example shows what the format could look like.

**EXAMPLE**

Milagro Corporation's accountant creates an expanded version of the statement of retained earnings in order to provide more visibility into activities involving equity. The statement follows:

Milagro Corporation
Statement of Retained Earnings
For the year ended 12/31/20X1

| | Common Stock, $1 par | Additional Paid-in Capital | Retained Earnings | Total Shareholders' Equity |
|---|---|---|---|---|
| Retained earnings at December 31, 20X0 | $10,000 | $40,000 | $100,000 | $150,000 |
| Net income for the year ended December 31, 20X1 | | | 40,000 | 40,000 |
| Dividends paid to shareholders | | | -25,000 | -25,000 |
| Retained earnings at December 31, 20X1 | $10,000 | $40,000 | $115,000 | $165,000 |

## Financial Statement Footnotes

Financial statement footnotes are the explanatory and supplemental notes that accompany the financial statements. The exact nature of these footnotes varies, depending on the financial framework used to construct the financial statements (such as GAAP or IFRS). Each of these financial frameworks mandates the use of somewhat different footnotes.

Footnotes are considered an integral part of the financial statements, and so must be issued to outside parties along with the financial statements. It is not necessary to include footnotes if the statements are only being distributed internally.

Footnotes are extremely valuable to the readers of financial statements, since they can discern from the footnotes how various accounting policies used by the company are impacting its reported results and financial position.

The number of possible footnote disclosures is extremely long. The following list touches upon the more common footnotes, and is by no means even remotely comprehensive. If a company is in a specialized industry, there may be a number of additional disclosures that are specific to that industry. The sample footnote list follows:

- *Accounting policies*. Describes the significant accounting policies being followed.
- *Accounting changes*. Notes the nature and justification of a change in accounting principle, and the effect of the change.
- *Related parties*. States the nature of the relationship with a related party, and the amounts due to or from the other party.
- *Contingencies and commitments*. Describes the nature of any reasonably possible losses, and any guarantees, including maximum liabilities.

- *Risks and uncertainties*. Notes the use of significant estimates in accounting transactions, as well as various business vulnerabilities.
- *Nonmonetary transactions*. Notes nonmonetary transactions and any resulting gains or losses.
- *Subsequent events*. Discloses the nature of subsequent events and estimates their financial effect.
- *Business combinations*. States the type of combination, the reason for the acquisition, the payment price, liabilities assumed, goodwill incurred, acquisition-related costs, and other factors.
- *Fair value*. Describes the amount of fair value measurements and various reconciliations.
- *Cash*. Notes any uninsured cash balances.
- *Receivables*. Discloses the carrying amount of any financial instruments that are used as collateral for borrowings, and concentrations of credit risk.
- *Investments*. Notes the fair value and unrealized gains and losses on investments.
- *Inventories*. Describes any cost flow assumptions used, as well as any losses incurred when market prices are lower than cost.
- *Fixed assets*. States the methods of depreciation used, the amount of capitalized interest, asset impairments, and related issues.
- *Goodwill and intangibles*. Reconciles any changes in goodwill during the period, and notes any asset impairment losses.
- *Liabilities*. Describes the amounts and types of larger accrued liabilities.
- *Debt*. Discloses loans payable, interest rates, and maturities occurring over the next five years.
- *Pensions*. Reconciles various elements of the company pension plan during the period, and describes the company's investment policies.
- *Leases*. Itemizes future minimum lease payments.
- *Stockholders' equity*. Describes the terms of any convertible equity, notes dividends in arrears, and reconciles changes in equity during the period.
- *Revenue recognition*. Notes the company's revenue recognition policies.

Even more extensive footnotes are required by the SEC of any publicly-held company when they issue their quarterly and annual financial statements in the Forms 10-Q and 10-K, respectively.

## Consolidated Financial Statements

Consolidated financial statements are the financial statements of a group of entities that are presented as being those of a single economic entity. The definitions are:

- A group is a parent entity and all of its subsidiaries
- A subsidiary is an entity that is controlled by a parent entity

Thus, consolidated financial statements are the combined financials for a parent entity and its subsidiaries.

These statements require considerable effort to construct, since they must exclude the impact of any transactions between the entities being reported on. Thus, if there is a sale of goods between the subsidiaries of a parent company, this intercompany sale must be eliminated from the consolidated financial statements. Another common intercompany elimination is when the parent company pays interest income to the subsidiaries whose cash it is using to make investments; this interest income must be eliminated from the consolidated financial statements.

Consolidated statements are useful for reviewing the financial position and results of an entire group of commonly-owned businesses. Otherwise, reviewing the results of individual businesses within the group does not give an indication of the financial health of the group as a whole.

## Interim Financial Statements

Interim financial statements are financial statements that cover a period of less than one year. Typically, this means a monthly or quarterly set of financial statements, though the concept can apply to any other period, such as the last five months. Technically, the "interim" concept does not apply to the balance sheet, since this financial statement only refers to the assets, liabilities, and equity as of a specific point in time, rather than over a period of time.

The interim financial statement concept is most commonly associated with publicly-held companies, which must issue these statements at quarterly intervals. In this situation, three sets of interim statements are issued per year, which are for the first, second, and third quarters. The final reporting period of the year is encompassed by the year-end financial statements, and so is not considered to be associated with interim financial statements.

Interim financial statements contain the same documents found in annual financial statements. The line items appearing in these statements will also match the ones found in annual financial statements. The main differences between interim and annual statements can be found in the following areas:

- *Disclosures*. Some accompanying disclosures are not required in interim financial statements, or can be presented in a more summarized format.
- *Accrual basis*. The basis upon which accrued expenses are made can vary within interim reporting periods. For example, an expense could be recorded entirely within one reporting period, or its recognition may be spread across multiple periods. These issues can make the results and financial positions contained within interim periods appear to be somewhat inconsistent when reviewed on a comparative basis.
- *Seasonality*. The revenues generated by a business may be significantly impacted by seasonality. If so, interim statements may reveal periods of major losses and profits, which are not apparent in the annual financial statements.

Interim financial statements are not usually audited. Given the cost and time required for an audit, only the year-end financial statements are audited. If a company is publicly-held, its quarterly statements are instead reviewed. The concepts of an audit and a review are addressed in the Financial Statement Audits, Reviews, and Compilations section later in this chapter.

## Pro Forma Financial Statements

Pro forma financial statements are the complete set of financial statements issued by an entity, incorporating assumptions or hypothetical conditions about events that may have occurred in the past or which may occur in the future. Here are several examples of pro forma financial statements:

- *Full-year pro forma projection.* This is a projection of a company's year-to-date results, to which are added expected results for the remainder of the year, to arrive at a set of full-year pro forma financial statements. This approach is useful for projecting expected results both internally to management and externally to investors and creditors.
- *Investment pro forma projection.* A company may be seeking funding, and wants to show investors how the company's results will change if they invest a certain amount of money in the business. This approach may result in several different sets of pro forma financial statements, each designed for a different investment amount.
- *Historical with acquisition.* This is a backward-looking projection of a company's results in one or more prior years that includes the results of another business that the company wants to purchase, net of acquisition costs and synergies. This approach is useful for seeing how a prospective acquisition could have altered the financial results of the acquiring entity. This method could also be used for a shorter look-back period, just to the beginning of the current fiscal year; doing so gives investors a view of how the company would have performed if a recent acquisition had been made as of the beginning of the year; this can be a useful extrapolation of the results that may occur in the next fiscal year.
- *Risk analysis.* It may be useful to create a different set of pro forma financial statements that reflect best-case and worst-case scenarios for a business, so that managers can see the financial impact of different decisions, and the extent to which they can mitigate those risks.
- *Adjustments to GAAP or IFRS.* Management may believe that the financial results it has reported under either GAAP or IFRS are inaccurate or do not reveal a complete picture of the results of their business. If so, they may issue pro forma financial statements that include the corrections they believe are necessary to provide a better view of the business. The SEC takes a dim view of this kind of adjusted reporting by publicly-held companies.

There can be a significant problem with issuing pro forma financial statements to the public, since they contain management's assumptions about business conditions that may vary substantially from actual events, and which may, in retrospect, prove to be extremely inaccurate. Generally, pro forma financial statements tend to portray a business as being more successful than it really is, and having more financial resources available than may actually be the case.

## Financial Statement Audits, Reviews, and Compilations

A financial statement audit is the examination of an entity's financial statements and accompanying disclosures by an independent auditor, with the result being a report by the auditor, attesting to the fairness of presentation of the financial statements and related disclosures. The auditor's report must accompany the financial statements when they are issued to the intended recipients.

The purpose of a financial statement audit is to add credibility to the reported financial position and performance of a business. The SEC requires that all publicly-held entities must file annual reports with it that are audited. Similarly, lenders typically require an audit of the financial statements of any entity to which they lend funds. Suppliers may also require audited financial statements before they will be willing to extend trade credit (though usually only when the amount of requested credit is substantial).

The primary stages of an audit are as follows:

- *Planning and risk assessment.* Involves gaining an understanding of the business and the environment in which it operates, and using this information to assess whether there may be risks that could impact the financial statements.
- *Internal controls testing.* Involves the assessment of the effectiveness of an entity's suite of controls, concentrating on such areas as proper authorization, the safeguarding of assets, and the segregation of duties. A high level of effectiveness allows the auditors to scale back some of their later audit procedures.
- *Substantive procedures.* Involves a broad array of investigative procedures, including a ratio analysis of financial information, bank reconciliations, inventory counts, the confirmation of payables with suppliers, the analysis of reserves, and so forth.

Audit fees can be quite high, so some organizations instead hire auditors to conduct a financial statement review. A review has a much more limited scope than an audit, and so does not provide much assurance that all significant matters have been discovered that would have been noted in an audit. Given its more limited scope, a review is generally not allowed by lenders and creditors, who instead want to see the result of a full audit. However, a review is much less expensive than an audit.

In a review, the auditor performs only those procedures necessary to provide a reasonable basis for obtaining limited assurance that no material changes are needed to bring the financial statements into compliance with the applicable financial reporting framework. These procedures are more heavily concentrated in areas where there are enhanced risks of misstatement. Examples of these procedures are ratio analysis, the investigation of unusual or complex accounting transactions, and the investigation of significant journal entries.

Audit firms may provide a financial statement compilation service. In a compilation, the auditors engage in no activities to obtain assurance that any material modifications to the financial statements are needed. Thus, auditors do not use inquiries, analytical procedures, or review procedures, nor do they need to obtain an understanding of internal controls or engage in other audit procedures. Lenders and creditors are most unlikely to give any credence to financial statements created through a compilation service.

## Summary

This chapter has discussed each of the financial statements and revealed a number of possible layouts for them. The manager should have a solid understanding of the purpose of each of the financial statements and the information contained within each one. The nature of the required disclosures that accompany the financial statements will vary by company, so consult with the company controller to determine which disclosures are applicable.

It can be difficult for a manager not having a detailed understanding of accounting to extract the maximum amount of information from the financial statements. For more assistance in discerning the story that financial statements tell, see the following Interpreting Financial Statements chapter.

# Chapter 4
# Interpreting Financial Statements

## Introduction

When reviewing the financial statements of a business, what interpretation can a manager extract from these statements? In this chapter, we cover several types of financial statement analysis, mostly related to the ratio comparison of different line items in the statements. By comparing these results, and especially over multiple reporting periods, we can arrive at a reasonable estimation of the financial results and condition of a business. We also include a cautionary discussion of the limitations of ratio analysis.

When reviewing the following ratios, keep in mind that most of them will be used by outsiders, such as credit analysts. Or, if a company is publicly-held, the ratios will be calculated by outside analysts. If a manager intends to deal with these individuals, it will be necessary to monitor the same ratios and understand how they are compiled.

## Interpretation of Financial Statements

There are two key techniques for analyzing financial statements. The first is the use of horizontal and vertical analysis. Horizontal analysis is the comparison of financial information over a series of reporting periods, while vertical analysis is the proportional analysis of a financial statement, where each line item on a statement is listed as a percentage of another item. Typically, this means that every line item on an income statement is stated as a percentage of gross sales, while every line item on a balance sheet is stated as a percentage of total assets. Thus, horizontal analysis is the review of the results of multiple time periods, while vertical analysis is the review of the proportion of accounts to each other within a single period. Later sections describe horizontal and vertical analysis more fully.

Another heavily-used technique is ratio analysis. Ratios are used to calculate the relative size of one number in relation to another. After a ratio is calculated, it can then be compared to the same ratio calculated for a prior period, or that is based on an industry average, to see if a company is performing in accordance with expectations. In a typical financial statement analysis, most ratios will be within expectations, leaving a small number of outlier ratios that require additional detailed analysis.

There are several general categories of ratios, each designed to examine a different aspect of a company's performance. These categories are:

- *Liquidity ratios*. This is the most fundamentally important set of ratios, because they measure the ability of a company to remain in business. Samples of ratios in this category are:

- *Cash coverage ratio*. Shows the amount of cash available to pay interest.
- *Current ratio*. Measures the amount of liquidity available to pay for current liabilities.
- *Quick ratio*. The same as the current ratio, but does not include inventory.
- *Liquidity index*. Measures the amount of time required to convert assets into cash.

- *Activity ratios*. These ratios are a strong indicator of the quality of management, since they reveal how well management is utilizing company resources. Samples of ratios in this category are:
  - *Accounts payable turnover ratio*. Measures the speed with which a company pays its suppliers.
  - *Accounts receivable turnover ratio*. Measures a company's ability to collect accounts receivable.
  - *Inventory turnover ratio*. Measures the amount of inventory needed to support a given level of sales.
  - *Fixed asset turnover ratio*. Measures a company's ability to generate sales from a certain base of fixed assets.
  - *Sales to working capital ratio*. Shows the amount of working capital required to support a given amount of sales.
- *Leverage ratios*. These ratios reveal the extent to which a company is relying upon debt to fund its operations, and its ability to pay back the debt. Samples of ratios in the category are:
  - *Debt to equity ratio*. Shows the extent to which management is willing to fund operations with debt, rather than equity.
  - *Fixed charge coverage*. Shows the ability of a company to pay for its fixed costs.
- *Profitability ratios*. These ratios measure how well a company performs in generating a profit. Samples of ratios in this category are:
  - *Breakeven point*. Reveals the sales level at which a company breaks even.
  - *Gross profit ratio*. Shows revenues minus the cost of goods sold, as a proportion of sales.
  - *Net profit ratio*. Calculates the amount of profit after taxes and all expenses have been deducted from net sales.
  - *Return on net assets*. Shows company profits as a percentage of fixed assets and working capital.
  - *Return on equity*. Reveals total profits as a percentage of shareholders' equity.

Each of these ratios is described in more detail in the following sections.

## Horizontal Analysis

Horizontal analysis is the comparison of historical financial information over a series of reporting periods, or of the ratios derived from this information. The analysis is most commonly a simple grouping of information that is sorted by period, but the numbers in each succeeding period can also be expressed as a percentage of the amount in the baseline year, with the baseline amount being listed as 100%.

When conducting a horizontal analysis, it is useful to conduct the analysis for all of the financial statements at the same time, to see the complete impact of operational results on the company's financial condition over the review period. For example, as noted in the next two examples, the income statement analysis shows a company having an excellent second year, but the related balance sheet analysis shows that it is having trouble funding growth, given the decline in cash, increase in accounts payable, and increase in debt.

Horizontal analysis of the income statement is usually in a two-year format such as the one shown in the next exhibit, with a variance also reported that states the difference between the two years for each line item. An alternative format is to simply add as many years as will fit on the page, without showing a variance, to see general changes by account over multiple years.

**Sample Income Statement Horizontal Analysis**

| | 20X1 | 20X2 | Variance |
|---|---|---|---|
| Sales | $1,000,000 | $1,500,000 | $500,000 |
| Cost of goods sold | 400,000 | 600,000 | -200,000 |
| Gross margin | 600,000 | 900,000 | 300,000 |
| | | | |
| Salaries and wages | 250,000 | 375,000 | -125,000 |
| Office rent | 50,000 | 80,000 | -30,000 |
| Supplies | 10,000 | 20,000 | -10,000 |
| Utilities | 20,000 | 30,000 | -10,000 |
| Other expenses | 90,000 | 110,000 | -20,000 |
| Total expenses | 420,000 | 615,000 | -195,000 |
| Net profit | $180,000 | $285,000 | $105,000 |

Horizontal analysis of the balance sheet is also usually in a two-year format, such as the one shown in the following exhibit, with a variance stating the difference between the two years for each line item. An alternative format is to add as many years as will fit on the page, without showing a variance, in order to see general changes by account over multiple years.

**Sample Balance Sheet Horizontal Analysis**

| | 20X1 | 20X2 | Variance |
|---|---:|---:|---:|
| Cash | $100,000 | $80,000 | -$20,000 |
| Accounts receivable | 350,000 | 525,000 | 175,000 |
| Inventory | 150,000 | 275,000 | 125,000 |
| Total current assets | 600,000 | 880,000 | 280,000 |
| | | | |
| Fixed assets | 400,000 | 800,000 | 400,000 |
| Total assets | $1,000,000 | $1,680,000 | $680,000 |
| | | | |
| Accounts payable | $180,000 | $300,000 | $120,000 |
| Accrued liabilities | 70,000 | 120,000 | 50,000 |
| Total current liabilities | 250,000 | 420,000 | 170,000 |
| | | | |
| Notes payable | 300,000 | 525,000 | 225,000 |
| Total liabilities | 550,000 | 945,000 | 395,000 |
| | | | |
| Capital stock | 200,000 | 200,000 | 0 |
| Retained earnings | 250,000 | 535,000 | 285,000 |
| Total equity | 450,000 | 735,000 | 285,000 |
| | | | |
| Total liabilities and equity | $1,000,000 | $1,680,000 | $680,000 |

## Vertical Analysis

Vertical analysis is the proportional analysis of a financial statement, where each line item on a financial statement is listed as a percentage of another item. Typically, this means that every line item on an income statement is stated as a percentage of gross sales, while every line item on a balance sheet is stated as a percentage of total assets.

The most common use of vertical analysis is within a financial statement for a single time period, to see the relative proportions of account balances. Vertical analysis is also useful for timeline analysis, to see relative changes in accounts over time, such as on a comparative basis over a five-year period. For example, if the cost of goods sold has a history of being 40% of sales in each of the past four years, a new percentage of 48% would be a cause for alarm. An example of vertical analysis for an income statement is shown in the far right column of the following condensed income statement

**Sample Condensed Income Statement**

| | $ Totals | Percent |
|---|---|---|
| Sales | $1,000,000 | 100% |
| Cost of goods sold | 400,000 | 40% |
| Gross margin | 600,000 | 60% |
| | | |
| Salaries and wages | 250,000 | 25% |
| Office rent | 50,000 | 5% |
| Supplies | 10,000 | 1% |
| Utilities | 20,000 | 2% |
| Other expenses | 90,000 | 9% |
| Total expenses | 420,000 | 42% |
| Net profit | $180,000 | 18% |

The information provided by this income statement format is primarily useful for spotting spikes in expenses.

The central issue when creating a vertical analysis of a balance sheet is what to use as the denominator in the percentage calculation. The usual denominator is the asset total, but the total of all liabilities can also be used when calculating all liability line item percentages, and the total of all equity accounts when calculating all equity line item percentages. An example of vertical analysis for a balance sheet is shown in the far right column of the following condensed balance sheet.

**Sample Condensed Balance Sheet**

| | 20X1 | Percent |
|---|---|---|
| Cash | $100,000 | 10% |
| Accounts receivable | 350,000 | 35% |
| Inventory | 150,000 | 15% |
| Total current assets | 600,000 | 60% |
| | | |
| Fixed assets | 400,000 | 40% |
| Total assets | $1,000,000 | 100% |
| | | |
| Accounts payable | $180,000 | 18% |
| Accrued liabilities | 70,000 | 7% |
| Total current liabilities | 250,000 | 25% |
| | | |
| Notes payable | 300,000 | 30% |
| Total liabilities | 550,000 | 55% |
| | | |
| Capital stock | 200,000 | 20% |
| Retained earnings | 250,000 | 25% |
| Total equity | 450,000 | 45% |
| | | |
| Total liabilities and equity | $1,000,000 | 100% |

The information provided by this balance sheet format is useful for noting changes in a company's investment in working capital and fixed assets over time, which may indicate an altered business model that requires a different amount of ongoing funding.

We now turn to an explanation of the ratios that may be of use to a manager. Each explanation is accompanied by an example to illustrate how the ratio can be employed.

## Cash Coverage Ratio

The cash coverage ratio is useful for determining the amount of cash available to pay for interest, and is expressed as a ratio of the cash available to the amount of interest to be paid. This is a useful ratio when the entity evaluating a company is a prospective lender. The ratio should be substantially greater than 1:1. To calculate this ratio, take the earnings before interest and taxes (EBIT) from the income statement, add back to it all non-cash expenses included in EBIT (such as depreciation and amortization), and divide by the interest expense. The formula is:

$$\frac{\text{Earnings before interest and taxes + Non-cash expenses}}{\text{Interest expense}}$$

There may be a number of additional non-cash items to subtract in the numerator of the formula. For example, there may have been substantial charges in a period to increase reserves for sales allowances, product returns, bad debts, or inventory obsolescence. If these non-cash items are substantial, be sure to include them in the calculation. Also, the interest expense in the denominator should only include the actual interest expense to be paid – if there is a premium or discount to the amount being paid, it is not a cash payment, and so should not be included in the denominator.

---

**EXAMPLE**

The controller of Currency Bank is concerned that a borrower has recently taken on a great deal of debt to pay for a leveraged buyout, and wants to ensure that there is sufficient cash to pay for its new interest burden. The borrower is generating earnings before interest and taxes of $1,200,000 and it records annual depreciation of $800,000. The borrower is scheduled to pay $1,500,000 in interest expenses in the coming year. Based on this information, the borrower has the following cash coverage ratio:

$$\frac{\$1{,}200{,}000 \text{ EBIT} + \$800{,}000 \text{ Depreciation}}{\$1{,}500{,}000 \text{ Interest expense}}$$

= 1.33 cash coverage ratio

The calculation reveals that the borrower can pay for its interest expense, but has very little cash left for any other payments.

---

## Current Ratio

One of the first ratios that a lender or supplier reviews when examining a company is its current ratio. The current ratio measures the short-term liquidity of a business; that is, it gives an indication of the ability of a business to pay its bills. A ratio of 2:1 is preferred, with a lower proportion indicating a reduced ability to pay in a timely manner. Since the ratio is current assets divided by current liabilities, the ratio essentially implies that current assets can be liquidated to pay for current liabilities.

To calculate the current ratio, divide the total of all current assets by the total of all current liabilities. The formula is:

$$\frac{\text{Current assets}}{\text{Current liabilities}}$$

The current ratio can yield misleading results under the following circumstances:

- *Inventory component.* When the current assets figure includes a large proportion of inventory assets, since these assets can be difficult to liquidate. This can be a particular problem if management is using aggressive accounting techniques to apply an unusually large amount of overhead costs to inventory, which further inflates the recorded amount of inventory.

- *Paying from debt*. When a company is drawing upon its line of credit to pay bills as they come due, which means that the cash balance is near zero. In this case, the current ratio could be fairly low, and yet the presence of a line of credit still allows the business to pay in a timely manner.

---

**EXAMPLE**

A supplier wants to learn about the financial condition of Lowry Locomotion. The supplier calculates the current ratio of Lowry for the past three years:

| | Year 1 | Year 2 | Year 3 |
|---|---:|---:|---:|
| Current assets | $8,000,000 | $16,400,000 | $23,400,000 |
| Current liabilities | $4,000,000 | $9,650,000 | $18,000,000 |
| Current ratio | 2:1 | 1.7:1 | 1.3:1 |

The sudden rise in current assets over the past two years indicates that Lowry has undergone a rapid expansion of its operations. Of particular concern is the increase in accounts payable in Year 3, which indicates a rapidly deteriorating ability to pay suppliers. Based on this information, the supplier elects to restrict the extension of credit to Lowry.

---

## Quick Ratio

The quick ratio formula matches the most easily liquidated portions of current assets with current liabilities. The intent of this ratio is to see if a business has sufficient assets that are immediately convertible to cash to pay its bills. The key elements of current assets that are included in the quick ratio are cash, marketable securities, and accounts receivable. Inventory is not included in the quick ratio, since it can be quite difficult to sell off in the short term. Because of the exclusion of inventory from the formula, the quick ratio is a better indicator than the current ratio of the ability of a company to pay its obligations.

To calculate the quick ratio, summarize cash, marketable securities and trade receivables, and divide by current liabilities. Do not include in the numerator any excessively old receivables that are unlikely to be paid. The formula is:

$$\frac{\text{Cash + Marketable securities + Accounts receivable}}{\text{Current liabilities}}$$

Despite the absence of inventory from the calculation, the quick ratio may still not yield a good view of immediate liquidity if current liabilities are payable right now, while receipts from receivables are not expected for several more weeks.

**EXAMPLE**

Rapunzel Hair Products appears to have a respectable current ratio of 4:1. The breakdown of the ratio components is:

| Item | Amount |
|---|---:|
| Cash | $100,000 |
| Marketable securities | 50,000 |
| Accounts receivable | 420,000 |
| Inventory | 3,430,000 |
| Current liabilities | 1,000,000 |
| | |
| Current ratio | 4:1 |
| Quick ratio | 0.57:1 |

The component breakdown reveals that nearly all of Rapunzel's current assets are in the inventory area, where short-term liquidity is questionable. This issue is only visible when the quick ratio is substituted for the current ratio.

## Liquidity Index

The liquidity index calculates the days required to convert a company's trade receivables and inventory into cash. The index is used to estimate the ability of a business to generate the cash needed to meet current liabilities. Use the following steps to calculate the liquidity index:

1. Multiply the ending trade receivables balance by the average collection period.
2. Multiply the ending inventory balance by the average inventory liquidation period. This includes the average days to sell inventory and to collect the resulting receivables.
3. Summarize the first two items and divide by the total of all trade receivables and inventory.

The liquidity index formula is:

$$\frac{(\text{Trade receivables} \times \text{Days to liquidate}) + (\text{Inventory} \times \text{Days to liquidate})}{\text{Trade receivables} + \text{Inventory}}$$

The liquidation days information in the formula is based on historical averages, which may not translate well to the receivables and inventory currently on hand. Actual cash flows may vary substantially around the averages indicated by the formula.

---

**EXAMPLE**

A credit analyst wants to understand the ability of a customer, Hassle Corporation, to convert its receivables and inventory into cash. Hassle has $400,000 of trade receivables on hand, which can normally be converted to cash within 50 days. Hassle also has $650,000 of inventory, which can be liquidated in an average of 90 days. When combined with the receivable collection period, this means it takes 140 days to fully liquidate inventory *and* collect the proceeds. Based on this information, the liquidity index is:

$$\frac{(\$400{,}000 \text{ Receivables} \times 50 \text{ Days to liquidate}) + (\$650{,}000 \text{ Inventory} \times \text{Days to liquidate})}{\$400{,}000 \text{ Receivables} + \$650{,}000 \text{ Inventory}}$$

= 106 Days to convert assets to cash

The larger proportion of inventory in this calculation tends to skew the number of days well past the liquidation days for trade receivables. In short, Hassle will require a lengthy period to convert several current assets to cash, which may impact its ability to pay bills in the short term.

---

It may appear difficult to obtain the liquidation days information required for this formula. However, using industry averages can yield a reasonable estimate of the liquidity index for a business.

## Accounts Payable Turnover Ratio

Accounts payable turnover measures the speed with which a company pays its suppliers. If the turnover ratio declines from one period to the next, this indicates that the business is paying its suppliers more slowly, and may be an indicator of worsening financial condition. A change in the turnover ratio can also indicate altered payment terms with suppliers, though this rarely has more than a slight impact on the overall outcome of the ratio. If a company is paying its suppliers very quickly, it may mean that the suppliers are demanding fast payment terms.

To calculate the ratio, summarize all purchases from suppliers during the measurement period, and divide by the average amount of accounts payable during that period. The formula is:

$$\frac{\text{Total supplier purchases}}{(\text{Beginning accounts payable} + \text{Ending accounts payable}) \div 2}$$

The formula can be modified to exclude cash payments to suppliers, since the numerator should include only purchases on credit from suppliers. However, the amount of up-front cash payments to suppliers is normally so small that this modification is not necessary.

---

**EXAMPLE**

An analyst is reviewing Mulligan Imports, and wants to determine the company's accounts payable turnover for the past year. In the beginning of this period, the accounts payable balance was $800,000, and the ending balance was $884,000. Purchases for the last 12 months were $7,500,000. Based on this information, the analyst calculates the accounts payable turnover as:

$$\frac{\text{\$7,500,000 Purchases}}{\text{(\$800,000 Beginning payables + \$884,000 Ending payables)} \div 2}$$

= 8.9 Accounts payable turns per year

To calculate the accounts payable turnover in days, the analyst divides the 8.9 turns into 365 days, which yields:

365 Days ÷ 8.9 Turns = 41 Days

---

## Accounts Receivable Turnover Ratio

Accounts receivable turnover measures the ability of a company to efficiently issue credit to its customers and collect it back in a timely manner. A high turnover ratio indicates a combination of a conservative credit policy and an aggressive collections department, while a low turnover ratio represents an opportunity to collect excessively old receivables that are tying up working capital. This is useful information, since a customer with its own collection problems is less likely to pay its suppliers on time.

To calculate accounts receivable turnover, add together the beginning and ending accounts receivable to arrive at the average accounts receivable for the measurement period, and divide this amount into the net credit sales for the year. The formula is:

$$\frac{\text{Net annual credit sales}}{\text{(Beginning accounts receivable + Ending accounts receivable)} \div 2}$$

If the receivables balance is quite variable over the measurement period, the use of just the beginning and ending receivable balances in the denominator may skew the measurement. In this case, consider using a larger number of data points to derive the average.

---

**EXAMPLE**

A credit analyst is investigating the credit application of Norrona Software, and wants to see if Norrona is experiencing any of its own collection problems. In the beginning of the measurement period, the beginning receivable balance was $316,000, and the ending balance was $384,000. Net credit sales for the last 12 months were $3,500,000. Based on this information, the analyst calculates the accounts receivable turnover as:

$$\frac{\$3{,}500{,}000 \text{ Net credit sales}}{(\$316{,}000 \text{ Beginning receivables} + \$384{,}000 \text{ Ending receivables}) \div 2}$$

= 10 Accounts receivable turns

To calculate the accounts receivable turnover in days, the analyst divides the 10 turns into 365 days, which yields:

365 Days ÷ 10 Turns = 36.5 Days

---

## Inventory Turnover Ratio

The inventory turnover ratio is the rate at which inventory is used over a measurement period. This is an important measurement, for many businesses are burdened by an excessively large investment in inventory, which can consume available cash.

When there is a low rate of inventory turnover, this implies that a business may have a flawed purchasing system that bought too many goods, or that stocks were increased in anticipation of sales that did not occur. In both cases, there is a high risk of inventory aging, in which case it becomes obsolete and has little residual value.

When there is a high rate of inventory turnover, this implies that the purchasing function is tightly managed. However, it may also mean that a business does not have the cash reserves to maintain normal inventory levels, and so is turning away prospective sales. The latter scenario is most likely when the amount of debt is unusually high and there are minimal cash reserves.

To calculate inventory turnover, divide the ending inventory figure into the annualized cost of sales. If the ending inventory figure is not a representative number, use an average figure instead. The formula is:

$$\frac{\text{Annual cost of goods sold}}{\text{Inventory}}$$

The result of this calculation can be divided into 365 days to arrive at days of inventory on hand. Thus, a turnover rate of 4.0 becomes 91 days of inventory.

---

**EXAMPLE**

An analyst is reviewing the inventory situation of the Hegemony Toy Company. The business incurred $8,150,000 of cost of goods sold in the past year, and has ending inventory of $1,630,000. Total inventory turnover is calculated as:

$$\frac{\$8,150,000 \text{ Cost of goods sold}}{\$1,630,000 \text{ Inventory}}$$

$$= 5 \text{ Turns per year}$$

The five turns figure is then divided into 365 days to arrive at 73 days of inventory on hand.

---

## Fixed Asset Turnover Ratio

The fixed asset turnover ratio is the ratio of net sales to net fixed assets. A high ratio indicates that a company is doing an effective job of generating sales with a relatively small amount of fixed assets. Conversely, if the ratio is declining over time, the company has either overinvested in fixed assets or it needs to issue new products to revive its sales. Another possible effect is for a company to make a large investment in fixed assets, with a time delay of several months to a year before the new assets start generating revenues. Finally, a lack of ongoing investment in fixed assets will yield an apparently high turnover ratio over time, as depreciation reduces the reported amount of net fixed assets; this issue can be spotted by reviewing the cash expenditures for fixed assets that are reported in the statement of cash flows.

To derive fixed asset turnover, subtract accumulated depreciation from gross fixed assets, and divide into net annual sales. It may be necessary to obtain an average fixed asset figure, if the amount varies significantly over time. Do not include intangible assets in the denominator, since it can skew the results. The formula is:

$$\frac{\text{Net annual sales}}{\text{Gross fixed assets} - \text{Accumulated depreciation}}$$

This ratio is of most use in a "heavy industry," such as manufacturing, where a large capital investment is required. It is less useful in a services or knowledge-intensive industry, where the amount of fixed assets may be quite small.

If accelerated depreciation is used, it can rapidly reduce the amount of net fixed assets in the denominator, which makes the turnover figure look higher than is really the case.

---

**EXAMPLE**

Latham Lumber has gross fixed assets of $5,000,000 and accumulated depreciation of $2,000,000. Sales over the last 12 months totaled $9,000,000. The calculation of Latham's fixed asset turnover ratio is:

$$\frac{\$9{,}000{,}000 \text{ Net sales}}{\$5{,}000{,}000 \text{ Gross fixed assets} - \$2{,}000{,}000 \text{ Accumulated depreciation}}$$

$$= 3.0 \text{ Fixed asset turnover per year}$$

---

## Sales to Working Capital Ratio

It usually takes a certain amount of invested cash to maintain sales. There must be an investment in accounts receivable and inventory, against which accounts payable are offset. Thus, there is typically a ratio of working capital to sales that remains fairly constant in a business, even as sales levels change. This relationship can be measured with the sales to working capital ratio, which should be reported on a trend line to more easily spot spikes or dips. A spike in the ratio could be caused by a decision to grant more credit to customers in order to encourage more sales, while a dip could signal the reverse. A spike might also be triggered by a decision to keep more inventory on hand in order to more easily fulfill customer orders.

The ratio is calculated by dividing annualized net sales by average working capital. The formula is:

$$\frac{\text{Annualized net sales}}{\text{Accounts receivable} + \text{Inventory} - \text{Accounts payable}}$$

---

**EXAMPLE**

A credit analyst is reviewing the sales to working capital ratio of Milford Sound, which has applied for credit. Milford has been adjusting its inventory levels over the past few quarters, with the intent of doubling inventory turnover from its current level. The result is shown in the following table:

| | Quarter 1 | Quarter 2 | Quarter 3 | Quarter 4 |
|---|---|---|---|---|
| Revenue | $640,000 | $620,000 | $580,000 | $460,000 |
| Accounts receivable | 214,000 | 206,000 | 194,000 | 186,000 |
| Inventory | 1,280,000 | 640,000 | 640,000 | 640,000 |
| Accounts payable | 106,000 | 104,000 | 96,000 | 94,000 |
| Total working capital | 1,388,000 | 742,000 | 738,000 | 732,000 |
| Sales to working capital ratio | 1.8:1 | 3.3:1 | 3.1:1 | 3.1:1 |

The table includes a quarterly ratio calculation that is based on annualized sales. The table reveals that Milford achieved its goal of reducing inventory, but at the cost of a significant sales reduction, probably caused by customers turning to competitors that offered a larger selection of inventory.

---

## Debt to Equity Ratio

The debt to equity ratio of a business is closely monitored by the lenders and creditors of the company, since it can provide early warning that an organization is so overwhelmed by debt that it is unable to meet its payment obligations. This may also be triggered by a funding issue. For example, the owners of a business may not want to contribute any more cash to the company, so they acquire more debt to address the cash shortfall. Or, a company may use debt to buy back shares, thereby increasing the return on investment to the remaining shareholders.

Whatever the reason for debt usage, the outcome can be catastrophic, if corporate cash flows are not sufficient to make ongoing debt payments. This is a concern to lenders, whose loans may not be paid back. Suppliers are also concerned about the ratio for the same reason. A lender can protect its interests by imposing collateral requirements or restrictive covenants; suppliers usually offer credit with less restrictive terms, and so can suffer more if a company is unable to meet its payment obligations to them.

To calculate the debt to equity ratio, simply divide total debt by total equity. In this calculation, the debt figure should also include all lease obligations. The formula is:

$$\frac{\text{Long-term debt} + \text{Short-term debt} + \text{Leases}}{\text{Equity}}$$

---

**EXAMPLE**

A credit analyst is reviewing the credit application of New Centurion Corporation. The company reports a $500,000 line of credit, $1,700,000 in long-term debt, and a $200,000 operating lease. The company has $800,000 of equity. Based on this information, New Centurion's debt to equity ratio is:

$$\frac{\$500{,}000 \text{ Line of credit} + \$1{,}700{,}000 \text{ Debt} + \$200{,}000 \text{ Lease}}{\$800{,}000 \text{ Equity}}$$

= 3:1 debt to equity ratio

The debt to equity ratio exceeds the 2:1 ratio threshold above which the analyst is not allowed to grant credit. Consequently, New Centurion is kept on cash in advance payment terms.

---

## Fixed Charge Coverage

A business may incur so many fixed costs that its cash flow is mostly consumed by payments for these costs. The problem is particularly common when a company has incurred a large amount of debt, and must make ongoing interest payments. In this situation, use the fixed charge coverage ratio to determine the extent of the problem. If the resulting ratio is low, it is a strong indicator that any subsequent drop in the profits of a business may bring about its failure.

To calculate the fixed charge coverage ratio, combine earnings before interest and taxes (EBIT) with any lease expense, and then divide by the combined total of interest expense and lease expense. The formula is:

$$\frac{\text{Earnings before interest and taxes} + \text{Lease expense}}{\text{Interest expense} + \text{Lease expense}}$$

---

**EXAMPLE**

Luminescence Corporation recorded earnings before interest and taxes of $800,000 in the preceding year. The company also recorded $200,000 of lease expense and $50,000 of interest expense. Based on this information, its fixed charge coverage is:

$$\frac{\$800{,}000 \text{ EBIT} + \$200{,}000 \text{ Lease expense}}{\$50{,}000 \text{ Interest expense} + \$200{,}000 \text{ Lease expense}}$$

$$= 4{:}1 \text{ Fixed charge coverage ratio}$$

---

## Breakeven Point

The breakeven point is the sales volume at which a business earns exactly no money. It is mostly used for internal analysis purposes, but is also useful for a credit analyst, who can use it to determine the amount of losses that could be sustained if a credit applicant were to suffer a sales downturn.

To calculate the breakeven point, divide total fixed expenses by the contribution margin. Contribution margin is sales minus all variable expenses, divided by sales. The formula is:

$$\frac{\text{Total fixed expenses}}{\text{Contribution margin percentage}}$$

A more refined approach is to eliminate all non-cash expenses (such as depreciation) from the numerator, so that the calculation focuses on the breakeven cash flow level.

---

**EXAMPLE**

A credit analyst is reviewing the financial statements of a customer that has a large amount of fixed costs. The industry is highly cyclical, so the analyst wants to know what a large downturn in sales will do to the customer. The customer has total fixed expenses of $3,000,000, sales of $8,000,000, and variable expenses of $4,000,000. Based on this information, the customer's contribution margin is 50%. The breakeven calculation is:

$$\frac{\$3{,}000{,}000 \text{ Total fixed costs}}{50\% \text{ Contribution margin}}$$

$$= \$6{,}000{,}000 \text{ Breakeven sales level}$$

Thus, the customer's sales can decline by $2,000,000 from their current level before the customer will begin to lose money.

---

## Gross Profit Ratio

The gross profit ratio shows the proportion of profits generated by the sale of goods or services before selling and administrative expenses. In essence, it reveals the ability of a business to create sellable products in a cost-effective manner. The ratio is of some importance from an analysis perspective, especially when tracked on a trend line, to see if a business is continuing to provide products to the marketplace for which customers are willing to pay.

The gross margin ratio is calculated as sales minus the cost of goods sold, divided by sales. The formula is:

$$\frac{\text{Sales} - \text{Cost of goods sold}}{\text{Sales}}$$

The ratio can vary over time as sales volumes change, since the cost of goods sold contains some fixed cost elements that will not vary with sales volume.

---

**EXAMPLE**

An analyst is reviewing a credit application from Quest Adventure Gear, which includes financial statements for the past three years. The analyst extracts the following information from the financial statements of Quest:

| | 20X1 | 20X2 | 20X3 |
|---|---|---|---|
| Sales | $12,000,000 | $13,500,000 | $14,800,000 |
| Cost of goods sold | $5,000,000 | $5,100,000 | $4,700,000 |
| Gross profit ratio | 42% | 38% | 32% |

The analysis reveals that Quest is suffering from an ongoing decline in its gross profits, which should certainly be a concern from the perspective of allowing credit.

---

## Net Profit Ratio

The net profit ratio is a comparison of after-tax profits to net sales. It reveals the remaining profit after all costs of production and administration have been deducted from sales, and income taxes recognized. As such, it is one of the best measures of the overall results of a firm, especially when combined with an evaluation of how well it is using its working capital. The measure is commonly reported on a trend line, to judge performance over time. It is also used to compare the results of a business with its competitors.

The net profit ratio is really a short-term measurement, because it does not reveal a company's actions to maintain profitability over the long term, as may be indicated by the level of capital investment or research and development expenditures. Also, a company may delay a variety of discretionary expenses, such as maintenance or training, to make its net profit ratio look better than it normally is. Consequently, evaluate this ratio alongside an array of other metrics to gain a full picture of a company's ability to continue as a going concern.

Another issue with the net profit ratio is that a company may intentionally keep it low through a variety of expense recognition strategies in order to avoid paying taxes. If so, review the statement of cash flows to determine the real cash-generating ability of the business.

To calculate the net profit ratio, divide net profits by net sales and then multiply by 100. The formula is:

(Net profit ÷ Net sales) × 100

---

**EXAMPLE**

Kelvin Corporation has $1,000,000 of sales in its most recent month, as well as sales returns of $40,000, a cost of goods sold of $550,000, and administrative expenses of $360,000. The income tax rate is 35%. The calculation of its net profit percentage is:

$1,000,000 Sales - $40,000 Sales returns = <u>$960,000 Net sales</u>

$960,000 Net sales - $550,000 Cost of goods - $360,000 Administrative expenses

= <u>$50,000 Income before tax</u>

$50,000 Income before tax × (1 – 0.35) = <u>$32,500 Profit after tax</u>

($32,500 Profit after tax ÷ $960,000 Net Sales) × 100

= <u>3.4% Net profit ratio</u>

---

## Return on Net Assets

The return on net assets measurement compares net profits to net assets to see how well a company is able to utilize its asset base to create profits. A high ratio is an indicator of excellent management performance.

To calculate the return on net assets, add together fixed assets and net working capital, and divide the result into net after-tax profits. Net working capital is defined as current assets minus current liabilities. It is best to eliminate unusual items from the calculation, since they can skew the results. The calculation is:

$$\frac{\text{Net profit}}{\text{Fixed assets} + \text{Net working capital}}$$

The fixed asset figure in the calculation can be net of depreciation, but the type of depreciation calculation used can skew the net amount significantly, since some accelerated depreciation methods can eliminate as much as 40% of an asset's value in its first full year of usage.

---

**EXAMPLE**

Quality Cabinets, an old maker of fine mahogany cabinets, has net income of \$2,000,000, which includes a one-time expense of \$500,000. It also has fixed assets of \$4,000,000 and net working capital of \$1,000,000. For the purposes of the return on net assets calculation, the one-time expense item is eliminated, which increases the net income figure to \$2,500,000. The calculation of return on net assets is:

$$\frac{\$2{,}500{,}000 \text{ Net income}}{\$4{,}000{,}000 \text{ Fixed assets} + \$1{,}000{,}000 \text{ Net working capital}}$$

= 50% return on net assets

---

## Return on Equity

The return on equity (ROE) ratio reveals the amount of return earned by investors on their investments in a business. It is one of the metrics most closely watched by investors. Given the intense focus on ROE, it is frequently used as the basis for bonus compensation for senior managers.

ROE is essentially net income divided by shareholders' equity. ROE performance can be enhanced by focusing on improvements to three underlying measurements, all of which roll up into ROE. These sub-level measurements are:

- *Profit margin*. Calculated as net income divided by sales. Can be improved by trimming expenses, increasing prices, or altering the mix of products or services sold.

- *Asset turnover*. Calculated as sales divided by assets. Can be improved by reducing receivable balances, inventory levels, and/or the investment in fixed assets, as well as by lengthening payables payment terms.
- *Financial leverage*. Calculated as assets divided by shareholders' equity. Can be improved by buying back shares, paying dividends, or using more debt to fund operations.

Or, stated as a formula, the return on equity is as follows:

$$\text{Return on Equity} = \frac{\text{Net income}}{\text{Sales}} \times \frac{\text{Sales}}{\text{Assets}} \times \frac{\text{Assets}}{\text{Shareholders' equity}}$$

---

**EXAMPLE**

Hammer Industries manufactures construction equipment. The company's return on equity has declined from a high of 25% five years ago to a current level of 10%. The CFO wants to know what is causing the problem, and assigns the task to a financial analyst, Wendy. She reviews the components of ROE for both periods, and derives the following information:

| | ROE | | Profit Margin | | Asset Turnover | | Financial Leverage |
|---|---|---|---|---|---|---|---|
| Five Years Ago | 25% | = | 12% | × | 1.2x | × | 1.75x |
| Today | 10% | = | 10% | × | 0.6x | × | 1.70x |

The information in the table reveals that the primary culprit causing the decline is a sharp reduction in the company's asset turnover. This has been caused by a large buildup in the company's inventory levels, which have been brought about by management's insistence on stocking larger amounts of finished goods in order to increase the speed of order fulfillment.

---

The multiple components of the ROE calculation present an opportunity for a business to generate a high ROE in several ways. For example, a grocery store has low profits on a per-unit basis, but turns over its assets at a rapid rate, so that it earns a profit on many sale transactions over the course of a year. Conversely, a manufacturer of custom goods realizes large profits on each sale, but also maintains a significant amount of component parts that reduce asset turnover. The following illustration shows how both entities can earn an identical ROE, despite having such a different emphasis on profits and asset turnover. In the illustration, we ignore the effects of financial leverage.

**Comparison of Returns on Equity**

| | ROE | | Profit Margin | | Asset Turnover |
|---|---|---|---|---|---|
| Grocery Store | 20% | = | 2% | × | 10x |
| Custom manufacturer | 20% | = | 40% | × | 0.5x |

Usually, a successful business is able to focus on either a robust profit margin *or* a high rate of asset turnover. If it were able to generate both, its return on equity would be so high that the company would likely attract competitors who want to emulate the underlying business model. If so, the increased level of competition usually drives down the overall return on equity in the market to a more reasonable level.

A high level of financial leverage can increase the return on equity, because it means a business is using the minimum possible amount of equity, instead relying on debt to fund its operations. By doing so, the amount of equity in the denominator of the return on equity equation is minimized. If any profits are generated by funding activities with debt, these changes are added to the numerator in the equation, thereby increasing the return on equity.

The trouble with employing financial leverage is that it imposes a new fixed expense in the form of interest payments. If sales decline, this added cost of debt could trigger a steep decline in profits that may end in bankruptcy. Thus, a business that relies too much on debt to enhance its shareholder returns may find itself in significant financial trouble. A more prudent path is to employ a modest amount of additional debt that a company can comfortably handle even through a business downturn.

---

**EXAMPLE**

The president of Finchley Fireworks has been granted a bonus plan that is triggered by an increase in the return on equity. Finchley has $2,000,000 of equity, of which the president plans to buy back $600,000 with the proceeds of a loan that has a 6% after-tax interest rate. The following table models this plan:

| | Before Buyback | After Buyback |
|---|---:|---:|
| Sales | $10,000,000 | $10,000,000 |
| Expenses | 9,700,000 | 9,700,000 |
| Debt interest expense | --- | 36,000 |
| Profits | 300,000 | 264,000 |
| Equity | 2,000,000 | 1,400,000 |
| Return on equity | 15% | 19% |

The model indicates that this strategy will work. Expenses will be increased by the new amount of interest expense, but the offset is a steep decline in equity, which increases the return on equity. An additional issue to be investigated is whether the company's cash flows are stable enough to support this extra level of debt.

---

A business that has a significant asset base (and therefore a low asset turnover rate) is more likely to engage in a larger amount of financial leverage. This situation arises because the large asset base can be used as collateral for loans. Conversely, if a company has high asset turnover, the amount of assets on hand at any point in time is relatively low, giving a lender few assets to designate as collateral for a loan.

> **Tip:** A highly successful company that spins off large amounts of cash may generate a low return on equity, because it chooses to retain a large part of the cash. Cash retention increases assets and so results in a low asset turnover rate, which in turn drives down the return on equity. Actual ROE can be derived by stripping the excess amount of cash from the ROE equation.

Return on equity is one of the primary tools used to measure the performance of a business, particularly in regard to how well management is enhancing shareholder value. As noted in this section, there are multiple ways to enhance ROE. However, we must warn against the excessive use of financial leverage to improve ROE, since the use of debt can turn into a considerable burden if cash flows decline.

A case can be made that ROE should be ignored, since an excessive focus on it may drive management to pare back on a number of discretionary expenses that are needed to build the long-term value of a company. For example, the senior management team may cut back on expenditures for research and development, training, and marketing in order to boost profits in the short term and elevate ROE. However, doing so impairs the ability of the business to build its brand and compete effectively over the long term. Some management teams will even buy their companies back from investors, so that they are not faced with the ongoing pressure to enhance ROE. In a buyback situation, managers see that a lower ROE combined with a proper level of reinvestment in the business is a better path to long-term value.

## Limitations of Ratio Analysis

Ratio analysis is a useful tool for the manager who needs to create a picture of the financial results and position of a business just from its financial statements. However, there are a number of limitations of ratio analysis to be aware of. They are:

- *Historical.* All of the information used in ratio analysis is derived from actual historical results. This does not mean that the same results will carry forward into the future. However, ratio analysis can be used on pro forma information and compared to historical results for consistency.
- *Historical versus current cost.* The information on the income statement is stated in current costs (or close to it), whereas some elements of the balance sheet may be stated at historical cost (which could vary substantially from current costs). This disparity can result in unusual ratio results.
- *Aggregation.* The information in a financial statement line item being used for a ratio analysis may have been aggregated differently in the past, so that running the ratio analysis on a trend line does not compare the same information through the entire trend period.

- *Operational changes*. A company may change its underlying operational structure to such an extent that a ratio calculated several years ago and compared to the same ratio today would yield a misleading conclusion. For example, if a constraint analysis system is implemented, this might lead to a reduced investment in fixed assets, whereas a ratio analysis might conclude that the company is letting its fixed asset base become too old.
- *Accounting policies*. Different companies may have different policies for recording the same accounting transaction. This means that comparing the ratio results of different companies may be like comparing apples and oranges. For example, one company might use accelerated depreciation while another company uses straight-line depreciation, or one company records a sale at gross while the other company does so at net.
- *Business conditions*. Place ratio analysis in the context of the general business environment. For example, 60 days of sales outstanding might be considered poor in a period of rapidly growing sales, but might be excellent during an economic contraction when customers are in severe financial condition and unable to pay their bills.
- *Interpretation*. It can be quite difficult to ascertain the reason for the results of a ratio. For example, a current ratio of 2:1 might appear to be excellent, until you realize that the company just sold a large amount of its stock to bolster its cash position. A more detailed analysis might reveal that the current ratio will only temporarily be at that level, and will probably decline in the near future.
- *Company strategy*. It can be dangerous to conduct a ratio analysis comparison between two firms that are pursuing different strategies. For example, one company may be following a low-cost strategy, and so is willing to accept a lower gross margin in exchange for more market share. Conversely, a company in the same industry is focusing on a high customer service strategy where its prices are higher and gross margins are higher, but it will never attain the revenue levels of the first company.
- *Point in time*. Some ratios extract information from the balance sheet. Be aware that the information on the balance sheet is only as of the last day of the reporting period. If there was an unusual spike or decline in the account balance on the last day of the reporting period, this can impact the outcome of the ratio analysis.

In short, ratio analysis has a variety of limitations. However, as long as there is awareness of these problems and alternative and supplemental methods are used to collect and interpret information, ratio analysis is still useful.

## Effect of the Number of Days in a Month

The financial results reported by a business can vary markedly by month, depending upon the number of business days within that month. This is because some months have a total of 28 days, while others have as many as 31 days. When the effects of federal holidays are included, the result is noted in the following table:

**Net Number of Business Days by Month**

| Month | Calendar Days | Business Days* | Holidays | Net Business Days |
|---|---|---|---|---|
| January | 31 | 23 | 2 | 21 |
| February | 28 | 20 | 1 | 19 |
| March | 31 | 21 | 0 | 21 |
| April | 30 | 22 | 0 | 22 |
| May | 31 | 22 | 1 | 21 |
| June | 30 | 21 | 0 | 21 |
| July | 31 | 23 | 1 | 22 |
| August | 31 | 21 | 0 | 21 |
| September | 30 | 22 | 1 | 21 |
| October | 31 | 23 | 1 | 22 |
| November | 30 | 20 | 2 | 18 |
| December | 31 | 22 | 1 | 21 |
| Totals | 365 | 260 | 10 | 250 |

* Will vary somewhat by year

When aggregated, the information in the preceding table yields the following distribution:

**Distribution of Business Days per Month**

| Number of Net Business Days | Number of Months | Proportion |
|---|---|---|
| 22 | 3 | 25% |
| 21 | 7 | 59% |
| 20 | 0 | 0% |
| 19 | 1 | 8% |
| 18 | 1 | 8% |
| Totals | 12 | 100% |

In some industries, there is a clear association between the net number of business days and the amount of revenue earned, while it is less of an issue in other industries. For example, the consulting business relies upon billable hours, and so a consulting firm's revenues are closely related to the net number of business days.

Conversely, a seasonal business will experience strong sales in certain months, irrespective of the net number of business days.

The number of business days is of particular concern to a manager if sales closely correlate with the net number of business days and the company has a high level of fixed costs. In this case, a company is likely to experience losses when there are fewer working days in a month. If the breakeven point only allows for a profit in a few months, the prudent manager will need to cut back on expenses and/or raise prices to ensure that profits can be achieved in every month of the year.

## Summary

Which of the preceding review methods are most critical, and which merely provide useful additional information? The answer depends upon the reason for the analysis. If the analysis is intended to determine the basic viability of a business, consider using the following tranches of analysis activities to obtain layers of information about a business:

- *Essential information.* The core requirement is to understand the short-term viability of a business. To find this information, use a combination of the quick ratio, accounts payable turnover ratio, and the net profit ratio.
- *Expanded information.* Supplement the first layer of analysis with the liquidity index, sales to working capital ratio, and fixed charge coverage analysis.
- *Long-term viability.* To understand the long-term viability of a business, add to the preceding analyses all asset turnover ratios, the debt to equity ratio, and the breakeven point.

When using these layers of analysis, always do so using trend line (horizontal) analysis. By doing so, any declines in profitability or financial position are much more apparent.

As noted in the introduction, the manager needs to understand all key ratios if there is a need to discuss them with outsiders. At a minimum, it is quite likely that the company controller will provide a supplemental analysis that highlights key points in the financial statements that should be of concern to the management team. This analysis is at a level of detail more refined than can be obtained through a simple ratio analysis.

# Chapter 5
# Evaluation of Responsibility Centers

## Introduction

One of the cornerstones of a system of management is the organizational structure of a business. A company must be structured in whatever manner allows it to compete and earn a reasonable profit. In most cases, this means organizing by functional area. Also, if the company is large enough, these functional areas may be clustered together into divisions. Once the organizational structure has been implemented, there will be a number of responsibility centers within the company, each of which (as the name implies) is responsible for a specific activity. From an accounting perspective, the methods used to assemble and report information must be based on the nature of these responsibility centers.

In this chapter, we define the responsibility center, as well as the functional and divisional organizational structures. We then note the chart of accounts formats most amenable to aggregating information for the designated responsibility centers, and finish with a discussion of the types of responsibility center information that should be issued.

We also describe how transfer pricing can impact the results of a company's divisions, and the methods available for setting transfer prices. In some cases, the type of transfer pricing method chosen can have a profound impact on the reported results of a responsibility center.

**Related Podcast Episode:** Episode 65 of the Accounting Best Practices Podcast discusses responsibility accounting. It is available at: **accounting-tools.com/podcasts** or **iTunes**

## Responsibility Reporting

Responsibility reporting is based on the assumption that every cost incurred must be the responsibility of one person somewhere in a business. For example, the cost of rent can be assigned to the person who negotiates and signs the lease, while the cost of an employee's salary is the responsibility of that person's direct manager. This concept also applies to the cost of products, for each component part has a standard cost, which it is the responsibility of the purchasing manager to obtain at the correct price. Similarly, scrap costs incurred at a machine are the responsibility of the shift manager.

At the upper levels of the organizational structure, it is common to find fewer responsibility reports being used. This is because there is a natural progression of reports that aggregate the information going to higher levels of authority. The aggregation is based on the following concepts:

1. *Revenue center*. A revenue center is solely responsible for generating sales. Typical revenue centers are the sales department and licensing department. This approach is not usually recommended, since someone solely tasked with boosting revenues may incur inordinate expenses to do so, resulting in net losses despite an increase in sales. For example, a salesperson could reduce prices in order to obtain a customer order, or spend an inordinate amount of time and cost to obtain an order.
2. *Cost center*. A cost center only has control over the costs incurred, and not revenues, profitability, or invested funds. There can be many cost centers, such as for a specific machine, an administrative task, or a building lease. Cost center reports can be sent to a large proportion of employees. While useful, this approach can focus an excessive amount of attention on cost reduction, rather than on fulfilling the strategic direction of the business. For example, a cost center manager may elect not to pay for an overnight delivery to a customer on the grounds that the cost is excessive, even though the customer is critical to the company's success.
3. *Profit center*. A profit center is responsible for both a set of costs and the revenue that those costs generate. This report tends to encompass a number of cost centers, so there are far fewer profit centers than cost centers. This approach is recommended, since it forces managers to balance the effects on both revenues and expenses when making decisions.
4. *Investment center*. An investment center is a profit center whose manager is also responsible for the funds invested in operations. One investment center can incorporate several profit centers, so there may only be one investment center in a business. This approach is the most comprehensive, since managers must now consider the use of invested funds along with all profit center considerations when making decisions.

By properly employing the responsibility center concept, reports can be tailored for each responsible person. For example, the manager of a work cell will receive a cost report that only itemizes the costs incurred by that specific cell, while the production manager will receive a different one that itemizes the costs of the entire production department, and the president will receive one that summarizes the results and return on investment of the entire organization.

Responsibility reporting is a subset of the overall organizational structure of a business. In the next two sections, we describe the most common of these organizational formats, the functional and divisional structures.

## Functional Organizational Structure

The functional organizational structure organizes the activities of a business around areas of specialization. For example, there may be a marketing department that focuses solely on marketing activities, a sales department that only engages in sales activities, and an engineering department that only designs products and manufacturing facilities. This approach involves a great deal of process standardization within a business.

The functional organizational structure is the dominant mode of organization in medium to large companies, since these entities deal with such large sales and production volumes that no other form of organizational structure would be nearly as efficient. It is particularly effective in the following situations:

- Large volume of standardized product or service sales
- Reduced level of change within the industry
- Large fixed asset base
- Minimal amount of entirely new product line introductions
- Minimal changes due to fashion or other changes in taste or technology
- Competition is primarily based on cost

---

**EXAMPLE**

Dude Skis has just passed $10 million in sales, and its president believes that this is a good time to restructure the business to improve efficiencies through job specialization. Accordingly, he clusters employees into the following functional areas:

| | | |
|---|---|---|
| Accounting department | Human resources department | Production department |
| Corporate department | Investor relations department | Public relations department |
| Engineering department | Legal department | Purchasing department |
| Facilities department | | Sales and marketing department |

---

The functional structure has a number of advantages, including the following:

- *Efficiencies*. When employees are allowed to focus on one specific functional area to the exclusion of all else, they can achieve significant efficiencies in terms of process flow and management methods.
- *Chain of command*. There is a very clear chain of command in this structure, so everyone knows which decisions they are allowed to make, and which ones to hand off to their supervisors.
- *Promotions*. It is easier to set up career paths for employees and monitor their progress toward the goals outlined for their functional areas.
- *Specialization*. A company can use this approach to cultivate a group of extraordinary specialists who can strongly impact the functions of the company.

- *Training*. It is easier to monitor and update the training of employees when they are focused on narrow functional areas.

Despite the advantages of the functional organizational structure, it can also twist the fundamental process and decision flow within a business, with the following results:

- *Fast growth*. When a company is growing rapidly and is therefore continually modifying its operations to meet changing conditions, the functional structure can reduce the speed with which changes are made. This is because requests for decisions must move up the organizational structure to a decision maker, and then back down to the person requesting a decision; if there are multiple levels in the organizational structure, this can take a long time.
- *Queue times*. When processes cross the boundaries of multiple functional areas, the queue times added by each area can greatly increase the time required to complete an entire transaction.
- *Silos*. There is a tendency toward poor communications across the various functional silos within a business, though this can be mitigated by using cross-functional teams.
- *Small businesses*. This approach is not needed in quite small businesses, where employees may be individually responsible for many functions at the same time.
- *Specialist viewpoint*. When everyone in the company is herded into clusters of functional silos, there are few people left who are capable of seeing the total strategic direction of the company, which can result in a very difficult decision making process.

From a responsibility center perspective, information is aggregated at the level of each department. This usually means that departments are treated as cost centers, while the entire organization is treated as a single profit center or investment center. The sales department may be treated as a revenue center.

## Divisional Organizational Structure

The divisional organizational structure organizes the activities of a business around geographical, market, or product and service groups. Thus, a company organized on divisional lines could have operating groups for the United States or Europe, or for commercial customers, or for the green widget product line. Each such division contains a complete set of functions. Thus, the green widget division would handle its own accounting, sales and marketing, engineering, production, and so forth.

This approach is useful when decision making should be clustered at the division level to react more quickly to local conditions. The divisional structure is especially useful when a company has many regions, markets, and/or products. However, it can cause higher total costs, and can result in a number of small, quarreling fiefdoms within a company that do not necessarily work together for the good of the entire entity.

**EXAMPLE**

Big Data Corporation has just passed $250 million in sales, and its president decides to adopt a divisional organizational structure in order to better service its customers. Accordingly, he adopts the following structure:

- *Commercial division.* Focuses on all commercial customers and has its own product development, production, accounting and sales employees.
- *Retail division.* Focuses on all retail customers in the United States, and has its own product development, production, accounting, and sales employees.
- *International division.* Focuses on all retail customers outside of the United States. It shares product development and production facilities with the retail division, and has its own accounting and sales employees.

---

The key points in favor of the divisional structure involve placing decision making as close to the customer as possible. The advantages are:

- *Accountability.* This approach makes it much easier to assign responsibility for actions and results. In particular, a division is run by its own management group, which looks out for the best interests of the division.
- *Competition.* The divisional structure works well in markets where there is a great deal of competition, where local managers can quickly shift the direction of their businesses.
- *Culture.* This structure can be used to create a culture at the divisional level that most closely meets the needs of the local market.
- *Local decisions.* The divisional structure allows decision making to be shifted downward in the organization, which may improve the company's ability to respond to local market conditions.
- *Multiple offerings.* When a company has a large number of product offerings, or different markets that it services, and they are not similar, it makes more sense to adopt the divisional structure.
- *Speed.* This approach tends to yield faster responses to local market conditions.

The key points against the divisional structure involve the cost of duplicating functions and a reduced focus on the overall direction of the company. The disadvantages are:

- *Cost.* When a complete set of functions is set up within each division, there are likely to be more employees in total than would be the case if the business had instead been organized under a purely functional structure. Also, there must still be a corporate organization, which adds more overhead cost to the business.
- *Economies of scale.* The company as a whole may not be able to take advantage of economies of scale, unless purchases are integrated across the entire organization.

- *Inefficiencies*. When there are a number of functional areas spread among many divisions, no one functional area will be as efficient as would have been the case if there had instead been one central organization for each function.
- *Rivalries*. The various divisions may have no incentive to work together, and may even work at cross-purposes, as some managers undercut the actions of other divisions in order to gain localized advantages.
- *Silos*. All skills are compartmentalized by division, so it can be difficult to transfer skills or best practices across the organization. It is also more difficult to cross-sell products and services between the divisions.
- *Strategic focus*. Each division will tend to have its own strategic direction, which may differ from the strategic direction of the company as a whole.

From a responsibility center perspective, information is aggregated at the level of each division. Since each division generates its own sales, this means that each division is treated as either a profit center or investment center. If there are departments within each division, the departments are treated as cost centers.

## The Structure of the Chart of Accounts

How do we organize information for responsibility center reporting? This is done through the chart of accounts, which is a listing of all accounts used in the general ledger, along with the account code assigned to each account. The general ledger is the central database of information that a company maintains about its business transactions. When information is entered into the general ledger, each transaction references an account number, which ties back to an account description.

The structure of the account number listed in the chart of accounts is crucial for responsibility reporting, since it allows a company to store information at the level of the individual responsibility center. Alternatively, if no attention is paid to the account code structure in the chart of accounts, it will not be possible to collect information in a manner that can be used to derive reports.

In essence, the chart of accounts at the most primitive level can employ three-digit account numbers to collect a basic set of information, but cannot store information by department or division. Five-digit account numbers allow for information storage at the department level, while seven-digit account numbers allow for storage at both the department and division levels. Thus, the account code structure needs to match the organizational structure of a business. The following sub-sections expand upon these concepts.

**Related Podcast Episode:** Episode 163 of the Accounting Best Practices Podcast discusses the chart of accounts. It is available at: **accountingtools.com/podcasts** or **iTunes**

## Three-Digit Chart of Accounts

A three-digit chart of accounts allows a business to create a numerical sequence of accounts that can contain as many as 1,000 potential accounts. The three-digit format is most commonly used by small businesses that do not break out the results of any departments or divisions in their financial statements. A sample three-digit chart of accounts is shown in the following exhibit.

**Sample Three-Digit Chart of Accounts**

| Account Number | Description |
|---|---|
| 010 | Cash |
| 020 | Petty cash |
| 030 | Accounts receivable |
| 040 | Reserve for doubtful accounts |
| 050 | Marketable securities |
| 060 | Raw materials inventory |
| 070 | Work-in-process inventory |
| 080 | Finished goods inventory |
| 090 | Reserve for obsolete inventory |
| 100 | Fixed assets – Computer equipment |
| 110 | Fixed assets – Computer software |
| 120 | Fixed assets – Furniture and fixtures |
| 130 | Fixed assets – Leasehold improvements |
| 140 | Fixed assets - Machinery |
| 150 | Accumulated depreciation – Computer equipment |
| 160 | Accumulated depreciation – Computer software |
| 170 | Accumulated depreciation – Furniture and fixtures |
| 180 | Accumulated depreciation – Leasehold improvements |
| 190 | Accumulated depreciation – Machinery |
| 200 | Other assets |
| 300 | Accounts payable |
| 310 | Accrued payroll liability |
| 320 | Accrued vacation liability |
| 330 | Accrued expenses liability – other |
| 340 | Unremitted sales taxes |
| 350 | Unremitted pension payments |
| 360 | Short-term notes payable |
| 370 | Other short-term liabilities |
| 400 | Long-term notes payable |
| 500 | Capital stock |
| 510 | Retained earnings |
| 600 | Revenue |

| Account Number | Description |
|---|---|
| 700 | Cost of goods sold – Materials |
| 710 | Cost of goods sold – Direct labor |
| 720 | Cost of goods sold – Manufacturing supplies |
| 730 | Cost of goods sold – Applied overhead |
| 800 | Bank charges |
| 805 | Benefits |
| 810 | Depreciation |
| 815 | Insurance |
| 825 | Office supplies |
| 830 | Salaries and wages |
| 835 | Telephones |
| 840 | Training |
| 845 | Travel and entertainment |
| 850 | Utilities |
| 855 | Other expenses |
| 860 | Interest expense |

In the example, each block of related accounts begins with a different set of account numbers. Thus, current liabilities begin with "300," revenue items begin with "600," and cost of goods sold items begin with "700." This numbering scheme makes it easier for the accounting staff to remember where accounts are located within the chart of accounts. This type of account range format is also required by the report writing module in many accounting software packages.

### Five-Digit Chart of Accounts

A five-digit chart of accounts is used by organizations that want to track information at the departmental level. With a five-digit code, they can produce a separate income statement for each department. This format duplicates the account codes found in a three-digit chart of accounts, but then adds a two-digit code to the left, which indicates specific departments. The three-digit codes for expenses (and sometimes also revenues) are then duplicated for each department for which management wants to record information. A sample of the five-digit chart of accounts format appears in the following exhibit, using the accounting and production departments to show how expense account codes can be duplicated.

**Sample Five-Digit Chart of Accounts**

| Account Number | Department | Description |
|---|---|---|
| 00-010 | xxx | Cash |
| 00-020 | xxx | Petty cash |
| 00-030 | xxx | Accounts receivable |
| 00-040 | xxx | Allowance for doubtful accounts |

| Account Number | Department | Description |
|---|---|---|
| 00-050 | xxx | Marketable securities |
| 00-060 | xxx | Raw materials inventory |
| 00-070 | xxx | Work-in-process inventory |
| 00-080 | xxx | Finished goods inventory |
| 00-090 | xxx | Reserve for obsolete inventory |
| 00-100 | xxx | Fixed assets – Computer equipment |
| 00-110 | xxx | Fixed assets – Computer software |
| 00-120 | xxx | Fixed assets – Furniture and fixtures |
| 00-130 | xxx | Fixed assets – Leasehold improvements |
| 00-140 | xxx | Fixed assets – Machinery |
| 00-150 | xxx | Accumulated depreciation – Computer equipment |
| 00-160 | xxx | Accumulated depreciation – Computer software |
| 00-170 | xxx | Accumulated depreciation – Furniture and fixtures |
| 00-180 | xxx | Accumulated depreciation – Leasehold improvements |
| 00-190 | xxx | Accumulated depreciation – Machinery |
| 00-200 | xxx | Other assets |
| 00-300 | xxx | Accounts payable |
| 00-310 | xxx | Accrued payroll liability |
| 00-320 | xxx | Accrued vacation liability |
| 00-330 | xxx | Accrued expenses liability – other |
| 00-340 | xxx | Unremitted sales taxes |
| 00-350 | xxx | Unremitted pension payments |
| 00-360 | xxx | Short-term notes payable |
| 00-370 | xxx | Other short-term liabilities |
| 00-400 | xxx | Long-term notes payable |
| 00-500 | xxx | Capital stock |
| 00-510 | xxx | Retained earnings |
| 00-600 | xxx | Revenue |
| 00-700 | xxx | Cost of goods sold – Materials |
| 00-710 | xxx | Cost of goods sold – Direct labor |
| 00-720 | xxx | Cost of goods sold – Manufacturing supplies |
| 00-730 | xxx | Cost of goods sold – Applied overhead |
| 10-800 | Accounting | Bank charges |
| 10-805 | Accounting | Benefits |
| 10-810 | Accounting | Depreciation |
| 10-815 | Accounting | Insurance |
| 10-825 | Accounting | Office supplies |
| 10-830 | Accounting | Salaries and wages |
| 10-835 | Accounting | Telephones |
| 10-840 | Accounting | Training |

| Account Number | Department | Description |
|---|---|---|
| 10-845 | Accounting | Travel and entertainment |
| 10-850 | Accounting | Utilities |
| 10-855 | Accounting | Other expenses |
| 10-860 | Accounting | Interest expense |
| 20-800 | Production | Bank charges |
| 20-805 | Production | Benefits |
| 20-810 | Production | Depreciation |
| 20-815 | Production | Insurance |
| 20-825 | Production | Office supplies |
| 20-830 | Production | Salaries and wages |
| 20-835 | Production | Telephones |
| 20-840 | Production | Training |
| 20-845 | Production | Travel and entertainment |
| 20-850 | Production | Utilities |
| 20-855 | Production | Other expenses |
| 20-860 | Production | Interest expense |

The preceding sample chart of accounts shows an exact duplication of accounts for each department listed. This is not necessarily the case in reality, since some departments have accounts for which they are the only probable users. For example, the accounting department in the example has an account for bank charges that the production department is unlikely to use. Thus, some accounts can be avoided by flagging them as inactive in the accounting system. By doing so, they do not appear in the formal chart of accounts.

## Seven-Digit Chart of Accounts

The seven-digit chart of accounts is needed by larger organizations in which management wants to track information about departments within divisions. The seven-digit coding structure requires the coding used for a five-digit system as its baseline, plus two additional digits that are placed to the left of the five-digit codes to designate company divisions. In those cases where a business also wants to track its assets and liabilities by division, it will be necessary to apply the additional two digits to balance sheet accounts. The seven-digit chart of accounts appearing in the following exhibit could be used.

**Sample Seven-Digit Chart of Accounts**

| Account Number | Division | Department | Description |
|---|---|---|---|
| 10-00-010 | Boston | xxx | Cash |
| 10-00-020 | Boston | xxx | Petty cash |
| 10-00-030 | Boston | xxx | Accounts receivable |
| 10-00-040 | Boston | xxx | Allowance for doubtful accounts |
| 10-00-050 | Boston | xxx | Marketable securities |
| 10-00-060 | Boston | xxx | Raw materials inventory |
| 10-00-070 | Boston | xxx | Work-in-process inventory |
| 10-00-080 | Boston | xxx | Finished goods inventory |
| 10-00-090 | Boston | xxx | Reserve for obsolete inventory |
| 10-00-100 | Boston | xxx | Fixed assets – Computer equipment |
| 10-00-110 | Boston | xxx | Fixed assets – Computer software |
| 10-00-120 | Boston | xxx | Fixed assets – Furniture and fixtures |
| 10-00-130 | Boston | xxx | Fixed assets – Leasehold improvements |
| 10-00-140 | Boston | xxx | Fixed assets – Machinery |
| 10-00-150 | Boston | xxx | Accumulated depreciation – Computer equipment |
| 10-00-160 | Boston | xxx | Accumulated depreciation – Computer software |
| 10-00-170 | Boston | xxx | Accumulated depreciation – Furniture and fixtures |
| 10-00-180 | Boston | xxx | Accumulated depreciation – Leasehold improvements |
| 10-00-190 | Boston | xxx | Accumulated depreciation – Machinery |
| 10-00-200 | Boston | xxx | Other assets |
| 10-00-300 | Boston | xxx | Accounts payable |
| 10-00-310 | Boston | xxx | Accrued payroll liability |
| 10-00-320 | Boston | xxx | Accrued vacation liability |
| 10-00-330 | Boston | xxx | Accrued expenses liability – other |
| 10-00-340 | Boston | xxx | Unremitted sales taxes |
| 10-00-350 | Boston | xxx | Unremitted pension payments |
| 10-00-360 | Boston | xxx | Short-term notes payable |
| 10-00-370 | Boston | xxx | Other short-term liabilities |
| 10-00-400 | Boston | xxx | Long-term notes payable |
| 10-00-500 | Boston | xxx | Capital stock |
| 10-00-510 | Boston | xxx | Retained earnings |
| 10-00-600 | Boston | xxx | Revenue |
| 10-00-700 | Boston | xxx | Cost of goods sold – Materials |
| 10-00-710 | Boston | xxx | Cost of goods sold – Direct labor |

| Account Number | Division | Department | Description |
|---|---|---|---|
| 10-00-720 | Boston | xxx | Cost of goods sold – Manufacturing supplies |
| 10-00-730 | Boston | xxx | Cost of goods sold – Applied overhead |
| 10-10-800 | Boston | Engineering | Bank charges |
| 10-10-805 | Boston | Engineering | Benefits |
| 10-10-810 | Boston | Engineering | Depreciation |
| 10-10-815 | Boston | Engineering | Insurance |
| 10-10-825 | Boston | Engineering | Office supplies |
| 10-10-830 | Boston | Engineering | Salaries and wages |
| 10-10-835 | Boston | Engineering | Telephones |
| 10-10-840 | Boston | Engineering | Training |
| 10-10-845 | Boston | Engineering | Travel and entertainment |
| 10-10-850 | Boston | Engineering | Utilities |
| 10-10-855 | Boston | Engineering | Other expenses |
| 10-10-860 | Boston | Engineering | Interest expense |
| 10-20-800 | Boston | Sales | Bank charges |
| 10-20-805 | Boston | Sales | Benefits |
| 10-20-810 | Boston | Sales | Depreciation |
| 10-20-815 | Boston | Sales | Insurance |
| 10-20-825 | Boston | Sales | Office supplies |
| 10-20-830 | Boston | Sales | Salaries and wages |
| 10-20-835 | Boston | Sales | Telephones |
| 10-20-840 | Boston | Sales | Training |
| 10-20-845 | Boston | Sales | Travel and entertainment |
| 10-20-850 | Boston | Sales | Utilities |
| 10-20-855 | Boston | Sales | Other expenses |
| 10-20-860 | Boston | Sales | Interest expense |
| 20-00-010 | Omaha | xxx | Cash |
| 20-00-020 | Omaha | xxx | Petty cash |
| 20-00-030 | Omaha | xxx | Accounts receivable |
| 20-00-040 | Omaha | xxx | Allowance for doubtful accounts |
| 20-00-050 | Omaha | xxx | Marketable securities |
| 20-00-060 | Omaha | xxx | Raw materials inventory |
| 20-00-070 | Omaha | xxx | Work-in-process inventory |
| 20-00-080 | Omaha | xxx | Finished goods inventory |
| 20-00-090 | Omaha | xxx | Reserve for obsolete inventory |
| 20-00-100 | Omaha | xxx | Fixed assets – Computer equipment |
| 20-00-110 | Omaha | xxx | Fixed assets – Computer software |
| 20-00-120 | Omaha | xxx | Fixed assets – Furniture and fixtures |
| 20-00-130 | Omaha | xxx | Fixed assets – Leasehold improvements |
| 20-00-140 | Omaha | xxx | Fixed assets – Machinery |

| Account Number | Division | Department | Description |
|---|---|---|---|
| 20-00-150 | Omaha | xxx | Accumulated depreciation – Computer equipment |
| 20-00-160 | Omaha | xxx | Accumulated depreciation – Computer software |
| 20-00-170 | Omaha | xxx | Accumulated depreciation – Furniture and fixtures |
| 20-00-180 | Omaha | xxx | Accumulated depreciation – Leasehold improvements |
| 20-00-190 | Omaha | xxx | Accumulated depreciation – Machinery |
| 20-00-200 | Omaha | xxx | Other assets |
| 20-00-300 | Omaha | xxx | Accounts payable |
| 20-00-310 | Omaha | xxx | Accrued payroll liability |
| 20-00-320 | Omaha | xxx | Accrued vacation liability |
| 20-00-330 | Omaha | xxx | Accrued expenses liability – other |
| 20-00-340 | Omaha | xxx | Unremitted sales taxes |
| 20-00-350 | Omaha | xxx | Unremitted pension payments |
| 20-00-360 | Omaha | xxx | Short-term notes payable |
| 20-00-370 | Omaha | xxx | Other short-term liabilities |
| 20-00-400 | Omaha | xxx | Long-term notes payable |
| 20-00-500 | Omaha | xxx | Capital stock |
| 20-00-510 | Omaha | xxx | Retained earnings |
| 20-00-600 | Omaha | xxx | Revenue |
| 20-00-700 | Omaha | xxx | Cost of goods sold – Materials |
| 20-00-710 | Omaha | xxx | Cost of goods sold – Direct labor |
| 20-00-720 | Omaha | xxx | Cost of goods sold – Manufacturing supplies |
| 20-00-730 | Omaha | xxx | Cost of goods sold – Applied overhead |
| 20-10-800 | Omaha | Engineering | Bank charges |
| 20-10-805 | Omaha | Engineering | Benefits |
| 20-10-810 | Omaha | Engineering | Depreciation |
| 20-10-815 | Omaha | Engineering | Insurance |
| 20-10-825 | Omaha | Engineering | Office supplies |
| 20-10-830 | Omaha | Engineering | Salaries and wages |
| 20-10-835 | Omaha | Engineering | Telephones |
| 20-10-840 | Omaha | Engineering | Training |
| 20-10-845 | Omaha | Engineering | Travel and entertainment |
| 20-10-850 | Omaha | Engineering | Utilities |
| 20-10-855 | Omaha | Engineering | Other expenses |
| 20-10-860 | Omaha | Engineering | Interest expense |
| 20-20-800 | Omaha | Sales | Bank charges |
| 20-20-805 | Omaha | Sales | Benefits |

| Account Number | Division | Department | Description |
|---|---|---|---|
| 20-20-810 | Omaha | Sales | Depreciation |
| 20-20-815 | Omaha | Sales | Insurance |
| 20-20-825 | Omaha | Sales | Office supplies |
| 20-20-830 | Omaha | Sales | Salaries and wages |
| 20-20-835 | Omaha | Sales | Telephones |
| 20-20-840 | Omaha | Sales | Training |
| 20-20-845 | Omaha | Sales | Travel and entertainment |
| 20-20-850 | Omaha | Sales | Utilities |
| 20-20-855 | Omaha | Sales | Other expenses |
| 20-20-860 | Omaha | Sales | Interest expense |

## Responsibility Center Information Reporting

Once responsibility centers have been identified and information collected for them, what information should be reported? Since these reports are entirely internal to a business, they are not governed in any way by the accounting standards that are targeted at the financial statements issued to third parties. Consequently, the focus can be on the most effective transfer of essential information, rather than on compliance with arcane reporting requirements. The nature of the information reported will vary, depending on the type of responsibility center.

In the rare case where a responsibility center is set up as a revenue center, the only basis upon which the manager is being judged is on revenue generated. In this situation, the manager will likely want to receive a large amount of detail about revenues, which may call for revenue reports that are presented in many different ways, such as:

- Sorted by customer
- Sorted by distribution warehouse
- Sorted by product line
- Sorted by promotion
- Sorted by region
- Sorted by salesperson

The most common responsibility center is the cost center, which can be applied to any department or sub-set of a department. In this case, expenses should be separately presented by cost type, at the level of detail at which the information is being collected in the general ledger. It makes little sense to aggregate information into a smaller number of line items for a cost center report, since the whole point of the report is to present cost information at the finest possible level of detail.

There are several ways to sort the information in a cost center report. One approach is alphabetical, which has the benefit of itemizing information in a customary format over an extended period of time, which makes it easier to locate information. An alternative is to re-sort the report in declining order by expenditure level, so that the largest items always appear at the top of the report. A third variation is similar to the alphabetical sorting, but with expenses clustered into groups of related items; for example, all compensation expenses, such as wages, benefits, and payroll taxes, can be listed under a compensation expense line sub-header. Any of these approaches will work – consult with the report recipients to see which version works best for them.

The reporting for a profit center essentially combines the reporting for a revenue center and a cost center, with the result being a traditional income statement that shows profits and losses. If the profit center manager demands the level of detail that a revenue manager wants to see, the additional revenue detail will need to be placed in a separate report – it will not fit on an income statement.

The reporting for an investment center is the same as for a profit center, with additional reporting for the return on investment. This information can be presented in either of the following ways:

- *Return on investment.* Divide net profits by the total amount of capital invested in the investment center to arrive at the return on investment. This approach makes the returns of different profit centers more comparable on a percentage basis.
- *Residual profit.* Subtract the cost of all capital employed in the investment center from net profits, to show any remaining residual profit or loss. This approach is useful for pointing out whether a profit center is reducing shareholder value by producing a return lower than the cost of capital.

---

**EXAMPLE**

The management of Barbary Coast Rifles creates a new division called Moroccan Muzzle Loaders, which crafts handmade "antique" muzzle loading guns in the Berber style for discerning collectors. Mr. Ball is assigned responsibility for the new division, which is designated as an investment center. In its first full year of operations, Moroccan generates profits of $1,000,000 on a total investment of $5,000,000. The parent company has a 15% cost of capital, which means that the cost of the capital invested in Moroccan is $750,000 (calculated as 15% cost of capital × $5,000,000 invested funds). This results in the following investment center measurements:

- Return on investment: $1,000,000 profit ÷ $5,000,000 capital = 20% return on investment
- Residual profit: $1,000,000 profit ÷ $750,000 cost of invested funds = $250,000 residual profit

---

Either approach to reporting the results of an investment center is designed to force the responsible manager to be prudent in his or her use of cash when running the business. For example, a stringent collections practice reduces the amount of accounts receivable outstanding, which means less cash is invested in accounts receivable, which increases both the return on investment and the residual profit.

All reports designed for any of these types of responsibility centers should be presented in a multi-period format, so that users can see the trend of revenues, costs, and profits over multiple periods, and thereby discern patterns in performance.

Ideally, all types of responsibility reports should only contain information about controllable costs. These are the costs that the recipient of a report can take action to adjust. Thus, a responsibility report should not include a cost allocation, on the grounds that any such allocation is out of the control of the recipient. If management insists on including non-controllable costs in a responsibility report, these costs should at least be separated from the other costs and clearly labeled as non-controllable.

---

**EXAMPLE**

The classic case of muddying the presentation of responsibility center reports is when the company president wants to allocate the cost of corporate overhead to individual profit centers. This allocation is not controllable by any of the profit center managers, since they cannot force the president to alter the cost of corporate overhead. Consequently, any allocation merely serves to reduce the reported profitability of all profit centers. If such a report were to be taken literally, a profitable activity might even be shut down, on the grounds that its operations net of the corporate allocation result in a loss. Shutting down such a profit center would merely leave fewer profit centers to shoulder the burden of corporate overhead.

---

**Tip:** Examine the formats of preliminary reports with those employees who are managing responsibility centers. If there is an assertion that any cost or investment item is not fully controllable by the designated employees, either alter the situation so that they *are* in control, or remove the offending item from the report.

## Transfer Pricing

In some organizations, goods and services may be sold by one subsidiary to another. If so, the prices at which these items are sold can have a major impact on the results of the buying and selling responsibility centers, as well as the decisions of the responsible managers. Consider the following situations:

- *Revenue basis*. The manager of a selling subsidiary treats such a sale in the same manner that he would the price of a product sold outside of the company. It forms part of the revenue of his subsidiary, and is therefore crucial to the financial performance on which he is judged.
- *Preferred customers*. If the manager of a selling subsidiary is given the choice of selling either to a downstream subsidiary or to outside customers, an excessively low transfer price will lead the manager to sell exclusively to outside customers, and to refuse orders originating from the downstream subsidiary.

- *Preferred suppliers*. If the manager of a buying (downstream) subsidiary is given the choice of buying either from an upstream subsidiary or an outside supplier, an excessively high transfer price will cause the manager to buy exclusively from outside suppliers. As a result, the upstream subsidiary may have too much unused capacity, and will have to cut back on its expenses in order to remain profitable.

Conversely, these issues are not important if corporate headquarters uses a central production planning system, and *requires* upstream subsidiaries to ship components to downstream subsidiaries, irrespective of the transfer price.

An additional topic that impacts the overall level of corporate profitability is the total amount of income taxes paid. If a company has subsidiaries located in different tax jurisdictions, it can use transfer prices to adjust the reported profit level of each subsidiary. Ideally, the corporate parent wants to recognize the most taxable income in those tax jurisdictions where corporate income taxes are lowest. It can achieve this by lowering the transfer prices of components going into the subsidiaries located in those tax jurisdictions having the lowest tax rates.

A company should adopt those transfer prices that result in the highest total profit for the consolidated results of the entire entity. Almost always, this means that the company sets the transfer price to be the market price of the component, subject to the issue just noted regarding the recognition of income taxes. By doing so, subsidiaries can earn more money for the company as a whole by having the option to sell to outside entities, as well as in-house. This gives subsidiaries an incentive to expand their production capacity to take on additional business.

---

**EXAMPLE**

Entwhistle Electric makes compact batteries for a variety of mobile applications. It was recently purchased by Razor Holdings, which also owns Green Lawn Care, maker of low-emission lawn mowers. The reason for Razor's purchase of Entwhistle was to give Green an assured supply of batteries for Green's new line of all-electric lawn mowers. Razor's corporate planning staff mandates that Entwhistle set a transfer price for batteries shipped to Green that equals its cost, and also requires that Entwhistle fulfill all of Green's needs before it can sell to any other customers. Green's orders are highly seasonal, so Entwhistle finds that it cannot fulfill orders from its other customers at all during the high point of Green's production season. Also, because the transfer price is set at cost, Entwhistle's management finds that it no longer has a reason to drive down its costs, and so its production efficiencies stagnate.

After a year, Razor's corporate staff realizes that Entwhistle has lost 80% of its previous customer base, and is now essentially relying upon its sales to Green to stay operational. Entwhistle's profit margin has vanished, since it can only sell at cost, and its original management team, faced with a contracting business, has left to work for competitors.

---

Transfer prices do not have to match the market price to achieve optimal results. There are cases where there is no market price at all, so a company needs to create a price in order to spur management behavior that is favorable to the company as a whole.

---

**EXAMPLE**

Entwhistle Electric creates five tons per year of black plastic shavings as part of its production of battery casings. Since there is no market for black plastic scrap, the company has traditionally thrown it into the trash. The annual trash haulage and environmental disposal fees associated with this scrap are about $1,000.

Entwhistle's fellow corporate subsidiary, Green Lawn Care, learns of the black plastic scrap situation, and offers to buy it from Entwhistle for a token $10 a ton, as well as haul it away for free. Green can melt down this scrap and use it in the black plastic trim on its electric lawn mowers.

Entwhistle agrees to the deal, not only because of the minor $50 in annual revenues, but also because of the eliminated disposal fees and the mitigated risk of having any environmental issues related to the scrap.

---

In short, transfer prices can have a significant impact on how the managers of subsidiaries run their operations, and on how much a company as a whole pays in income taxes. Though we have pointed out that market prices are the best basis for developing transfer prices, there are a number of pricing methods available. We will explore both market pricing and these other methods next.

## Market Price Basis

The simplest and most elegant transfer price is to use the market price. By doing so, the upstream subsidiary can sell either internally or externally and earn the same profit with either option. It can also earn the highest possible profit, rather than being subject to the odd profit vagaries that can occur under mandated pricing schemes. Downstream subsidiaries will also be indifferent to the source of their components, since the price is the same from all suppliers. If the price is simple to obtain, such as through industry trade journals or price sheets, there is also little reason for buying and selling subsidiaries to argue over the price.

However, market-based prices are not always available. Here are several areas of concern:

- *Product differentiation.* The most common problem is that the products being sold in the market are differentiated from each other by a variety of unique features, so there is no standard market price.
- *Quality differentiation.* Product features may be the same, but quality differences between products cause significant pricing disparities.

- *Specialty products*. The components in question may be of such a highly specialized nature that there is no market for them at all.
- *Internal costs*. The cost of selling internally to another subsidiary is somewhat lower than the cost of selling to an external customer, since there are fewer selling costs and bad debts associated with an internal sale; this means that comparing potential sales based just on the market price is not entirely correct.
- *Corporate planning*. If there is a centralized planning staff, they may not want the subsidiaries to make decisions based on the market price, because they want all components routed to internal subsidiaries to relieve supply shortages. This is not necessarily a problem, as long as the internal sales are conducted at the market price.

In short, market-based pricing is highly recommended, but it does not apply in many situations. If market pricing cannot be used, consider using one of the alternative methods outlined in the following sections.

### Adjusted Market Price Basis

If it is not possible to use the market pricing technique just noted, consider using the general concept, but incorporating some adjustments to the price. For example, reduce the market price to account for the presumed absence of bad debts, since corporate management will likely intervene and force a payment if there is a risk of non-payment. Also, reduce the market price to account for the absence of any sales staff in transactions, since these internal sales should not require any sales effort to complete – a sale is reduced to some paperwork between the purchasing and planning staffs of the two subsidiaries.

If these bad debt and selling costs are actually eliminated from the selling subsidiary and the buying subsidiary can make purchases at lower prices, both entities benefit from the price reductions. The result may be a tendency to prefer selling within the company rather than to outside parties, which is what corporate managers want to see.

The main problem with adjusted market prices will be arguments between the subsidiaries over the size of the downward adjustments. There should be a procedure in place for how the adjustments are determined. If not, the subsidiary manager with the better negotiating ability will win, which may result in the other subsidiary taking its business elsewhere. The corporate staff should monitor these negotiations and intervene as necessary.

### Negotiated Basis

It may be necessary to negotiate a transfer price between subsidiaries without using any market price as a baseline. This situation arises when there is no discernible market price because the market is very small or the goods are highly customized.

Negotiated prices can vary wildly, depending on the negotiating skills of the participants. The variable cost of production for the selling subsidiary should be used as the minimum possible price, so that it does not lose money. The resulting price usually gives both participants some ability to earn a profit. However, there are some issues with it:

- *Unfairness*. If the negotiated price excessively favors one subsidiary, the other subsidiary will likely search outside of the company for better deals.
- *Negotiation time*. If a component represents a large amount of revenue for the selling subsidiary, or a large cost for the buying subsidiary, they may spend an inordinate amount of time negotiating the price.

For the reasons noted here, negotiated prices are considered to be a suboptimal solution, and so should only be used in a minority of transfer pricing situations for items representing a small proportion of total business activity.

**Contribution Margin Basis**

If there is no market price at all from which to derive a transfer price, an alternative is to create a price based on a component's contribution margin. To do so, follow these steps:

1. Determine the price at which a finished product will sell to an outside entity after all subsidiaries of the company have finished their processing of the product.
2. Determine the contribution margin of the finished product. This is revenues minus all variable costs associated with the product.
3. Allocate the contribution margin back to the various subsidiaries that contributed to its construction, based on each subsidiary's share of the total cost incurred.

This approach creates a fair allocation of the contribution margin to the subsidiaries. However, it also suffers from the following problems:

- *Allocation methodology*. Since the allocation of contribution margin is based on each subsidiary's share of the total cost, a subsidiary can increase its share if it *increases* its costs. Also, if a subsidiary reduces its costs, the cost savings is essentially apportioned among all of the subsidiaries, which gives a subsidiary little reason to reduce its costs. Thus, the allocation method drives subsidiaries to engage in behavior that does not benefit the company as a whole.
- *Complicated allocation*. If a company has many subsidiaries, there may be so many transfers of parts associated with a specific product that it is difficult to determine which subsidiaries should be credited with the contribution margin, or the amount of the allocation. This also requires a large amount of accounting staff time, as well as an allocation procedure that is rigidly ad-

hered to; otherwise, the subsidiaries will bicker over how much contribution margin they receive.

Despite the problems noted here, the contribution margin approach can be a workable alternative to using market prices to develop transfer prices.

**Cost Plus Basis**

If there is no market price at all on which to base a transfer price, consider using a system that creates a transfer price based on the cost of the components being transferred. The best way to do this is to add a margin onto the cost, where you compile the standard cost of a component, add a standard profit margin, and use the result as the transfer price. While this method is useful, be aware of two flaws that can cause problems:

- *Cost basis*. When the pricing system is based on adding a margin to the underlying cost, there is no incentive to reduce the underlying cost. If anything, subsidiary managers will be tempted to alter their cost accounting systems to shift more costs *into* those components being sold to another subsidiary, thereby dumping costs onto a different entity.
- *Standard margin*. The margin added to the cost may not relate to the margin that a subsidiary earns on its sales to outside customers. If it is too low, subsidiary managers have no incentive to manufacture the component. If the margin is too high, and this margin is incorporated into the final product price, the subsidiary selling the completed product may find that its cost is too high to earn a profit.

Despite the issues noted here, the cost plus method can still work, as long as corporate management mandates ongoing cost reductions throughout the company, and also verifies whether the margins added to costs are reasonable. Also, it may work if there are so few transfers that the economic benefits to be gained from rigging the system are minimal.

**Cost Anomalies in a Cost-Based Transfer Price**

Of the transfer pricing methods described here, the contribution margin basis and the cost plus basis both involve cost inputs. When collecting the cost information used to derive transfer prices, be aware of several issues that can impact costs, and which may result in a great deal of variability in the transfer price. These issues are:

- *Cost allocations*. When a selling subsidiary can shift its costs to a buying subsidiary, there is a tendency to shift more overhead costs into the components being sold to the buying subsidiary.
- *Cost reduction incentive*. When the manager of a selling subsidiary knows he can sell products to a buying subsidiary and cover his costs, there is no incentive to reduce those costs. It would be egregious to let costs increase, but there is no longer any incentive to decrease costs. This problem is less

critical if the selling subsidiary still sells most of its products to outside entities, since it must still maintain control over its costs in order to be competitive.

- *Volume changes.* If the unit volume ordered by a buying subsidiary changes substantially over time, the selling subsidiary will have to manufacture parts in varying batch sizes, which may result in very different costs, depending on the volume produced. If the transfer price is fixed for a relatively long-term period, the selling subsidiary may find itself either benefiting from these volume changes or experiencing very low profits that are caused by small batch sizes.

A partial solution to several of these problems is to agree on a standard cost at the beginning of the year, and review it periodically. Corporate management should be involved in this process, both to impose cost reduction goals and to verify whether any shifting of overhead costs to downstream subsidiaries is being attempted. Using a standard cost allows buying subsidiaries to plan for costs with considerable certainty, while selling subsidiaries can improve their profits if they reduce costs to below the agreed-upon standard costs.

**Pricing Problems Caused by Transfer Pricing**

Transfer pricing between subsidiaries causes a problem for the marketing department of whichever subsidiary is selling the final product to outside customers, because it does not know which part of the transferred-in price is comprised of variable costs, and which is fixed costs. If the marketing department is developing long-term sustainable costs, it knows the price needs to be higher than both types of costs combined, in order to assure long-term sustainable profitability. However, this is not the case for short-term pricing situations where a customer may be asking for a pricing discount in exchange for a large order. In the latter situation, the costing system needs to clearly differentiate which product costs are variable, and which are not.

Another issue with price setting arises when several subsidiaries in a row add as many costs as they can to the transfer price, as well as a profit margin. By the time the final product arrives at the subsidiary that sells it to an outside customer, the cost may be so high that the last subsidiary cannot possibly earn a profit on the sale. The following example illustrates the problem.

---

**EXAMPLE**

Razor Holdings adopts a transfer pricing policy under which each of its subsidiaries can add a 30% margin to the additional costs transferred to buying subsidiaries. In the following scenario, its Lead Supply subsidiary sends lead components to Entwhistle Electric, which incorporates the lead into its batteries. Entwhistle sends the batteries to Green Lawn Care, which includes the batteries in its electric lawn shears.

| | Lead Supply | Entwhistle Electric | Green Lawn Care |
|---|---|---|---|
| Transferred cost | $0 | $5.85 | 13.98 |
| Additional cost | 4.50 | 6.25 | 15.00 |
| 30% markup | 1.35 | 1.88 | 1.02 |
| Transfer price | $5.85 | $13.98 | $30.00 |

Unfortunately, the market price for electric lawn shears is $30, so the Green Lawn Care subsidiary will only earn a profit of $1.02, or 3%, on each sale. However, the company as a whole will earn a profit of $4.25 ($1.35 for Lead Supply + $1.88 for Entwhistle + $1.02 for Green), or 14%.

Thus, Green Lawn Care likely questions why it is bothering to sell electric lawn shears, while corporate management is somewhat more pleased with the overall result.

---

Possible solutions are to allow the furthest downstream subsidiary to buy its components elsewhere, or to have corporate management reduce the margins allowed to upstream subsidiaries.

**Tax Impact of Transfer Prices**

We have discussed various methods for developing transfer prices in most of the preceding commentary, but they may all be overridden by corporate management if it wants to achieve the lowest possible amount of income taxes paid. This is a major area of corporate planning, because it causes a permanent reduction in income taxes paid, not just a deferral of tax payments to a later period.

The essential tax management concept is to set a high transfer price for buying subsidiaries located in tax jurisdictions that have a high income tax rate, so they report a high cost of goods sold, and therefore pay the minimum amount of high-percentage income tax. Conversely, the transfer price should be as low as possible for those buying subsidiaries located in tax jurisdictions that have a low income tax rate, so they report a low cost of goods sold, and therefore pay the maximum amount of low-percentage income tax. The overall impact for the corporate parent should be a reduction in income taxes paid.

---

**EXAMPLE**

Razor Holdings owns Entwhistle Electric, which is located in the United States, and Green Lawn Care, which is located in Ireland. The corporate tax rate in the United States is 35%, and the rate in Ireland is 12.5%. Because of the disparity in tax rates, Razor wants Entwhistle to sell all of its components to Green at a low price. By doing so, Entwhistle earns a minimal profit on these inter-company sales and therefore has minimal income on which to pay taxes, while Green has a very low cost of goods sold and a correspondingly high net profit, on which it pays the reduced Irish income tax. Razor implements this strategy for the current fiscal year, with the following results:

| | Entwhistle Subsidiary (United States) | Green Lawn Care (Ireland) |
|---|---:|---:|
| Revenue | $10,000,000 | $35,000,000 |
| Cost of goods sold and administrative expenses | 8,000,000 | 21,000,000 |
| Profit | $2,000,000 | $14,000,000 |
| Profit % | 20% | 40% |
| | | |
| Income tax rate | 35% | 12.5% |
| Income tax | $700,000 | $1,750,000 |

If Entwhistle had sold its products to other customers, rather than internally, it would have realized a profit of an additional $1,000,000, which would have called for an additional $350,000 income tax payment to the United States government. However, the transfer pricing strategy essentially shifted the additional $1,000,000 of profit to the Ireland tax jurisdiction, which was then taxed at only 12.5%. Thus, Razor created a permanent tax savings of $225,000 through its transfer pricing strategy, which is calculated as:

(35% United States tax rate – 12.5% Ireland tax rate) × $1,000,000 Taxable profit

---

The practices just noted could lead a company to adopt outrageous transfer pricing practices that shift virtually all profits to whichever tax jurisdictions have the lowest tax rates. To keep such egregious behavior from occurring, the Internal Revenue Service has issued guidelines in Section 482 of the Internal Revenue Code that specify how transfer prices can be formulated. Section 482 contains multiple alternative formulations, with the preferred practice being to use market rates as the transfer price, followed by variations on the cost plus profit methodology. These formulations allow for the inclusion of a variety of adjustments, which can alter a transfer price significantly. A company usually takes advantage of the Section 482 guidelines to the greatest extent possible in order to achieve the lowest possible consolidated tax payment. The IRS prefers to have companies use transfer prices that are largely based on market prices, leaving the minimum amount of additional adjustments for a company's accountants to manipulate.

There is always a chance that auditors from a taxing jurisdiction will take issue with the transfer pricing methods used by a company, which may lead to substantial fines and penalties. This is a particular problem when a company is being audited by multiple tax jurisdictions, with each one trying to maximize its tax receipts at the expense of the other jurisdictions.

To avoid these audit costs, larger companies frequently enter into an advance pricing agreement (APA) with multiple tax jurisdictions, which is known as a *bilateral APA*. The APA outlines in advance the procedure that a company will take to establish its transfer prices. An APA application involves a presentation by the company of why it plans to use a certain transfer pricing method, why alternate methods were not chosen, and a description of the transactions to which the transfer pricing method will be applied. Having an APA in place means that a company will be much less likely to incur penalties and fines, though it may still be subject to audits to ensure that it is complying with the terms of the APA.

In short, transfer pricing can have a major impact on the amount of income tax payments that a company must make, by shifting reported net income amongst subsidiaries located in various tax jurisdictions. The transfer prices used to create these tax reductions are subject to regulation by the various tax jurisdictions, which can lead to an ongoing series of audits. To avoid the aggravation of audits and any resulting additional payments, consider entering into bilateral advance pricing agreements.

## Accounting Issues Related to Responsibility Centers

The accounting standards do not mandate any type of reporting in relation to responsibility centers, so it is technically possible for responsibility reporting to be completely unrelated to the more rigidly-defined financial statements. However, the information on which responsibility reports are based usually comes from the general ledger, which is also used to create the financial statements (which *are* controlled by the accounting standards). This means that the recognition of revenue and expenses that appear in the responsibility reports is the same as the recognition used in the financial statements.

There is nothing wrong with having both types of reports come from the same source material. However, the manager should be cognizant of the timing of accounting entries in the general ledger to create financial statements. Many adjusting entries are made as of the last day of the reporting period. Prior to that date, the revenue and expense information in the general ledger is not necessarily correct. Consequently, mandating that responsibility reports be issued prior to the financial statements (such as on a weekly basis) is probably not a good idea, since those reports may contain incorrect or misleading information.

---

**EXAMPLE**

The president of the Black Cat Ladder Company wants to issue responsibility reports to the managers of the company's five profit centers at the end of each week. One of the key expenses for each profit center is compensation expense. Since the company pays its employees every other week, this means the accounting staff only records compensation expense in the general ledger every other week. Consequently, the first and third weekly reports of the month contain no compensation expense, while the expense reported in the second and fourth weeks is doubled. To rectify the issue, the president can either have the accounting staff provide weekly compensation expense accruals, or only issue responsibility reports on a monthly basis.

---

## Summary

The use of functional and divisional organizational structures is clearly useful for many companies, since it drives responsibility for activities well down into an organization, allowing for a less rigid top-down management structure. To support this more effective model, responsibility centers can be created and bolstered with an appropriate system of reporting. If a responsibility center is created, but there is no feedback loop that informs that center of its performance, there is no way to conduct effective management operations. Consequently, the consideration of such an arcane subject as the structure of the chart of accounts is of interest to the manager, who must ensure that the correct information is being accumulated in the correct format to produce supporting reports.

In some situations, the manner in which transfer prices are formulated can have a major impact on the reported results of profit centers, since price setting can shift profitability between profit centers, irrespective of how well the centers are being managed. However, the effects of transfer pricing on profit center results may be of little consequence to management if the overriding goal is to alter prices to minimize the corporate-wide total tax liability.

# Chapter 6
# Overview of Selected Accounting Standards

## Introduction

The typical manager may feel that the standards governing the accounting profession are too lengthy and arcane to be worth learning. Instead, the usual approach is to depend upon the company's chief financial officer, controller, or outside auditors, who provide summarizations of issues that may impact how a business is managed. Accounting standards are lengthy, and their contents might indeed be considered arcane. However, few of these standards directly impact the management of a business; instead, they are more likely to be concerned with the proper presentation of the financial statements and the accompanying disclosures. In this chapter, we have culled from the mass of accounting standards a set of topics that are likely to be of interest to the manager. We have also eliminated from the discussion any mention of accounting specifics that are best left to the accounting staff. Instead, the following discussion items (presented in alphabetical order by topic) are intended only to inform the manager of the general concepts associated with certain accounting standards.

The information in this chapter is derived from the GAAP framework, which is widely used in the United States. The information presented may vary somewhat from the mandates of the other main accounting framework, International Financial Reporting Standards.

## Accounting Changes and Error Corrections

Accounting principles are the rules to be followed when reporting financial information. There is an assumption in GAAP that, once an accounting principle has been adopted by a business, the principle shall be consistently applied in recording transactions and events from that point forward. Consistent application is a cornerstone of accounting, since it allows the readers of financial statements to compare the results of multiple accounting periods. Given how important it is to maintain consistency in the application of accounting principles, a business should only change an accounting principle in one of the two following situations:

- The change is required by an update to GAAP
- The use of an alternative principle is preferable

Whenever there is a change in accounting principle, retrospective application of the new principle to prior accounting periods is required, unless it is impracticable to do so. If it is impracticable to retroactively apply changes to prior interim periods of the current fiscal year, the change in accounting principle can only be made as of the start of a subsequent fiscal year. The activities required for retrospective application are:

1. Alter the carrying amounts of assets and liabilities for the cumulative effect of the change in principle as of the beginning of the first accounting period presented.
2. Adjust the beginning balance of retained earnings to offset the change noted in the first step.
3. Adjust the financial statements for each prior period presented to reflect the impact of the new accounting principle.

If it is impracticable to make these changes, do so as of the earliest reported periods for which it is practicable to do so. It is considered impracticable to make a retrospective change when any of the following conditions apply:

- *Assumptions*. Making a retrospective application calls for assumptions about what management intended to do in prior periods, and those assumptions cannot be independently substantiated.
- *Efforts made*. The company has made every reasonable effort to do so.
- *Estimates*. Estimates are required, which are impossible to provide due to the lack of information about the circumstances in the earlier periods.

When making prior period adjustments due to a change in accounting principle, do so only for the direct effects of the change. A direct effect is one that is *required* to switch accounting principles.

---

**EXAMPLE**

Armadillo Industries changes from the last in, first out method of inventory accounting to the first in, first out method (see the Inventory section). Doing so calls for an increase in the ending inventory in the preceding period, which in turn increases net profits for that period. Altering the inventory balance is a direct effect of the change in principle.

An indirect effect of the change in principle would be a change in the corporate accrual for profit sharing in the prior period. Since it is an indirect effect, Armadillo does not record the change.

---

A change in accounting estimate occurs when there is an adjustment to the carrying amount of an asset or liability, or the subsequent accounting for it. Examples of changes in accounting estimate are changes in:

- Reserve accounts
- The useful life of depreciable assets (see the Fixed Assets section)
- The salvage values of depreciable assets (see the Fixed Assets section)
- The amount of expected warranty obligations

Changes in accounting estimate occur relatively frequently, and so would require a considerable effort to make an ongoing series of retroactive changes to prior financial statements. Instead, GAAP only requires that changes in accounting estimate be accounted for in the period of change and thereafter. Thus, no retrospective change is required or allowed.

## Advertising

Advertising is the promotion of a business or its products, with the intent of creating a positive image or stimulating customer purchases. The costs incurred for advertising can be aggregated into two areas, which are the production of advertisements and their dissemination. The accounting for advertising costs is as follows:

- *Production costs*. Charge advertising production costs to expense as incurred or when the related advertising first takes place.
- *Dissemination costs*. Charge advertising costs to expense as used. For example, charge the cost to air a television advertisement to expense as the airtime is used.

This treatment is based on the belief that the beneficial effects of advertising are short-lived, and because it is difficult to determine the number of periods over which the resulting benefits can be measured. This guidance does *not* apply to direct-response advertising.

There are cases when a business engages in direct-response advertising, where the recognition of some costs can be deferred. Examples of costs that may be eligible for deferral are the third-party billings and in-house labor costs associated with idea development, writing ad copy, artwork, printing magazine space, and mailing.

This situation arises when there is a reliable and demonstrated relationship between costs incurred and future benefits achieved. For example, a company may have a history of obtaining a 1% response rate on all direct mail pieces mailed out. Thus, the cost of obtaining that 1% response rate can be associated with the total cost of the mailing.

A business can defer the expense recognition for direct-response advertising if both of the following conditions are met:

- The advertising is intended to generate sales for which customers can be shown to have responded specifically to the advertising by tracking the names of respondents and the specific advertising that triggered their response, such as a coupon or response card; and
- The advertising results in probable future benefits, which requires persuasive evidence of historical patterns of similar results for the business (historical patterns for the industry as a whole are not allowed). Test market results can be used.

To defer expenses related to direct-response advertising, accumulate costs separately for each significant advertising effort, so that costs can be recognized in direct proportion to the receipt of related customer sales. Each set of accumulated costs is then recognized based on the proportion of actual revenues generated by the campaign to the total revenues expected from the campaign. The estimated amount of total revenues to be received may change over time, which can alter the remaining amortization calculation; prior period results are not altered if there is a subsequent change in the estimated amount of total revenues to be received.

If the recorded amount of advertising costs exceeds the associated amount of remaining net revenues yet to be realized, charge the excess amount of advertising costs to expense in the current period.

## Capitalized Interest

Interest is a cost of doing business, and if a company incurs an interest cost that is directly related to a fixed asset (see the Fixed Assets section), it is reasonable to capitalize this cost, since doing so provides a truer picture of the total investment in the asset. Since a business would not otherwise have incurred the interest if it had not acquired the asset, the interest is essentially a direct cost of owning the asset.

Conversely, if a business does not capitalize this interest cost and instead charges it to expense, the company would be unreasonably reducing the amount of reported earnings during the period when the company incurred the expense, and increasing earnings during later periods, when it would otherwise have been charging the capitalized interest to expense through depreciation.

The value of the information provided by capitalizing interest may not be worth the effort of the incremental accounting cost associated with it. Here are some issues to consider when deciding whether to capitalize interest:

- How many assets would be subject to interest capitalization?
- How easy is it to separately identify those assets that would be subject to interest capitalization?
- How significant would be the effect of interest capitalization on the company's reported resources and earnings?

Thus, one should only capitalize interest when the informational benefit derived from doing so exceeds the cost of accounting for it. The positive impact of doing so is greatest for construction projects, where:

- Costs are separately compiled
- Construction covers a long period of time
- Expenditures are large
- Interest costs are considerable

Capitalize interest that is related to the following types of fixed assets:

- Assets that are constructed for the company's own use. This includes assets built for the company by suppliers, where the company makes progress payments or deposits.
- Assets that are constructed for sale or lease, and which are constructed as discrete projects.

GAAP specifically does *not* allow one to capitalize interest for inventory items that are routinely manufactured in large quantities on a repetitive basis.

---

**EXAMPLE**

Milford Sound builds a new corporate headquarters. The company hires a contractor to perform the work, and makes regular progress payments to the contractor. Milford should capitalize the interest expense related to this project.

Milford Sound creates a subsidiary, Milford Public Sound, which builds custom-designed outdoor sound staging for concerts and theatre activities. These projects require many months to complete, and are accounted for as discrete projects. Milford should capitalize the interest cost related to each of these projects.

---

If a company is undertaking activities to develop land for a specific use, capitalize interest related to the associated expenditures for as long as the development activities are in progress.

## Compensated Absences

A business should accrue an expense for employee compensation related to future absences if all of the following conditions are present:

- *Estimation*. The amount of the compensation can be reasonably estimated.
- *Probable payment*. It is probable that the compensation will be paid.
- *Service basis*. The future obligation is based on employee services already rendered to the company.
- *Vesting or accumulation*. Employee rights that vest or accumulate over time are the basis for the obligation. Vesting is the process of earning a non-forfeitable right.

The accrual should account for anticipated forfeitures (if allowed), which will reduce the amount of the accrual. Also, the accrual should be recognized in the year in which employees earn the compensated absence, not when they take the absence.

---

**EXAMPLE**

A new employee receives a vested right to one month of paid vacation at the beginning of the second year of her employment. The employer does not grant any pro rata payout if she is terminated prior to the vesting date.

The compensated absence is considered to be earned in the first year of the person's employment, so the employer should accrue an expense for the vacation pay during her first year of employment, reduced by an allowance for expected forfeitures that are caused by employee departures.

---

If the right to a compensated absence expires (as commonly occurs when a company grants "use it or lose it" vacation time), do not accrue a liability for future absences in the period prior to when the right expires. This is because any later payout cannot be attributed to employee services from prior periods. However, if compensated absences are cumulative, accrue a liability in an amount that is reasonably probable that employees will be paid in later periods, and if the amount can be reasonably estimated.

---

**EXAMPLE**

There is already an existing accrued balance of 40 hours of unused vacation time for Fred Smith on the books of Armadillo Industries. In the most recent month, Fred accrued an additional five hours of vacation time (since he is entitled to 60 hours of accrued vacation time per year, and 60 ÷ 12 = five hours per month). He also used three hours of vacation time during the month. This means that, as of the end of the month, Armadillo should have accrued a total of 42 hours of vacation time for him, which is calculated as:

40 Hours existing balance + 5 Hours additional accrual – 3 Hours used

Mr. Smith is paid $30 per hour, so his total vacation accrual should be $1,260 (42 hours × $30/hour). The beginning liability balance for him is $1,200 (40 hours × $30/hour), so Armadillo accrues an additional $60 of vacation liability.

---

## Contingencies

A loss contingency arises when there is a situation for which the outcome is uncertain, and which should be resolved in the future, possibly creating a loss. Examples of contingent loss situations are:

- Injuries that may be caused by a company's products, such as when it is discovered that lead-based paint has been used on toys sold by the business
- The threat of asset expropriation by a foreign government, where compensation will be less than the carrying amount of the assets that will probably be expropriated
- A threatened lawsuit

When deciding whether to account for a loss contingency, the basic concept is to only record a loss that is probable, and for which the amount of the loss can be reasonably estimated. If the best estimate of the amount of the loss is within a range, accrue whichever amount appears to be a better estimate than the other estimates in the range. If there is no "better estimate" in the range, accrue a loss for the minimum amount in the range.

If it is not possible to arrive at a reasonable estimate of the loss associated with an event, only disclose the existence of the contingency in the notes accompanying the financial statements. Or, if it is not probable that a loss will be incurred, even if it is possible to estimate the amount of a loss, only disclose the circumstances of the contingency, without accruing a loss.

---

**EXAMPLE**

Armadillo Industries has been notified by the local zoning commission that it must remediate abandoned property on which chemicals had been stored in the past. Armadillo has hired a consulting firm to estimate the cost of remediation, which has been documented at $10 million. Since the amount of the loss has been reasonably estimated and it is probable that the loss will occur, the company can record the $10 million as a contingent loss. If the zoning commission had not indicated the company's liability, it may have been more appropriate to only mention the loss in the disclosures accompanying the financial statements.

**EXAMPLE**

Armadillo Industries has been notified that a third party may begin legal proceedings against it, based on a situation involving environmental damage to a site once owned by Armadillo. Based on the experience of other companies who have been subjected to this type of litigation, it is probable that Armadillo will have to pay $8 million to settle the litigation. A separate aspect of the litigation is still open to interpretation, but could potentially require an additional $12 million to settle. Given the current situation, Armadillo should accrue a loss in the amount of $8 million for that portion of the situation for which the outcome is probable, and for which the amount of the loss can be reasonably estimated.

---

If the conditions for recording a loss contingency are initially not met, but are met during a later accounting period, the loss should be accrued in the later period. Do not make a retroactive adjustment to an earlier period to record a loss contingency.

GAAP does not allow the recognition of a gain contingency, since doing so might result in the recognition of revenue before the contingent event has been settled.

## Deferred Compensation

If a deferred compensation arrangement is based on employee performance during a specific time period, accrue the cost of the deferred compensation in that performance period. If the deferred compensation is based on both current and future service, only accrue an expense for that portion of the compensation attributable to current service. As of the full eligibility date for the deferred compensation, the employer should have accrued the present value of those benefits expected to be paid in the future.

---

**EXAMPLE**

Armadillo Industries creates a deferred compensation agreement for its CEO, under which he will become eligible for the benefits stated in the contract after five years have passed. The terms of the agreement indicate that the CEO will render services for five years in order to earn the deferred compensation, so Armadillo accrues the cost of the contract over the intervening five years.

---

## Fixed Assets

The vast majority of the expenditures that a company makes are for consumables, such as office supplies, wages, or products that it sells to customers. The effects of these items pass through a company quickly – they are used or sold and converted to cash, and they are recorded as expenses immediately or with a slight delay (if they involve inventory). Thus, the benefits they generate are short-lived.

Fixed assets are entirely different. These are items that generate economic benefits over a long period of time. Because of the long period of usefulness of a fixed asset, it is not justifiable to charge its entire cost to expense when incurred. Instead, the *matching principle* comes into play. Under the matching principle, recognize both the benefits and expenses associated with a transaction (or, in this case, an asset) at the same time. To do so, we convert an expenditure into an asset, and use depreciation to gradually charge it to expense over time.

By designating an expenditure as a fixed asset, we are shifting the expenditure away from the income statement, where expenditures normally go, and instead place it in the balance sheet. As we gradually reduce its recorded cost through depreciation, the expenditure slowly flows from the balance sheet to the income statement. Thus, the main difference between a normal expenditure and a fixed asset is that the fixed asset is charged to expense over a longer period of time.

The process of identifying fixed assets, recording them as assets, and depreciating them is time-consuming, so it is customary to build some limitations into the process that will route most expenditures directly to expense. One such limitation is to charge an expenditure to expense immediately unless it has a useful life of at least one year. Another limitation is to only recognize an expenditure as a fixed asset if it exceeds a certain dollar amount, known as the *capitalization limit*. These limits keep the vast majority of expenditures from being classified as fixed assets, which reduces the work of the accounting department.

---

**EXAMPLE**

Armadillo Industries incurs expenditures for three items, and must decide whether it should classify them as fixed assets. Armadillo's capitalization limit is $2,500. The expenditures are:

- It buys a used mold for its plastic injection molding operation for $5,000. Armadillo expects that the mold only has two months of useful life left, after which it should be scrapped. Since the useful life is so short, the controller elects to charge the expenditure to expense immediately.
- It buys a laptop computer for $1,500, which has a useful life of three years. This expenditure is less than the capitalization limit, so the controller charges it to expense.
- It buys a 10-ton injection molding machine for $50,000, which has a useful life of 10 years. Since this expenditure has a useful life of longer than one year and a cost greater than the capitalization limit, the controller records it as a fixed asset, and will depreciate it over its 10-year useful life.

---

A business should initially record a fixed asset at the historical cost of acquiring it, which includes the costs to bring it to the condition and location necessary for its intended use. If these preparatory activities will occupy a period of time, one can also include in the cost of the asset the interest costs related to the cost of the asset during the preparation period (see the Capitalized Interest section).

The activities involved in bringing a fixed asset to the condition and location necessary for its intended purpose include the following:

- Physical construction of the asset
- Demolition of any preexisting structures
- Renovating a preexisting structure to alter it for use by the buyer
- Administrative and technical activities during preconstruction for such activities as designing the asset and obtaining permits
- Administrative and technical work after construction commences for such activities as litigation, labor disputes, and technical problems

---

**EXAMPLE**

Nascent Corporation constructs a solar observatory. The project costs $10 million to construct. Also, Nascent takes out a loan for the entire $10 million amount of the project, and pays $250,000 in interest costs during the six-month construction period. Further, the company incurs $500,000 in architectural fees and permit costs before work begins.

All of these costs can be capitalized into the cost of the building asset, so Nascent records $10.75 million as the cost of the building asset.

---

The purpose of depreciation is to charge to expense a portion of an asset that relates to the revenue generated by that asset. There are three factors to consider in the calculation of depreciation, which are:

- *Useful life*. This is the time period over which the company expects that an asset will be productive. Past its useful life, it is no longer cost-effective to continue operating the asset, so the company would dispose of it or stop using it. Depreciation is recognized over the useful life of an asset.
- *Salvage value*. When a company eventually disposes of an asset, it may be able to sell the asset for some reduced amount, which is the salvage value. Depreciation is calculated based on the asset cost, less any estimated salvage value. If salvage value is expected to be quite small, it is generally ignored for the purpose of calculating depreciation.

---

**EXAMPLE**

Pensive Corporation buys an asset for $100,000, and estimates that its salvage value will be $10,000 in five years, when it plans to dispose of the asset. This means that Pensive will depreciate $90,000 of the asset cost over five years, leaving $10,000 of the cost remaining at the end of that time. Pensive expects to then sell the asset for $10,000, which will eliminate the asset from its accounting records.

---

- *Depreciation method.* One can calculate depreciation expense using an accelerated depreciation method, or evenly over the useful life of the asset. The advantage of using an accelerated method is that more depreciation can be recognized early in the life of a fixed asset, which defers some income tax expense recognition into a later period. The advantage of using a steady depreciation rate is the ease of calculation.

## Inventory

When a company produces more goods than it can immediately sell, it records the cost of the excess number of units as an inventory asset. When these goods are later sold, their associated cost is charged to expense.

The typical inventory asset is comprised of many identical parts that may have been acquired or constructed during different time periods. In each of these time periods, it is likely that the costs incurred varied somewhat from those incurred in other time periods. The result is a mish-mash of inventory items that all look the same, but which have different costs associated with them. How can one decide which costs to charge to expense when goods are sold? A possible solution is the cost layering concept. Under cost layering, we assume that different tranches of costs have been incurred to construct or acquire certain clusters of inventory. The following example illustrates the concept.

---

**EXAMPLE**

Milford Sound acquires speakers from a contract manufacturer, for sale through Milford's on-line store. An especially popular speaker is the home theater subwoofer model. Over the past three months, Milford made the following purchases of this model from its contract manufacturer:

| Date | Quantity | Price/each |
|---|---|---|
| 1/05/X3 | 3,200 | $89.00 |
| 1/29/X3 | 850 | 90.25 |
| 2/15/X3 | 1,700 | 91.00 |
| 3/09/X3 | 1,350 | 91.00 |

Since the first two purchases were made at different prices, the units in each of these purchases can be considered a separate cost layer. Since the last two purchases were made at the same price, they can be aggregated into the same cost layer, or they may be treated as separate cost layers.

Depending on the cost layering system that Milford chooses to use (see the next sub-sections), the company can assume that the cost of a subwoofer that is charged to the cost of goods sold may come from the first of these cost layers (the first in, first out system), from the last of the cost layers (the last in, first out system) or from an average of these costs (the weighted-average system).

---

Several methods for calculating the cost of inventory that employ the cost layering concept are shown in the next few sub-sections. Several were referenced in the last example.

## First In, First Out Method

The first in, first out (FIFO) method of inventory valuation operates under the assumption that the first goods purchased are also the first goods sold. In most companies, this accounting assumption closely matches the actual flow of goods, and so is considered the most theoretically correct inventory valuation method.

Under the FIFO method, the earliest goods purchased are the first ones removed from the inventory account. This results in the remaining items in inventory being accounted for at the most recently incurred costs, so that the inventory asset recorded on the balance sheet contains costs quite close to the most recent costs that could be obtained in the marketplace. Conversely, this method also results in older historical costs being matched against current revenues and recorded in the cost of goods sold, so the gross margin (i.e., sales minus the cost of goods sold) does not necessarily reflect a proper matching of revenues and costs.

---

**EXAMPLE**

Milagro Corporation decides to use the FIFO method for the month of January. During that month, it records the following transactions:

| | Quantity Change | Actual Unit Cost | Actual Total Cost |
|---|---|---|---|
| Beginning inventory (layer 1) | +100 | $210 | $21,000 |
| Sale | -75 | | |
| Purchase (layer 2) | +150 | 280 | 42,000 |
| Sale | -100 | | |
| Purchase (layer 3) | +50 | 300 | 15,000 |
| Ending inventory | = 125 | | $78,000 |

The cost of goods sold in units is calculated as:

100 Beginning inventory + 200 Purchased – 125 Ending inventory = 175 Units

Milagro's controller uses the information in the preceding table to calculate the cost of goods sold for January, as well as the cost of the inventory balance as of the end of January. The calculations appear in the following table:

| | Units | Unit Cost | Total Cost |
|---|---|---|---|
| **Cost of goods sold** | | | |
| FIFO layer 1 | 100 | $210 | $21,000 |
| FIFO layer 2 | 75 | 280 | 21,000 |
| Total cost of goods sold | 175 | | $42,000 |
| | | | |
| **Ending inventory** | | | |
| FIFO layer 2 | 75 | 280 | $21,000 |
| FIFO layer 3 | 50 | 300 | 15,000 |
| | | | |
| Total ending inventory | 125 | | $36,000 |

Thus, the first FIFO layer, which was the beginning inventory layer, is completely used up during the month, as well as half of Layer 2, leaving half of Layer 2 and all of Layer 3 to be the sole components of the ending inventory.

Note that the $42,000 cost of goods sold and $36,000 ending inventory equals the $78,000 combined total of beginning inventory and purchases during the month.

---

From a database management perspective, the FIFO method results in the smallest number of cost layers to track, since the oldest layers are constantly being eliminated.

## Last In, First Out Method

The last in, first out (LIFO) method operates under the assumption that the last item of inventory purchased is the first one sold. Picture a store shelf where a clerk adds items from the front, and customers also take their selections from the front; the remaining items of inventory that are located further from the front of the shelf are rarely picked, and so remain on the shelf – that is a LIFO scenario.

The trouble with the LIFO scenario is that it is rarely encountered in practice. If a company were to use the process flow embodied by LIFO, a significant part of its inventory would be very old, and likely obsolete. Nonetheless, a company does not actually have to experience the LIFO process flow in order to use the method to calculate its inventory valuation.

The reason why companies use LIFO is the assumption that the cost of inventory increases over time, which is reasonable in inflationary periods. If LIFO were to be used in such a situation, the cost of the most recently acquired inventory would always be higher than the cost of earlier purchases, so the ending inventory balance would be valued at earlier costs, while the most recent costs appear in the cost of goods sold. By shifting high-cost inventory into the cost of goods sold, a company can reduce its reported level of profitability, and thereby defer its recognition of income taxes. Since income tax deferral is the only justification for LIFO in most situations, it is banned under IFRS (though it is still allowed in the United States under the approval of the Internal Revenue Service).

---

**EXAMPLE**

Milagro Corporation decides to use the LIFO method for the month of March. The following table shows the various purchasing transactions for the company's Elite Roasters product. The quantity purchased on March 1 actually reflects the inventory beginning balance.

| Date Purchased | Quantity Purchased | Cost per Unit | Units Sold | Cost of Layer #1 | Cost of Layer #2 | Total Cost |
|---|---|---|---|---|---|---|
| March 1 | 150 | $210 | 95 | (55 × $210) | | $11,550 |
| March 7 | 100 | 235 | 110 | (45 × $210) | | 9,450 |
| March 11 | 200 | 250 | 180 | (45 × $210) | (20 × $250) | 14,450 |
| March 17 | 125 | 240 | 125 | (45 × $210) | (20 × $250) | 14,450 |
| March 25 | 80 | 260 | 120 | (25 × $210) | | 5,250 |

The following bullet points describe the transactions noted in the preceding table:

- *March 1.* Milagro has a beginning inventory balance of 150 units, and sells 95 of these units between March 1 and March 7. This leaves one inventory layer of 55 units at a cost of $210 each.
- *March 7.* Milagro buys 100 additional units on March 7, and sells 110 units between March 7 and March 11. Under LIFO, we assume that the latest purchase was sold first, so there is still just one inventory layer, which has now been reduced to 45 units.
- *March 11.* Milagro buys 200 additional units on March 11, and sells 180 units between March 11 and March 17, which creates a new inventory layer that is com-

prised of 20 units at a cost of $250. This new layer appears in the table in the "Cost of Layer #2" column.

- *March 17*. Milagro buys 125 additional units on March 17, and sells 125 units between March 17 and March 25, so there is no change in the inventory layers.
- *March 25*. Milagro buys 80 additional units on March 25, and sells 120 units between March 25 and the end of the month. Sales exceed purchases during this period, so the second inventory layer is eliminated, as well as part of the first layer. The result is an ending inventory balance of $5,250, which is derived from 25 units of ending inventory, multiplied by the $210 cost in the first layer that existed at the beginning of the month.

---

Before implementing the LIFO system, consider the following points:

- *Consistent usage*. The Internal Revenue Service states that a company using LIFO for its tax reporting must also use LIFO for its financial reporting. Thus, a company wanting to defer tax recognition through early expense recognition must show those same low profit numbers to the outside users of its financial statements. This may not be a problem in a privately-held company that does not release its financial results to outsiders.
- *Covenant compliance*. When LIFO has been used for a long period of time and materials prices have increased during that period, the reported inventory asset may be so low that a company has trouble meeting the terms of its loan covenants that require a certain amount of current assets.
- *Just-in-time conversion*. If a company using LIFO subsequently converts to a just-in-time production system that emphasizes minimal on-hand inventories, it is likely that the oldest inventory layers will be accessed, resulting in the recognition of many out-of-date costs.
- *Layering*. Since the LIFO system is intended to use the most recent layers of inventory, the company may never access earlier layers, which can result in an administrative problem if there are many layers to document.
- *Profit fluctuations*. If early layers contain inventory costs that depart substantially from current market prices, a company could experience sharp changes in its profitability if those layers are ever accessed.

In summary, LIFO is only useful for deferring income tax payments in periods of cost inflation. It does not reflect the actual flow of inventory in most situations, and may even yield unusual financial results that differ markedly from reality.

### Weighted Average Method

When using the weighted average method, divide the cost of goods available for sale by the number of units available for sale, which yields the weighted-average cost per unit. In this calculation, the cost of goods available for sale is the sum of beginning inventory and net purchases. This weighted-average figure is then used to assign a cost to both ending inventory and the cost of goods sold.

The singular advantage of the weighted average method is the complete absence of any inventory layers, which avoids the record keeping problems encountered with either the FIFO or LIFO methods described earlier.

---

**EXAMPLE**

Milagro Corporation elects to use the weighted-average method for the month of May. During that month, it records the following transactions:

| | Quantity Change | Actual Unit Cost | Actual Total Cost |
|---|---|---|---|
| Beginning inventory | +150 | $220 | $33,000 |
| Sale | -125 | | |
| Purchase | +200 | 270 | 54,000 |
| Sale | -150 | | |
| Purchase | +100 | 290 | 29,000 |
| Ending inventory | = 175 | | $116,000 |

The actual total cost of all purchased or beginning inventory units in the preceding table is $116,000 ($33,000 + $54,000 + $29,000). The total of all purchased or beginning inventory units is 450 (150 beginning inventory + 300 purchased). The weighted average cost per unit is therefore $257.78 ($116,000 ÷ 450 units).

The ending inventory valuation is $45,112 (175 units × $257.78 weighted average cost), while the cost of goods sold valuation is $70,890 (275 units × $257.78 weighted average cost). The sum of these two amounts (less a rounding error) equals the $116,000 total actual cost of all purchases and beginning inventory.

---

### Specific Identification Method

The cost layering concept operates under the assumption that costs cannot be traced to specific inventory items. This assumption is largely true, since there may be hundreds of identical items in stock. However, in cases where a business only retains uniquely identifiable inventory items, it is perfectly acceptable to assign a cost to each individual unit of inventory. When an item is sold, the cost specifically linked to that item is charged to the cost of goods sold. The result is a highly accurate inventory accounting system that precisely matches inventory costs with revenues. For this system to work, it should have the following attributes:

- *Unique inventory items.* Each item in stock must be uniquely identified. This typically limits use of the specific identification method to custom-made or uniquely-configured items, such as jewelry or automobiles.
- *Cost linkage.* When goods are acquired or built, the costing system must accumulate costs at the individual unit level.
- *Expensive items.* Because of the extra cost of accumulating and tracking costs at the individual unit level, this system is only cost-effective when the

items being tracked are quite expensive. Thus, it is a reasonable system for a custom watch manufacturer, but not for someone who custom-manufactures Christmas tree ornaments.

## Research and Development

Research and development involves those activities that create or improve products or processes. Examples of activities typically considered to fall within the research and development functional area are noted in the following exhibit.

**Sample Research and Development Activities**

| | |
|---|---|
| Research to discover new knowledge | Modifying formulas, products, or processes |
| Applying new research findings | Designing and testing prototypes |
| Formulating product and process designs | Designing tools that involve new technology |
| Testing products and processes | Designing and operating a pilot plant |

The basic problem with research and development expenditures is that the future benefits associated with these expenditures are sufficiently uncertain that it is difficult to record the expenditures as an asset. Given these uncertainties, GAAP mandates that all research and development expenditures be charged to expense as incurred. The chief variance from this guidance is in a business combination, where the acquirer can recognize the fair value of research and development assets.

The basic rule of charging all research and development expenditures to expense is not entirely pervasive, since there are exceptions, as noted in the following bullet points:

- *Assets.* If materials or fixed assets have been acquired that have alternative future uses, record them as assets. The materials should be charged to expense as consumed, while depreciation should be used to gradually reduce the recorded cost of the fixed assets.
- *Computer software.* If computer software is acquired for use in a research and development project, charge the cost to expense as incurred. However, if there are future alternative uses for the software, capitalize its cost and depreciate the software over its useful life.
- *Purchased intangibles.* If intangible assets are acquired from third parties and these assets have alternative uses, they are to be accounted for as intangible assets. However, if the intangibles are purchased for a specific research project and there are no alternative future uses, charge them to expense as incurred.

## Subsequent Events

A subsequent event is an event that occurs after a reporting period, but before the financial statements for that period have been issued or are available to be issued. The two types of subsequent events are:

- *Additional information*. An event provides additional information about conditions in existence as of the balance sheet date, including estimates used to prepare the financial statements for that period.
- *New events*. An event provides new information about conditions that did not exist as of the balance sheet date.

GAAP states that the financial statements should include the effects of all subsequent events that provide additional information about conditions in existence as of the balance sheet date. This rule requires that all entities evaluate subsequent events through the date when financial statements are available to be issued, while a public company should continue to do so through the date when the financial statements are actually filed with the Securities and Exchange Commission. Examples of situations calling for the adjustment of financial statements are:

- *Lawsuit*. If events take place before the balance sheet date that trigger a lawsuit, and lawsuit settlement is a subsequent event, consider adjusting the amount of any contingent loss already recognized to match the amount of the actual settlement.
- *Bad debt*. If a company issues invoices to a customer before the balance sheet date, and the customer goes bankrupt as a subsequent event, consider adjusting the bad debts reserve account to match the amount of receivables that will likely not be collected.

If there are subsequent events that provide new information about conditions that did not exist as of the balance sheet date, and for which the information arose before the financial statements were available to be issued or were issued, these events should not be recognized in the financial statements. Examples of situations that do not trigger an adjustment to the financial statements if they occur after the balance sheet date but before financial statements are issued or are available to be issued are:

- A business combination
- Changes in the value of assets due to changes in exchange rates
- Destruction of company assets
- Entering into a significant guarantee or commitment
- Sale of equity
- Settlement of a lawsuit where the events causing the lawsuit arose after the balance sheet date

## Stock-Based Compensation

Managers routinely issue shares to their employees, but do not understand the accounting ramifications of doing so. The precise terms of each arrangement can have a drastic impact on how it must be accounted for, so the manager should be aware of the accounting ramifications before writing up a stock-based compensation agreement.

In essence, a share issuance is not free to the business – when these payments are made, the essential accounting is to recognize the cost of the related services as they are received by the company, at their fair value. The following issues relate to the measurement and recognition of stock-based compensation:

Essential Concepts

- *Grant date.* The date on which a stock-based award is granted is assumed to be the date when the award is approved under the corporate governance requirements. The grant date can also be considered the date on which an employee initially begins to benefit from or be affected by subsequent changes in the price of a company's stock, as long as subsequent approval of the grant is considered perfunctory.

---

**EXAMPLE**

The board of directors of Coronary Associates approves a stock option award to Dr. Jones, who is an employee of Coronary. The board meeting date on which the award is approved is March 15. This is the grant date.

---

- *Service period.* The service period associated with a stock-based award is considered to be the vesting period, but the facts and circumstances of the arrangement can result in a different service period for the purpose of determining the number of periods over which to accrue compensation expense. This is called the *implicit service period.*

---

**EXPENSE**

Mrs. Smith is granted 10,000 stock options by the board of directors of Uncanny Corporation, which vest over 24 months. There is no service specified under the arrangement, so the service period is assumed to be the 24-month vesting period. Thus, the fair value of the award should be recognized ratably over the vesting period.

---

Costs to be Recognized

- *Expense accrual.* When the service component related to a stock issuance spans several reporting periods, accrue the related service expense based on the probable outcome of the performance condition. A performance condition is a condition that affects the determination of the fair value of an award. Thus, the expense is accrued when it is probable that the condition will be achieved. Also, the expense is accrued over the initial best estimate of the employee service period, which is usually the service period required in the arrangement related to the stock issuance.

---

**EXAMPLE**

The board of directors of Armadillo Industries grants stock options to its president that have a fair value of $80,000, which will vest in the earlier of four years or when the company achieves a 20% market share in a new market that the company wants to enter. Since there is not sufficient historical information about the company's ability to succeed in the new market, the controller elects to set the service period at four years, and accordingly accrues $20,000 of compensation expense in each of the next four years.

If both performance conditions had been required before the stock options would be awarded, and there was no way of determining the probability of achieving the 20% market share condition, the controller would only begin to accrue any compensation expense after it became probable that the market share condition could be achieved. In this latter case, compensation expense would be recognized at once for all of the earlier periods during which no compensation expense had been accrued.

---

- *Service rendered prior to grant date.* If some or all of the requisite service associated with stock-based compensation occurs prior to the grant date, compensation expense is accrued during these earlier reporting periods, based on the fair value of the award at each reporting date. When the grant date is reached, the compensation accrued to date is adjusted based on the per-unit fair value assigned on the grant date. Thus, the initial recordation is a best guess of what the eventual fair value will be.
- *Service rendered prior to performance target completion.* An employee may complete the required amount of service prior to the date when the associated performance target has been achieved. If so, the compensation expense is recognized when it becomes probable that the target will be achieved. This recognition reflects the service already rendered by the employee.
- *Service not rendered.* If an employee does not render the service required for an award, the employer may then reverse any related amount of compensation expense that had previously been recognized.

---

**EXAMPLE**

Uncanny Corporation grants 5,000 restricted stock units (RSUs) to its vice president of sales, with a three-year cliff vesting provision. The fair value of the RSUs on the grant date is $60,000, so the company accrues $20,000 of compensation expense per year for three years.

One week prior to the cliff vesting date, the vice president of sales unexpectedly resigns. Since the award has not yet vested, the company reverses all of the accrued compensation expense.

---

- *Employee payments.* If an employee pays the issuer an amount in connection with an award, the fair value attributable to employee service is net of the amount paid. For example, if a stock option has a fair value on the grant date of $100, and the recipient pays $20 for the option, the award amount attributable to employee service is $80.

---

**EXAMPLE**

Armadillo Industries issues 1,000 shares of common stock to Mr. Jones, the vice president of sales, at a large discount from the market price. On the grant date, the fair value of these shares is $20,000. Mr. Jones pays $1,000 to the company for these shares. Thus, the amount that can be attributed to Mr. Jones' services to the company is $19,000 (calculated as $20,000 fair value - $1,000 payment).

---

- *Noncompete agreement.* If a share-based award contains a non-compete agreement, the facts and circumstances of the situation may indicate that the non-compete is a significant service condition. If so, accrue the related amount of compensation expense over the period covered by the non-compete agreement.

---

**EXAMPLE**

Armadillo Industries grants 200,000 restricted stock units (RSUs) to its chief high-pressure module design engineer, which are vested on the grant date. The fair value of the grant is $500,000, which is triple his compensation for the past year. Under the terms of the arrangement, the RSUs will only be transferred to the engineer ratably over the next five years if he complies with the terms of the non-compete agreement.

Since the RSUs are essentially linked to the noncompete agreement, and the amount of the future payouts are quite large, it is evident that the arrangement is really intended to be compensation for future services yet to be rendered to the company. Consequently, the appropriate accounting treatment is not to recognize the expense at once, but rather to recognize it ratably over the remaining term of the noncompete agreement.

---

- *Clawback arrangements*. There may be an arrangement under which an employee is required to return shares or profits from the sale of shares. This is called a clawback arrangement, and most commonly occurs as a noncompete mechanism, so that employees will not leave to work for a competitor for a certain period of time. This arrangement is not considered in the grant date fair value of an equity award; instead, it is accounted for only when the contingent event actually occurs. If such a return payment is made, it is recognized as a credit in the income statement, and is limited to the lesser of the compensation cost already recognized for the returned payment, or the fair value of the consideration received.
- *Payroll taxes*. A liability for the payroll taxes associated with stock-based compensation is accrued as of the date of the event that triggered measurement of the compensation.
- *Expired stock options*. If stock option grants expire unused, the related amount of compensation expense is not reversed.
- *Subsequent changes*. If the circumstances later indicate that the number of instruments to be granted has changed, the change in compensation cost is recognized in the period in which the change in estimate occurs. Also, if the initial estimate of the service period turns out to be incorrect, the expense accrual is adjusted to match the updated estimate.

---

**EXAMPLE**

The board of directors of Armadillo Industries initially grants 5,000 stock options to the engineering manager, with a vesting period of four years. The shares are worth $100,000 at the grant date, so the controller plans to recognize $25,000 of compensation expense in each of the next four years. After two years, the board is so pleased with the performance of the engineering manager that they accelerate the vesting schedule to the current date. The controller must therefore accelerate the remaining $50,000 of compensation expense that had not yet been recognized to the current date.

---

If a stock-based award is modified, treat the modification as an exchange of the original award for an entirely new award. Thus, the company is assumed to buy back the original award and exchange it for an award of equal or greater value. The accounting for a modified award includes the following points:

- *Fair value basis*. If there is an incremental change in value between the "old" and "new" awards, this is treated as additional compensation expense. The amount of expense is calculated by determining the fair value of the "old" award immediately prior to the terms modification, and subtracting it from the fair value of the modified award.
- *Short-term inducements*. If the company offers short-term inducements to convince employees to accept an alteration of their stock-based compensation plans, only treat these inducements as modifications if they are accepted by employees.

- *Equity restructuring.* If there is an equity restructuring and awards are replaced with new ones that have the same fair values, the existing accounting is not altered. However, if the fair values have changed, the effects of the equity restructuring are treated as a modification.
- *Cancellation and replacement.* If the company cancels a stock-based award and concurrently grants a replacement award or other form of payment, treat these two events as the modification of terms of the original award.
- *Award cancellation.* If the company cancels an award outright, without any offer to replace the award, the recognition of any remaining unrecognized compensation expense is accelerated to the cancellation date.

---

**EXAMPLE**

Armadillo Industries issues 10,000 stock options to various employees in 20X1. The designated exercise price of the options is $25, and the vesting period is four years. The total fair value of these options is $20,000, which the company charges to expense ratably over four years, which is $5,000 per year.

One year later, the market price of the stock has declined to $15, so the board of directors decides to modify the options to have an exercise price of $15.

Armadillo incurs additional compensation expense of $30,000 for the amount by which the fair value of the modified options exceeds the fair value of the original options as of the date of the modification. The accounting department adds this additional expense to the remaining $15,000 of compensation expense associated with the original stock options, which is a total unrecognized compensation expense of $45,000. The company recognizes this amount ratably over the remaining three years of vesting, which is $15,000 per year.

---

## Taxes

A company may find that it has more tax deductions or tax credits from an operating loss than it can use in the current year's tax return. If so, it has the option of offsetting these amounts against the taxable income or tax liabilities of the tax returns in earlier periods or in future periods. Carrying these amounts back to the tax returns of prior periods is always more valuable, since the company can apply for a tax refund at once. Thus, these excess tax deductions or tax credits are carried back first, with any remaining amounts being reserved for use in future periods. Carryforwards eventually expire, if not used within a certain number of years. A company should recognize a receivable for the amount of taxes paid in prior years that are refundable due to a carryback. A deferred tax asset can be realized for a carryforward, but possibly with an offsetting valuation allowance that is based on the probability that some portion of the carryforward will not be realized.

---

**EXAMPLE**

Spastic Corporation has created $100,000 of deferred tax assets through the diligent generation of losses for the past five years. Based on the company's poor competitive stance, management believes it is more likely than not that there will be inadequate profits (if any) against which the deferred tax assets can be offset. Accordingly, Spastic recognizes a valuation allowance in the amount of $100,000 that fully offsets the deferred tax assets, resulting in no net change in the balance sheet.

---

A tax position is a stance taken by a company in its tax return that measures tax assets and liabilities, and which results in the permanent reduction or temporary deferral of income taxes. When constructing the proper accounting for a tax position, the accounting staff follows these steps:

1. Evaluate whether the tax position taken has merit, based on the tax regulations.
2. If the tax position has merit, measure the amount that can be recognized in the financial statements.
3. Determine the probability and amount of settlement with the taxing authorities. Recognition should only be made when it is more likely than not (i.e., more than 50% probability) that the company's tax position will be sustained once it has been examined by the governing tax authorities.
4. Recognize the tax position, if warranted.

---

**EXAMPLE**

Armadillo Industries takes a tax position on an issue and determines that the position qualifies for recognition, and so should be recognized. The following table shows the estimated possible outcomes of the tax position, along with their associated probabilities:

| Possible Outcome | Probability of Occurrence | Cumulative Probability |
|---|---|---|
| $250,000 | 5% | 5% |
| 200,000 | 20% | 25% |
| 150,000 | 40% | 65% |
| 100,000 | 20% | 85% |
| 50,000 | 10% | 95% |
| 0 | 5% | 100% |

Since the benefit amount just beyond the 50% threshold level is $150,000, Armadillo should recognize a tax benefit of $150,000.

---

If a company initially concludes that the probability of a tax position being sustained is less than 50%, it should not initially recognize the tax position. However, it can recognize the position at a later date if the probability increases to be in excess of 50%, or if the tax position is settled through interaction with the taxing authorities, or the statute of limitations keeps the taxing authorities from challenging the tax position. If a company subsequently concludes that it will change a tax position previously taken, it should recognize the effect of the change in the period in which it alters its tax position. An entity can also derecognize a tax position that it had previously recognized if the probability of the tax position being sustained drops below 50%.

---

**EXAMPLE**

Armadillo Industries takes a tax position under which it accelerates the depreciation of certain production equipment well beyond the normally-allowed taxable rate, resulting in a deferred tax liability* after three years of $120,000.

After three years, a tax court ruling convinces Armadillo management that its tax position is untenable. Consequently, the company recognizes a tax liability for the $120,000 temporary difference**. At the company's current 35% tax rate, this results in increased taxes of $42,000 and the elimination of the temporary difference.

* A deferred tax liability is income taxes payable in a future period.

** A temporary difference is the difference between the recorded cost of an asset or liability and its basis for tax purposes.

---

If there is a change in the tax laws or tax rates, a business cannot recognize alterations in its income tax liability in advance of the enactment of these laws and rates. Instead, the company must wait until enactment has been completed, and can then recognize the changes on the enactment date.

## Summary

The topics summarized in this chapter comprise a tiny fraction of the total content of the accounting standards. However, they constitute many of the issues that managers are most likely to raise with the accounting staff, especially in terms of how management actions will alter the financial results of the organization. For example, a decision to purchase a large number of laptop computers for the staff may or may not result in a large charge to office supplies in the current period, depending upon the capitalization limit that the company uses.

If other issues arise that are not covered in this chapter, the best source of advice is the company's auditors, who usually have the most up-to-date knowledge of accounting standards.

# Chapter 7
# Sales and Marketing Decisions

## Introduction

A business may incur fixed costs that do not vary with activity volume, or variable costs that *do* change in relation to activity volume. In this chapter, we integrate fixed and variable costs into several tools that can be used to review the results and projections of a business. The concept of contribution margin is examined first. We then use contribution margin to derive the breakeven point of a business, and discuss the uses to which breakeven analysis can be put. The breakeven concept is then extended to calculate the margin of safety. These issues are all components of cost-volume-profit analysis, for which we provide a number of examples. Finally, we address sales mix, which impacts the results of a cost-volume-profit analysis. These topics are intended to provide the reader with a view of how sales volumes interact with the cost structure of a business to achieve profitability.

In addition, there are several pricing methodologies that are based on accounting cost. We discuss the nature of these methods, including the advantages and disadvantages of each one. We conclude the chapter with several elasticity of demand topics; they play a significant role in the relationship of price points to sales volume.

## Contribution Margin

The contribution margin is a product's price minus its variable costs, resulting in the incremental profit earned for each unit sold. The total contribution margin generated by an entity represents the total earnings available to pay for fixed expenses and generate a profit. The contribution margin concept can be applied throughout a business, for individual products, product lines, profit centers, subsidiaries, and for an entire organization.

The measure is useful for determining whether to allow a lower price in special pricing situations. If the contribution margin is excessively low or negative, it would be unwise to continue selling a product at that price point. It is also useful for determining the profits that will arise from various sales levels (see the next example). Further, the concept can be used to decide which of several products to sell if they use a common bottleneck resource, so that the product with the highest contribution margin is sold.

To determine the amount of contribution margin for a product, subtract all variable costs of a product from its revenues, and divide by its revenue. The calculation is:

$$\frac{\text{Product revenue} - \text{Product variable costs}}{\text{Product revenue}}$$

---

**EXAMPLE**

The Iverson Drum Company sells drum sets to high schools. In the most recent period, it sold $1,000,000 of drum sets that had related variable costs of $400,000. Iverson had $660,000 of fixed costs during the period, resulting in a loss of $60,000.

| | |
|---|---:|
| Revenue | $1,000,000 |
| Variable expenses | 400,000 |
| Contribution margin | 600,000 |
| Fixed expenses | $660,000 |
| Net loss | -$60,000 |

Iverson's contribution margin is 60%, so if it wants to break even, the company needs to either reduce its fixed expenses by $60,000 or increase its sales by $100,000 (calculated as the $60,000 loss divided by the 60% contribution margin).

**EXAMPLE**

The president of Giro Cabinetry is examining the gross margins on the five products that his company sells. A summary of this information is:

| Product | Sales Price | Variable Cost | Fixed Cost | Gross Margin | Contribution Margin |
|---|---:|---:|---:|---:|---:|
| A | $100 | 60 | 30 | 10% | 40% |
| B | 200 | 100 | 60 | 20% | 50% |
| C | 75 | 25 | 23 | 36% | 67% |
| D | 400 | 300 | 120 | -5% | 25% |
| E | 325 | 230 | 98 | -1% | 29% |

Fixed costs are comprised of factory overhead, which are assigned to products based on their prices. Thus, a high-priced product will be assigned more fixed cost than a lower-priced product. However, there is no linkage between price and fixed cost, so the fixed cost allocations are artificial.

Based on the information in the table, the president might be tempted to cancel products D and E, since both have negative gross margins. However, if he were to do so, the factory overhead would still remain, and would now be allocated among the smaller number of remaining products, which would reduce their gross margins. Only by examining the contribution margin is it obvious that *all* of the products are profitable, and should be retained in order to generate sufficient profits to offset the total amount of fixed costs incurred by the company.

---

## Breakeven Point

The breakeven point is the sales volume at which a business earns exactly no money, where all contribution margin earned is needed to pay for the company's fixed costs. The concept is most easily illustrated in the following chart, where fixed costs occupy a block of expense at the bottom of the table, irrespective of any sales being generated. Variable costs are incurred in concert with the sales level. Once the contribution margin on each sale cumulatively matches the total amount of fixed costs, the breakeven point has been reached. All sales above that level directly contribute to profits.

### Breakeven Table

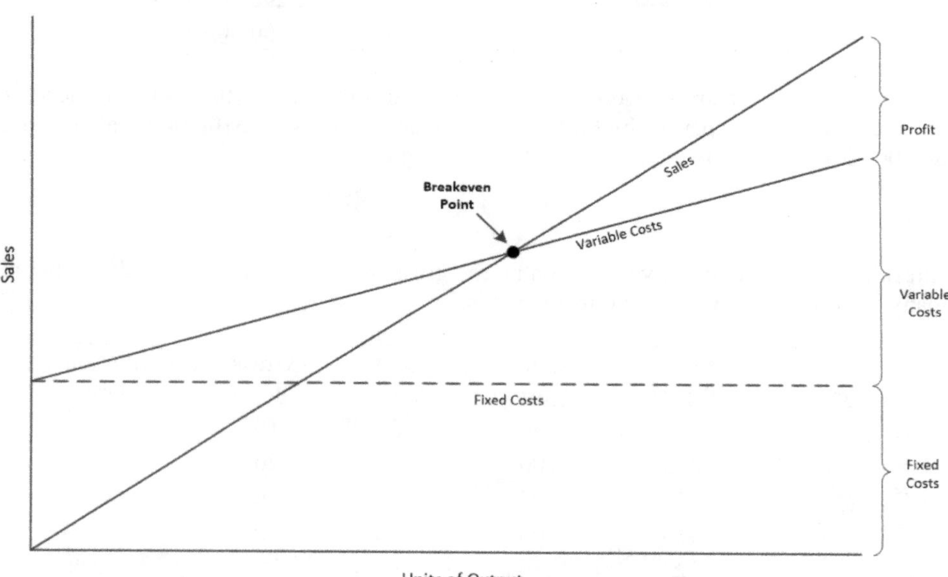


Knowledge of the breakeven point is useful for the following reasons:

- Determining the amount of remaining capacity after the breakeven point is reached, which reveals the maximum amount of profit that can be generated.
- Determining the impact on profit if automation (a fixed cost) replaces labor (a variable cost).
- Determining the change in profits if product prices are altered.
- Determining the amount of losses that could be sustained if the business suffers a sales downturn.

In addition, the breakeven concept is useful for establishing the overall ability of a company to generate a profit. When the breakeven point is near the maximum sales level of a business, this means it is nearly impossible for the company to earn a profit even under the best of circumstances.

Management should constantly monitor the breakeven point, particularly in regard to the last item noted, in order to reduce the breakeven point whenever possible. Ways to do this include:

- *Cost analysis*. Continually review all fixed costs, to see if any can be eliminated. Also review variable costs to see if they can be eliminated, since doing so increases margins and reduces the breakeven point.
- *Margin analysis*. Pay close attention to product margins, and push sales of the highest-margin items, thereby reducing the breakeven point.
- *Outsourcing*. If an activity involves a fixed cost, consider outsourcing it in order to turn it into a per-unit variable cost, which reduces the breakeven point.
- *Pricing*. Reduce or eliminate the use of coupons or other price reductions, since they increase the breakeven point.
- *Technologies*. Implement any technologies that can improve the efficiency of the business, thereby increasing capacity with no increase in cost.

To calculate the breakeven point, divide total fixed expenses by the contribution margin (which was described in an earlier section). The formula is:

$$\frac{\text{Total fixed expenses}}{\text{Contribution margin percentage}}$$

A more refined approach is to eliminate all non-cash expenses (such as depreciation) from the numerator, so that the calculation focuses on the breakeven cash flow level. The formula is:

$$\frac{\text{Total fixed expenses} - \text{Depreciation} - \text{Amortization}}{\text{Contribution margin percentage}}$$

Another variation on the formula is to focus instead on the number of units that must be sold in order to break even, rather than the sales level in dollars. This formula is:

$$\frac{\text{Total fixed expenses}}{\text{Average contribution margin per unit}}$$

**EXAMPLE**

The management of Ninja Cutlery is interested in buying a competitor that makes ceramic knives. The company's due diligence team wants to know if the competitor's breakeven point is too high to allow for a reasonable profit, and if there are any overhead cost opportunities that may reduce the breakeven point. The following information is available:

| | |
|---|---|
| Maximum sales capacity | $5,000,000 |
| Current average sales | $4,750,000 |
| Contribution margin percentage | 35% |
| Total operating expenses | $1,750,000 |
| Breakeven point | $5,000,000 |
| | |
| Operating expense reductions | $375,000 |
| Revised breakeven level | $3,929,000 |
| Maximum profits with revised breakeven point | $375,000 |

The analysis shows that the competitor has an inordinately high breakeven point that allows for little profit, if any. However, there are several operating expense reductions that can trigger a steep decline in the breakeven point. The management of Ninja Cutlery makes an offer to the owners of the competitor, based on the cash flows that can be gained from the reduced breakeven level.

---

A potential problem with the breakeven concept is that it assumes the contribution margin in the future will remain the same as the current level, which may not be the case. A breakeven analysis can be modeled using a range of contribution margins to gain a better understanding of possible future profits and losses at different unit sales levels. See the Sales Mix section for a discussion of variations in contribution margin.

---

**EXAMPLE**

Milford Sound sells a broad range of audio products. The financial analyst is concerned that the average contribution margin of these products has been slipping over the past few years, as customers have been switching to personal audio devices. The current average contribution margin is 38%, but the declining trend indicates that the margin could be 30% within two years. The analyst uses this information to construct the following breakeven analysis for the company:

| | Current Case | Projected Case |
|---|---|---|
| Total fixed costs | $20,000,000 | $20,000,000 |
| ÷ Contribution margin | 38% | 30% |
| = Breakeven sales | $52,632,000 | $66,667,000 |

The calculation shows that the breakeven point will increase by $14 million over the next two years. Since Milford's current sales level is $58,000,000, this means that the company faces the alternatives of driving a massive sales increase, fixed cost reductions, or margin improvements in order to remain profitable.

---

## Margin of Safety

The margin of safety is the reduction in sales that can occur before the breakeven point of a business is reached. The amount of this buffer is expressed as a percentage.

The margin of safety concept is especially useful when a significant proportion of sales are at risk of decline or elimination, as may be the case when a sales contract is coming to an end. By knowing the amount of the margin of safety, management can gain a better understanding of the risk of loss to which a business is subjected by changes in sales. The opposite situation may also arise, where the margin of safety is so large that a business is well-protected from sales variations.

To calculate the margin of safety, subtract the current breakeven point from sales, and divide the result by sales. The breakeven point is calculated by dividing the contribution margin into total fixed expenses. The formula is:

$$\frac{\text{Total current sales} - \text{Breakeven point}}{\text{Total current sales}}$$

To translate the margin of safety into the number of units sold, use the following formula instead:

$$\frac{\text{Total current sales} - \text{Breakeven point}}{\text{Selling price per unit}}$$

If the margin of safety is expressed as the number of units sold, the result works best if a company only sells one type of product. Otherwise, it can be difficult to translate the result into a range of products that have different price points and contribution margins.

---

**EXAMPLE**

Lowry Locomotion is considering the purchase of new equipment to expand the production capacity of its toy tractor product line. The addition will increase Lowry's operating costs by $100,000 per year, though sales will also be increased. Relevant information is noted in the following table:

| | Before Machinery Purchase | After Machinery Purchase |
|---|---:|---:|
| Sales | $4,000,000 | $4,200,000 |
| Contribution margin percentage | 48% | 48% |
| Fixed expenses | $1,800,000 | $1,900,000 |
| Breakeven point | $3,750,000 | $3,958,000 |
| Profits | $120,000 | $116,000 |
| Margin of safety | 6.3% | 5.8% |

The table reveals that both the margin of safety and profits worsen slightly as a result of the equipment purchase, so expanding production capacity is probably not a good idea.

---

## Cost-Volume-Profit Analysis

Cost-volume-profit (CVP) analysis is designed to show how changes in product margins, prices, and unit volumes impact the profitability of a business. It is one of the fundamental financial analysis tools for ascertaining the underlying profitability of a business. The components of cost-volume-profit analysis are:

- *Activity level.* This is the total number of units sold in the measurement period.
- *Price per unit.* This is the average price per unit sold, including any sales discounts and allowances. The price per unit can vary substantially from period to period, based on changes in the mix of products and services, which may be caused by old product terminations, new product introductions, and the seasonality of sales.
- *Variable cost per unit.* This is the totally variable cost per unit sold, which is usually just the amount of direct materials and the sales commission associated with a unit sale. Nearly all other expenses do not vary with sales volume, and so are considered fixed costs.
- *Total fixed cost.* This is the total fixed cost of the business within the measurement period. This figure tends to be relatively steady from period to period, unless there is a step cost transition where the company has elected

to incur an entirely new cost in response to a change in activity level (such as adding a production line).

These components can be mixed and matched in a variety of ways to arrive at different types of analysis. For example:

- What is the breakeven unit volume of a business? We divide the total fixed cost of the company by its contribution margin per unit. Thus, if a business has $50,000 of fixed costs per month, and the average contribution margin of a product is $50, the necessary unit volume to reach a breakeven sales level is 1,000 units.
- What unit quantity is needed to achieve $__ in profits? We add the target profit level to the total fixed cost of the company, and divide by its contribution margin per unit. Thus, if the CEO of the business in the last example wants to earn $20,000 per month, we add that amount to the $50,000 of fixed costs, and divide by the average contribution margin of $50 to arrive at a required unit sales level of 1,400 units.
- If I add a fixed cost, what sales are needed to maintain profits of $__? We add the new fixed cost to the target profit level and original fixed cost of the business, and divide by the unit contribution margin. To continue with the last example, the company is planning to add $10,000 of fixed costs per month. We add that to the $70,000 baseline fixed costs and profit and divide by the $50 average contribution margin to arrive at a new required sales level of 1,600 units per month.
- If I cut unit prices by $__, how many additional units must be sold to maintain profit levels? To continue with the last example, the baseline fixed costs are $60,000, profits are $20,000, and the contribution margin is $50 per unit. The plan is to reduce the unit price by $10 in an attempt to increase sales. Doing so will decrease the contribution margin to $40. To calculate the total number of unit sales required, we divide the $40 contribution margin per unit into the combined fixed costs and profits to arrive at total unit sales of 2,000. Thus, if prices are cut by $10, unit sales must increase by 400 units from the last example in order to maintain profit levels.

In short, the various components of CVP analysis can be used to uncover the financial results arising from many possible scenarios.

---

**EXAMPLE**

The president of Micron Metallic is working through the annual budgeting process, and wants to know how many stamping machines the company must produce in the upcoming year in order to earn a target before-tax profit of $3,000,000. The business has $24,000,000 of fixed costs, and its contribution margin per unit is $20,000. The calculation of units to sell is:

$$\frac{\$24{,}000{,}000 \text{ Fixed costs} + \$3{,}000{,}000 \text{ Target profit}}{\$20{,}000 \text{ Contribution margin per unit}}$$

$$= 1{,}350 \text{ Units}$$

---

The analysis can be refined to include the impact of income taxes, so that the formula for establishing a target after-tax profit for a certain number of units sold becomes:

$$\frac{\text{Fixed costs} + (\text{Target profit} \div (1 - \text{Tax \%}))}{\text{Contribution margin per unit}}$$

---

**EXAMPLE**

To continue with the last example, the president of Micron Metallic wants to determine the number of stamping machines that must be sold in order to achieve an *after-tax* profit of $3,000,000, using the same information. The tax rate is 35%. The calculation is:

$$\frac{\$24{,}000{,}000 \text{ Fixed costs} + (\$3{,}000{,}000 \text{ Target profit} \div (1 - 35\%))}{\$20{,}000 \text{ Contribution margin per unit}}$$

$$= 1{,}431 \text{ Units}$$

---

We do not present a single cost-volume-profit formula, for there is no single formula that applies to all situations. Instead, the basic concept must be revised to meet the requirements of each financial analysis topic as it arises.

## Sales Mix

Sales mix refers to the proportions of different products and services that comprise the total sales of a company. In most cases, each product or service that a company provides has a different contribution margin, so changes in sales mix (even if the total sales level remains the same) usually result in differing amounts of profit.

---

**EXAMPLE**

The financial analyst of Creekside Industrial is examining the sales and profit figures for the past two months, and is having difficulty understanding why sales were identical, but profits were radically different in the two months. He creates the following analysis of sales of the company's two types of batteries:

| | January | | | February | | |
|---|---|---|---|---|---|---|
| | Product A | Product B | Total | Product A | Product B | Total |
| Sales | $2,000,000 | $3,500,000 | $5,500,000 | $4,000,000 | $1,500,000 | $5,500,000 |
| Variable costs | 1,600,000 | 1,400,000 | 3,000,000 | 3,200,000 | 600,000 | 3,800,000 |
| Variable cost % | 80% | 40% | 55% | 80% | 40% | 69% |
| Contribution | 400,000 | 2,100,000 | 2,500,000 | 800,000 | 900,000 | 1,700,000 |
| Fixed costs | | | 2,000,000 | | | 2,000,000 |
| Profit (loss) | | | $500,000 | | | -$300,000 |

Because sales have shifted between the two products, which have radically different contribution margins, the profit level is heavily impacted by the sales mix.

---

If a company introduces a new product that has a low profit, and which it sells aggressively, it is quite possible that profits will decline even as sales increase. Conversely, if a company elects to drop a low-profit product line and instead push sales of a higher-profit product line, total profits can increase even as total sales decline.

**Tip:** Sales managers must be aware of sales mix when they devise commission plans for the sales staff, since the intent should be to incentivize the sales staff to sell high-profit items. Otherwise, a poorly-constructed commission plan could push the sales staff in the direction of selling the wrong products, which alters the sales mix and results in lower profits.

A cost accounting variance called the *sales mix variance* is used to measure the difference in unit volumes in the actual sales mix from the planned sales mix. Follow these steps to calculate it at the individual product level:

1. Subtract budgeted unit volume from actual unit volume and multiply by the budgeted contribution margin.
2. Do the same for each of the products sold.
3. Aggregate this information to arrive at the sales mix variance for the company.

The formula is:

(Actual unit sales – Budgeted unit sales) × Budgeted contribution margin

---

**EXAMPLE**

Oberlin Acoustics expects to sell 100 platinum harmonicas, which have a contribution margin of $12 per unit, but actuals sells only 80 units. Also, Oberlin expects to sell 400 stainless steel harmonicas, which have a contribution margin of $6, but actually sells 500 units. The sales mix variance is:

Platinum harmonica: (80 actual units – 100 budgeted units)
× $12 contribution margin = -$240

Stainless steel harmonica: (500 actual units – 400 budgeted units)
× $6 contribution margin = $600

Thus, the aggregated sales mix variance is $360, which reflects a large increase in the sales volume of a product having a lower contribution margin, combined with a decline in sales for a product that has a higher contribution margin.

---

## Accounting Inputs to Price Formulation

When the price of a product or service is created, it does not necessarily have to relate in any way to the underlying cost of the product or service. The price can simply be set at whatever level the market will bear, or perhaps the company intends to set a loss-leader price to attract customers. However, some pricing systems make active use of product cost information. In this section, we note several pricing formulations in which accounting information is used.

### Cost Plus Pricing

Cost plus pricing is a price-setting method under which the costs of direct materials, direct labor, and overhead are added together for a product; then a markup percentage is added in order to derive the price of the product. It can also be used under a contract with a customer, where the customer reimburses the seller for all costs incurred and also pays a negotiated profit in addition to the costs incurred.

---

**EXAMPLE**

Hammer Industries has designed a product that contains the following costs:

- Direct material costs = $20.00
- Direct labor costs = $5.50
- Allocated overhead = $8.25

The company applies a standard 30% markup to all of its products. To derive the price of this product, Hammer adds together the stated costs to arrive at a total cost of $33.75, and then multiplies this amount by (1 + 0.30) to arrive at the product price of $43.88.

---

The following are advantages to using the cost plus pricing method:

- *Assured contract profits.* Any contractor is willing to accept this method for a contractual agreement with a customer, since it is assured of having its costs reimbursed and of making a profit. There is no risk of loss on such a contract.
- *Justifiable.* In cases where the supplier must persuade its customers of the need for a price increase, the supplier can point to an increase in its costs as the reason for the price increase.
- *Simple.* It is quite easy to derive a product price using this method, though the overhead allocation method should be defined in order to be consistent in calculating the prices of multiple products.

The following are disadvantages of using the cost plus method:

- *Contract cost overruns.* From the perspective of any government entity that hires a supplier under a cost plus pricing arrangement, the supplier has no incentive to curtail its expenditures - on the contrary, it will likely include as many costs as possible in the contract so that it can be reimbursed. Thus, a contractual arrangement should include cost-reduction incentives for the supplier.
- *Ignores competition.* A company may set a product price based on the cost plus formula and then be surprised when it finds that competitors are charging substantially different prices. This has a huge impact on the market share and profits that a company can expect to achieve. The company either ends up pricing too low and giving away potential profits, or pricing too high and achieving minor revenues.
- *Product cost overruns.* Under this method, the engineering department has no incentive to prudently design a product that has the appropriate feature set and design characteristics for its target market. Instead, the department simply designs what it wants and launches the product.

This method is not acceptable for deriving the price of a product that is to be sold in a competitive market, primarily because it does not factor in the prices charged by competitors. Thus, this method is likely to result in a seriously overpriced product. Further, prices should be set based on what the market is willing to pay - which could result in a substantially different margin than the standard margin typically assigned to a product.

Cost plus pricing is a more valuable tool in a contractual situation, since the supplier has no downside risk. However, be sure to review which costs are allowable for reimbursement under the contract; it is possible that the terms of the contract are so restrictive that the supplier must exclude many costs from reimbursement, and so can potentially incur a loss.

**Time and Materials Pricing**

Time and materials pricing is used in service industries to bill customers for a standard labor rate per hour used, plus the actual cost of materials used. The standard labor rate per hour being billed does not necessarily relate to the underlying cost of the labor; instead, it may be based on the market rate for the services of someone having a certain skill set. Thus, a computer technician may bill out at $100 per hour, while costing $30 per hour, while a cable television mechanic may only bill out at $80 per hour, despite costing the same amount per hour. The cost of materials charged to the customer is for any materials actually used during the performance of services for the customer. This cost may be at the supplier's actual cost, or it may be a marked-up cost that includes a fee for the overhead cost associated with ordering, handling, and holding the materials in stock.

Under the time and materials pricing methodology, a single hourly rate may be charged irrespective of the experience level of the person performing the services, but usually there are different rates for different experience levels within the company. Thus, an associate consultant will have a lower billing rate than a consulting manager, who in turn has a lower billing rate than a consulting partner.

Industries in which time and materials pricing are used include:

- Accounting, auditing, and tax services
- Consulting services
- Legal work
- Medical services
- Vehicle repair

If a company chooses to base its labor rate under time and materials pricing on its underlying costs, rather than the market rate, it can do so by adding together the following:

- The cost of compensation, payroll taxes, and benefits per hour for the employee providing billable services
- An allocation of general overhead costs
- An additional factor to account for the proportion of expected unbillable time

---

**EXAMPLE**

Hammer Industries has an equipment repair group that charges out its staff at a level that covers the cost of labor, plus a profit factor. In the past year, Hammer incurred $2,000,000 of salary expenses, plus $140,000 of payroll taxes, $300,000 of employee benefits, and $500,000 of office expenses; this totaled $2,940,000 of expenses for the year. In the past year, the company had 30,000 billable hours, which is roughly what it expects to bill out in the near future. Hammer wants the division to earn a 20% profit. Based on this information, the division charges $122.50 per hour for each of its repair personnel. The calculation of the labor price per hour is:

$2,940,000 annual costs ÷ (1 - 20% profit percentage) = $3,675,000 revenue needed

$3,675,000 revenue needed ÷ 30,000 billable hours = $122.50 billing rate

---

The following are advantages of using the time and materials pricing method:

- *Assured profits*. If a company can keep its employees billable, this pricing structure makes it difficult *not* to earn a profit. However, the reverse situation can arise if the proportion of billable hours declines (see below).
- *High risk situations*. This pricing method is excellent in situations where the outcome of the work is in such doubt that the supplier will only take on the work if it can be properly reimbursed.

The following are disadvantages of using the time and materials pricing method:

- *Cost basis ignores market prices*. If a company sets its time and materials prices based on its internal cost structure, it may be setting prices lower than the market rate, thereby potentially losing profits. The reverse situation may also occur, where market prices are lower than internally-compiled prices. If so, a business will find itself unable to generate much business.
- *Customers will not allow*. This pricing format allows a company to potentially run up its hours billed and charge more than the customer expects. Thus, customers prefer a fixed price to time and materials pricing.
- *Lost profits*. A company that provides highly value-added services could potentially use value based pricing, where prices are set based on the perceived value delivered to the customer. Not using this approach could result in lost profits.
- *Low billable hours situations*. The basis of the time and materials pricing system is that a company will be able to bill enough hours to offset its fixed costs (usually the salaries of its employees). If the number of billable hours declines and headcount does not decline in proportion, the company will lose money.
- *Price negotiations*. More sophisticated customers will negotiate reductions in the billable rate per hour, eliminate any mark-up on materials, and impose

a "not to exceed" clause in any time and materials contract, thereby limiting profits.

Time and materials pricing is a standard practice in many services businesses and works well, as long as the company sets sufficiently competitive prices and maintains a high rate of billable hours. Otherwise, the amount of revenue generated will not offset the fixed costs of the business, resulting in losses.

**Breakeven Pricing**

Breakeven pricing is the practice of setting a price point at which a business will earn zero profits on a sale. The intention behind the use of breakeven pricing is to gain market share and drive competitors from the marketplace. By doing so, a company may be able to increase its production volumes to such an extent that it can reduce costs and then earn a profit at what had been the breakeven price. Alternatively, once it has driven out competitors, the company can raise its prices sufficiently to earn a profit, but not so high that the increased price is tempting for new market entrants.

The concept is also useful for establishing the lowest acceptable price, below which the seller will begin to lose money on a sale. This information is useful when responding to a customer that is demanding the lowest possible price.

The breakeven price can be calculated based on the following formula:

(Total fixed cost ÷ Production unit volume) + Variable cost per unit

This calculation allows one to calculate the price at which a business will earn exactly zero profit, assuming that a certain number of units are sold. In practice, the actual number of units sold will vary from expectations, so the true breakeven price may prove to be somewhat different.

It is especially common for a new entrant into a market to engage in breakeven pricing in order to obtain market share. It is particularly likely when the new entrant has a product that it cannot differentiate from the competition in a meaningful way, and so differentiates on price.

A business intent on following the breakeven pricing strategy should have substantial financial resources, since it may incur significant losses during the early stages of this strategy.

---

**EXAMPLE**

Hansen Industrial wants to enter the market for yellow one-sided widgets. The fixed cost of manufacturing these widgets is $50,000, and the variable cost per unit is $5.00. Hansen's president expects to sell 10,000 of the widgets. Therefore, the breakeven price of the widgets is:

($50,000 fixed costs ÷ 10,000 units) + $5.00 variable cost

= $10.00 breakeven price

Assuming that Hansen actually sells 10,000 units in the period, $10.00 will be the price at which the company breaks even. Alternatively, if Hansen were to sell fewer units, it would incur a loss, because the price point does not cover fixed costs. Or, if Hansen were to sell more units, it would earn a profit, because the price point covers more than the fixed costs.

---

The following are advantages of using the breakeven pricing method:

- *Entry barrier*. If a company continues with its breakeven pricing strategy, possible new entrants to the market will be deterred by the low prices.
- *Reduces competition*. Financially weaker competitors will be driven out of the market.
- *Market dominance*. It is possible to achieve a dominant market position with this strategy, if it can be used to increase production volumes and thereby reduce costs and earn a profit.

The following are disadvantages of using the breakeven pricing method:

- *Customer loss*. If a company only engages in breakeven pricing without also improving its product quality or customer service, it may find that customers leave if/when it raises prices.
- *Perceived value*. If a company reduces prices substantially, it creates a perception among customers that the product or service is no longer as valuable, which may interfere with any later actions to increase prices.
- *Price war*. Competitors may respond with even lower prices, so that the company does not gain any market share.

This method is most useful for those companies with sufficient resources to lower prices and fight off attempts by competitors to undercut them. It is à difficult approach for a smaller, resource-poor company that cannot survive for long with zero margins.

## Price Elasticity of Demand

Price elasticity is the degree to which changes in price impact the unit sales of a product or service. The demand for a product is considered to be *inelastic* if changes in price have minimal impact on unit sales volume. Conversely, the demand for a product is considered to be *elastic* if changes in price have a large impact on unit sales volume. This concept can be a key determinant of the underlying profitability of a business. In particular, a high level of price elasticity can directly correlate with low profit margins.

A product is more likely to have inelastic demand if customers buy it for reasons other than price. This typically involves high-end luxury goods, or the "latest and greatest" products that are impacted by style considerations, where there are no obvious substitutes for the product. Thus, altering the price of a custom-made watch may not appreciably alter the amount of unit sales volume, since roughly the same number of potential customers will still be interested in buying it, irrespective of the price.

A product is more likely to have elastic demand when it is a commodity that is offered by many suppliers. In this situation, there is no way to differentiate the product, so customers only buy it based on price. Thus, if a company were to raise prices on a product that has elastic demand, unit volume would likely plummet as customers go elsewhere to find a better deal. Examples of products having elastic demand are gasoline and many of its byproducts, corn, wheat, and cement. The key considerations in whether a product will have elastic or inelastic demand are:

- *Duration*. Over time, consumers will alter their behavior to avoid excessively expensive goods. This means that the price for a product may be inelastic in the short term and increasingly elastic over the long term. For example, the owner of a fuel-inefficient vehicle will be forced to pay for higher gasoline prices in the short term, but may switch to a more fuel-efficient vehicle over the long term in order to buy less fuel.
- *Necessity*. If something must be purchased (such as a drug for a specific medical condition), the consumer will buy it, irrespective of price.
- *Payer*. People who can have their purchases reimbursed by someone else (such as the company they work for) are more likely to exhibit price inelastic behavior. For example, an employee is more likely to stay at an expensive hotel if the company is paying for it.
- *Percent of income*. If something involves a significant proportion of the income of the consumer, the consumer is more likely to look for substitute products, which makes a product more price elastic.
- *Uniqueness*. If there is no ready substitute for a product, it will be more price inelastic. This is particularly true where intensive marketing is used to make the product appear indispensable in the minds of consumers.

The elasticity or inelasticity of demand is a consideration in the pricing of products. Clearly, inelastic demand gives a company a great deal of room in price setting, whereas elastic demand means that the appropriate price is already defined by the market. Products having inelastic demand tend to have smaller markets, whereas products with elastic demand can involve much larger sales volume. Thus, a company pursuing a strategy of only selling products with inelastic demand may be limiting its potential sales growth.

From a practical perspective, companies are most likely to set prices based on what competitors are charging for their products, modified by the perceived value of certain product features. Price elasticity can also be used to fine-tune prices, but it is still more of a theoretical concept than one that has practical applicability.

The formula for the price elasticity of demand is the percent change in unit demand as a result of a one percent change in price. The calculation is:

$$\frac{\%\text{ Change in unit demand}}{\%\text{ Change in price}}$$

A product is said to be price inelastic if this ratio is less than one, and price elastic if the ratio is greater than one. Revenue should be maximized when a company can set the price to have an elasticity of exactly one.

---

**EXAMPLE**

Hammer Industries wants to test the price elasticity of demand for two of its products. It alters the price of its steel construction hammer by 3%, which generates a reduction in unit volume of 2%. This indicates some inelasticity of demand, since the company can raise prices and experience a smaller offsetting reduction in sales.

Hammer then tests the price inelasticity of its home screwdriver set by altering its price by 2%. This results in a reduction in unit volume of 4%. The result indicates significant elasticity of demand, since unit sales drop twice as fast as the increase in price.

---

## Cross Price Elasticity of Demand

Cross price elasticity of demand is the percentage change in the demand for one product when the price of a different product changes. This concept is useful for many companies that sell a multitude of products and services, since what at first may appear to be an isolated price change can have a ripple effect on other parts of the business. The manager should be aware of these interrelationships and how they can impact profits. The cross price elasticity formula is:

$$\frac{\text{Percentage change in demand of one product}}{\text{Percentage change in price of a different product}}$$

If there is no relationship between the two products, this ratio will be zero. However, if a product is a valid *substitute* for the product whose price has changed, there will be a positive ratio - that is, a price increase in one product will yield an increase in demand for another product. Conversely, if two products are typically purchased together (known as *complementary* products), a price change will result in a negative ratio - that is, a price increase in one product will yield a decrease in demand for the other product. Here are examples of different ratio results for the cross price elasticity of demand:

- *Positive ratio.* When the admission price at a movie theater increases, the demand for downloaded movies increases, because downloaded movies are a substitute for a movie theater.
- *Negative ratio.* When the admission price at a movie theater increases, the demand at the nearby parking garage also declines, because fewer people are parking there to go to the movie theater. These are complementary products.
- *Zero ratio.* When the admission price at a movie theater increases, the demand at a nearby furniture store is unchanged, because the two are unrelated.

A company can use the concept of cross price elasticity of demand in its pricing strategies. For example, the food served in a movie theater has a strong complementary relationship with the number of theater tickets sold, so it may make sense to drop ticket prices in order to attract more movie viewers, which in turn generates more food sales. Thus, the net effect of lowering ticket prices may be more total profit for the theater owner.

A business can also use heavy branding of its product line to mitigate the substitution effect. Thus, by spending money on advertising, a business can make customers want to buy its products so much that a price increase will not send them out to buy substitute products (at least not within a certain price range).

## Non-Price Determinants of Demand

What if customers have other reasons than price for buying products or services? The following list enumerates several non-price determinants of demand. These factors are important, because they can change the number of units sold, irrespective of price points. As such, they can provide great value to a company, and so should be a factor in ongoing company planning and pricing discussions. The determinants are:

- *Available income.* If the amount of available buyer income changes, it alters their propensity to purchase. Thus, if there is an economic boom, someone is more likely to buy, irrespective of price.
- *Branding.* Sellers can use advertising, product differentiation, customer service, and so forth to create such robust brand images that buyers have a strong preference for their goods.
- *Complementary goods.* If there is a price change in a complementary item, it can impact the demand for a product. Thus, a change in the price of popcorn in a movie theatre could impact the demand for movies.
- *Demographics.* A change in the proportions of the population in different age ranges can alter demand in favor of those groups increasing in size (and vice versa). Thus, an aging population will increase the demand for arthritis drugs.

- *Future expectations.* If buyers believe that the market will change in the future, such as may happen with an anticipated constriction of supplies, this can alter their purchasing behavior now. Thus, an expected constriction in the supply of rubber might increase the demand for tires now.
- *Market size.* If the market is expanding rapidly, customers may be compelled to purchase based on other factors than price, simply because the supply of goods is not keeping up with demand.
- *Seasonality.* The need for goods varies by time of year; for example, there is a strong demand for lawn mowers in the spring, but not in the fall.

These determinants will alter the demand for goods and services, but only within certain price ranges. For example, if non-price determinants are driving increased demand, but prices are very high, it is likely that buyers will be driven to look at substitute products.

## Summary

The interaction of unit costs, fixed costs, sales volumes, and contribution margins is critical to an understanding of how a business earns a profit. By altering the inputs to a cost-volume-profit model, one can estimate how the results of a business will change, which affects management's decisions to invest in fixed assets, withdraw products, cut back business units, hire staff, and so forth.

A note of caution must be inserted into this discussion. Cost-volume-profit analysis assumptions are not entirely under the control of an organization. It may be possible to adhere to planned changes in costs, but unit sales and product price points may not be accepted by customers, rendering a financial model invalid. Consequently, it may be necessary to revise these models frequently in response to pilot tests in the market; alternatively, incorporate worst-case scenarios for unit sales and price points, in case customer acceptance of a new company initiative is indifferent.

# Chapter 8
# Human Resources Decisions

## Introduction

In most organizations, employees are one of the most essential factors in the success of operations. Accordingly, managers may spend a substantial portion of their time on human resources issues, perhaps relating to promotions, transfers, pay rate changes, and so forth. There are also many accounting issues related to human resources that any manager should be aware of. These issues primarily relate to payroll activities and the cost of employees. This chapter presents those human resources issues relating to accounting that can be informative to the manager. In addition, we make note of a number of compensation cost reduction issues, which can be of use when a company is contemplating the reduction of expenses.

**Related Podcast Episode:** Episode 54 of the Accounting Best Practices Podcast discusses payroll cycles. It is available at: **accountingtools.com/podcasts** or **iTunes**

## Payroll Cycles

One of the more important payroll management decisions is how long to set the payroll cycle. Each payroll requires a great deal of effort by the payroll staff to collect information about time worked, locate and correct errors, process wage rate and deduction changes, calculate pay, and issue payments. Consequently, it makes a great deal of sense to extend the duration of payroll cycles.

If payrolls are spaced at short intervals, such as weekly, the payroll staff has to prepare 52 payrolls per year. Conversely, paying employees once a month reduces the payroll staff's payroll preparation activities by approximately three-quarters. Since paying employees just once a month can be a burden on the employees, companies frequently adopt a half-way measure, paying employees either twice a month (the *semimonthly* payroll) or once every two weeks (the *biweekly* payroll). The semimonthly payroll cycle results in processing 24 payrolls per year, while the biweekly payroll cycle requires the processing of 26 payrolls per year.

An example of a weekly payroll cycle is shown in the following exhibit, where employees are paid every Tuesday for the hours they worked in the preceding week.

**Weekly Payroll Cycle**

| January | | | | | | |
|---|---|---|---|---|---|---|
| S | M | T | W | T | F | S |
| | 1 | 2 | 3 | 4 | 5 | 6 |
| 7 | 8 | 9 | 10 | 11 | 12 | 13 |
| 14 | 15 | 16 | 17 | 18 | 19 | 20 |
| 21 | 22 | 23 | 24 | 25 | 26 | 27 |
| 28 | 29 | 30 | 31 | | | |

An example of a biweekly payroll cycle is shown in the following exhibit, where employees are paid every other Tuesday for the hours worked in the preceding two weeks:

**Biweekly Payroll Cycle**

| January | | | | | | |
|---|---|---|---|---|---|---|
| S | M | T | W | T | F | S |
| | 1 | 2 | 3 | 4 | 5 | 6 |
| 7 | 8 | 9 | 10 | 11 | 12 | 13 |
| 14 | 15 | 16 | 17 | 18 | 19 | 20 |
| 21 | 22 | 23 | 24 | 25 | 26 | 27 |
| 28 | 29 | 30 | 31 | | | |

An example of a semimonthly payroll cycle is shown in the following exhibit, where employees are paid on the 15$^{th}$ and last days of the month.

**Semimonthly Payroll Cycle**

| January | | | | | | |
|---|---|---|---|---|---|---|
| S | M | T | W | T | F | S |
| | 1 | 2 | 3 | 4 | 5 | 6 |
| 7 | 8 | 9 | 10 | 11 | 12 | 13 |
| 14 | 15 | 16 | 17 | 18 | 19 | 20 |
| 21 | 22 | 23 | 24 | 25 | 26 | 27 |
| 28 | 29 | 30 | 31 | | | |

An example of a monthly payroll cycle is shown in the following exhibit, where employees are paid on the last day of the month.

**Monthly Payroll Cycle**

| January | | | | | | |
|---|---|---|---|---|---|---|
| S | M | T | W | T | F | S |
| | 1 | 2 | 3 | 4 | 5 | 6 |
| 7 | 8 | 9 | 10 | 11 | 12 | 13 |
| 14 | 15 | 16 | 17 | 18 | 19 | 20 |
| 21 | 22 | 23 | 24 | 25 | 26 | 27 |
| 28 | 29 | 30 | 31 | | | |

An argument in favor of the biweekly payroll is that employees become accustomed to receiving two paychecks per month, plus two "free" paychecks during the year, which has a somewhat more positive impact on employee morale. Nonetheless, the semimonthly payroll represents a slight improvement over the biweekly payroll from the perspective of payroll department efficiency, and is therefore recommended.

If employees are accustomed to a weekly payroll cycle and the company switches them to one of a longer duration, expect to have some employees complain about not having enough cash to see them through the initial increased payroll cycle. This problem can be mitigated by extending pay advances to employees during the initial conversion to the longer payroll cycle. Once employees receive their larger paychecks under the new payroll cycle, they should be able to support themselves and will no longer need an advance.

A further issue is when a company operates a different payroll cycle for different groups of employees. For example, hourly employees may be paid on a weekly cycle and salaried employees on a semimonthly cycle. To complicate matters further, a company may have acquired other businesses and retained the payroll cycles used for their employees. Retaining all of these payroll cycles places the payroll staff in the position of perpetually preparing payrolls, so that it never has time for other activities. To avoid this problem, convert all of the different payroll cycles to a single one that applies to all employees. This may take a large amount of effort, but is mandatory if the intent is to unburden the payroll staff from base-level data entry activities.

## Time Tracking Issues

The main input to the payroll system is documentation of the hours worked by employees, which is used to derive compensation payments. Depending upon the level of detail demanded, the aggregate amount of documentation time required by employees throughout the company can be so substantial that it interferes with the overall profitability of the business. If so, time tracking becomes a notable issue for every manager in the company. In this section, we explore the extent to which time tracking should be used, how to exclude employees from the time tracking system, and whether the amount of information collected can be pared back.

## Time Tracking Scope

A key issue in developing a time tracking system is to determine the extent of the time tracking that is *really* required. An overly conservative payroll manager may feel that it is necessary to have every employee submit a time report for every day worked, detailing the time spent on every activity. If so, consider whether this is really necessary. Are management decisions being made that are based on this information? Is the information required by law? Does a customer want to see the information as part of the periodic billings that the company sends it? In most cases, the answer is no. And even if the answer is yes, there are ways to mitigate the amount of information collected. Consider the following example:

---

**EXAMPLE**

Luminescence Corporation operates an LED manufacturing facility. Management is concerned about employee productivity, and wants to have all employees fill out a time sheet each day, detailing their activities. The payroll manager of Luminescence points out that the time required to fill out these timesheets will surely contribute to a further decline in productivity, and suggests the following set of alternatives:

- Limit the timesheets to the engineering and production departments, where the productivity issue appears to be worst;
- Use standardized activity codes, in order to reduce the time required to fill out the time sheets; and
- Limit this time keeping requirement to one month per year.

---

In the preceding example, the last alternative (to limit the time tracking period) was the most crucial. When management demands that employees report more information through the time tracking system, it may take action on the resulting information for a short period of time, but will likely stop doing so fairly soon, once it achieves whatever goal it initially set. From that point onward, the only valid reason for continuing to collect the information is to verify that employees are not deviating from the current use of their time; this is a control point, and can be easily reviewed by sampling employee activities at fairly lengthy intervals. Thus, continuing to require *all* employees to record a large set of data in perpetuity is highly inefficient.

What about a requirement by a customer to report certain information to it that calls for employee timekeeping? This requirement arises occasionally in consulting projects, where customers want to know exactly what activities the company's employees are engaged in. One can reduce the scope of such customer-imposed requirements by comparing customer demands to the current set of information already being tracked by the corporate timekeeping system, and negotiating with the customer to modify their requirements to match your system. This is most effectively done before the contract is signed with the customer.

**Employee Exclusions**

Whenever possible, try to exclude employees from the time tracking system. Instead, create a standard amount of hours worked, and only have them record their time worked if it varies from the predetermined amount. This is time tracking by exception, and works well for many positions where employees engage in essentially the same activities every day, and for the same period of time. Time tracking by exception is an excellent solution when employees do not see the need to continually submit time reports that document the same activities; in this situation, employees are much less likely to submit their time sheets on a timely basis, so the payroll staff must spend extra time reminding them to do so.

Another form of employee exclusion is to switch employees from being paid on an hourly basis to being paid on a salaried basis. By doing so, the company eliminates the need to track their time at all, at least for the purpose of computing their pay. However, if employees are salaried but their time is billed to customers (as is the case for a consultant), it is still necessary to track their time.

Converting an employee to salaried status will likely only apply to a very small proportion of all employees, since this status is governed by federal regulations. The key guidelines for designating a person as being eligible for a salary are as follows:

- *Administrative*. Those in charge of an administrative department, even if they supervise no one, and anyone assisting management with long-term strategy decisions.
- *Executive*. Those who manage more than 50% of the time and supervise at least two employees.
- *Professional*. Those who spend at least 50% of their time on tasks requiring knowledge obtained through a four-year college degree (including systems analysis, design, and programming work on computer systems, even if a four-year degree was not obtained). The position must also allow for continued independent decision making and minimal close supervision.

Even if an employee has been identified as being potentially convertible from an hourly to a salaried position, the employee may perceive this as an attempt to deny him overtime pay. If so, the company may have to offer a higher salary to mollify the employee, which may be large enough to negate any possible efficiency improvement from having to no longer track the person's hours worked. Thus, converting employees from hourly to salaried pay is an interesting concept, but is only applicable in a few situations.

**Data Collection Scope**

An employee time tracking system may be used to collect more information than hours worked. A time tracking system is a data collection system, and so can be used to collect information about anything. However, do not be tempted to overuse this capability, since collecting additional data requires more data entry time by employees. Instead, question the need for any additional data collection above the bare minimum amount. Ideally, this means the company is collecting the identification number of each employee and his time worked – and nothing else.

Above the baseline data collection level just noted, the next most common item to be collected is the pay code, which identifies hours worked as falling into a pay category, such as holidays, bereavement leave, jury duty, and vacation time. If the decision is made to use pay codes, do not overwhelm employees with a multitude of these codes, since they will be more likely to record the wrong codes.

In the production area and materials management departments, it may be necessary to use activity codes for such tasks as receiving, putaways to stock, picking from stock, inventory counting, manufacturing, rework, and shipping. Resist the urge to use activity codes, because employees tend to spend their time in the same proportions on the same activities over time – collecting information to confirm that nothing has changed is a waste of time. Ideally, only require hourly production workers to clock in and clock out, and do not waste their time recording any additional time tracking information – with the possible exception of the next item.

If the cost of production jobs is being accumulated, employees may record the time they spend on individual jobs. These systems can be quite elaborate, with every conceivable cost being assigned to jobs. Such detailed record keeping may be required by customers, but if it is not, does the business really need the information? In a custom production environment, the answer may very well be yes, since management needs to know how well the company is setting prices and controlling its production process. However, if the company is largely selling standardized products, consider strictly limiting the job tracking system to just those jobs that truly require custom work, and for which management regularly compares the budgeted to actual cost and takes action on this information.

---

**EXAMPLE**

Grubstake Brothers manufactures backhoes that are moderately customized to fit the needs of its customers. Management is considering whether to have the production staff track their time on specific jobs. The production manager asserts that the average employee works on three jobs per day, and so would need to track his time against each of the three jobs. There are 500 production employees, and they work an average of 20 days per month. Thus, timekeeping would change from two transactions per day per employee (clocking in and clocking out) to eight transactions per day (clocking in and out for each job). This translates into the following volumes per month:

Current: 500 employees × 20 days × 2 transactions = **20,000** time tracking transactions

With job tracking: 500 employees × 20 days × 8 transactions = **80,000** time keeping transactions

In addition, the payroll staff must collect and correct the increased volume of time keeping transactions, which may require it to hire an additional payroll clerk.

---

One way to deal with job costing is to split it away from the time tracking system, so that only those employees actively involved with custom jobs are required to track their time on a job-specific basis. This approach also means that job information can be collected at different intervals from when payroll-specific information is being collected, which reduces the amount of time-critical information that the payroll staff must deal with as part of its payroll processing activities.

## Payroll Deduction Issues

A company may use an array of benefits to tempt job candidates to join the organization. From a competitive perspective, it may be necessary to offer the broadest possible range of benefits. These benefits are expensive, so the company usually pays for part of each one, while employees pay for the remainder through ongoing payroll deductions. However, maintaining a complex set of benefits can be difficult from an accounting perspective, since each employee may enroll in a different mix of benefits, each of which requires a different deduction from employee pay. The result can be a high error rate in the processing of payroll deductions, as well as an inordinate amount of payroll staff time to enter and monitor these deductions. In this section, we address how payroll deductions can be properly managed.

Whenever there are deductions from an employee's pay, this involves setting up the deduction as well as a goal amount that terminates the deduction when the total amount of the deductions (the goal) is reached. These additions to the payroll processing function require the time of the payroll staff to set up, and may include errors that require further investigation and correction. Ideally, the goal should be to minimize the number of deductions, so that the payroll staff has more time available for other, more value-added, activities. Here are several methods to consider that can reduce the number of deductions:

- *Benefit deductions*. There may be many deductions associated with employee benefits, such as the employee-paid portion of medical insurance, dental insurance, life insurance, and supplemental life insurance. These deductions are usually set up once a year, when insurance rates change, and are then copied forward automatically in all future payrolls until the next change in rates. These deductions can amount to a massive number of revisions when insurance rates change. One way to reduce the number of these deductions is to eliminate the employee-paid part of a benefit, so that the company pays the entire amount of the insurance. Since this can be expensive, a simpler and less expensive alternative is to merge all benefits into a single package, and require just one deduction from employees for the entire package. A third option is to eliminate some lesser-used benefits, and thereby the deductions associated with them.
- *Employee advances*. Those employees with minimal cash reserves may get into the habit of requesting a pay advance from the company, which is then deducted from their next paycheck. If the company allows these advances, it can reasonably expect some employees to make continuing use of them,

with an ongoing series of advances and offsetting deductions. This can be quite a problem for the payroll staff, since these entries cannot be automated. Further, the company loses any unpaid advances if an employee suddenly leaves the company. It is best to avoid this problem entirely by not allowing *any* employee advances. Instead, refer employees to a selection of local lenders who provide short-term loans.

- *Employee purchases*. If a company allows its employees to buy products from the company, or from other companies on their behalf, it is common practice to allow employees to pay for these purchases with a series of deductions from their paychecks. Some employees will take advantage of this situation to effectively use the company as their private bank, making a series of such purchases and requesting an unending stream of deductions from their paychecks to pay for the purchases. Also, employees may request that their deductions be altered (usually to extend the reimbursement period), which calls for more deduction calculations by the payroll staff. Since there is no operational need for these purchases, consider not allowing employees to buy anything through the company without paying for the purchases up front, in cash.

A manager outside of the accounting area should be aware of the issues and possible resolutions noted in this section, if only to understand the accounting viewpoint in regard to the difficulty of handling payroll deductions.

## Payroll Tax Remittance Issues

An employer has a legal obligation to forward to the government all income taxes that it has withheld from employee pay, as well as social security and Medicare taxes. In this section, we review when tax deposits should be remitted to the government and the penalties associated with not making timely remittances.

There are two deposit schedules, known as the *monthly deposit schedule* and the *semiweekly deposit schedule*, which state when to deposit payroll taxes. The deposit schedule to be used is based on the total taxes (i.e., federal income taxes withheld, social security taxes, and Medicare taxes) reported in the Form 941 in a four-quarter lookback period. The lookback period begins on July 1 and ends on June 30. The decision tree for selecting a deposit period is:

- If $50,000 or less of taxes was reported during the lookback period, use the monthly deposit schedule.
- If $50,000 or more of taxes was reported during the lookback period, use the semiweekly deposit schedule.

If a business qualifies to use the monthly deposit schedule, deposit employment taxes on payments made during a month by the 15$^{th}$ day of the following month. If an employer qualifies to use the semiweekly deposit schedule, remit payroll taxes using the information in the following exhibit.

**Semi-Weekly Deposit Schedule**

| Payment Date | Corresponding Deposit Date |
|---|---|
| Wednesday, Thursday, or Friday | Following Wednesday |
| Saturday, Sunday, Monday, Tuesday | Following Friday |

Note that the semiweekly deposit method does not mean that an employer is required to make two tax deposits per week – it is simply the name of the method. Thus, if a company has one payroll every other week, it would remit taxes only every other week.

The differentiating factor between the monthly and semiweekly deposit schedules is that an employer must remit taxes much more quickly under the semiweekly method. The monthly method uses a simpler and more delayed tax deposit schedule, which is ideal for smaller businesses.

An employer can be penalized if it makes a tax deposit too late, or in an amount that is less than the required amount. The penalties are noted in the following exhibit.

**Payroll Penalties**

| Penalty Amount | Description |
|---|---|
| 2% | Deposits are made 1 to 5 days late. |
| 5% | Deposits are made 6 to 15 days late. |
| 10% | Deposits are made more than 15 days late. Also applicable for amounts paid within 10 days of the first IRS notice date regarding a tax due. |
| 10% | Deposits are paid directly to the IRS or paid with the employer's tax return. |
| 15% | Amounts still unpaid more than 10 days after the date of the first IRS notice date regarding a tax due, or the date of receipt of a demand for immediate payment. |

In addition to the penalties just noted, the IRS also charges interest on the unpaid tax balance from the date when it was due for remittance to the government. The IRS formulates the interest rate as follows:

- *Underpayment*. The interest rate is the federal short-term rate plus three percentage points.
- *Underpayment by large corporate filers*. The interest rate is the federal short-term rate plus five percentage points.

---

**EXAMPLE**

Spud Potato Farms does not remit payroll taxes of $10,000 for September (due October 15) until November 20. Thus, the deposit is made 35 days late. Spud has not received a tax due notice from the IRS. The IRS assesses the following failure to pay penalty against Spud:

| | | |
|---|---|---|
| Failure to pay tax ($10,000 × 10%) | = | $1,000.00 |
| Interest on taxes due ($10,000 × 5% × 35/365) | = | 47.95 |
| Total penalty | = | $1,047.95 |

The official IRS interest rate during the penalty period was 5%.

---

If an employer does not deposit the federal income, social security, and Medicare taxes that it owes to the United States Treasury, the government can apply the *trust fund recovery penalty*. This penalty is the full amount of the tax owed. It can apply to individuals if the government cannot collect the applicable taxes from the business. The trust fund recovery penalty is an enormous issue, since employees can be held personally liable for unpaid taxes owed by the business.

The IRS can impose the trust fund recovery penalty on anyone to whom both of the following circumstances apply:

- The person is responsible for collecting, accounting for, and paying the taxes. The IRS defines this person as an officer or employee of a business, an accountant, or a volunteer director or trustee. It can also include anyone who signs checks for the business, or who has the authority to cause the spending of business funds.
- The person acted willfully (i.e., voluntarily, consciously, and intentionally) in not paying the taxes. Such a person knows the required actions are not taking place, and either intentionally disregarded the law or was indifferent to its requirements.

The IRS can take collection action against a person's personal assets under this penalty, including such actions as a federal tax lien or the seizure of assets.

---

**EXAMPLE**

Mr. Arlan Spud is running short of cash to run his business, Spud Potato Farms, of which he is the president, and uses unremitted payroll taxes to pay his other creditors. This action falls within the IRS definition of acting willfully to not deposit taxes, and leaves Mr. Spud personally liable for the trust fund recovery penalty.

---

We present the issue of payroll tax remittances mostly to inform the manager of the extent of the associated penalties, as well as the possibility that this liability could become a personal liability. Thus, it is essential to plan for upcoming tax remittances to ensure that they are paid promptly, in accordance with the designated deposit schedule.

## Definition of an Employee

A common human resources issue that every manager must deal with at some point is whether someone working for the company is an employee or a contractor. If a person is defined as an employee, the company must deduct social security and Medicare taxes from that person's pay, as well as withhold income taxes. If the company does not do so, it is liable for the payment of these items to the government. Further, the company is responsible for the full employer share of all social security and Medicare taxes. Conversely, a company is not liable for any of these withholdings, taxes, or remittances if someone is designated as a contractor.

Clearly, a manager needs to understand the definitions of an employee and a contractor. There are several ways to define an employee, as noted in the following bullet points:

- *Common-law employee.* Under common-law rules, someone is an employee if the company has the right to control what will be done and how it will be done, even if the individual has a considerable degree of freedom of action. A person who meets these criteria is considered an employee, irrespective of all other considerations.
- *Statutory employee.* A worker is considered an employee if he or she falls into one of the following categories:
    - A driver who delivers food, beverages (other than milk), laundry, or dry cleaning for someone else. This person may be on a commission form of compensation.
    - A full-time life insurance salesperson who sells primarily on behalf of one company.
    - Someone who works at home under guidelines issued by the entity for which the work is done, with materials furnished by and returned to that entity.
    - A traveling salesperson who works full-time for one entity to obtain orders from customers. These orders must be for items for either resale or use as supplies in the customer's business. The customers must either be contractors, retailers, wholesalers, or operators of hotels, restaurants, or any other businesses dealing with food or lodgings.

  In addition, the service contract must state or imply that substantially all of the services are to be performed personally by the worker, the worker does not have a substantial investment in the assets used to perform the service, and the service is performed on a continuing basis for the same payer.

The definition of a statutory employee is of particular significance, because a company only deducts payroll taxes from the wages of statutory employees; it does not withhold federal income taxes from their wages.

To determine whether a person can be classified as an independent contractor, review the entire working relationship between the company and the person, and arrive at a decision based on the complete body of evidence. There are three categories of facts to consider, which are:

- *Behavioral control.* A person is an employee if the business has the right to direct and control how the person does the task for which he was hired. The amount of control is based on the level of instruction regarding such issues as when and where to work, what equipment to use, which employees to use, where to buy supplies, what sequence of tasks to follow, and so forth. Behavioral control can include training by the company to perform services in a particular way.
- *Financial control.* Facts indicative of financial control by the company are the extent to which a worker is reimbursed for business expenses, the amount of investment by the worker in the business, the extent to which the worker sells his services to other parties, whether the amount paid to the person is based on time worked rather than for a work product, and whether the worker can participate in a profit or loss.
- *Type of relationship.* A person is more likely to be considered an independent contractor if there is a written contract describing the relationship of the parties, the business does not provide benefits to the person, the relationship is not permanent, and the services performed are not a key aspect of the regular business of the company.

---

**EXAMPLE**

Mr. David Stringer is a securities attorney who specializes in the issuance of bonds. He has been paid on an hourly basis for the last ten years by his sole client, Heavy Lift Corporation (HLC), and is reimbursed by HLC for expenses incurred. The CFO of HLC does not attempt to control the work habits of Mr. Stringer. There is no contract between the two parties; instead, Mr. Stringer simply issues an invoice to HLC at the end of each month, and the company pays it. HLC does not pay any benefits to Mr. Stringer. HLC is not in the business of selling bonds – it only does so periodically in order to raise capital.

The cumulative evidence in this situation is in favor of Mr. Stringer being an independent contractor. HLC does not exercise behavioral control, though there is some evidence of financial control that would be reduced if Mr. Stringer had any additional clients. The type of relationship is more firmly in favor of independent contractor status, since HLC does not pay benefits and Mr. Stringer's area of specialization is outside of the regular business of the company.

**EXAMPLE**

Myron Sotherby hires Ames Whitmore to supervise the construction of his new garage. Mr. Sotherby pays suppliers directly, carries workers' compensation coverage for Mr. Whitmore, supervises the work on a daily basis, and pays Mr. Whitmore on an hourly basis, irrespective of the status of the project. Mr. Whitmore cannot work on other projects until the garage has been completed. Mr. Whitmore is an employee of Mr. Sotherby.

**EXAMPLE**

Waylon Price has signed a contract with Milford Sound to provide concrete pouring services for several of Milford's public stadium projects. Under the terms of the contract, Mr. Price's firm will be paid a flat fee once specific tasks have been completed, and is liable for any subsequent issues with the concrete through a one-year warranty period. Mr. Price carries workers' compensation insurance for his business, and he employs several people. Mr. Price is an independent contractor.

**EXAMPLE**

Hubble Corporation lays off Red Miller, and then agrees to pay him a flat fee to design trajectory tracking software for one of Hubble's telescopes. Hubble does not provide Mr. Miller with any specific work instructions, and only sets a target date for delivery of the software. He is not required to attend any meetings of the programming department. He has signed an agreement with Hubble, which specifically states that he is an independent contractor, and will receive no benefits from the company. Mr. Miller is an independent contractor.

**EXAMPLE**

Vern Tucker is a paint specialist who works in the auto repair shop of a large auto sales company. He works a 40-hour week and is paid 40% of the amount billed to each customer. The auto sales company provides all of his equipment and paint supplies, and also monitors the time he takes in comparison to the estimates given to customers. Mr. Tucker is an employee.

**EXAMPLE**

Gene Brooks is a taxi cab driver. He pays Ultimate Cab Company $150 per day to rent a cab from it, which includes a sophisticated on-line dispatching service. Ultimate Cab also advertises its vehicles to the general public. Mr. Brooks pays for the ongoing servicing of the cab, as well as fuel. He keeps all fares that he receives from customers. Mr. Brooks is an independent contractor.

---

## Accrued Bonuses

An expense that can have a significant impact on the financial results of a business is the reported amount of accrued bonuses. A bonus expense is accrued in advance in expectation of employees earning a bonus, usually at the end of the year. Given the financial impact of bonus accruals, managers should be aware of the related accounting rules.

A bonus expense should be accrued whenever there is an expectation that the financial or operational performance of a company at least equals the performance levels required in any active bonus plans.

The decision to accrue a bonus calls for considerable judgment, for the entire period of performance may encompass many future months, during which time a person may *not* continue to achieve his bonus plan objectives, in which case any prior bonus accrual should be reversed. Here are some alternative ways to treat a bonus accrual during the earlier stages of a bonus period:

- Accrue no expense at all until there is a reasonable probability that the bonus will be achieved.
- Accrue a smaller expense early in a performance period to reflect the higher risk of performance failure, and accrue a larger expense later if the probability of success improves.

Do *not* accrue a significant bonus expense in a situation where the probability that the bonus will be awarded is low; such an accrual is essentially earnings management, since it creates a false expense that is later reversed when the performance period is complete.

## The Common Paymaster Rule

When a parent company owns a number of subsidiary entities, there is a possibility that employees will transfer between the various subsidiaries during a calendar year. If so, and payroll is computed at each individual subsidiary, and the transferring employees are paid more than the social security wage cap, too much of the social security tax will be deducted from their pay, and the company as a whole will match all of that extra deduction. This is a problem for the employee, who is having too much tax deducted, and for the company, which is incurring an excessive payroll expense. Though an employee can recover the excess amount deducted, the employer cannot do so. Given the potential for this extra expenditure, managers of company subsidiaries should be aware of the issue, and how it can be avoided.

---

**EXAMPLE**

Milford Sound, the audio equipment company, has two subsidiaries, Puget Sound and Long Island Sound. Mr. Arnold Saxon works for the Puget Sound subsidiary from January 1 to June 30 of 2019 as the division manager, and is paid compensation of $100,000 during that time. He then transfers to the Long Island Sound subsidiary and works there from July 1 to December 31 of 2019, earning another $100,000. The payroll department of the Puget Sound subsidiary deducts $6,200 from his pay, and the payroll department of the Long Island Sound subsidiary does the same. Since the 2019 social security wage cap is $132,900, the maximum amount that should have been deducted from his pay is $8,240, rather than the $12,400 that was actually deducted. Mr. Saxon can apply for a return of the excess $4,160 deducted from his pay, but Milford Sound cannot recover the matching amount of $4,160 that it also paid.

---

If a business experiences this problem and is organized as a corporation, it can take advantage of the common paymaster rule to eliminate the excess amount of taxes paid. Under this rule, the parent company calculates payroll taxes for any employees being paid by more than one subsidiary as though they are being paid by a single entity for the entire calendar year. To do so, the parent company designates one entity within its group of controlled businesses to pay the employees. This designated entity is called the *common paymaster.*

The common paymaster is responsible not only for paying designated employees, but also for maintaining the payroll records for them. It is allowable for the common paymaster to pay an employee with a single paycheck, despite that person working for multiple entities, or it may pay them with separate checks that are drawn on the bank accounts or the entities for which an employee works. The common paymaster's administrative duties also include remitting payroll taxes to the government.

**Tip:** The only risk involved in using the common paymaster rule is that all subsidiaries using a common paymaster are jointly and severally liable for their shares of payroll taxes to be remitted. Thus, if one subsidiary were to fall behind on its payroll tax remittances to the government, the government could force a different subsidiary to pay the overdue amount.

In order to qualify for the common paymaster rule, a business must meet *all* of the following conditions:

- The parties paying employees must be related, where:
  - One company owns at least half the stock of the other related companies; or
  - At least 30% of the employees of one company must be concurrently employed by the other company; or
  - At least half of the officers of one company must be officers of the other company.

- If a company is a non-stock corporation, at least half of the board of directors of one company must serve on the board of directors of the other company.
- All payments made to employees must be made through a single legal entity. This means that an employee cannot be individually paid by more than one payroll department within the same company.

## Unemployment Insurance Issues

Each state has its own unemployment insurance program, which evaluates unemployment claims and administers the payment of benefits to individuals. Each of the states has its own rules regarding unemployment eligibility, the amounts to be paid out, and the duration of these benefits. Depending on the rules, the amount of unemployment insurance that a company must pay can vary markedly from state to state. In this section, we identify the specific unemployment rates charged by each state and the resulting impact on company profitability. Any manager tasked with rolling out new company locations should be aware of this issue, since it can materially impact company profits.

State governments impose a state-level unemployment tax on employers that can be quite high. A state typically assigns a relatively high default tax rate to a new business, and then subsequently adjusts that rate based on the history of unemployment claims made by employees of the business (known as the *experience rating*). If a business rarely lays off its staff, it will eventually be assigned a lower tax rate, with the reverse being true for a business with an uneven employment record. The amount of wages subject to taxation and the range of applicable tax rates are noted by state in the following table.

**Summary of State Unemployment Taxes as of December 2018**[1]

| State | Wages Subject to Tax | Minimum Tax Rate | Maximum Tax Rate | New Employer Rate |
|---|---|---|---|---|
| Alabama | $8,000 | 0.65% | 6.80% | 2.70% |
| Alaska | 39,800 | 1.00% | 5.40% | 1.73% |
| Arizona | 7,000 | 0.04% | 10.59% | 2.00% |
| Arkansas | 12,000 | 0.40% | 14.30% | 3.20% |
| California | 7,000 | 1.50% | 6.20% | 3.40% |
| Colorado | 12,500 | 0.77% | 10.10% | 2.11% |
| Connecticut | 15,000 | 1.90% | 6.80% | 3.90% |
| Delaware | 18,500 | 0.30% | 8.20% | 1.70% |
| District of Columbia | 9,000 | 1.60% | 7.00% | 2.70% |
| Florida | 7,000 | 0.10% | 5.40% | 2.70% |
| Georgia | 9,500 | 0.04% | 8.10% | 2.70% |
| Hawaii | 44,000 | 0.00% | 5.60% | 2.40% |

[1] Source: ADP Fast Wage and Tax Facts

| State | Wages Subject to Tax | Minimum Tax Rate | Maximum Tax Rate | New Employer Rate |
|---|---|---|---|---|
| Idaho | 37,800 | 0.40% | 5.40% | 1.40% |
| Illinois | 12,960 | 0.55% | 7.35% | 3.45% |
| Indiana | 9,500 | 0.50% | 7.40% | * |
| Iowa | 29,300 | 0.00% | 8.00% | 1.00% |
| Kansas | 14,000 | 0.20% | 7.60% | 2.70% |
| Kentucky | 10,200 | 0.60% | 9.75% | 2.70% |
| Louisiana | 7,700 | 0.10% | 6.20% | * |
| Maine | 12,000 | 0.55% | 5.46% | 1.83% |
| Maryland | 8,500 | 0.30% | 7.50% | 2.60% |
| Massachusetts | 15,000 | 0.73% | 11.13% | * |
| Michigan | 9,000 | 0.06% | 10.30% | 2.70% |
| Minnesota | 32,000 | 0.10% | 9.00% | 1.44% |
| Mississippi | 14,000 | 0.20% | 5.60% | 1.20% |
| Missouri | 13,000 | 0.00% | 9.00% | 2.70% |
| Montana | 31,400 | 0.13% | 6.30% | * |
| Nebraska | 9,000 | 0.00% | 5.40% | 1.25% |
| Nevada | 29,500 | 0.30% | 5.40% | 3.00% |
| New Hampshire | 14,000 | 0.10% | 7.50% | 1.70% |
| New Jersey | 33,500 | 0.50% | 5.80% | 2.80% |
| New Mexico | 24,300 | 0.33% | 5.40% | 1.00% |
| New York | 10,900 | 1.30% | 9.10% | 4.00% |
| North Carolina | 23,100 | 0.06% | 5.76% | 1.00% |
| North Dakota | 35,100 | 0.49% | 11.43% | 2.34% |
| Ohio | 9,000 | 0.30% | 8.80% | 2.70% |
| Oklahoma | 17,700 | 0.10% | 5.50% | 1.50% |
| Oregon | 38,400 | 1.20% | 5.40% | 2.60% |
| Pennsylvania | 9,750 | 2.64% | 11.26% | 3.68% |
| Puerto Rico | 7,000 | 2.20% | 5.40% | 3.20% |
| Rhode Island | 22,400 | 0.99% | 9.59% | 1.83% |
| South Carolina | 14,000 | 0.06% | 5.46% | 1.23% |
| South Dakota | 15,000 | 0.00% | 9.50% | 1.20% |
| Tennessee | 8,000 | 0.01% | 10.00% | 2.70% |
| Texas | 9,000 | 0.59% | 8.21% | 2.70% |
| Utah | 33,100 | 0.20% | 7.20% | * |
| Vermont | 17,300 | 1.10% | 7.70% | 1.00% |
| Virginia | 8,000 | 0.13% | 6.23% | 2.53% |
| Virgin Islands | 23,500 | 1.50% | 6.00% | 2.00% |
| Washington | 45,000 | 0.13% | 7.73% | * |
| West Virginia | 12,000 | 1.50% | 8.50% | 2.70% |
| Wisconsin | 14,000 | 0.00% | 12.00% | * |
| Wyoming | 25,400 | 0.34% | 8.84% | * |

* Industry average or a variable rate

The difference in wage base can have a dramatic effect on the amount of state unemployment tax that a business pays, as noted in the following example:

---

**EXAMPLE**

Albatross Flight Systems is considering moving its 100 employees to a facility in another state. The average annual pay of its employees is $55,000 and no one earns less than $30,000. The best sites selected by the CEO of Albatross are Nevada and Colorado. Assuming that Albatross is assigned a new employer rate when it moves, the calculation of the annual amount of state unemployment taxes that it would pay is:

| State | Expense Calculation | | Total Expense |
|---|---|---|---|
| Colorado | 100 staff × $12,500 wage base × 2.11% rate | = | $26,375 |
| Nevada | 100 staff × $29,500 wage base × 3.00% rate | = | $88,500 |

Thus, the lower state unemployment tax for Colorado could pay for an additional staff person, when compared to the rate for Nevada.

---

**Tip:** If management is contemplating expanding into a new state, and the cost of state unemployment taxes is a significant factor in the decision, peruse the preceding summary table of state unemployment taxes to see which ones have a combination of the lowest amount of wages subject to tax and the lowest new employer rate.

## The Employee Cost Object

A cost object is an item for which a cost is compiled. One of the most commonly-reviewed cost objects is the employee, since there are a large number of costs associated with employees, and because compensation can be the largest expense that a business incurs. A complete analysis of the employee cost object should include all of the expenses noted in the following exhibit.

**Costs to Assign to an Employee**

| +/- | Assignable Cost | Commentary |
|---|---|---|
| + | Base compensation | Base compensation is always included in the cost of an employee |
| + | Historical overtime | If a person has a history of incurring overtime, include the average amount of this overtime, plus applicable payroll taxes |
| + | Bonuses | Only include the amount of bonuses that are likely to be earned, plus applicable payroll taxes |
| - | Increased compensation elsewhere | If an employee is to be let go, consider the cost of increased overtime for those employees remaining, as well as the payroll taxes associated with that overtime |
| + | Payroll taxes | This includes the social security, Medicare, and federal unemployment taxes paid by the employer |
| + | Benefits | This is the net cost of benefits paid by the company, after employee payroll deductions are subtracted |
| + | Travel and entertainment | This includes the historical average cost of travel and entertainment incurred by the employee |

Several costs should not always be included in an employee cost analysis, since they would still remain if an employee were to be let go. Consider retaining the following costs if an analysis is compiled for the purpose of calculating cost savings from an employee termination:

- *Cell phones*. If a cell phone is considered common property that is simply passed along to a different person when one individual leaves the company, its cost should not be assigned to a specific individual.
- *Commissions*. In many cases, a customer will be assigned to a different salesperson if the original salesperson is let go, so the company continues to incur a commission. However, if each sale is unique and there is no transfer of customers to a replacement salesperson, the cost of commissions could be assigned to an employee.
- *Depreciation*. The depreciation on computer equipment and furniture used by an employee will remain if the position is eliminated, so do not assign the cost to an employee.
- *Profit sharing*. If an employee were to be laid off, profits would simply be shared with someone else who remains on the staff.
- *Square footage allocation*. The department to which an employee is assigned may be charged for the square footage occupied by an employee. Since this cost would remain even if an employee were not on staff, it should not be considered an employee-specific cost.

A particularly large point that is frequently missed is to assign the *actual* net cost of benefits to employees, rather than the *average* net cost per employee. For example, it is entirely likely that an employee taking family medical insurance is much more expensive than one taking single coverage, since there is such a large disparity in the costs of these two variations on medical insurance.

## The True Variability of Direct Labor

A common analysis by any management team involves the variable cost of a sale. This information is needed in order to properly price a customer request for the company's best possible price. If the company bids too high, the purchase order may be given to a competitor. If the bid is too low, the company is essentially losing money on every unit sold. Consequently, the variable cost of a sale must be determined with some precision.

The variable cost of goods sold has traditionally been considered to only include three costs, which are direct materials, direct labor, and the commission (if any) resulting from a sale. There is no question that direct materials and commissions are truly variable costs, since these costs are not incurred if there is no sale. However, is that the case for direct labor? People employed within the direct labor job classification are typically paid a daily wage even in the absence of any work; otherwise, a company would be at risk of losing valuable skilled staff who can find steadier employment elsewhere. That being the case, the cost of direct labor does not really vary in proportion to sales. Instead, direct labor can more appropriately be considered either a cost associated with the period, or a component of factory overhead.

The one situation in which direct labor *is* a variable cost is when employees are paid under the piece-rate system. Under this approach, employees are paid based on the number of units produced. If the number produced varies, so too does their pay. Based on the characteristics of this type of compensation, it can be considered a variable cost.

## Compensation Cost Reduction

Depending on the type of business, the cost of compensation may be the largest cost incurred. Compensation can be a particularly pernicious cost, because it tends to increase every year through inflationary increases, even in the absence of improvements in employee productivity to offset the costs. In this section, we look at a number of techniques for mitigating the cost of compensation. These techniques are divided into the areas of employee hiring, temporary cost reductions designed for financial downturns, and more permanent solutions. Every manager needs to be aware of these techniques, to keep compensation costs under control.

**Proactive Hiring Solutions**

Some compensation costs can be avoided by being extremely prudent about hiring decisions. The initial compensation level at which someone is hired is extremely important, for it sets the base case upon which future pay raises will be founded. There are also options available for completely avoiding or delaying the hiring of employees. Consider the following techniques:

- *Temporary workers for overflow work.* When activity levels are increasing within a business, do not automatically hire new full-time employees to assist with the work load. If this is done, the current activity level may not be sufficient to keep the new staff busy. Instead, bring in temporary staff to handle the incremental work load. If the activity level drops, remove the temporary workers with a call to the temp agency that supplied them. If activity levels prove to be more permanent, it is time to replace the temporary workers with permanent positions.
- *Temporary workers for evaluation.* New hires are typically based on several interviews, a background check, and phone calls to a few references. While useful, these activities do not give a sufficiently clear impression of the work habits and knowledge base of a prospective employee. An alternative that will provide this information is hiring people on a temporary basis, and then hiring them into a full-time position after a probationary period. This approach gives the existing staff a much more detailed view of an applicant, and so tends to result in hires that are less likely to result in an early termination. The trouble is that people applying for the more senior positions are not likely to agree to a temporary work arrangement; consequently, it is more commonly used for hiring into lower-level positions.
- *Subcontract work.* If there are tasks to be done that are not central to the mission of the business, is it possible to subcontract the work to another company? Doing so means that the business is only paying for work that needs to be done, and that the contract work can be shifted elsewhere to a different provider if the work product does not meet the company's standards. This approach is particularly effective when an entire department of non-core activities is subcontracted, since the larger amount of work gives the company enough leverage to impose higher levels of performance and reasonable contract prices.
- *Delay start dates.* If new recruits have been offered positions with the company, consider asking them to start several months later. This approach can be made less unpalatable by issuing signing bonuses that the recruits can use to cover some portion of their expenses until the delayed start date arrives.
- *Require lengthy hiring review.* When a new hire does not work out, it can take months or even years for management to overcome the usual reluctance to fire someone, resulting in a long-term waste of cash while the person is still being employed. One way to avoid this is to require multiple interviews by a number of the staff, psychological testing, and an extensive background

check before anyone is hired. The intent is to spend a moderate amount of time and money up front in order to detect flaws in recruits, thereby saving much more cash later on related to lost productivity and termination costs.

The main thrust of these points is to only hire on a full-time basis when absolutely necessary, and to be extremely careful when hiring into those positions that absolutely must be filled.

## Temporary Cost Reductions

When a company has encountered financial problems, the most common solution is for the president to enact some form of temporary compensation cost reduction, which is only intended to be in effect for the duration of the crisis. The intent of these measures is to retain as many employees as possible, on the theory that the knowledge base of the pool of employees is too valuable to lose. If this approach is taken, consider using a mix of the following tactics:

- *Stop hiring*. For the duration of the crisis, simply stop all hiring. Instead, as some employees leave the company, allocate their work among the remaining staff. This is not the best solution, for a significant imbalance may develop between the amount of work to be done and the number of available employees, resulting in large amounts of overtime and employee stress.
- *Cut bonuses*. If there is no obligation to pay bonuses, issue a notice that bonuses will not be paid. This should not be a problem for those employees whose base pay is adequate, but could be an issue if bonuses comprise a large part of their annual compensation. An alternative is to defer bonuses, so that they are paid on a later date. In the latter case, do not announce a specific date by which bonuses will be paid, so the company has the leeway to continue to defer the payments.
- *Cut management compensation*. When there is financial hardship, the management team should always set an example by taking the largest compensation cuts in the company. Doing so focuses the attention of managers on correcting the business, and also makes it easier for other employees to accept any pay cuts that may be assigned to them. Reductions in management compensation should certainly involve large portions (or all) of their bonuses, as well as notable reductions in their base pay.
- *Cut pay in general*. It may be necessary to institute a pay cut throughout the company. If so, avoid promising to pay back employees for lost wages when the good times return, since doing so merely imposes a large burden on the company at a later date. Instead, make it clear that the pay cut will continue in effect, and will be reviewed at regular intervals to see if an improvement in the company's fortunes will allow it to reinstitute the original pay levels at some later date.
- *Freeze pay*. It may be possible to simply freeze the pay of employees for the duration of the crisis. Doing so does not severely impact employees, since their current compensation is untouched. By simply stopping all increases

for a period of time, the business has avoided the impact of inflationary increases until such time as pay raises are started again.

- *Reduce the amount of planned pay increases*. If the financial decline is a modest one, it may be sufficient to merely reduce the rate of planned pay increases. The resulting cost savings will initially appear to be relatively minor, but also have a beneficial long-term effect, since future pay increases will be based on the somewhat lower compensation of employees.
- *Shift to part time*. The work situation of some employees may allow them to accept part-time status for a certain period of time, perhaps due to a family situation, such as supporting elderly parents. The amount of benefits paid to them can be negotiated. This approach should be treated as a call for volunteers, rather than a mandatory cut-back to part-time status.
- *Cut working hours*. If the overall amount of work to be completed declines, consider reducing the work hours for the entire company, such as switching from an eight-hour day to a seven-hour day. This approach means that management wants to retain all employees for a certain period of time, after which it expects to be able to ramp up activity to the normal work period again. This technique may not work well when the work force is mostly comprised of low-wage employees who cannot afford even a small reduction in their pay.
- *Use vacation time*. The company can strongly recommend to employees that this would be a good time to use their accrued vacation time. Doing so does not reduce the amount of cash being paid as compensation to employees, but it does reduce the company's obligation to pay employees for unused vacation time if they were to be laid off at a later date. Thus, this is good advance preparation for reduced cash payouts if a downsizing is considered possible.
- *Offer voluntary unpaid days off*. If there is clearly too much work capacity available within a business, it may be possible to simply offer unpaid days off to all employees, and see who takes the offer. There may be employees who want to take occasional days off to supplement their vacations, and whose financial circumstances make an unpaid absence an agreeable alternative. However, be aware that this may result in a dearth of employees in the workplace in the periods adjacent to major holidays and weekends.
- *Lay off employees*. If no other alternatives appear to yield sufficient cost savings, it may be necessary to lay off employees. Before doing so, consider the full cost of a termination, which includes residual benefit payments, termination pay, increased unemployment insurance, and so forth.
- *Offer a hire-back bonus*. If there is an expectation that business will eventually pick back up, and if the people to be laid off have significant skills, it may make sense to offer them a bonus if they are hired back. This means that the company incurs no immediate cost, but will pay a bonus if it hires back an employee. The advantage of doing so is that employees may be more willing to subsist on temporary work until they are hired back.

While these methods are useful for retaining staff during difficult economic times, employees cannot subsist on reduced compensation forever. Consequently, expect the effectiveness of these measures to gradually decline over time, as increasing numbers of employees abandon the company to find work elsewhere.

**Permanent Cost Reductions**

The most valuable compensation cost reductions are those that represent permanent cuts that will not be given back to employees. Here are several alternatives:

- *Pay more commissions*. Moving a larger proportion of employee pay to a commission basis means that the company is only obligated to pay if a sale is made. Though useful, there are still several problems to consider. First, not many employees generate revenue, so a commission plan will not apply to most of the staff. Also, commission payments must be made as stated in the commission agreement, which may call for cash payments when the company has no cash.
- *Pay more bonuses*. If employees are accustomed to a large proportion of their pay being in wages and salaries, there is an assumption that this form of pay will at least receive a boost to compensate for inflation, so there is an ongoing spiral of increasing compensation costs. To avoid some of the inflationary impact, shift a large part of compensation into bonuses, which are only paid when the company's results are sufficiently good to generate the cash for the bonuses. Also, bonuses are not necessarily subject to inflationary increases.
- *Restrict bonus eligibility*. An alternative to the last point is to restrict the number of people who are eligible to receive bonuses. Ideally, only those people who have a direct impact on the performance of the company should be eligible for a bonus. If other positions have gradually crept into the bonus pool, even though these employees are essentially being paid extra in exchange for no performance, weed them out of the bonus pool.
- *Pay more stock options*. When a company is publicly held, a viable alternative to the basic compensation package is to pay lower wages in exchange for stock options. This approach works best in a startup company, where there is a reasonable prospect that the options will gain appreciably in value, resulting in major gains for the recipients. An added benefit is that the company not only has no cash payout obligation, but is *paid* cash when employees convert their shares to options. They pay the company the exercise price at which a stock option allows them to buy shares from the company, and then sell the shares to investors on the open market.
- *Stop paying overtime*. Any overtime payment requires a substantial boost over the normal pay rate, so it is tempting for employees to delay their work somewhat in order to stay later and qualify for overtime pay. To prevent this behavior, mandate senior management approval for any overtime hours worked.

- *Tighten merit pay criteria*. The top-performing employees should certainly be paid in accordance with their abilities. However, outsized pay increases should be confined to the most deserving group. All too frequently, merit pay criteria are reduced to the point where far too many employees are receiving merit pay increases. This is an especially pernicious problem, since the merit increases enhance their base pay, so that their compensation over time becomes much too high.
- *Put hard cap on pay ranges*. If employees are classified as having certain types of jobs, put a hard cap on the maximum wage or salary that can be paid. Thus, an engineer grade three might be allowed a maximum salary of $90,000. Any pay above the hard cap is prohibited, though bonuses may be allowed. The concept is intended to avoid stratospherically high compensation levels for those employees who have been in the same job classification for a long time, and who have been receiving routine pay increases that no longer equate to their underlying skill sets.
- *Install a two-tier wage structure*. If some of the work force is protected from a wage reduction, it may still be possible to set up a two-tiered structure where new hires are paid substantially less than the workers who were hired at an earlier date.
- *Match pay to target turnover levels*. If turnover levels are inordinately low, it may mean that the company's compensation levels are so high that employees would be foolish to leave the company. This is not necessarily a cost-effective solution to employee turnover. Instead, derive an acceptable target turnover level, and gradually allow compensation levels to drift down to the point where that employee turnover level is achieved. This analysis may also find that excessively high turnover in some key areas may warrant an increase in compensation levels.
- *Outsource work*. It may be substantially less expensive to shift some work to a low-wage location, where an outsourcing firm handles local hiring and management on behalf of the company. An alternative is for the company to open its own facility in a low-wage location, so that it can impose its own human resources practices on the local staff.
- *Pay hiring bonuses*. If a quality candidate for a position is pushing for an initial pay level that is too high, the result will be a base rate of pay on which merit and inflationary increases will subsequently be based, so that the company bears the burden of the increased cost for years to come. To avoid this issue, offer a standard rate of pay, plus a hiring bonus. Doing so drives down the recruit's initial base pay, which reduces compensation levels in future years.

There is no single tactic that is likely to trigger a decline in compensation costs. Instead, a broad range of concepts may have to be followed, and even then the impact may be only a reduced rate of increase in compensation costs. To achieve any favorable results, the management team must consistently follow selected compensation control tactics for a long time, with few exceptions.

## Summary

Realistically, the most common human resources issue that a manager will deal with is maintaining a prudent level of compensation expenditures, which is why this chapter contains so many cost control suggestions. In addition, we have presented several other topics that are more subtle background issues that managers tend to be less aware of, but which can have a significant long-term impact on the efficiency and cost structure of a business. Paying attention to the reduction of employee time tracking and the duration of the payroll cycle can yield an especially high return.

# Chapter 9
# Investment Decisions

## Introduction

One of the most critical manager decisions is whether to invest funds. The wrong choice can result in a notable drain of company resources, while the right choice can yield a higher level of profitability, improved capacity, and/or the ability to compete in new areas. There are a number of tools available for examining prospective investments. In this chapter, we pay particular attention to several types of discounted cash flow analysis, as well as alternative tools that can be used in niche areas, such as for large investments, research and development situations, and highly complex environments. In conclusion, we note the unusually conservative accounting rules relating to investment decisions.

**Related Podcast Episodes:** Episode 147 of the Accounting Best Practices Podcast discusses net present value analysis, while Episode 145 addresses capital budgeting with minimal cash, and Episode 214 covers discounted cash flows. They are available at: **accountingtools.com/podcasts** or **iTunes**

## The Investment Decision

A manager can invest funds in three main types of investments, which are as follows:

- *Fixed assets*. This includes the replacement of worn-out equipment, the expansion of production capacity, or assets mandated by regulatory requirements. Generally, this is the main focus of investment decisions, and so is the primary focus of this chapter. Fixed asset investments are also known as *capital budgeting*.
- *Securities*. This is the investment of excess funds in securities, usually with the intent of earning a modest return on low-risk investments that are highly liquid.
- *Other business entities*. This involves the outright or partial acquisition of an ownership interest in another entity, and is addressed in detail in the Acquisition Decisions chapter.

Ultimately, the investment decision is based on overall corporate strategy, rather than any accounting rules or analysis techniques. For example, if management wants to outsource the entire production area, there will be no need to conduct an analysis of cash flows for production equipment. However, once a strategic decision has been made, the manager must adopt a method for determining how to invest funds in specific assets. In this chapter, we focus attention on the profits or cash flows from a prospective investment as being the primary determinants of an investment decision. The examination of these profits or cash flows can be made in a number of ways. Generally, calculation methods fall into these categories:

- *Abbreviated.* There are several "back of the envelope" methods, including payback analysis and the accounting rate of return, that can be calculated in a few moments, and which can provide a general level of information about risk and return. They are not recommended as the only type of analysis to be used.
- *Discounted cash flows.* This approach requires one to assemble all inbound and outbound cash flows related to a prospective investment, and determine the net change in cash flows, adjusted for the time value of money. The bulk of this chapter is devoted to discounted cash flows, with topics covering the time value of money, present and future value tables, net present value, the internal rate of return, the incremental internal rate of return, and terminal value.
- *Real options.* This approach is the most sophisticated one, involving a review of many different scenarios that could alter the outcome of a decision. Discounted cash flows are likely to be included in this analysis. Given the amount of time involved in real options analysis, this approach is typically reserved for larger investments.

In the following sections, we cover a number of investment analysis techniques in detail.

## Payback Analysis

The simplest and least accurate capital expenditure evaluation technique is the payback method. This approach is still heavily used, because it provides a very fast "back of the envelope" calculation of how soon a company will earn back its investment. This means that it provides a rough measure of how long a company will have its investment at risk before earning back the original amount expended. Thus, it is a rough measure of risk. There are two ways to calculate the payback period, which are:

1. *Simplified.* Divide the total amount of an investment by the average resulting cash flow. This approach can yield an incorrect assessment, because a proposal with cash flows skewed far into the future can yield a payback period that differs substantially from when actual payback occurs.
2. *Manual calculation.* Manually deduct the forecasted positive cash flows from the initial investment amount from Year 1 forward, until the investment is paid back. This method is slower, but ensures a higher degree of accuracy.

A decision rule can be added to the payback calculation, where an investment is rejected if the payback period exceeds a certain threshold amount. For example, if a business has a three-year threshold for its investments, all proposed investments having paybacks longer than three years will be rejected.

---

**EXAMPLE**

Milagro Corporation's CFO has received a proposal from a manager, asking to spend $1,500,000 on equipment that will result in cash inflows in accordance with the following table:

| Year | Cash Flow |
|---|---|
| 1 | +$150,000 |
| 2 | +150,000 |
| 3 | +200,000 |
| 4 | +600,000 |
| 5 | +900,000 |

The total cash flows over the five-year period are projected to be $2,000,000, which is an average of $400,000 per year. When divided into the $1,500,000 original investment, this results in a payback period of 3.75 years. However, the briefest perusal of the projected cash flows reveals that the flows are heavily weighted toward the far end of the time period, so the results of this calculation cannot be correct.

Instead, the CFO runs the calculation year by year, deducting the cash flows in each successive year from the remaining investment. The results of this calculation are:

| Year | Cash Flow | Net Invested Cash |
|---|---|---|
| 0 | | -$1,500,000 |
| 1 | +$150,000 | -1,350,000 |
| 2 | +150,000 | -1,200,000 |
| 3 | +200,000 | -1,000,000 |
| 4 | +600,000 | -400,000 |
| 5 | +900,000 | 0 |

The table indicates that the real payback period is located somewhere between Year 4 and Year 5. There is $400,000 of investment yet to be paid back at the end of Year 4, and there is $900,000 of cash flow projected for Year 5. The CFO assumes the same monthly amount of cash flow in Year 5, which means that he can estimate final payback as being just short of 4.5 years.

---

The payback method is not overly accurate, does not provide any estimate of how profitable a project may be, and does not take account of the time value of money. Further, it ignores all cash flows occurring after the payback period has been achieved, so that it has a bias against longer-term projects. Nonetheless, its extreme simplicity makes it a perennial favorite in many companies.

**Discounted Payback**

The accuracy of the payback method can be improved by incorporating the time value of money into the cash flows expected in each future year, which is known as discounted payback. However, doing so increases the complexity of this analysis method. To apply the time value of money to the calculation, follow these steps:

1. Create a table in which is listed the expected cash outflow related to the investment in Year 0.
2. In the following lines of the table, enter the cash inflows expected from the investment in each subsequent year.
3. Multiply the expected annual cash inflows in each year in the table by the applicable discount rate, using the same interest rate for all of the periods in the table. No discount rate is applied to the initial investment, since it occurs at once.
4. Create a column on the far right side of the table that lists the cumulative discounted cash flow for each year. The calculation in this final column is to add back the discounted cash flow in each period to the remaining negative balance from the preceding period. The balance is initially negative because it includes the cash outflow to fund the project.
5. When the cumulative discounted cash flow becomes positive, the time period that has passed up until that point represents the payback period.

---

**EXAMPLE**

We will continue with the preceding example. Milagro has a cost of capital of 7%, so the present value factor for 7% (see the Discounted Cash Flow Analysis chapter) is included in the payback table, with the following results:

| Year | Cash Flow | 7% Present Value Factor | Cash Flow Present Value | Net Invested Cash |
|---|---|---|---|---|
| 0 | | | | -$1,500,000 |
| 1 | +$150,000 | 0.9346 | +$140,190 | -1,359,810 |
| 2 | +150,000 | 0.8734 | +131,010 | -1,228,800 |
| 3 | +200,000 | 0.8163 | +163,260 | -1,065,540 |
| 4 | +600,000 | 0.7629 | +457,740 | -607,800 |
| 5 | +900,000 | 0.7130 | +641,700 | -33,900 |

The discounted payback calculation reveals that the payback period will be slightly longer than the five years of cash flows presented in the manager's original proposal.

---

The concept of discounted payback does have some value, for it indicates the point in time at which the initial investment has been recouped on a discounted basis. If a project is still expected to have a significant useful life after this point has been reached, then there is ample opportunity for additional returns to be generated. Alternatively, if the discounted payback is late in the useful life of an investment, then there is a substantial risk that no positive returns will ever be generated. From this viewpoint, a project with (for example) a discounted payback of two years with two additional years remaining in its useful life could be a better investment than a project with a discounted payback of three years with one additional year remaining thereafter in its useful life.

## Accounting Rate of Return

The accounting rate of return is used in capital budgeting to estimate whether to proceed with an investment. The calculation is the accounting profit from an investment, divided by the initial investment in the project. A project would be accepted if the measure yields a percentage that exceeds a certain hurdle rate used by the company as its minimum rate of return. The formula for the accounting rate of return is:

Average annual accounting profit ÷ Initial investment = Accounting rate of return

In this calculation, the average annual accounting profit is calculated as the profit related to the investment using all accruals and non-cash expenses (thus, it includes the costs of depreciation and amortization). If the investment involves cost reduction instead of earning a profit, the numerator is the amount of cost savings generated by the project. In essence, then, profit is calculated using the accrual basis of accounting, not the cash basis.

In the calculation, the initial investment is considered to be the initial cash investment, plus any change in working capital caused by the investment.

The result of the calculation is expressed as a percentage. Thus, if a company projects that it will earn an average annual profit of $70,000 on an initial investment of $1,000,000, the project has an accounting rate of return of 7%.

There are several serious problems with the accounting rate of return, which are:

- *Time value of money.* The measure does not factor in the time value of money. Thus, if there is currently a high market interest rate, the time value of money could completely offset any profit reported by a project – but the accounting rate of return does not incorporate this factor, so it clearly overstates the profitability of proposed investments.
- *Cash flow.* The measure includes all non-cash expenses, such as depreciation and amortization, and so does not reveal the return on actual cash flows.
- *Time-based risk.* There is no consideration of the increased risk in the variability of forecasts that arises over a long period of time.

In short, the accounting rate of return is not by any means a perfect method for evaluating an investment, and so should be used (if at all) only in concert with other evaluation tools.

## Time Value of Money

In the following sections, we will describe discounted cash flow analysis. The foundation of this analysis is the concept that cash received today is more valuable than cash received at some point in the future. The reason is that someone who agrees to receive payment at a later date foregoes the ability to invest that cash right now. The only way for someone to agree to a delayed payment is to pay them for the privilege, which is known as interest income.

For example, if a person owns \$10,000 now and invests it at an interest rate of 10%, she will have earned \$1,000 by having use of the money for one year. If she were instead to *not* have access to that cash for one year, she would lose the \$1,000 of interest income. The interest income in this example represents the time value of money.

To extend the example, what is the current payout of cash at which the person would be indifferent to receiving cash now or in one year? In essence, what is the amount that, when invested at 10%, will equal \$10,000 in one year? The general formula used to answer this question, known as the *present value of 1 due in N periods*, is:

$$\frac{1}{(1 + \text{Interest rate})^{\text{Number of years}}}$$

The calculation for the example is:

$$\frac{\$10{,}000}{(1 + 10\%)^{1 \text{ year}}}$$

$$= \$9{,}090.91$$

In essence, if the person receives \$9,090.91 now and invests it at a 10% interest rate, her cash balance will have increased to \$10,000 in one year.

The effect of the present value formula becomes more pronounced if the receipt of cash is delayed to a date even further in the future, because the period during which the recipient of the cash cannot invest the cash is prolonged.

The concept of the time value of money also works in reverse, for expenditures.. There is a monetary value associated with delaying the payment of cash, which is known as the *future amount of 1 due in N periods*. The general formula used to address this situation is:

$$\text{Amount deferred} \times (1 + \text{Interest rate})^{\text{Number of years}}$$

For example, if a person could delay the expenditure of $10,000 for one year and could invest the funds during that year at a 10% interest rate, the value of the deferred expenditure would be $11,000 in one year.

One of the common uses of the time value of money is to derive the present value of an annuity. An annuity is a series of payments that occur in the same amounts and at the same intervals over a period of time. An annuity is a common feature of an investment analysis, where a consistent stream of cash flows is expected for multiple years if a fixed asset is purchased. For example, a company is contemplating the purchase of a production line for $3,000,000, which will generate net positive cash flows of $1,000,000 per year for the next five years. This stream of incoming cash flows is an annuity. The formula used to derive the present value of an *ordinary annuity of 1 per period* is:

$$\frac{1 - \dfrac{1}{(1 + \text{Interest rate})^{\text{Number of years}}}}{\text{Interest rate}}$$

The preceding formula is for an *ordinary annuity*, which is an annuity where payments are made at the end of each period. If cash were instead received at the beginning of each period, the annuity would be called an *annuity due*, and would be formulated somewhat differently.

## Present and Future Value Tables

In the last section, we discussed the general concept of the time value of money, and how this value can be translated into the present value formula. The concept is most commonly employed in an electronic spreadsheet. For example, the present value formula in Excel is:

(1/(1+Interest rate)^Number of years

As an example, if the discount rate is 10% and you want to determine the discount for cash flows that will occur three years in the future, the Excel calculation is:

(1/(1+0.1)^3) = 0.75131

The easiest way to calculate present value is to use the preceding formula in Excel for the monetary amount and time period in question. However, what if an electronic spreadsheet is not available? The present value discount factor can also be derived from a present value table, which is commonly available in textbooks and on the Internet. The following present value table states the discount factors for the present value of 1 due in N periods for a common range of interest rates.

**Present Value Factors for 1 Due in N Periods**

| Number of Years | 6% | 7% | 8% | 9% | 10% | 11% | 12% |
|---|---|---|---|---|---|---|---|
| 1 | 0.9434 | 0.9346 | 0.9259 | 0.9174 | 0.9091 | 0.9009 | 0.8929 |
| 2 | 0.8900 | 0.8734 | 0.8573 | 0.8417 | 0.8265 | 0.8116 | 0.7972 |
| 3 | 0.8396 | 0.8163 | 0.7938 | 0.7722 | 0.7513 | 0.7312 | 0.7118 |
| 4 | 0.7921 | 0.7629 | 0.7350 | 0.7084 | 0.6830 | 0.6587 | 0.6355 |
| 5 | 0.7473 | 0.7130 | 0.6806 | 0.6499 | 0.6209 | 0.5935 | 0.5674 |
| 6 | 0.7050 | 0.6663 | 0.6302 | 0.5963 | 0.5645 | 0.5346 | 0.5066 |
| 7 | 0.6651 | 0.6228 | 0.5835 | 0.5470 | 0.5132 | 0.4817 | 0.4524 |
| 8 | 0.6274 | 0.5820 | 0.5403 | 0.5019 | 0.4665 | 0.4339 | 0.4039 |
| 9 | 0.5919 | 0.5439 | 0.5003 | 0.4604 | 0.4241 | 0.3909 | 0.3606 |
| 10 | 0.5584 | 0.5084 | 0.4632 | 0.4224 | 0.3855 | 0.3522 | 0.3220 |
| 11 | 0.5268 | 0.4751 | 0.4289 | 0.3875 | 0.3505 | 0.3173 | 0.2875 |
| 12 | 0.4970 | 0.4440 | 0.3971 | 0.3555 | 0.3186 | 0.2858 | 0.2567 |
| 13 | 0.4688 | 0.4150 | 0.3677 | 0.3262 | 0.2897 | 0.2575 | 0.2292 |
| 14 | 0.4423 | 0.3878 | 0.3405 | 0.2993 | 0.2633 | 0.2320 | 0.2046 |
| 15 | 0.4173 | 0.3625 | 0.3152 | 0.2745 | 0.2394 | 0.2090 | 0.1827 |

To use the table, move to the column representing the relevant interest rate, and move down to the "number of years" row indicating the discount rate to apply to the applicable year of cash flow. Thus, if an analysis were to indicate $100,000 of cash flow in the fourth year, and the interest rate were 10%, multiply the $100,000 by 0.6830 to arrive at a present value of $68,300 for those cash flows.

The same type of table format is available for determining the future amount of 1 due in N periods. This table is used to derive the amount that one would accept on a future date in exchange for delaying the receipt of cash. The multipliers for this calculation are noted in the following table.

**Future Value Factors for 1 Due in N Periods**

| Number of Years | 6% | 7% | 8% | 9% | 10% | 11% | 12% |
|---|---|---|---|---|---|---|---|
| 1 | 1.0600 | 1.0700 | 1.0800 | 1.0900 | 1.1000 | 1.1100 | 1.1200 |
| 2 | 1.1236 | 1.1449 | 1.1664 | 1.1881 | 1.2100 | 1.2321 | 1.2544 |
| 3 | 1.1910 | 1.2250 | 1.2597 | 1.2950 | 1.3310 | 1.3676 | 1.4049 |
| 4 | 1.2625 | 1.3108 | 1.3605 | 1.4116 | 1.4641 | 1.5181 | 1.5735 |
| 5 | 1.3382 | 1.4026 | 1.4693 | 1.5386 | 1.6105 | 1.6851 | 1.7623 |
| 6 | 1.4185 | 1.5007 | 1.5869 | 1.6771 | 1.7716 | 1.8704 | 1.9738 |
| 7 | 1.5036 | 1.6058 | 1.7138 | 1.8280 | 1.9487 | 2.0762 | 2.2109 |
| 8 | 1.5939 | 1.7182 | 1.8509 | 1.9926 | 2.1436 | 2.3045 | 2.4760 |
| 9 | 1.6895 | 1.8385 | 1.9990 | 2.1719 | 2.3580 | 2.5580 | 2.7731 |
| 10 | 1.7909 | 1.9672 | 2.1589 | 2.3674 | 2.5937 | 2.8394 | 3.1059 |
| 11 | 1.8983 | 2.1049 | 2.3316 | 2.5804 | 2.8531 | 3.1518 | 3.4786 |
| 12 | 2.0122 | 2.2522 | 2.5182 | 2.8127 | 3.1384 | 3.4985 | 3.8960 |
| 13 | 2.1329 | 2.4099 | 2.7196 | 3.0658 | 3.4523 | 3.8833 | 4.3635 |
| 14 | 2.2609 | 2.5785 | 2.9372 | 3.3417 | 3.7975 | 4.3104 | 4.8871 |
| 15 | 2.3966 | 2.7590 | 3.1722 | 3.6425 | 4.1773 | 4.7860 | 5.4736 |

To use the table, move to the column representing the relevant interest rate, and move down to the "number of years" row indicating the multiplier to apply to the applicable year of cash flow. Thus, if the option were available to delay the receipt of $10,000 for five years, and the funds could be invested at 8% in the meantime, multiply the $10,000 by 1.4693 to arrive at a future value of $14,693 for those cash flows.

The same table format is also available for determining the present value of an ordinary annuity of 1 per period. This table is used to derive the present value of a series of annuity payments. The multipliers for this calculation are noted in the following table.

**Present Value Factors for Ordinary Annuity of 1 per Period**

| Number of Years | 6% | 7% | 8% | 9% | 10% | 11% | 12% |
|---|---|---|---|---|---|---|---|
| 1 | 0.9434 | 0.9346 | 0.9259 | 0.9174 | 0.9091 | 0.9009 | 0.8929 |
| 2 | 1.8334 | 1.8080 | 1.7833 | 1.7591 | 1.7355 | 1.7125 | 1.6901 |
| 3 | 2.6730 | 2.6243 | 2.5771 | 2.5313 | 2.4869 | 2.4437 | 2.4018 |
| 4 | 3.4651 | 3.3872 | 3.3121 | 3.2397 | 3.1699 | 3.1024 | 3.0373 |
| 5 | 4.2124 | 4.1002 | 3.9927 | 3.8897 | 3.7908 | 3.6959 | 3.6048 |
| 6 | 4.9173 | 4.7665 | 4.6229 | 4.4859 | 4.3553 | 4.2305 | 4.1114 |
| 7 | 5.5824 | 5.3893 | 5.2064 | 5.0330 | 4.8684 | 4.7122 | 4.5638 |
| 8 | 6.2098 | 5.9713 | 5.7466 | 5.5348 | 5.3349 | 5.1461 | 4.9676 |
| 9 | 6.8017 | 6.5152 | 6.2469 | 5.9952 | 5.7590 | 5.5370 | 5.3282 |
| 10 | 7.3601 | 7.0236 | 6.7101 | 6.4177 | 6.1446 | 5.8892 | 5.6502 |
| 11 | 7.8869 | 7.4987 | 7.1390 | 6.8052 | 6.4951 | 6.2065 | 5.9377 |
| 12 | 8.3838 | 7.9427 | 7.5361 | 7.1607 | 6.8137 | 6.4924 | 6.1944 |
| 13 | 8.8527 | 8.3577 | 7.9038 | 7.4869 | 7.1034 | 6.7499 | 6.4235 |
| 14 | 9.2950 | 8.7455 | 8.2442 | 7.7862 | 7.3667 | 6.9819 | 6.6282 |
| 15 | 9.7122 | 9.1079 | 8.5595 | 8.0607 | 7.6061 | 7.1909 | 6.8109 |

The annuity table contains a multiplier specific to the number of payments over which you expect to receive a series of equal payments and at a certain discount rate. When this factor is multiplied by one of the payments, it yields the present value of the stream of payments. For example, if you expect to receive five payments of $10,000 each and use a discount rate of 8%, the factor would be 3.9927 (as noted in the preceding table in the intersection of the 8% column and the row for five years). Then multiply the 3.9927 factor by $10,000 to arrive at a present value of the annuity of $39,927.

## Net Present Value

Net present value (NPV) analysis is useful for determining the current value of a stream of cash flows that extend out into the future. It can also be used to compare several such cash flows to decide which has the largest present value. NPV is commonly used in the analysis of investments, to see if an initial payment for fixed assets and other expenditures will generate net positive cash flows over time. To calculate net present value, we use the following formula:

$$NPV = X \times [(1+r)^n - 1]/[r \times (1+r)^n]$$

Where:

X = The amount received per period
n = The number of periods
r = The rate of return

It is not that difficult to estimate the amount of cash received per period, as well as the number of periods over which cash will be received. The difficult inclusion in the formula is the rate of return. This is generally considered to be a company's average cost of capital, but can also be considered its incremental cost of capital, or a risk-adjusted cost of capital. In the latter case, this means that several extra percentage points are added to the corporate cost of capital for those cash flow situations considered to be unusually risky. The cost of capital is the weighted-average cost of a company's outstanding debt and equity.

---

**EXAMPLE**

The CFO of Franklin Drilling is interested in the NPV associated with a production facility that the CEO wants to acquire. In exchange for an initial $10 million payment, Franklin should receive payments of $1.2 million at the end of each of the next 15 years. Franklin has a corporate cost of capital of 9%. To calculate the NPV, he inserts the cash flow information into the NPV formula, as follows:

$$\$1,200,000 \times ((1+0.09)\verb|^|15-1)/(0.09 \times (1+0.09)\verb|^|15) = \$9,672,826$$

The present value of the cash flows associated with the investment is $327,174 lower than the initial investment in the facility, so Franklin should not proceed with the investment.

---

The NPV calculation can be massively more complicated than the simplified example just shown. In reality, it may be necessary to include the present values of the cash flows related to the following additional items:

- Ongoing expenditures related to the investment
- Variable amounts of cash flow being received over time, rather than the same amount every time
- Variable timing for the receipt of cash, rather than the consistent receipt of a payment on the same date
- The amount of working capital required for the project, as well as the release of working capital at the end of the project
- The amount at which the investment can be resold at the end of its useful life
- The tax value of depreciation on the asset that was purchased

All of the preceding factors should be considered when evaluating NPV for an investment proposal. In addition, consider generating several models to account for the worst case, most likely, and best case scenarios for cash flows (see the following Real Options section).

## Internal Rate of Return

The internal rate of return (IRR) is the rate of return at which the present value of a series of future cash flows equals the present value of all associated costs. IRR is commonly used in investment analysis to discern the rate of return on the estimated cash flows arising from a prospective investment. The project having the highest IRR is selected for investment purposes.

The easiest way to calculate the internal rate of return is to open Microsoft Excel and follow these steps:

1. Enter in any cell a negative figure that is the amount of cash outflow in the first period. This is normal when acquiring fixed assets, since there is an initial expenditure to acquire and install the asset.
2. Enter the subsequent cash flows for each period following the initial expenditure in the cells immediately below the cell where the initial cash outflow figure was entered.
3. Access the IRR function and specify the cell range into which entries were just made. The internal rate of return will be calculated automatically. It may be useful to use the Increase Decimal function to expand the number of decimal places appearing in the calculated internal rate of return, thereby providing a more detailed answer.

As an example, a company is reviewing a possible investment, for which there is an initial expected investment of $20,000 in the first year, followed by incoming cash flows of $12,000, $7,000 and $4,000 in the next three years. If this information is entered into the Excel IRR function, it returns an IRR of 8.965%.

The IRR formula in Excel is extremely useful for quickly deriving a possible rate of return. However, it can be used for a less ethical purpose, which is to artificially model the correct amounts and timing of cash flows to produce an IRR that meets a company's investment guidelines. In this case, a manager is fudging the results in his or her cash flow model in order to gain acceptance of a project, despite knowing that it may not be possible to achieve those cash flows.

## Incremental Internal Rate of Return

The incremental internal rate of return is an analysis of the financial returns where there are two competing investment opportunities involving different amounts of investment. The analysis is applied to the difference between the costs of the two investments. Thus, the cash flows associated with the less expensive alternative would be subtracted from the cash flows associated with the more expensive alternative to arrive at the cash flows applicable to the difference between the two alternatives; an internal rate of return analysis would then be conducted on this difference.

Based just on quantitative analysis, select the more expensive investment opportunity if it has an incremental internal rate of return higher than the minimum return considered acceptable. However, there are qualitative issues to consider as well, such as whether there is an incremental increase in risk associated with the more expensive investment.

If there is a considerable amount of additional risk associated with the more expensive investment opportunity, adjust for this risk by increasing the minimum return considered acceptable. For example, the minimum rate of return threshold for a low-risk investment might be 5%, while the threshold might be 10% for a high-risk investment.

---

**EXAMPLE**

Hassle Corporation is considering obtaining a color copier, and it can do so either with a lease or an outright purchase. The lease involves a series of payments over the three-year useful life of the copier, while the purchase option involves more cash up-front and some continuing maintenance, but it also has a resale value at the end of its useful life. The following analysis of the incremental differences in the cash flows between the two alternatives reveals that there is a positive incremental internal rate of return for the purchasing option. Barring any other issues (such as available cash to buy the copier), the purchasing option therefore appears to be the better alternative.

| Year | Lease | Buy | Difference |
|---|---|---|---|
| 0 | -$7,000 | -$29,000 | -$22,000 |
| 1 | -7,000 | -1,500 | 5,500 |
| 2 | -7,000 | -1,500 | 5,500 |
| 3 | -7,000 | -1,500 | 5,500 |
| Resale | | +15,000 | 15,000 |
| | | Incremental IRR | 13.3% |

---

## Terminal Value

The cash flows associated with an analysis may not have a discernible time horizon – that is, there is no expectation that they will end. In this case, it is customary to derive a terminal value, which is the aggregation of all cash flows beyond the date range for which cash flows are being predicted. Terminal value is then included in the cash flow analysis. Terminal value can be calculated with the *perpetuity formula*, which employs the following steps:

1. Estimate the cash flows associated with the final year of projections, and eliminate from this amount any unusual items that are not expected to occur again in later years.
2. Estimate a reasonable growth rate for this adjusted cash flow figure for later years. The amount should approximate the rate of growth for the entire economy. The rate of sustainable growth should be quite small, and may even be zero or a negative figure.

3. Subtract this growth rate from the company's cost of capital, and divide the result into the adjusted cash flows for the final year. The formula is:

$$\frac{\text{Adjusted final year cash flow}}{\text{Cost of capital} - \text{Growth rate}} = \text{Terminal value}$$

---

**EXAMPLE**

Glow Atomic is reviewing the projected income stream from a new type of fusion plant that could generate electricity in perpetuity. The analysis is broken into annual cash flows for the first 20 years, followed by a terminal value. The expected cash flow for the 20$^{th}$ year is $10,000,000. Glow expects these cash flows to increase at a rate of 1% thereafter. The company has a 15% cost of capital. Based on this information, the terminal value of the investment opportunity is:

$$\frac{\$10{,}000{,}000 \text{ Final year cash flow}}{15\% \text{ Cost of capital} - 1\% \text{ Growth rate}} = \$71{,}429{,}000 \text{ Terminal value}$$

---

## Real Options

Another way to review an investment decision is to examine the value embedded in different strategic alternatives. This concept is known as a *real option*, which refers to the decision options available for a tangible asset. Most businesses ignore the real option concept, instead choosing to construct a net present value analysis for a single possible outcome. Instead, use the real options concept to examine a whole range of outcomes. For example, a traditional investment analysis in an oil refinery would probably use a single price per barrel of oil for the entire investment period, whereas the actual price of oil will likely fluctuate far outside of the initial estimated price point over the course of the investment. An analysis based on real options would instead focus on the range of profits and losses that may be encountered over the course of the investment period as the price of oil changes over time.

A comprehensive real options analysis begins with a review of the risks to which a project will be subjected, and then models for each of these risks or combinations of risks. To continue with the preceding example, an investor in an oil refinery project could expand the scope of the analysis beyond the price of oil to also encompass the risks of possible new environmental regulations on the facility, the downtime caused by a supply shutdown, and the risk of damage caused by a hurricane.

A logical outcome of real options analysis is to be more careful in placing large bets on a single likelihood of probability. Instead, it can make more sense to place a series of small bets on different outcomes, and then alter the portfolio of investments over time as more information about the various risks becomes available. Once the key risks have been resolved, the best investment is easier to discern, so that a "bet the bank" investment can be made.

---

**EXAMPLE**

An agriculture company wants to develop a new crop strain for either wheat or barley, to be sold for export. The primary intended market is an area in which wheat is currently the preferred crop. The company estimates that it can generate a 20% return on investment by developing a new wheat variant at a cost of $30 million. Since wheat is already the primary type of crop being planted, the odds of success are high. However, if the company can successfully develop a barley variant at a total cost of $50 million, its projected profits are 50%. The key risk with the barley project is farmer acceptance. Given the high profits that could be derived from selling barley, the company makes a small initial investment in a pilot project. If the level of farmer acceptance appears reasonable, the company can then invest an additional $8 million for a further roll out of the concept.

This use of real options allows the company to invest a relatively small amount to test its assumptions regarding a possible alternative investment. If the test does not work, the company has only lost $1 million. If the test succeeds, the company can pursue an alternative that may ultimately yield far higher profits than the more assured investment in wheat.

---

A concern with using real options is that competitors may be using the same concept at the same time, and may use the placing of small bets to arrive at the same conclusions as the company. The result may be that several competitors will enter the same market at approximately the same time, driving down the initially rich margins that management may have assumed were associated with a real option. Thus, the parameters of real options change constantly, and so must be re-evaluated at regular intervals.

Another concern relates to the last point that competitors may jump into the same market. This means that a business cannot evaluate the results of its options analyses in a leisurely manner. Instead, each option must be evaluated quickly and decisions made to make additional investments (or not) before the competition gets a jump on the situation.

## Complex Systems Analysis

When analyzing a possible investment, it is useful to also analyze the system into which the investment will be inserted. If the system is unusually complex, it is likely to take longer for the new asset to function as expected within the system. The reason for the delay is that there may be unintended consequences that ripple through the system, requiring adjustments in multiple areas that must be addressed before any gains from the initial investment can be achieved.

It may initially appear that the multitude of factors to consider in a complex system can be accounted for by creating an equally complex analysis model. However, virtually all models, no matter how complex, are not entirely complete; there are always additional factors that have not been considered that can impact a model in unexpected ways, resulting in outcomes that are well outside of what the analyst might expect.

---

**EXAMPLE**

ABC Airlines is modeling whether to offer its customers a new route into Denver from Kansas City. ABC must consider a number of factors that can impact flight service, such as the impact of snowfall on the number of travelers to the area's ski resorts, whether a new high-speed train from Kansas City to Denver will impact the number of paying passengers, the extent to which upstart low-cost airlines may drive down prices, and how the price of aviation fuel will drive up ticket prices. ABC elects not to provide service, after which the International Olympic Committee grants Denver the next winter Olympics, which triggers an upsurge in travel even in advance of the games. Thus, an outlier event arises that would not normally have been factored into the decision, but which has an impact on the decision.

---

A basic rule of investing in a complex environment is that it is impossible to understand the full impact of the investment. There may be any number of adjustments required that will call for additional investments of both time and money. Consequently, the more complex the environment, the more time and money should be allocated to an investment, even if there may not appear to be any immediate need for the additional investment.

## Research and Development Funding Analysis

The funding process for research and development (R&D) projects tends to result in the funding of less-risky projects. The reason is that there is usually not enough cash available to fund all proposed investments, so a ranking system must be imposed to determine which projects will receive funding. The ranking is driven by a discounted cash flows analysis, for which a higher discount rate is imposed on the riskier projects. Since this analysis tends to reduce the cash flows associated with riskier projects, only safer R&D projects are funded. The typical result is that a business pours more cash into the extension of its existing product lines, which are considered safe investments, and little cash into real innovation.

One way to break through this safety-driven selection process is to deliberately allocate cash to several classifications of R&D projects, of which one is for high-risk endeavors. The amount allocated to each classification will vary, depending on management's willingness to lose money on high-risk projects. In general, this concept will increase the probability that a business will come up with a breakthrough product that can lead to an entirely new product line.

When cash is deliberately invested in high-risk R&D projects, there will inevitably be a number of project failures, either because the results will not be commercially viable or because the project is an outright failure. The real problem is when there are *few* failures, because it indicates that the company is not investing in sufficiently risky projects, with their attendant high returns.

To determine the amount of project failure being experienced, summarize the total expense related to projects that have been cancelled (known as *R&D waste*). While this metric can be deliberately altered by delaying the date on which a project is cancelled, it can still provide relevant input into the amount of project risk being incurred over multiple periods.

Even when the allocation of funding into different classifications increases the odds of funding a riskier R&D project, it is still necessary to allocate funds *within* each classification. A possible approach for deciding between projects is to use *expected commercial value* (ECV), which amalgamates the probabilities of success into a more standard net present value calculation. The formula is:

(((Project net present value × probability of commercial success) – commercialization cost)

× (probability of technical success)) – product development cost

---

**EXAMPLE**

Entwhistle Electric is considering an investment in a tiny battery for cell phone applications. There is some risk that the battery cannot be developed in the necessary size. Facts pertaining to the project are:

| | |
|---|---:|
| Project net present value | \$8,000,000 |
| Probability of commercial success | 90% |
| Commercialization cost | \$1,500,000 |
| Probability of technical success | 75% |
| Product development cost | \$3,500,000 |

Entwhistle's financial analyst derives the following ECV for the project from the preceding information:

((($8,000,000 Project NPV × 90% probability of commercial success)

– $1,500,000 commercialization cost)

× (75% probability of technical success)) – $3,500,000 product development cost

Expected commercial value = $775,000

---

An ECV analysis will inevitably result in some projects not being funded. However, not being funded does not necessarily equate to being permanently cancelled. These projects might become more tempting prospects for funding at a later date, depending on changes in such areas as:

- Competitor actions
- Legal liability
- Price points for adjacent products
- Raw materials availability
- Technical advances

Because of these issues, it may make more sense to schedule an occasional review of prospective investments that have failed the ECV test, to see if circumstances now make them worthy of an investment.

## Accounting Issues Related to Investment Decisions

The central accounting issue related to investment decisions is whether to write down an investment under impairment rules. The concept applies somewhat differently to investments in fixed assets, securities, and other entities. We make note of each situation in the following sub-sections.

### Impairment of Fixed Assets

Under the impairment concept, a business must periodically test its fixed assets to see if they are still as valuable as the costs at which they are currently stated on the books. If not, reduce the recorded cost of these assets by recognizing a loss. Also, it is not allowable to reverse an impairment loss.

Under the impairment rules, a loss must be recognized for the difference between the sum of the undiscounted cash flows expected to result from the use (and eventual disposition) of an asset over its remaining useful life, and its current carrying amount. If there are a number of possible cash flow outcomes, a probability-weighted cash flow analysis can be used.

---

**EXAMPLE**

Luminescence Corporation operates a small floodlight manufacturing facility. Luminescence considers the entire facility to be a reporting unit, so it conducts an impairment test on the entire operation. The test reveals that a continuing decline in the market for floodlights (caused by the surge in LED lights in the market) has caused a $2 million impairment charge. Luminescence allocates the charge to the four assets in the facility as follows:

| Asset | Carrying Amount | Proportion of Carrying Amounts | Impairment Allocation | Revised Carrying Amount |
|---|---|---|---|---|
| Ribbon machine | $8,000,000 | 67% | $1,340,000 | $6,660,000 |
| Conveyors | 1,500,000 | 13% | 260,000 | 1,240,000 |
| Gas injector | 2,000,000 | 16% | 320,000 | 1,680,000 |
| Filament inserter | 500,000 | 4% | 80,000 | 420,000 |
| Totals | $12,000,000 | 100% | $2,000,000 | $10,000,000 |

---

**Tip:** Given the difficulty of calculation, impairment charges are usually only recognized when there is a notable loss involved. Smaller impairment charges that have no material impact on the financial results of a business are typically ignored. From a practical perspective, this means that smaller fixed assets cannot trigger a large enough impairment loss to be worth testing.

## Impairment of Securities

A business most commonly invests in securities that it intends to sell in the short term for a profit. This type of investment is known as a *trading security*. Trading securities are recognized at their fair value on the balance sheet, and all unrealized gains and losses on these holdings are recognized in earnings. This adjustment is made in every reporting period.

A company may also invest in a security that is classified as either held-to-maturity or available-for-sale. As the name implies, *held-to-maturity* means that the company intends to hold a security until its maturity date. The *available-for-sale* designation is a catch-all category that applies to any investments that are not either held to maturity or designated as trading securities. If a company has invested in held-to-maturity or available-for-sale securities, and there is a decline in their market value below their carrying amounts, it may be necessary to recognize an impairment loss.

The key issue in this determination is whether such a decline is other than temporary. If an impairment loss on an *equity security* is considered to be other than temporary, recognize a loss in the amount of the difference between the carrying amount and fair value of the security. Once the impairment is recorded, this becomes the new cost basis of the security, and cannot be adjusted upward if there is a subsequent recovery in the fair value of the security. If an impairment loss on a *debt security* is considered to be other than temporary, the amount of the loss recognized is based on the following criteria:

- If the business intends to sell the security or it is more likely than not that it will be forced to do so before there has been a recovery of the amortized cost of the security, recognize a loss in earnings in the amount of the difference between the amortized cost and fair value of the security.
- If the business does not intend to sell the security and it is more likely than not that it will not have to do so before there has been a recovery of the amortized cost of the security, separate the impairment into the amount representing a credit loss and the amount relating to all other causes. Then recognize that portion of the impairment representing a credit loss in earnings. Recognize the remaining portion of the impairment in other comprehensive income, net of taxes.

Once the impairment is recorded, this becomes the new amortized cost basis of the debt security, and cannot be adjusted upward if there is a significant recovery in the fair value of the security.

This impairment analysis for securities designated as held-to-maturity or available-for-sale must be performed in every reporting period.

---

**EXAMPLE**

Armadillo Industries buys $250,000 of the equity securities of Currency Bank. A national liquidity crisis causes a downturn in Currency's business, so a major credit rating agency lowers its rating for the bank's securities. These events cause the quoted price of Armadillo's holdings to decline by $50,000. The CFO of Armadillo believes that the liquidity crisis will end soon, resulting in a rebound of the fortunes of Currency Bank, and so authorizes the recordation of the $50,000 valuation decline in other comprehensive income. The following entry records the transaction:

| | Debit | Credit |
|---|---|---|
| Loss on available-for-sale securities (recorded in other comprehensive income) | 50,000 | |
| Investments – Available-for-sale | | 50,000 |

In the following year, the prognostication abilities of the CFO are unfortunately not justified, as the liquidity crisis continues. Accordingly, the CFO authorizes shifting the $50,000 loss from other comprehensive income to earnings.

---

### Impairment of Investments in Other Entities

When a company owns an interest in another business that it does not control (such as a corporate joint venture), it may use the *equity method* to account for its ownership interest. The equity method is designed to measure changes in the economic results of the investee by requiring the investor to recognize its share of the profits or losses recorded by the investee. The equity method is a more complex technique of accounting for ownership, and so is typically used only when there is a significant ownership interest that enables an investor to have influence over the decision-making of the investee.

The key determining factor in the use of the equity method is having significant influence over the operating and financial decisions of the investee. The primary determinant of this level of control is ownership of at least 20% of the voting shares of the investee, though this measurement can be repudiated by evidence that the investee opposes the influence of the investor. Other types of evidence of significant influence are controlling a seat on the board of directors, active participation in the decisions of the investee, or swapping management personnel with the investee.

The essential accounting under the equity method is to initially recognize an investment in an investee at cost, and then adjust the carrying amount of the investment by recognizing its share of the earnings or losses of the investee in earnings over time. The following additional guidance applies to these basic points:

- *Dividends*. The investor should subtract any dividends received from the investee from the carrying amount of the investor's investment in the investee.
- *Investee losses*. It is possible that the investor's share of the losses of an investee will exceed the carrying amount of its investment in the investee. If

so, the investor should report losses up to its carrying amount, as well as any additional financial support given to the investee, and then discontinue use of the equity method. However, additional losses can be recorded if it appears assured that the investee will shortly return to profitability. If there is a return to profitability, the investor can return to the equity method only after its share of the profits has been offset by those losses not recognized when use of the equity method was halted.

- *Other write-downs*. If an investor's investment in an investee has been written down to zero, but it has other investments in the investee, the investor should continue to report its share of any additional investee losses, and offset them against the other investments, in sequence of the seniority of those investments (with offsets against the most junior items first). If the investee generates income at a later date, the investor should apply its share of these profits to the other investments in order, with application going against the most senior items first.

---

**EXAMPLE**

Armadillo Industries purchases 30% of the common stock of Titanium Barriers, Inc. Armadillo controls two seats on the board of directors of Titanium as a result of this investment, so it uses the equity method to account for the investment. In the next year, Titanium earns $400,000. Armadillo records its 30% share of the profit with the following entry:

| | Debit | Credit |
|---|---|---|
| Investment in Titanium Barriers | 120,000 | |
| Equity in Titanium Barriers income | | 120,000 |

A few months later, Titanium issues a $50,000 cash dividend to Armadillo, which the company records with the following entry:

| | Debit | Credit |
|---|---|---|
| Cash | 50,000 | |
| Investment in Titanium Barriers | | 50,000 |

**EXAMPLE**

Armadillo Industries has a 35% ownership interest in the common stock of Arlington Research. The carrying amount of this investment has been reduced to zero because of previous losses. To keep Arlington solvent, Armadillo has purchased $250,000 of Arlington's preferred stock and extended a long-term unsecured loan of $500,000.

During the next year, Arlington incurs a $1,200,000 loss, of which Armadillo's share is 35%, or $420,000. Since the next most senior level of Arlington's capital after common stock is its preferred stock, Armadillo first offsets its share of the loss against its preferred stock investment. Doing so reduces the carrying amount of the preferred stock to zero, leaving

$170,000 to be applied against the carrying amount of the loan. This results in the following entry by Armadillo:

| | Debit | Credit |
|---|---|---|
| Equity method loss | 420,000 | |
| Preferred stock investment | | 250,000 |
| Loan | | 170,000 |

In the following year, Arlington records $800,000 of profits, of which Armadillo's share is $280,000. Armadillo applies the $280,000 first against the loan write-down, and then against the preferred stock write-down with the following entry:

| | Debit | Credit |
|---|---|---|
| Preferred stock investment | 110,000 | |
| Loan | 170,000 | |
| Equity method income | | 280,000 |

The result is that the carrying amount of the loan is fully restored, while the carrying amount of the preferred stock investment is still reduced by $140,000 from its original level.

---

## Summary

Many of the tools described in this chapter are intended to assist the manager in deciding upon where to invest funds. Unfortunately, many organizations decide in advance how they want to invest funds, without conducting any quantitative analysis to see if this is a good idea. Instead, "gut feel" is the main basis for an investment decision. Alternatively, an analysis tool may be used to severely restrict the range of potential investments, with other investments whose results are somewhat sub-standard being summarily dismissed. In reality, overall strategy should be used to set the boundaries for which investments are acceptable, while the detailed techniques noted in this chapter are then employed to determine which specific investments to pursue.

In addition, it is essential for the manager to be aware of the accounting for investments, for the accounting rules are particularly conservative in this area, requiring write-downs that can seriously impair the state of a company's balance sheet. These write-downs can give investors and creditors the impression that a business' financial condition has declined within a short period of time.

# Chapter 10
# Acquisition Decisions

## Introduction

The manager must be concerned with an immense number of issues when engaging in acquisition activities, from the establishment of an acquisition strategy through the proper integration of an acquired business. Accounting issues play a large part in these acquisition decisions, including the investigation of accounting-related topics as part of the due diligence investigation, mitigating tax effects, and integrating the accounting operations of the acquirer and acquiree. We deal with all of these topics in the following sections, with particular emphasis on the tax structure of a proposed deal.

**Related Podcast Episodes:** Episodes 80, 88, 166, and 254 of the Accounting Best Practices Podcast discuss due diligence, acquisition types, whose accounting system to use in an acquisition, and merger integration, respectively. They are available at: **accountingtools.com/podcasts** or **iTunes**

## Accounting Due Diligence

An essential part of any acquisition is due diligence, which is the investigation of all aspects of the target company. It is addressed immediately after the parties have agreed in principle to deal, but before a binding agreement has been signed. Doing so tells the acquirer if there are any issues that might alter its valuation of the business, or which might scuttle the deal entirely. It also produces useful information for the eventual integration of the business into the acquirer.

The first type of information that many acquirers request is the financial statements, since they show the financial results, current financial position, and cash flows of the business. In short, they represent the financial health and productivity of the organization. However, the financial statements are presented at an aggregate level, so it is only possible to draw general conclusions from them. The due diligence team must dig deeper, using the additional items noted in this section, to arrive at a thorough understanding of the financial aspects of a business. Key financial issues to address include:

- *Annual financial statements*. Ideally, there should be financial statements for the past five years, which the team should translate into a trend-line comparison for the full five years. Doing so makes it easier to spot long-term changes in the business. In addition, at least the most recent fiscal year's financial statements should be audited; this means that an outside auditor has examined the accounting records for that period, and judges the information shown in the financial statements to fairly represent the results and ending financial position of the company.

- *Monthly financial statements*. Obtain all financial statements for each month of the year-to-date. This gives the team a good view of short-term trends in the business. It may also be useful to obtain the monthly results for the preceding year, just to obtain an idea of the seasonality to which the business is subjected over a full year. Seasonality could be important, if the acquirer finds that it may need to provide funding to the company at certain times of the year when its cash flow is negative.

**Tip:** If the company has not supplied financial results for the last few months, this is evidence that the business may be suffering a financial decline. It is especially likely if the business is withholding this information because it is concerned about "confidentiality". Therefore, do not complete due diligence without financial statements that are current through the immediately preceding month.

- *Cash flow analysis*. A key part of the financial statements is the statement of cash flows. This document reveals the sources and uses of cash. Be mindful of the information in this report when reviewing the income statement, for the target may report substantial profits even while burning through its cash reserves. Investigate the statement of cash flows for unusual one-time payments, such as owner distributions or asset purchases from related parties.
- *Cash restrictions*. Is cash restricted from use in any way? For example, the local bank may have issued a performance bond on behalf of the company, and has restricted a corresponding amount of the company's cash. Another example would be a cash restriction in order to fund a letter of credit. These restrictions can severely impact the amount of cash that an acquirer might expect to extract from an acquisition transaction.
- *Non-operating results*. Identify all non-operating transactions that arose during the review period, and strip them out of the financial results to see how the core operations of the business performed. This includes proceeds from insurance claims and legal settlements, gains or losses on asset sales, and so forth.
- *Expenses categorized as non-operational*. A company may shift expenses into a non-operational expense category, such as one-time expenses, in order to make its earnings from operations look more impressive. Be sure to examine all expenses claimed to be non-operational, and reclassify them as operational, if necessary.
- *One-time events*. See if there were any operational events that are unlikely to occur again, and strip them out of the results of operations. This is a common problem for one-time sales to large customers, such as the sale of a large number of software licenses to the federal government. This is a particular problem, because target companies have an annoying habit of putting themselves up for sale immediately after such sales, on the assumption that

buyers will assume a continuing sales level in the future, and accordingly pay a higher price for the business.

- *Adjusting entries.* Examine the financial statements for unusual adjusting entries that have been used to prop up the results of the business, such as accrued revenue, expenses shifted into a prepaid expenses account, or liabilities that were not accrued.

**Acquisition Story:** The author once reviewed the financial statements of a software development company as part of a due diligence investigation, and found an unusual $1 million asset on its balance sheet for internally developed software. The company's management team had decided that its latest product was worth $1 million, so it recorded the asset; doing so also changed its equity balance from a negative to a positive number.

- *Restructuring charges.* The target may have created an expense accrual for restructuring charges, which is essentially the pre-recognition of expenses that do not happen until a future accounting period. This is a warning flag that managers are reducing expenses in future periods, possibly to spruce up profits in anticipation of a sale.
- *Disclosures.* Audited financial statements should include a set of disclosures on various topics. Review these disclosures in detail, since they can reveal a great deal more information about a company than is shown in its income statement and balance sheet.
- *Public filings.* If a company is publicly-held, it must file the Form 10-K annual report, Form 10-Q quarterly report, and a variety of other issues on the Form 8-K. All of these reports are available on the website of the Securities and Exchange Commission, which is www.sec.gov. These documents are a treasure trove of information, and describe the results of a business in considerable detail.
- *Management letters.* After an audit has been completed, the auditors sometimes compile a set of recommendations into a management letter, which they distribute to the CEO and audit committee. Any such letters issued for the past few years are worth reading, since they contain suggestions to rectify deficiencies found in the company's practices.
- *Margin analysis.* Nearly every viable business has one product, product line, or business segment that generates outsized profits in comparison to the rest of the company. The review team needs to find this "golden goose," to ensure that the acquirer does not take any steps following the acquisition that will interfere with its flow of profits. Conversely, this analysis may also reveal a number of other aspects of the business that consistently lose money. In short, margin analysis can be used in entirely different ways – to bolster profitable parts of a business and restructure or even shut down money-losing operations.

Near the end of the due diligence investigation, adjust the reported results of the company for any synergies found, resulting in pro forma financial statements that reveal what its financial results would have been for the past year if the acquisition had taken place at the beginning of the year. Pro forma financial statements are the complete set of financial statements issued by an entity, incorporating assumptions or hypothetical conditions about events that may have occurred in the past or which may occur in the future. If there is some concern about the ability to implement certain synergies, prepare pro forma statements based on best case, most likely, and worst case scenarios.

After constructing the pro forma financial statements, also develop a one-year cash flow forecast for the business, incorporating the best estimates of revenues and changes caused by synergies. This information is needed to ensure that the target will begin generating sufficient cash flows to make it worthwhile to proceed with the acquisition.

## Impact on Earnings per Share

The investment community may take the simplistic approach of evaluating the structure of an acquisition deal based solely on the resulting earnings per share (EPS) of the combined entity. In reality, the impact of a business combination may not be fully realized for years, whereas EPS has more of a historical orientation. Nonetheless, it is useful to understand the calculation of the combined EPS in order to anticipate the reaction of investors and analysts. The calculation is:

$$\frac{\text{Acquirer earnings} + \text{Acquiree earnings}}{\text{Total shares outstanding following acquisition}} = \text{Combined earnings per share}$$

---

**EXAMPLE**

High Noon Armaments acquires Barbary Coast Rifles for 250,000 shares of its common stock. Barbary earned $250,000 in its most recent year of operations. Just prior to the acquisition, High Noon had 2,000,000 shares outstanding, and earned $1,500,000 in its most recent year of operations. The before-and-after earnings per share of High Noon are calculated as follows:

| Before Acquisition | After Acquisition |
|---|---|
| $1,500,000 profit ÷ 2,000,000 shares<br>= $0.75 earnings per share | $1,750,000 profit ÷ 2,250,000 shares<br>= $0.78 earnings per share |

Earnings per share have increased as a result of the acquisition transaction, which is received favorably by the investment community.

---

In any acquisition where the resulting changes in profits and shares outstanding results in a decline in earnings per share, the acquisition is said to be *dilutive* to earnings. When the reverse situation occurs, the acquisition is said to be *accretive* to earnings.

## Tax Issues in an Acquisition

There are significant taxation issues related to acquisitions that can allow an astute seller to defer the recognition of income taxes for many years, or create an immediate (and large) tax liability for an uninformed seller. There are lesser, though still important, tax issues that impact the acquirer. The central tax issues related to an acquisition are noted in the following sub-sections.

### Tax Issues for the Seller

The seller wants to delay the taxation of any gains it may realize through an acquisition transaction. Delaying taxes has value, since income taxes paid in the future have a smaller present value than taxes paid now. The tax treatments of the various forms of compensation are as follows:

- *Stock-for-stock*. In a stock-for-stock exchange, income taxes are deferred until such time as the recipient of the stock of the acquirer sells that stock (which could be years in the future). If the recipient waits for a sufficiently long time to sell the stock (typically one year), the transaction is recognized as a long-term capital gain, for which a much lower tax rate is paid.
- *Cash*. A cash payment requires the immediate recognition of income taxes.
- *Debt*. Debt payments are taxable when received. Thus, there is a tax deferral aspect to this type of payment.
- *Other consideration*. If some other form of consideration is paid, the recipient is likely to owe income taxes at once if the recipient realizes a gain on the difference between the value of the consideration received and the cost basis of the stock given up.

If the consideration received in an acquisition is a combination of the preceding elements, some elements will be taxable and others will have deferred taxation.

**Note:** There are instances where the tax basis of the seller is higher than the price to be paid, in which case there is no gain on which income taxes would be paid. In this situation, the seller is much more likely to want a cash payment.

### Tax Issues for the Acquirer

Tax issues have a much smaller impact on the acquirer than the acquiree. Nonetheless, the acquirer should certainly be aware of the following issues:

- *Asset step up*. The acquirer wants to step up the recorded value of any assets it acquires to their fair market values, which allows it to use a higher level of depreciation expense to shield more profits from taxation. This is allowable in a taxable transaction, and not allowed in a tax-free transaction. However, if the fair market value of acquired assets is *less than* their net book values, the acquirer has no opportunity to engage in a step up transaction.

- *Net operating loss carry forwards*. The acquirer can gain access to unused net operating losses (NOLs) incurred by the seller, which the acquirer can use to shield the profits of the acquiree. However, these losses can only be recognized over lengthy periods, and so do not play a major role in the acquisition decision or how it is structured. Ultimately, an acquisition should be based primarily on other factors than the use of an NOL.

The tax issues pointed out in this section are not minor; in some acquisitions, the seller will be so insistent upon a particular legal structure to take advantage of a tax situation that the deal will fail without it. The reason is that income taxes can cut deeply into the gains of selling shareholders.

## Issues with Stock Purchases

Most of the legal structures described in the following sections are based on a desire to purchase the shares of the seller, rather than its assets. Buying shares means that the acquirer will then own the seller's business entity, rather than just its assets. This has the following ramifications:

- *Contracts*. Since the seller's business is presumably going to continue in operation as a subsidiary of the acquirer, the acquirer also obtains both the customer and supplier contracts of the seller. This can be useful if the seller has a large backlog of customer orders. However, some business partners include a "change of control" clause in their contracts, under which they have the option to terminate a contract if there is a change of control of the business. This does not necessarily mean that those business partners will terminate the contracts, but the acquirer will probably have to negotiate new ones.
- *Liabilities*. The downside of purchasing an entire business is that the acquirer is now responsible for all of its liabilities, even those that are not documented. It may have the right to obtain reimbursement from the seller for undocumented liabilities, but nonetheless, this presents a risk to the acquirer.
- *Net operating loss carry forwards*. Since a stock purchase shifts ownership of the seller entity to the acquirer, the acquirer also gains any NOLs owned by the seller.
- *Goodwill amortization*. Goodwill is the difference between the purchase price of an acquisition and the amount of the price not assigned to the assets and liabilities obtained in the acquisition. When the acquirer buys the stock of the seller, it cannot amortize any goodwill associated with the transaction for tax purposes. Since goodwill can comprise a large part of the amount paid, this can substantially increase the amount of income taxes that the acquirer pays.

## General IRS Requirements to Avoid Gain Recognition

The Internal Revenue Service (IRS) stipulates in its Internal Revenue Code (IRC) a number of acquisition structures that can allow the deferral of gain recognition. A proposed transaction must incorporate all three of the following concepts into an IRS-approved acquisition structure before gain deferral will be allowed:

- *Bona fide purpose*. The proposed transaction must have a genuine business purpose other than the deferral or complete avoidance of taxes.
- *Continuity of business enterprise*. The acquirer must continue to operate the acquired entity, or at least use a large proportion of the acquired assets in a business.
- *Continuity of interest*. The shareholders of an acquired business must receive a sufficient amount of stock in the acquiring entity (generally considered to be at least 50% of the purchase price) to have a continuing financial interest in it.

It is possible to circumvent the continuity of interest rule to some extent by issuing the minimum stock requirement to the seller in the form of preferred stock. Doing so gives recipients a periodic dividend, so that they receive some cash flow in the short term.

The IRS acquisition models that can be used to defer income taxes are called Type A, B, C, or D reorganizations (we will refer to them as acquisition types, rather than reorganization types). The IRS requirements for these acquisition structures are described in the following four sections.

## The Type "A" Acquisition

An acquisition transaction can be designed to follow the IRS guidelines for a Type "A" acquisition, which are stated in Section 368(a)(1) of the IRC (paragraph A). This acquisition has the following characteristics:

- At least 50% of the payment must be in the stock of the acquirer
- The selling entity is liquidated
- The acquirer acquires all assets and liabilities of the seller
- It must meet the bona fide purpose rule
- It must meet the continuity of business enterprise rule
- It must meet the continuity of interest rule
- It must be approved by the boards of directors of both entities, plus the shareholders of the selling entity

This transaction type is among the more flexible alternatives available, since it allows for a mix of payment types. It also allows selling shareholders to defer the recognition of income taxes related to those shares exchanged for acquirer stock. However, shareholders must recognize income on all non-equity payments made to them. Also, because the acquired entity is liquidated, this terminates any acquiree contracts that had not yet expired, which could cause problems for the acquirer.

The Type "A" acquisition is most useful in situations where the seller wants to receive a mix of cash and stock from the acquirer, which allows it to defer a portion of the related taxable income. Acquirers tend to be less enamored of this approach, since they run the risk of losing any contracts held by the acquired entity when it is liquidated.

## The Type "B" Acquisition

An acquisition transaction can be designed to follow the IRS guidelines for a Type "B" acquisition. This acquisition is defined as follows in Section 368(a)(1) of the IRC (paragraph B):

> "The acquisition by one corporation, in exchange solely for all or a part of its voting stock (or in exchange solely for all or a part of the voting stock of a corporation which is in control of the acquiring corporation), of stock of another corporation if, immediately after the acquisition, the acquiring corporation has control of such other corporation (whether or not such acquiring corporation had control immediately before the acquisition)."

The transaction has the following characteristics:

- Cash cannot exceed 20% of the total consideration
- At least 80% of the acquiree's stock must be acquired with the acquirer's voting stock
- The acquirer must buy at least 80% of the acquiree's outstanding stock
- Acquiree shareholders cannot be given the option of being paid in cash instead of stock, if the result could potentially be that less than 80% of the acquiree's stock is acquired with the acquirer's voting stock; even having this option available disallows the use of the Type "B" acquisition
- The selling entity becomes a subsidiary of the acquirer
- It must meet the bona fide purpose rule
- It must meet the continuity of business enterprise rule
- It must meet the continuity of interest rule
- It must be approved by the boards of directors of both entities, plus the shareholders of the selling entity

It is possible to have a creeping Type "B" acquisition, if the stock of the acquiree is purchased within a 12-month period and there is a plan to acquire it as a result of these transactions. There are two additional rules related to a creeping acquisition, which are:

- The acquirer can only use stock-for-stock purchases; cash is not allowed

- The acquirer could have used cash to buy shares in the acquiree at some point in the past, as long as those purchases were not part of a plan to acquire the business at that time

The Type "B" acquisition is most useful when the seller needs to keep operating the seller's business and its contracts. However, it forces the seller to accept nearly all acquirer stock in payment for the acquisition.

## The Type "C" Acquisition

An acquisition transaction can be designed to follow the IRS guidelines for a Type "C" acquisition. This acquisition is defined as follows in Section 368(a)(1) of the IRC (paragraph C):

> "The acquisition by one corporation, in exchange solely for all or a part of its voting stock (or in exchange solely for all or a part of the voting stock of a corporation which is in control of the acquiring corporation), of substantially all of the properties of another corporation, but in determining whether the exchange is solely for stock the assumption by the acquiring corporation of a liability of the other shall be disregarded."

In essence, this is the transfer of the assets of the seller to the acquirer in exchange for the voting stock of the acquirer. This acquisition has the following characteristics:

- The acquirer must buy at least 80% of the fair market value of the acquiree's assets
- The acquirer can use cash only if it uses its voting stock to buy at least 80% of the fair market value of the acquiree's assets
- The selling entity must be liquidated
- It must meet the bona fide purpose rule
- It must meet the continuity of business enterprise rule
- It must meet the continuity of interest rule
- The acquirer may not have to gain the approval of its shareholders for the transaction, since this is an asset purchase. The acquired entity must gain the approval of its shareholders for the transaction.

A problem with the Type "C" acquisition is that dissenting shareholders can demand that their shares be appraised and paid for in cash. If the resulting cash payments are more than 20% of the total compensation paid, this violates the Type "C" requirements and invalidates its use as a tax-deferral method for those shareholders receiving stock.

The Type "C" acquisition is most useful when the acquirer wants to treat the transaction as an asset purchase, and the seller wants to be paid primarily in stock in order to defer the recognition of income taxes.

## The Type "D" Acquisition

A Type "D" acquisition is defined as follows in Section 368(a)(1) of the IRC (paragraph D):

> "A transfer by a corporation of all or a part of its assets to another corporation if immediately after the transfer the transferor, or one or more of its shareholders (including persons who were shareholders immediately before the transfer), or any combination thereof, is in control of the corporation to which the assets are transferred; but only if, in pursuance of the plan, stock or securities of the corporation to which the assets are transferred are distributed in a transaction which qualifies under [Sections 354, 355, or 356]."

This transaction is designed primarily to subdivide a business into smaller components, which are then spun off to shareholders. The following are variations on the type "D" concept:

- *Spin-off.* A company is divided into at least two entities, and existing shareholders receive shares in the new entities.
- *Split-off.* A company is split into different entities, with some shareholders only retaining their shares in the original entity, while others turn in their shares in exchange for shares in the new entity.
- *Split-up.* A company creates several new entities, transfers its assets and liabilities to them, and liquidates itself. Shareholder interests transfer to the new entities.

All of the variations noted here are designed for the internal restructuring of a business, rather than the acquisition of an outside entity.

## Triangular Mergers

All of the preceding acquisition arrangements suffer from a potential problem, which is that there may be some dissenting shareholders who disagree with the deal, and refuse to participate in it. If so, they may elect to continue as minority shareholders, or demand appraisal rights, or vote against the deal in the stockholder vote that is required for most types of acquisitions. In addition, it can be hard to contact the many shareholders of a public company to obtain their votes.

Appraisal rights are the legal right of dissenting shareholders to not accept an offer to buy their shares, but instead to have their shares appraised and purchased – typically in cash. Appraisal rights may not be allowed, depending upon the state of incorporation of the selling entity. Appraisal rights can cause trouble in some types of acquisitions, since the amount of cash paid for these shares may invalidate the type of acquisition structure being used.

It is possible to get around the problems posed by dissenting shareholders, as well as the sheer volume of shareholders in a public company, through the use of a merger transaction, rather than an acquisition transaction. In a merger, all shareholders are required to accept the price offered by the acquirer if the seller's board of directors approves the deal. In this section, we present two types of mergers – the triangular merger and the reverse triangular merger.

**The Triangular Merger**

In a triangular merger, the acquirer creates a wholly-owned subsidiary, which in turn merges with the selling entity. The selling entity then liquidates. The acquirer is the sole remaining shareholder of the subsidiary. The characteristics of the transaction are the same as those for a Type "A" acquisition, which are:

- At least 50% of the payment must be in the stock of the acquirer
- The selling entity is liquidated
- The acquirer acquires all assets and liabilities of the seller
- It must meet the bona fide purpose rule
- It must meet the continuity of business enterprise rule
- It must meet the continuity of interest rule
- It must be approved by the boards of directors of both entities

**The Reverse Triangular Merger**

A reverse triangular merger is the same as a triangular merger, except that the subsidiary created by the acquirer merges into the selling entity and then liquidates, leaving the selling entity as the surviving entity, and a subsidiary of the acquirer. Its characteristics are:

- At least 50% of the payment must be in the stock of the acquirer
- The subsidiary created by the acquirer is liquidated
- The acquirer acquires all assets and liabilities of the seller
- It must meet the bona fide purpose rule
- It must meet the continuity of business enterprise rule
- It must meet the continuity of interest rule
- It must be approved by the boards of directors of both entities

The reverse triangular merger is used much more frequently than the triangular merger, because the reverse version retains the seller entity, along with any business contracts it may have. It is also useful when there are a large number of shareholders and it is too difficult to acquire their shares through a Type "A" acquisition.

## The Asset Acquisition

The preceding legal structures were based on the assumption that the acquirer wants to control the business entity of the seller. What if that is not the case, and the acquirer only wants to purchase the assets of the seller? Doing so has the following ramifications:

- *Contracts*. If the acquirer only buys the assets of the seller, it is not acquiring any contracts with the business partners of the seller. This can cause havoc if the acquirer intends to continue doing business with the customers and suppliers of the seller, since all contracts will have to be renegotiated.
- *Liabilities*. An asset acquisition actually means that the acquirer buys only those assets *and liabilities* specifically stated in the purchase agreement. Thus, there may be a transfer of liabilities. However, it will not include undocumented or contingent liabilities; this is the main reason for an asset acquisition.
- *Asset step-up*. The acquirer records any assets acquired at their fair market values, and depreciates these (presumably) stepped-up values for tax purposes. If the fair market value of the assets acquired is *less than* their net book values, there is no tax benefit. In addition, the acquirer can amortize any goodwill associated with the acquisition for tax purposes.
- *Net operating loss carry forwards*. Since the acquirer is not purchasing the seller's business entity, it does not obtain the NOLs associated with that entity.

**Note:** If an acquirer elects to purchase the assets of an acquiree, this means that it must obtain the title to each individual asset that it purchases – which can involve a substantial amount of legal work if there are many fixed assets. Also, it may be necessary to have liens removed from the acquired assets, which may call for negotiations with the creditors of the acquiree.

It may not be possible to disassociate the liability for environmental cleanup from an asset purchase. In some situations, environmental regulations state that the cost of future hazardous waste remediation can attach to assets, as well as legal entities. Consequently, if the acquirer is planning to buy real estate as part of an asset purchase, it should engage in considerable due diligence for environmental problems.

In summary, an acquirer may insist on an asset acquisition if it believes that the risk of acquiring additional liabilities is too great. It may also be a useful method if the acquirer only wants to pluck a specific "crown jewel" asset out of the seller, such as a key patent.

The shareholders of the seller are opposed to asset acquisitions, for the following reasons:

- *Remainders*. They end up owning any residual parts of the seller (usually its liabilities).
- *Double taxation*. The seller must pay income taxes on any gains realized from the sale of its assets. Then, if the entity chooses to pass through these gains to its shareholders, it does so with a dividend, which is taxed again. To make matters worse, if the seller had previously claimed an investment tax credit on the assets it is now selling, it may have to give back some of the credit, which increases its tax liability. Double taxation does not occur if the selling entity is organized as a subchapter "S" or similar organization (see the next section).

The asset acquisition can be useful when the acquirer only wants to buy a small piece of the selling entity, such as a specific product line. If so, the only way to complete the transaction will probably be an asset sale, because there is no entity that owns just the desired assets and no others.

## Impact of the Acquiree Organizational Form

There is a difference in the value of an acquiree, depending on whether it has been organized as an "S" Corporation or a "C" Corporation. The key difference is that the acquirer can more readily step up the recorded cost of the assets acquired from an "S" corporation.

The regulation that applies to this situation is Internal Revenue Code Section 338(h)(10). In essence, this section of the IRC allows the acquirer to purchase the shares of an "S" corporation while treating the transaction from a tax perspective as the purchase of its assets. This has two ramifications:

- The acquirer can step up the value of the acquiree's assets
- The acquiree entity is not terminated, so its contractual arrangements are now owned by the acquirer (though the contracts may still be subject to change of control clauses that terminate the contracts)

This means that the price an acquirer is willing to pay for an "S" corporation is likely to be higher than if the same entity were organized as a "C" corporation. The increase in price is based on the present value of the tax savings that the acquirer will generate from the incremental increase in the asset depreciation of the stepped-up assets it acquired in the transaction.

Thus, organizing a selling business as a subchapter "S" corporation increases its value to an acquirer, and so should raise the price paid for it.

The same situation applies to a limited liability corporation and a limited partnership, though the applicable text in the IRC is in Section 754.

## Summary of Legal Structures

There are many types of legal structures available to the buyer and seller, each offering a different mix of features. The legal structure selected will be the result of negotiations between the parties, and perhaps an alteration of the mix and amount of compensation paid in order to match the structure selected. The following bullet points note the key features of each legal structure described in this chapter:

- *Type "A" acquisition.* Allows for a mix of payment types, and deferred tax recognition on stock payments. However, the selling entity is liquidated, which may terminate key contracts to which the seller was a party.
- *Type "B" acquisition.* Requires payment mostly in stock, so there is little liquidity for the seller. However, the selling entity is retained, so the acquirer does not lose any contracts held by the seller. This is a popular legal structure.
- *Type "C" acquisition.* Requires payment mostly in stock, so there is little liquidity for the seller. This is essentially an asset sale. Dissenting shareholders who are paid cash can keep this type of deal from being completed.
- *Type "D" acquisition.* Ideal for splitting apart a company; rarely used for acquisitions.
- *Triangular merger.* Useful for avoiding dissenting shareholders. Also allows for a mix of payment types, and deferred tax recognition on stock payments. However, the selling entity is liquidated, which may terminate key contracts to which the seller was a party.
- *Reverse triangular merger.* Useful for avoiding dissenting shareholders. Also allows for a mix of payment types, and deferred tax recognition on stock payments. The selling entity is retained, so the acquirer does not lose any contracts held by the seller. This is a popular legal structure.
- *Asset purchase.* Mostly of interest to the acquirer, which only buys the assets it wants, thereby reducing its risk of incurring undocumented liabilities. Also allows for the step-up of assets to their fair market values. Involves double taxation to the shareholders of the seller, who therefore generally oppose this method.

## Accounting Integration

The accounting function can be one of the more difficult areas in which to integrate the operations of the acquirer and acquiree. If the acquirer prefers to have a well-integrated accounting system, all of the following integration steps must be followed. However, if the acquirer is willing to leave the acquiree alone and just asks for a trial balance that it can record in the consolidated records of the parent company, few of the following items need to be addressed. Thus, the extent of accounting integration work depends on the organizational structure of the acquirer. The more important integration tasks are as follows:

- *Account definitions.* It is quite possible for two organizations to store different information in the same account, because they define the account differently. This problem can arise between a parent company and an acquiree, so the integration team must meet with the general ledger accountant to precisely define which transactions are recorded in which accounts. The result may be a change in the default accounts used for certain transactions in the accounting software.
- *Accounting policies.* Even if the acquirer plans to leave its acquiree alone in most respects, it should impose a standard set of accounting policies. Examples of such policies are a uniform capitalization limit and a variety of revenue recognition rules. Otherwise, the acquiree might report financial results that are entirely inconsistent with those produced by other subsidiaries of the parent company.
- *Accounts payable.* If payments are to be processed from a central location, contact all suppliers to notify them of the new remittance address to which they should send their invoices.
- *Bank accounts.* Does the acquirer want to retain existing bank accounts? Many acquirers have preferred banking relationships, and so will want to shift over to new accounts at those banks. The conversion process can be lengthy, and typically includes the following steps:
    - Open new accounts
    - Order check stock for the new accounts
    - Record the new account number in the accounts payable software module
    - Shred the check stock for the old accounts
    - Move recurring ACH debits from the old accounts to the new accounts
    - Wait for checks outstanding to clear the old accounts
    - Close the old accounts
- *Best practices.* Investigate the practices of the acquiree's department and extract unique best practices for use elsewhere in the organization. Also, implement the acquirer's standard set of best practices.
- *Budget.* If the acquirer requires the use of a budget, oversee the budgeting process to create a budget for the remainder of the current year.
- *Capitalization limit.* Assign the acquirer's capitalization limit to the company, so that purchases of a similar dollar amount are treated in the same way – either charged to expense or recorded as fixed assets. This may be easier if handled on a go-forward basis, rather than applying it retrospectively to existing fixed assets.

- *Chart of accounts*. The acquirer's controller will probably want to impose a standard chart of accounts to assist in more rapidly closing the books of the parent company. This means that the company's old chart of accounts must be transitioned to the new one. This can involve a significant amount of work, such as:
    - Reset the default expense account in each vendor master file record
    - Reset the default sales account in each customer master file record
    - Reset the cash account used in the accounts payable module
    - Reset the account numbers in all journal entry templates
    - Reset the account numbers in recurring journal entries
    - Deactivate the old account numbers
    - Reset the account number ranges in all financial reports generated by the accounting software
- *Closing schedule*. The controller of the parent company very likely operates under a tight schedule when closing the books, and so will impose a specific set of due dates on the acquiree, stating the dates and times by which certain reports (primarily its final trial balance) are to be delivered.
- *Collections*. Investigate collection procedures and the state of the aged receivables to see if collection activities are adequate. If not, impose additional procedures to accelerate collections. If the acquirer sends all seriously overdue accounts to a single collection agency, it should route the same types of accounts from this acquiree to the same agency.
- *Common paymaster rule*. If there is an expectation that employees may be paid by different subsidiaries of the parent company, the acquirer should designate a single entity within its business infrastructure to pay those employees. This entity becomes the "common paymaster." Doing so avoids the duplicate withholding of payroll taxes beyond their maximum annual levels. This saves money for the organization as a whole, since it would otherwise be matching the excess amount of payroll taxes.
- *Controls*. Compare the controls used by the company to those required by the acquirer, and implement any missing controls. The team could also make inquiries about fraud that has happened in the past, in order to gain some idea of process weaknesses that may require particular attention. If the acquirer is publicly-held, it may be necessary to conduct a full controls review, to see if the acquiree is compliant with the provisions of Section 404 of the Sarbanes-Oxley Act.

> **Tip:** There are more likely to be control breaches if the acquiree was run by the founder, using a top-down management hierarchy. The founder would have been able to circumvent any controls, so the control analysis should be especially comprehensive.
>
> There are also likely to be weak controls in small businesses, which have not yet grown to the point where they would have found it necessary to enact more comprehensive controls.

- *Metrics.* The acquirer likely uses a somewhat different set of operational and financial metrics, and will want the acquiree to use them, as well. The accounting department is usually tasked with compiling this information. Doing so involves imposing standard calculation methods for the metrics – otherwise, the acquiree may adopt alternative calculation methods that skew the results.

> **Tip:** Do not throw out the acquiree's metrics without some consideration of why they were used. It is possible that the business environment and operations of the company mandated the use of certain metrics, whose use should be continued.

- *Payroll cycles.* If the acquirer wants to standardize payroll, it will probably demand standardized payroll cycles (which is the length of time between payrolls), such as paying employees on a biweekly basis. It is not especially difficult to change the length of a payroll cycle.
- *Payroll systems.* If the acquirer wants to operate a single, centralized payroll system, consider converting to the corporate system only at the beginning of the calendar year; by doing so, the company can accumulate annual pay information within a single system and issue a single tax withholding report to employees for the full year. Centralizing payroll calls for the transfer of the following information (and more) to the corporate system:
    - Annual salary and hourly wage information
    - Tax withholdings taken
    - Garnishments
    - Tax levies
    - Insurance deductions
    - Pension deductions
    - Direct deposit information
- *Processes (general).* The theoretically most logical way to integrate the accounting processes of an acquiree is to compare its systems to those of the acquirer, and devise the most efficient combination of the two. In reality, the integration team is in a hurry, and so only has two options, which are:
    - *Impose standard systems.* If the acquirer is expanding fast, it needs to apply the same, standardized system everywhere. This means that

potentially excellent local systems may be thrown out in favor of "cookie cutter" processes.
  - *Retain existing systems.* The acquirer may not care what systems the acquiree has, as long as it submits monthly summary-level reports on a timely basis. In this case, the integration team will probably verify that sufficient controls are in place, and take no further action.

- *Public reporting.* If the acquirer is a publicly-held company, it has four business days in which to file a Form 8-K with the Securities and Exchange Commission, in which it announces the acquisition.
- *Reports.* Rewrite all financial reports so that they match the standard report template used elsewhere in the organization. This may include the addition of entirely new reports.

**Tip:** If the acquisition takes place near the end of the acquirer's fiscal year, it may be more cost-effective to let the company continue to operate its own systems, and make most changes effective as of the beginning of the new fiscal year. This avoids the need for any retrospective alteration of financial reports from earlier in the year.

- *Software.* A potentially massive project is to switch to the accounting software used by the acquirer. The level of devastation imposed on the acquiree's accounting staff will depend upon how thoroughly the existing accounting software is integrated into the company; ripping it out and imposing a new system will likely overwhelm any other project that the accounting employees may be tasked with for many months.
- *Signatories.* Does the acquirer want to retain the current set of check signers and wire transfer authorizers? If not, the team should notify the company's bank of the change in control, cancel the current list of authorizers, and replace them with a new set of names.
- *Training.* If the acquirer is intent on installing new systems and procedures within the acquiree, it must support these changes with an appropriate level of training. Even if there are few systemic changes, training may still be needed because of the need to report information to the parent company. For example, what if the acquirer is located in a different country? Currency translation issues now arise that had never previously been a concern. In such cases, training will be needed to avoid the risk of having business transactions either being ignored or incorrectly accounted for.

Once all changes have been made, have the acquirer's internal audit team schedule a series of reviews of the accounting operations, to ensure that standard practices have been properly installed and are operational.

The preceding points about integrating the accounting function are based on the assumption that the acquirer will retain at least some local accounting functions. However, if it wants to centralize *all* accounting at the corporate level, the integration process is substantially different. In that case, the key steps are more likely to include the following:

- *Retention plans*. The acquiree's accounting staff is told that the department will be closed. Retention bonuses are promised to keep the staff on-site through the conversion process.
- *Vendor master file transfer*. The vendor master file from the acquiree's accounts payable system is converted into the format used for the same file in the acquirer's accounting system, and transferred to that file.
- *Payables transfer*. All open accounts payable are shifted to the acquirer's accounts payable system. The historical records for paid payables are also transferred.
- *Supplier contacts*. Suppliers are contacted and asked to forward their invoices to the central corporate accounts payable function.
- *Expense report inputting*. If the corporate parent uses a centralized employee expense reporting system, the acquiree's employees must be contacted and instructed in how to use the system to submit their expense reports.
- *Payment method transfer*. If payments to suppliers and employees are made by ACH direct deposit, shift the direct deposit information to the corporate payment system.
- *Customer master file transfer*. The customer master file from the acquiree's accounts receivable system is converted into the format used for the same file in the acquirer's accounting system, and transferred to that file.
- *Receivables transfer*. All open accounts receivable are shifted to the acquirer's accounts receivable system. The historical records for paid receivables are also forwarded.
- *Customer contacts*. Customers are contacted and asked to forward their invoice payments to the central corporate cash receipts function, or to a designated lockbox or bank account.
- *Collections database*. All accumulated information related to customer collection activities is forwarded to the central corporate collections group, along with contact information for each customer.
- *Fixed assets transfer*. All fixed assets listed in the fixed assets register, as well as all related accumulated depreciation amounts, are shifted to the acquirer's fixed assets system.
- *Mapping*. All general ledger accounts used by the acquiree are mapped to those used by the acquirer.
- *General ledger transfer*. At a minimum, all general ledger summary totals are shifted to the corporate general ledger system. A better alternative, though more complex to transfer, is to shift over the supporting detail as well for all periods used in the financial statements.
- *Reconciliation documentation*. The accounting staff of the acquiree should complete any remaining reconciliations of general ledger accounts, and forward the reconciliations to the corporate staff.

The preceding steps only indicate the major actions needed to move an entire accounting department into the central corporate system, but should give an idea of the large amount of work required to effect a comprehensive transfer.

It may be necessary to keep some accounting clerical staff on-site at the acquiree, irrespective of the determination to centralize, since some information (such as timekeeping data) is best accumulated locally. It may also be useful to retain an on-site financial analyst, to investigate variances from expectations and report findings back to corporate headquarters.

## Summary

The accounting function is deeply involved in any acquisition transaction. The accounting staff's opinion regarding the financial condition of a candidate acquiree will likely make or break the transaction. Also, if the management team wants to engage in a full integration of the accounting departments of both organizations, doing so will be a long and complicated process that may require the support of senior management to achieve. Finally, the tax objectives of the owners of the acquiree will likely play the dominant role in the structure of the payment used to purchase the acquiree entity. For all of these reasons, managers should have a deep understanding of the accounting issues involved in an acquisition.

# Chapter 11
# Cost Accounting Tools and Concepts

## Introduction

A manager must have a numerical basis upon which to make decisions. Some of this information is available from the financial statements and other ongoing reports provided by the accounting department. However, these financially-oriented reports are not sufficient for some of the more detailed management decisions. Instead, fine-grained information about costs must be considered in order to determine the corporate direction in such areas as which customers to retain, whether to expand sales, and when to outsource.

To assist in this decision-making, we present in this chapter the concepts of direct costing and activity-based costing. Each of these concepts represents a useful managerial tool.

**Related Podcast Episode:** Episode 256 of the Accounting Best Practices Podcast discusses how to derive a product cost. It is available at: **accountingtools.com/podcasts** or **iTunes**

## Direct Costing

Direct costing is a specialized form of cost analysis that only uses variable costs to make decisions. It is extremely useful for short-term decisions, but can lead to harmful results if used for long-term decision making. In the following sections, we will describe the concept, as well as those situations in which it is most useful, and the scenarios where direct costing can lead to incorrect conclusions.

In brief, direct costing is the analysis of incremental costs. An incremental cost is the extra cost associated with manufacturing one additional unit of production, or the cost that will change as the result of a decision. Direct costs are most easily illustrated through examples, such as:

- The costs actually consumed when a product is manufactured
- The incremental increase in costs when production is ramped up
- The costs that disappear when a production line is shut down
- The costs that disappear when an entire subsidiary is shut down

The examples show that direct costs can vary based upon the level of analysis. For example, when reviewing the direct cost of a single product, the only direct cost may be the materials used in its construction. However, if management is contemplating shutting down an entire company, the direct costs are *all* costs incurred by that company – including all of its production and administrative costs. The main point to remember is that a direct cost is any cost that changes as the result of either a decision or a change in volume.

Direct costs do not necessarily align with the way in which costs are accumulated in an accounting system, which calls for some selective cost extraction from various sources to arrive at the proper set of direct costs.

---

**EXAMPLE**

The management of Dude Skis wants to know how much it will cost to increase production of its Drag Knuckle Skis from 5,000 units to 8,000 units, so that it can sell the additional 3,000 skis for a wholesale price (in aggregate) of $900,000. The most obvious direct cost is the cost of the wood core and graphite laminate used in the skis, at a cost of $150 per pair of skis. In addition, the company will require three additional staff whose labor cost will be $25 per pair of skis. Finally, the company must lease a lamination machine for $30,000, which it can then return to the lessor after the production run is complete.

For the purposes of this specific production-increase decision, then, the associated direct costs are:

| | |
|---|---:|
| Incremental revenue | $900,000 |
| Cost of materials ($150 × 3,000 units) | 450,000 |
| Cost of labor ($25 × 3,000 units) | 75,000 |
| Cost of lamination machine | 30,000 |
| Total of all direct costs | 555,000 |
| Contribution margin | $355,000 |

---

Note in the preceding example that the manager could probably obtain the cost of materials from the existing bill of materials for the Drag Knuckle ski, but would have to obtain the labor cost from the production manager, and the lamination machine's lease cost from the industrial engineering manager. Thus, it is clear that much of the information needed for a direct costing analysis does not come from the accounting database; in addition, it may involve nothing more than estimated costs, since the analysis involves an action that has not yet taken place, and for which there is no exact cost information.

A key issue with direct costing is the large variety of costs that are ignored. In the preceding example, note the absence of any costs related to the management of the production facility, or an administrative charge, or machine setup labor by the engineering staff. The reason these costs are not included is that the costs are the same, whether or not the company elects to increase its ski production. Only costs exhibiting incremental changes as a result of the decision are included in a direct costing analysis.

## Direct Costing as a Managerial Tool

Direct costing is of great use as a managerial tool. The following decisions all involve the use of direct costs as inputs to decision models. What is immediately noticeable in the examples accompanying these decision models is the simplicity and clarity of the direct costing format, because it deals with only a small subset of total costs – those that are impacted by the decision. All other costs are irrelevant for the purposes of the decision being addressed, and so can be excluded from the model. In particular, they contain no allocations of overhead, which are not only irrelevant for many short-term decisions, but which can be difficult to explain to someone not trained in accounting.

### Automation Investments

A common scenario is for a company to invest in automated production equipment in order to reduce the amount it pays to its direct labor staff. Under direct costing, the key information to collect is the incremental labor cost of any employees who will be terminated, as well as the new period costs to be incurred as part of the equipment purchase, such as the depreciation on the equipment and maintenance costs.

---

**EXAMPLE**

Dude Skis plans to acquire an automated graphics lamination machine, which it will use to laminate graphics onto its high-end skis. It plans to eliminate three direct labor positions and add one maintenance technician as a result of this change. The lamination machine costs $100,000 and will be depreciated over five years. The fully burdened cost of all three direct labor positions is $90,000, while the fully burdened cost of the new maintenance technician is $55,000. Dude's president constructs the following table to summarize the situation:

| **Direct cost additions** | |
|---|---|
| Annual machine depreciation | +$20,000 |
| Maintenance technician | +55,000 |
| | |
| **Direct cost deductions** | |
| Direct labor positions | -90,000 |
| | |
| **Net change in direct costs** | -$15,000 |

The table reveals that Dude should install the machine, since there will be a net decline in direct costs. Additional factors to consider might be any history of machine breakdowns that could lead to the rehire of the laid off workers, as well as the risk that the machine's manufacturer will go out of business and can therefore no longer support the machine. These are qualitative risk factors.

---

## Cost Reporting

Direct costing is very useful for controlling variable costs, because a variance analysis report can be created that compares the actual variable cost to what the variable cost per unit should have been. Fixed costs are not included in this analysis, since they are associated with the period in which they are incurred, and so are not direct costs. A simple reporting format follows, which focuses the attention of management solely on direct costs.

---

**EXAMPLE**

Dude Skis closely tracks the direct cost of its skis, and does so by comparing actual variable costs per unit to budgeted costs. The following report shows its direct cost analysis for January production of its low-cost line of children's introductory skis.

| Actual unit production = 2,703 ski pairs | | | |
|---|---|---|---|
| Variable Cost Item | Actual Cost per Unit | Budgeted Cost per Unit | Variance per Unit |
| Wood core | $42.50 | $41.75 | -$0.75 |
| Fiberglas wrap | 38.84 | 37.52 | -1.32 |
| Edging | 4.11 | 4.03 | -0.08 |
| Tip and tail caps | 0.39 | 0.42 | +0.03 |
| Lamination | 4.72 | 4.73 | +0.01 |
| Totals | $90.56 | $88.45 | -$2.11 |

The report does not include direct labor, since Dude's management does not feel that labor costs vary sufficiently with production volumes to warrant being included in the report.

---

The example only showed direct costs. Management will likely want to also track its ability to control fixed costs, so it can use a separate report for those items that itemizes total period costs by expense type as compared to budgeted amounts. For example:

| Fixed Cost Item | Actual Cost | Budgeted Cost | Variance |
|---|---|---|---|
| Accounting and legal | $12,500 | $12,000 | -$500 |
| Insurance | 7,400 | 7,200 | -200 |
| Salaries, administration | 29,000 | 27,400 | -1,600 |
| Rent | 18,000 | 18,000 | 0 |
| Utilities | 4,700 | 4,000 | -700 |
| Totals | $71,600 | $68,600 | -$3,000 |

Note that the direct cost variance analysis report was designed for costs at the individual unit level, while the fixed cost variance analysis report was designed for total costs in a period. It is easier for management to take remedial action by using these differing formats for different types of costs.

## Customer Profitability

Some customers require a great deal of support, but also place such large orders that a company still earns a profit from the relationship. If there are such resource-intensive situations, it makes sense to occasionally calculate how much money the company really earns from each customer. This analysis may reveal that the company would be better off eliminating some of its customers, even if this results in a noticeable revenue decline.

---

**EXAMPLE**

Dude Skis sells to Stuffy Skis, which is a high-end retailer of the most expensive all-mountain skis, as well as Warehouse Sports, which retails the lowest-cost skis through many outlets to beginner skiers. The skis that Dude sells to Stuffy have the highest margins, and Stuffy requires little administrative support. Warehouse buys in massive volume, but only buys low-margin items, and returns 20% of its purchases under various pretexts in order to clear out its inventory at the end of the season. Dude's management wants to know how much it earns from each customer, and whether it should drop either one. Dude's chief operating officer constructs the following table:

| | Stuffy Customer | Warehouse Customer |
|---|---|---|
| Revenue | $520,000 | $2,780,000 |
| Direct costs | | |
| Materials | 210,000 | 1,390,000 |
| Direct labor | 100,000 | 550,000 |
| Customer service cost | 0 | 130,000 |
| Sales returns cost | 0 | 600,000 |
| Total direct costs | 310,000 | 2,670,000 |
| Contribution margin ($) | $210,000 | $110,000 |
| Contribution margin (%) | 40% | 4% |

In the table, there is no customer service cost at all for Stuffy Skis, since no customer service positions would be eliminated if Dude were to drop Stuffy as a customer. On the other hand, there are four customer service employees assigned to the Warehouse Sports account that would be laid off if Dude were to drop that account.

The analysis reveals that Stuffy Skis produces far more contribution margin than Warehouse Sports, despite much lower revenues. However, this does not mean that Dude should eliminate Warehouse as a customer, since it still produces $110,000 of contribution margin. If Dude has a large amount of overhead to cover, it may be necessary to continue dealing with Warehouse Sports in order to retain the associated amount of contribution margin.

---

The preceding format can be expanded to include not just a single customer, but also sales for an entire region or product line.

### Profit-Volume Relationship

Direct costing is useful for plotting changes in profit levels as sales volumes change. It is relatively simple to create a direct costing table, such as the one in the following example, which points out the volume levels at which additional direct costs will be incurred, so that management can estimate the amount of profit at different levels of corporate activity.

---

**EXAMPLE**

Dude Skis is conducting its annual budgeting process, and the accounting manager is called upon to create a profit-volume table that shows the amount of profit before taxes that Dude is likely to earn at different unit volume sales levels. The company currently produces 50,000 pairs of skis per year, and this figure is unlikely to decline. He learns that the company can produce an additional 10,000 pairs of skis without incurring any additional overhead costs. However, if the company expands production by an additional 20,000 pairs, it will incur an additional $750,000 in annual overhead expenses, and will likely also have to reduce its prices by 10% in order to achieve that volume level. Based on this information, he constructs the following table:

| | Number of Skis Sold | | |
|---|---|---|---|
| Number of ski pairs | 50,000 | 60,000 | 70,000 |
| Direct cost per pair of skis | $210 | $210 | $210 |
| Net sales price per pair sold | 380 | 380 | 342 |
| Total revenue | 19,000,000 | 22,800,000 | 23,940,000 |
| Total direct cost | 10,500,000 | 12,600,000 | 14,700,000 |
| Total period cost | 8,000,000 | 8,000,000 | 8,750,000 |
| Profit | $500,000 | $2,200,000 | $490,000 |
| Profit % | 3% | 10% | 2% |

The analysis reveals that Dude should certainly make every effort to increase its sales by an additional 10,000 units, since this will result in a significant improvement in its profitability. However, expanding by yet another 10,000 units may be a bad idea, since the company must accept lower per-unit prices as well as more overhead. In fact, the additional growth by 20,000 units, when coupled with an increased need for working capital and reduced profitability, may put the company in serious operating difficulties.

---

As just noted in the preceding example, include a working capital analysis with any profit-volume analysis, so that management can see the cost of expansion in terms of the increased investment in accounts receivable, payable, and inventory. Working capital is the amount of an entity's current assets minus its current liabilities, and is considered to be a prime measure of its level of liquidity.

---

**EXAMPLE**

To continue with the preceding example, the management of Dude Skis is concerned about the working capital impact of expanding the business by 20,000 pairs of skis, and so it asks the accounting staff for a revised analysis that includes projected working capital costs for the baseline scenario of 50,000 units, and for the highest-volume scenario of 70,000 units. The following table presents this information:

| | Number of Skis Sold | |
|---|---:|---:|
| Number of ski pairs | 50,000 | 70,000 |
| Total revenue | $19,000,000 | $23,940,000 |
| Profit | 500,000 | 490,000 |
| | | |
| Working capital components | | |
| + Accounts receivable | +$1,600,000 | +$2,400,000 |
| + Inventory | +3,200,000 | +4,000,000 |
| - Accounts payable | -1,100,000 | -1,300,000 |
| Total working capital | $3,700,000 | $5,100,000 |

The working capital assumptions in the table are that the same proportions of inventory and accounts payable will carry forward from the 50,000 unit activity level to the 70,000 unit activity level. However, the accounts receivable investment is assumed to increase, since the company will be making many of the incremental sales to a new group of retailers who are assumed to pay slower than the current group of retailers.

The working capital analysis reveals that Dude Skis would have to invest an extra $1,400,000 in its business in order to grow to a 70,000 unit level, while earning a somewhat lower profit. Clearly, the company should avoid this expansion, though the 60,000 unit sales level noted in the preceding example has a much better payoff, and should be considered.

---

## Outsourcing

Direct costing is useful for deciding whether to manufacture an item in-house or maintain a capability in-house, or whether to outsource it. If the decision involves manufacturing in-house or elsewhere, it is crucial to determine how many staff and which machines will actually be eliminated; in many cases, these resources are simply shifted elsewhere within the company, so there is no net profit improvement by shifting production to a supplier.

**EXAMPLE**

Dude Skis currently has a small plastic injection molding operation in-house, from which it molds the tip and tail guards for its skis. A local plastic injection molding firm visits Dude Skis and offers to produce these items for $0.41 per set. Management asks the accounting staff to determine whether this will result in improved profits for the company, using the assumption that the company would sell its injection molding machine if the supplier's offer is accepted.

According to Dude's cost records, the cost of a set of tip and tail guards is $0.56, which is comprised of the following items:

| Cost Items | Direct Costs | Overhead |
|---|---|---|
| Resin | $0.25 | |
| Color | 0.02 | |
| Scrap | 0.01 | |
| Injection molder depreciation | 0.03 | |
| Injection molder maintenance | 0.02 | |
| Injection molding labor | 0.05 | |
| Injection molding labor benefits | 0.01 | |
| Manufacturing overhead | | $0.12 |
| Administrative overhead | | 0.5 |
| Total | $0.39 | $0.17 |

In the preceding table, the injection molder depreciation cost of $0.03 per unit would not have been included if the company had chosen to keep the machine. However, since it plans to sell the machine if it accepts the supplier's offer, the depreciation is directly related to the decision, and so is a direct cost.

The costs comprising the overhead allocations will not decline if the company outsources this component, so the overhead is not a direct cost.

The table reveals that the direct costs associated with the analysis are lower than the supplier's offered price, so the company should reject the outsourcing option and continue to produce the tip and tail guards in-house. This decision is also reasonable from a risk management perspective, since Dude Skis would otherwise be permanently eliminating its capability to produce the part in-house, which could potentially leave it at the mercy of any price increases later imposed by the supplier.

## Direct Costing Pitfalls

Direct costing is an analysis tool, but it is only usable for certain types of analysis. In some situations, it can provide incorrect results. This section describes the key issues with direct costing to be aware of. They are:

- *Increasing costs.* Direct costing is sometimes targeted at whether to increase production by a specific amount in order to accept an additional customer order. For the purposes of this specific decision, the usual assumption is that the direct cost of the decision will be the same as the historical cost. However, the cost may actually increase. For example, if a machine is already running at 80% of capacity and a proposed decision will increase its use to 90%, this incremental difference may very well result in a disproportionate increase in the maintenance cost of the machine. Thus, be aware that a specific direct costing scenario may contain costs that are only relevant within a narrow range; outside of that range, costs may be substantially different.

---

**EXAMPLE**

Dude Skis has received an inquiry from a Japanese ski manufacturer that wants to outsource a production run of 5,000 skis. The total revenue from the proposed deal is $1,000,000 and Dude's direct cost is projected to be $800,000, which is based on the $700,000 of materials and $100,000 of labor required to manufacture the skis. Therefore, it initially appears that Dude can earn $200,000 on the deal.

However, Dude's production equipment is fully utilized during its single shift of operation, so this order will require employing a second shift that is paid a 10% shift differential, as well as an on-site supervisor and maintenance technician. There will also be an assumed 10% scrap rate caused by having a less well-trained work force on that shift. These additional costs are:

| Cost Item | Amount |
|---|---|
| Overtime | $10,000 |
| Scrap | 70,000 |
| Supervisor | 65,000 |
| Maintenance technician | 45,000 |
| Total | $190,000 |

Given that these additional costs leave a paltry $10,000 profit, Dude should either reject the inquiry or negotiate a higher price. The increased costs associated with the production being outside of Dude's normal operating range cause the deal (as proposed) to fail.

---

- *Indirect costs.* Direct costing does not account for indirect costs, because it is designed for short-term decisions where indirect costs are not expected to change. However, all costs change over the long term, which means that a decision that can impact a company over a long period of time should address long-term changes in indirect costs. Consequently, if a company uses an ongoing series of direct cost analyses to drive its pricing decisions, it may end up with an overall pricing structure that is too low to pay for its overhead costs. This is an especially pernicious problem for companies with a very high proportion of overhead costs, such as information technology companies that invest heavily in new products.

---

**EXAMPLE**

Dude Skis has a new software development group that has created a downloadable software product that allows skiers to track which runs they have skied each day, when tied into the global positioning chips on their smart phones. Under a direct costing analysis, the only cost to the company when a sale is made is a 2% credit card fee. However, Dude's programming team costs $200,000 per year, and charging a vanishingly small fee for the product will never pay for the overhead cost.

Instead, Dude's marketing manager conducts a survey of the market, learns that there is a potential market of 50,000 users at a price point of $10 per download, and accordingly prices the product at $10. This approach comfortably generates enough cash to pay for the related amount of overhead, also creates an additional profit, and is not based in any way on the direct cost of the product.

---

- *Relevant range.* A direct costing analysis is usually only valid within the constraints of the current capacity level. It requires a more sophisticated form of direct costing analysis to account for changes in costs as sales volumes or production volumes increase. This shortcoming can be overcome by consulting with the industrial engineering staff to determine additional capacity costs.

---

**EXAMPLE**

Dude Skis is considering an expansion of a prototype skiing platform for disabled skiers. It constructed 100 units as a pilot project, and sold them easily at a price of $2,000 and a direct cost of $750 each. Initial forecasts indicate that Dude could sell 5,000 units per year. Thus, the initial analysis indicates that Dude could earn a contribution margin of $6,250,000 on this new opportunity.

The trouble is that the direct costing analysis is based on the costs incurred during a pilot project. Launching a fully-equipped and properly managed product line will introduce an additional $1,000,000 per year of depreciation costs, as well as $4,000,000 of overhead costs that are directly related to the product. Consequently, the new product will be more likely to earn $1,250,000 per year than the $6,250,000 that was initially indicated.

---

## The Problem with Overhead Allocation

The major accounting frameworks mandate that a company record inventory items at their full cost. Full cost is the aggregation of all costs associated with a product, so that one can see the total cost of all materials, labor, and overhead that relate to that item. Most companies deal with this requirement by accumulating all of their manufacturing overhead costs into a spreadsheet and allocating it to products by any means – they really do not care what allocation method is used, since they are just fulfilling an accounting requirement.

Over time, the amount of overhead as a proportion of a company's costs has swelled, until it comprises the bulk of all expenditures. When managers are interested in interpreting where these costs come from, their accountants dredge up the same allocation model used for allocating costs to inventory, and apply it to every question that managers ask. For example, if a manager wants to know the cost of a specific product, the answer is to apply the entire pool of overhead costs to that product, so that the allocation includes a number of expenses that bear no relationship to the product at all.

Managers usually react to these generic allocations in one of two ways. They may feel that the accountants do not know what they are doing and throw out the allocations as pure rubbish. Or, they may believe that the accountants are experts, and therefore trust their pronouncements with the same gravity accorded those of a religious leader. The first reaction is unfortunate but justified, while the second can result in a dangerous dependence on information that is not appropriately matched to the circumstances.

We have thus far addressed the general problem posed by overhead – it is an amorphous mass that is difficult to apply to specific situations. Here are more targeted issues:

- *Automation cost allocation.* If a company uses automated production equipment to eliminate direct labor personnel and it is using direct labor as its basis of allocation, overhead costs will be under-applied to those jobs using the automation and over-applied to those jobs not using automation. The reason is that the automated jobs use less direct labor, so the allocation system will not assign them as much overhead. Meanwhile, jobs not using the automation are still using a sizeable amount of direct labor, so a proportionally greater amount of overhead (which is also increased by the depreciation expense associated with the automated machinery) is allocated to those jobs. This makes labor-intensive jobs look less profitable than they really are, while the reverse situation occurs for jobs using more automation.

---

**EXAMPLE**

Lowry Locomotion produces toy cars. Its engineering manager is considering installing an automated packaging machine on one production line located in its Chicago facility that makes toy fire trucks. Doing so will require an investment in new machinery that will add \$50,000 of depreciation to overhead, and will eliminate \$1.50 per unit of direct labor. The company currently allocates overhead based on the amount of direct labor consumed.

After the installation is complete, the total amount of overhead has increased from \$450,000 to \$500,000, while the total amount of direct labor consumed by a toy fire truck has declined from \$6.00 to \$4.50. The total direct labor used throughout the Chicago facility has declined from \$400,000 to \$350,000. The calculation of its overhead allocation before and after the installation of automated equipment is:

| Overhead Per Dollar of Direct Labor Calculation | |
|---|---|
| Before automation | \$450,000 overhead ÷ \$400,000 labor = \$1.13 per \$ of direct labor |
| After automation | \$500,000 overhead ÷ \$350,000 labor = \$1.43 per \$ of direct labor |

Before automation, the toy fire truck consumed \$6.00 of direct labor, so the amount of overhead assigned to each truck was \$6.78 (\$6.00 direct labor × \$1.13 overhead allocation). After automation, the toy fire truck consumes \$4.50 of direct labor, so the amount of overhead assigned to each truck declines to \$6.44 (\$4.50 direct labor × \$1.43 overhead allocation). Consequently, the method of overhead allocation drives down the full cost of the fire truck.

After automation, the entire Chicago facility still uses \$350,000 of direct labor, of which \$250,000 is used on another production line that manufactures toy racing cars. Prior to the automation, the racing car line had a total overhead allocation of \$282,500 (\$250,000 direct labor × \$1.13 overhead allocation). Following automation, the racing car line still uses the same amount of labor, but its overhead allocation has increased to \$357,500 (\$250,000 direct labor × \$1.43 overhead allocation).

Thus, the overhead allocation to the fire truck has declined because its allocation base has declined, while the additional overhead has now shifted to the racing car product, simply because its allocation base did not decline. The shift in allocation between the two product lines is so extreme that the racing car line is now absorbing an additional \$75,000 of overhead, even though the total amount of overhead only increased by \$50,000; this is because the racing car line has proportionally more of the allocation base than it did before the automation project was completed.

---

**Note:** An allocation base is the basis upon which an entity allocates its overhead costs. It takes the form of a quantity, such as machine hours used, kilowatt hours consumed, or square footage occupied. The allocation base should be a cause, or driver, of the cost being allocated. A good indicator that an allocation base is appropriate is when changes in the allocation base roughly correspond to changes in the actual cost. Thus, if machine usage declines, so too should the actual cost incurred to operate the machine.

- *Batch-level allocations.* A large amount of overhead cost is associated with the initiation and termination of product batches, which involve machine configurations and testing, as well as the pre-positioning of materials and tools at the production line. Consequently, small-batch jobs have high batch costs on a per-unit basis, while large-batch jobs have low batch costs on a per-unit basis. When an overhead application system only has one basis of allocation, overhead costs are under-applied to small jobs and over-applied to large jobs, so that the smaller jobs look more profitable. This mis-allocation may lead management to seek out smaller orders from customers, which ultimately lowers overall profitability.

---

**EXAMPLE**

Lowry Locomotion's Denver facility has two product lines. One produces toy tractors, and the other manufactures toy dump trucks. The toy tractors are produced in a multitude of different sizes and features, since customers demand it. Customers are less discriminating with dump trucks, so that Lowry can operate very long-term production runs of the same model. The facility produces 20,000 tractors and 280,000 dump trucks per year.

The total cost of batch setups in the Denver facility is $150,000, which is spread across the 300,000 toys produced at a standard overhead charge of $0.50 per unit. The trouble is that the dump trucks have run under a single batch setup for the entire year, while there have been 299 batch setups for the tractor line. Consequently, the allocation is wildly incorrect. Nearly all of the batch setup cost should be charged to the tractors. The calculation is:

$150,000 Total setup cost × (299 ÷ 300) = $149,500 Setup cost related to tractors

The $149,500 should be allocated to the 20,000 tractors that were produced in the measurement period, which is $7.48 per unit, rather than the $0.50 that is currently used.

---

- *Large proportion of overhead to allocation base.* A very common problem is that the amount of overhead to be allocated greatly exceeds the size of the allocation base, so that a small change in the allocation base results in a large change in the amount of overhead applied. The most common example is using direct labor as the allocation base – if the amount of direct labor in a company is $1 million and the amount of overhead is $5 million, $5 of overhead is being allocated to a product that only uses $1 of direct labor.

This situation can arise with any excessively small allocation base, and results in unjustifiable swings in applied overhead costs.

- *Single allocation base*. There can be a great variety of costs in overhead, and many of them have no cause-and-effect relationship with the single allocation base that is normally used. For example, the most common allocation base is direct labor, and yet such common overhead costs as rent, depreciation, and utilities are not impacted in any way by direct labor.

After perusing this list of allocation problems, one will likely feel that any overhead allocation is only accurate by mistake, because the typical system is not really designed to allocate overhead with any degree of precision. Activity-based costing was designed to side-step these shortcomings and provide overhead allocations that represent meaningful costing information. We address this concept in the next section.

## Activity-Based Costing

Activity-based costing (ABC) is designed to give better information about how to allocate overhead costs. It works best in complex environments, where there are many machines and products, and tangled processes that are not easy to sort out. ABC has nothing to do with the assignment of direct materials or direct labor to products or services; that assignment is already handled adequately by bills of material and labor routings, which identify the specific materials and labor steps required to produce a product.

Activity-based costing is best explained by walking through its various steps. They are:

1. *Identify costs*. The first step in ABC is to identify those costs that we want to allocate. This is the most critical step in the entire process, since we do not want to waste time with an excessively broad project scope. For example, if we want to determine the full cost of a distribution channel, we will identify advertising and warehousing costs related to that channel, but will ignore research costs, since they are related to products, not channels.
2. *Load secondary cost pools*. A cost pool is a grouping of individual costs, typically by department or service center. Create cost pools for those costs incurred to provide services to other parts of the company, rather than directly supporting a company's products or services. The contents of these secondary cost pools typically include computer services and administrative salaries, and similar costs. These costs are later allocated to other cost pools that more directly relate to products and services. There may be several secondary cost pools, depending upon the nature of the costs and how they will be allocated. For example, if there is a large cost associated with computer services, store these costs separately in a cost pool and allocate them based on computer usage. If there is another cost pool that contains building costs, allocate these costs based on square footage used.

3. *Load primary cost pools.* Create a set of cost pools for those costs more closely aligned with the production of goods or services. It is very common to have separate cost pools for each product line, since costs tend to occur at this level. Such costs can include research and development, advertising, procurement, and distribution. Similarly, consider creating cost pools for each distribution channel, or for each facility. If production batches are of greatly varying lengths, consider creating cost pools at the batch level, to assign costs based on batch size. It is not common to create cost pools at the individual product level, since only direct material and direct labor costs are usually aggregated at this level.
4. *Measure activity drivers.* An activity driver is the most significant cause of an activity. An example of an activity driver is the number of customer orders, which is used to allocate order entry costs to individual customers. A defensible activity driver is one where there is a strong causal relationship between the cost pool and the activity. Thus, if the activity does not occur, the cost in the related cost pool is not incurred. Use a data collection system to collect information about the activity drivers that are used to allocate the costs in secondary cost pools to primary cost pools, as well as to allocate the costs in primary cost pools to cost objects. It can be expensive to accumulate activity driver information, so use activity drivers for which information is already being collected, where possible.
5. *Allocate costs in secondary pools to primary pools.* Use activity drivers to apportion the costs in the secondary cost pools to the primary cost pools.
6. *Charge costs to cost objects.* A cost object is any item for which costs are separately being measured. Examples of cost objects are products, services, departments, machining operations, processes, suppliers, customers, distribution channels, and geographic regions. Use an activity driver to allocate the contents of each primary cost pool to cost objects. There will be a separate activity driver for each cost pool. To allocate the costs, divide the total cost in each cost pool by the total amount of activity in the activity driver, to establish the cost per unit of activity. Then allocate the cost per unit to the cost objects, based on their use of the activity driver.
7. *Formulate reports.* Convert the results of the ABC system into reports for management consumption. For example, if the system was originally designed to accumulate overhead information by geographical sales region, report on revenues earned in each region, all direct costs, and the overhead derived from the ABC system. This gives management a full cost view of the results generated by each region.
8. *Act on the information.* The most common management reaction to an ABC report is to reduce the quantity of activity drivers used by each cost object. Doing so should reduce the amount of overhead cost being used.

We have now arrived at a complete ABC allocation of overhead costs to those cost objects that deserve to be charged with overhead costs. By doing so, managers can see which activity drivers need to be reduced in order to shrink a corresponding amount of overhead cost. For example, if the cost of a single purchase order is $100, managers can focus on letting the production system automatically place purchase orders, or on using procurement cards as a way to avoid purchase orders. Either solution results in fewer purchase orders and therefore lower purchasing department costs.

---

**EXAMPLE**

Lowry Locomotion's president commissions a benchmarking study of various company processes, which concludes that the company's purchasing function is more expensive than the purchasing functions of competing companies. The president supports the creation of an ABC project to determine why Lowry's purchasing is so expensive.

The project is assigned to the purchasing manager, David Johnston. Mr. Johnston accesses the general ledger accounts for the purchasing department, and finds that its annual expenditures are:

| Expense Item | Amount |
|---|---|
| Salaries | $500,000 |
| Benefits | 75,000 |
| Travel and entertainment | 65,000 |
| Payroll taxes | 40,000 |
| Rent | 20,000 |
| Office supplies | 10,000 |
| Total | $710,000 |

He then conducts a time study in the purchasing department to determine which activities consume the staff's time. He compiles the following information:

| Purchasing Activity | Time Spent |
|---|---|
| Researching purchase orders | 50% |
| Purchase order follow up | 30% |
| Supplier visits | 20% |
| Total | 100% |

Mr. Johnston creates a separate cost pool for each of the three activities and allocates the $710,000 of expenses consumed by the department to them, using the following calculation:

| Cost Pool | Time Spent | Direct Allocation | Proportional Allocation | Total Allocation |
|---|---|---|---|---|
| Research purchase orders | 50% | | $322,500 | $322,500 |
| Purchase order follow up | 30% | | 193,500 | 193,500 |
| Supplier visits | 20% | $65,000 | 129,000 | 194,000 |
| Totals | 100% | $65,000 | $645,000 | $710,000 |

The travel and entertainment portion of the department's expenses are clearly associated with the supplier visits activity, so he shifts that entire cost to the Supplier Visits cost pool. All remaining costs are allocated among the cost pools based on the staff time spent on each one.

Mr. Johnston then investigates which activity drivers would be most appropriate for each cost pool. His conclusions are:

| Cost Pool | Activity Driver | Reasoning |
|---|---|---|
| Researching purchase orders | Number of jobs released | Purchase orders are compiled and issued at the start of every production job |
| Purchase order follow up | Number of purchase orders | The department has a policy of contacting suppliers about every purchase order one week before they are due for delivery |
| Supplier visits | Number of suppliers | The department visits every supplier once every three years |

Next, Mr. Johnston compiles volume information for the activity drivers. Job information is readily available from the logistics department, purchase orders are already compiled within the purchasing department, and the supplier count is available in the accounting database. Thus, all three activity measures cost little to monitor. He then adds the activity volume to the following table to derive the cost per unit of activity driver:

| Activity Driver | Activity Volume | Related Cost Pool | Cost in Related Cost Pool | Activity Driver Cost/Unit |
|---|---|---|---|---|
| Number of jobs released | 3,000 | Researching purchase orders | $322,500 | $107.50 |
| Number of purchase orders | 20,000 | Purchase order follow up | 193,500 | 9.68 |
| Number of suppliers | 400 | Supplier visits | 194,000 | 485.00 |
| Total | | | $710,000 | |

At this point, there is no need to allocate the purchasing costs even further, at the product level. There are several obvious conclusions from the research project, which Mr. Johnston includes in the following memo to the president:

- *Researching purchase orders*. Purchase orders are tied to job releases, and it is unlikely that the company will substantially alter the number of jobs.
- *Purchase order follow up*. Follow up calls are based on a department policy to follow up on 100 percent of all purchase orders. This can be restricted to monitor only those suppliers who have a history of faulty deliveries.

**Recommendation:** Create a receiving procedure to create a supplier ranking system, and eliminate all suppliers who persist in faulty deliveries. The result should be the complete elimination of purchase order follow up.

- *Supplier visits*. There is a substantial $485 cost associated with visiting every supplier on a rotating basis. This is a policy issue, and so can be fixed with a policy change.

**Recommendation:** To only visit those suppliers with whom the company spends at least $100,000 per year. This will eliminate 75% of the supplier visits, and thereby reduce costs by $145,500 (300 eliminated visits × $485 per visit).

The ABC study indicates high costs at the activity driver level for all three cost pools. The key issue was how the ABC research uncovered the existence of two purchasing department policies that were significant factors in driving up the cost of the department. By altering the policies, Lowry was able to eliminate a large part of its purchasing expense.

---

The inner workings of an ABC system can directly affect its cost. Here are several issues to consider:

- *Number of cost pools*. It is quite possible for an overly enthusiastic accountant to create a blizzard of cost pools, and end up monitoring dozens of them. This introduces too much complexity to the ABC calculations. Instead, try to limit the system to no more than a dozen cost pools.
- *Refresh rate for activity drivers*. Consider the amount of time it takes to accumulate information about activity drivers, and incorporate this information into the number of times per year that an update is conducted. For example, if the purchasing staff spends 40% of its time creating purchase orders, and this number rarely varies more than a few percent from month to month, do not impose a timekeeping regimen on the purchasing staff to refresh this information every month. Instead, just conduct an annual study. Many activity levels do not change much, and so can be refreshed only at long intervals and minimal cost.

---

**EXAMPLE**

Lowry Locomotion's accountant staff has not installed an ABC system before, and is overcome with zeal to create a highly detailed system with many cost pools and associated activity drivers. The first iteration of the implementation plan calls for data collection in the following areas:

- *Purchasing*. Track the number of purchase orders issued, reminder contacts made to suppliers, and supplier visits.
- *Manufacturing*. Track the number of machine minutes per batch, the number of machine setups, and the amount of time spent on rework.
- *Engineering*. Track the time spent on production line layouts, engineering change orders, and research and development.
- *Marketing*. Track the time spent on designing new ad campaigns, the number of ad placements, and the time spent on target costing projects.

In short, the staff wants to track everything about everyone. The best estimate of the cost of tracking the time usage of the 300 affected employees is one hour per week, at an average cost per hour of $30. The total data collection cost is therefore $468,000 (300 employees × $30/hour × 52 weeks). After learning of the projected data entry cost, the president prevails upon the controller to begin with a pilot project that only encompasses the purchase order activity in the purchasing department. Since the purchasing department already tracks the number of purchase orders created, there is no additional data entry cost at all.

---

- *Use existing activity drivers*. Few companies already compile information about activity volumes, so deciding to use a new activity driver for cost pool allocation purposes means that a new data collection system will be needed. To avoid this cost, see if there is an existing activity driver already in use that has a reasonable causal relationship with the cost pool in question, and use that instead. A causal relationship is a situation where one event is brought about by another. Thus, an activity causes specific changes elsewhere.
- *Focus on strong causal relationships*. If there is a strong causal relationship between an activity driver and a cost pool, by all means use it! A causal relationship means that a change in the activity driver changes the amount of costs incurred in the related cost pool. Therefore, if management focuses on reducing the number of activity driver occurrences, total costs will decline.

There are many possible activity drivers to choose from. The following table shows a selection of some more commonly used activity drivers.

**Sampling of Activity Drivers**

| Department Cost | Activity Driver with Causal Relationship |
|---|---|
| Accounts payable | Number of supplier invoices processed |
| | Number of checks paid |
| Accounts receivable | Number of customer invoices issued |
| | Number of collection calls made |
| | Number of cash receipts recorded |
| Facilities | Square footage used |
| Human resources | Number of full-time equivalent employees |
| | Number of training hours |
| Logistics | Number of purchase orders |
| | Number of parts in stock |
| | Number of receipts |
| | Number of shipments |
| | Number of warehouse picks |
| Order entry | Number of customer orders processed |
| | Number of customer service contacts |
| Product engineering | Hours charged to product design |
| | Number of engineering change orders |
| | Hours charged to product line process design |
| Production | Number of jobs scheduled |
| | Number of machine hours |
| | Number of maintenance work orders |
| Quality control | Number of receiving inspections |
| | Number of supplier certification visits |

To summarize activity-based costing, we shift costs from expense accounts into cost pools and then allocate these costs to cost objects using activity drivers. The activity drivers have a direct impact on changes in the cost pools with which they are associated. Cost objects are anything that incurs costs and which management wants to collect information about, such as products and services.

## Activity-Based Management

The mechanics of activity-based costing have just been noted, but what has been described thus far is really just a tool, and creates no benefit unless it is actively used. A formal methodology for doing so is activity-based management (ABM), which uses ABC information to improve company operations. ABM focuses on several key improvement areas, which are:

1. *Eliminate secondary activities*. Determine which activities are directly related to the production of products or services, and which are administrative (secondary) activities, and then work on reducing the proportion of costs spent on administrative activities. A ratio of 80:20 for production-related activities to administrative activities is very good. Activity-based costing information is needed to determine the full cost of both types of activities.
2. *Enhance customer value*. Work on reducing service backlogs by compressing the speed required to complete activities. It may also be possible to adjust activities to improve the quality of the goods and services being provided. In either case, customers are experiencing enhanced value, which may allow the company to increase its prices to reflect the improved value proposition.
3. *Reduce waste*. Determine which activities (in both the production and administrative areas) cause waste in terms of either excessive costs or time used, and work on process streamlining that reduces or eliminates these costs. This concept can be extended into the design of new products, to avoid areas in which waste occurs.
4. *Reinforce change*. Set up policies and procedures to reinforce all changes made, as well as periodic training sessions. The internal audit staff reviews the improved areas periodically and reports to management about whether the changes are taking hold in the organization. This may result in follow-up actions if slippage is detected.

---

**EXAMPLE**

An analysis team at Backwoods Survival Corporation is focusing on reducing the overhead costs associated with warehousing operations. They find that survival products are being packed into excessively large boxes. After sourcing a set of boxes whose dimensions more closely match what is being shipped, the company is able to eliminate an entire warehouse, as well as the associated overhead costs.

**EXAMPLE**

An examination of the standard reports at Catenary Corporation reveals that half of the reports compiled for use by management are never read. The president authorizes the termination of these reports, and also requires a quarterly review of the remaining reports to see if any additional ones should be eliminated. This reduction in report distribution allows the company to permanently terminate one accounting position.

---

**EXAMPLE**

The engineering manager of Active Exercise Machines examines the reports produced by the company's ABC system, and concludes that it is possible to develop an extremely low-cost and durable treadmill by avoiding a number of features that would otherwise add an excessive amount of complexity (and resource consumption) to the product. The result is a highly-popular basic treadmill that does not employ an Internet connection, fans, heart rate monitor, radio, or television connection.

---

The ABM activities just noted are all oriented inward, toward the reduction of a company's cost structure. However, it can also be used to force management thinking outward, toward better product pricing. For example, it may show that profitability on a customer order is closely tied to the frequency of delivery, the distance to the customer, and/or the size of the order. Management can then structure its pricing policies to take account of these factors.

---

**EXAMPLE**

Lowry Locomotion conducts several ABC studies and learns that a large proportion of its distributors are located outside of the local United Parcel Service (UPS) shipping zone, so that the standard shipping fee charged by Lowry is lower than the actual freight cost that it incurs. Accordingly, Lowry determines the specific UPS shipping zone for all of its customers, loads this information into the customer master file for each customer, and charges them a more accurate freight fee based on the shipping zone in which they are located.

---

In short, there are many decision areas at which ABM can be targeted. Examples of these areas are:

- How to alter the mix of goods and services being offered to increase profits
- How to design new products at specific price points that will achieve targeted margins
- How to set prices for goods and services
- Where to target process improvement and reengineering efforts
- Whether a proposed investment is justified
- Whether production facilities are competitive
- Whether to accept pricing proposals from customers
- Whether to outsource certain activities
- Whether to set minimum run sizes and make-to-order quantities
- Which activities to focus on in order to achieve a target price
- Whether costs will be affected by process changes or changes in transaction volumes
- Which customers to pursue and which ones to drop
- Which distribution channels to emphasize and which ones to de-emphasize

- Which goods and services to push and which ones to de-emphasize
- Which marketing tools are yielding the best returns, and which should be dropped
- Which prices to charge for the use of internal service departments
- Which properties produce the most income, and which ones should be sold off

Given the broad range of decision areas in which improvements can be obtained, ABM should be considered a significant tool in the enhancement of decisions throughout a business. A likely outcome is that profits will improve; even a profit increase of a few percent can represent the difference between a painful decline and long-term success in many industries.

Most organizations do not track the cost of their activities. Instead, they are more inclined to aggregate costs at the level of a department, so that they have an understanding of the total cost of (for example) the engineering department or the production department. A smaller business may instead choose to track costs by expense type, such as for bank fees, compensation, or benefits. In neither case is there any visibility into the cost of the activities that comprise the actual operations of the business. In the following exhibit, we note how these reporting structures differ. The exhibit reveals three ways to report on the expenses incurred by a manufacturing business.

**Types of Cost Reporting**

| Departmental Reporting | | Expense Reporting | | Activity Reporting | |
|---|---|---|---|---|---|
| Department | Expense | Expense Type | Expense | Activity | Expense |
| Accounting | $35,000 | Compensation | $250,000 | Assemble goods | $540,000 |
| Engineering | 25,000 | Depreciation | 50,000 | Bill customers | 20,000 |
| Legal | 10,000 | Direct materials | 345,000 | Order materials | 95,000 |
| Marketing | 20,000 | Rent | 80,000 | Receive goods | 70,000 |
| Production | 610,000 | Travel | 30,000 | Ship goods | 50,000 |
| Purchasing | 100,000 | Utilities | 45,000 | Take orders | 25,000 |
| | $800,000 | | $800,000 | | $800,000 |

In the preceding exhibit, the total reported amount is the same for all three types of cost reporting. Each type of reporting is useful, for different reasons. The manager responsible for the accounting department wants to see the total expense performance for that department, and so might prefer the departmental format. The expense reporting format provides an additional level of detail, and so would likely be in high demand as well. However, neither one clarifies *why* an expense exists – that is where activity reporting becomes the best available reporting method, since it is a strong indicator of the areas in a business that require attention.

In the following exhibit, we compare the traditional expense reporting format for a payroll department to an activity reporting format. When the traditional format is used, no obvious cost reduction possibilities are apparent. However, the activity reporting approach zeroes in on the high-cost activities at once, which strongly suggests what should be done.

**Comparison of Payroll Department Expense and Activity Reporting**

| Expense Reporting Format | | Activity Reporting Format | |
|---|---|---|---|
| Compensation and benefits | $350,000 | Collect and approve timesheets | $280,000 |
| Occupancy | 80,000 | Calculate payroll | 105,000 |
| Bank fees | 25,000 | Process tax filings | 40,000 |
| Postage | 20,000 | Correct data entry errors | 35,000 |
| Office supplies | 15,000 | Enter deduction changes | 30,000 |
| Data processing | 10,000 | Distribute paychecks | 10,000 |
| Total | $500,000 | | $500,000 |

In the preceding exhibit, the activity report shows that the primary target for expense reductions must be the collection and approval of timesheets, which comprises more than half the costs of the payroll department. Several other activities also represent opportunities for improvement, but the amount of potential savings associated with them is much lower than for the timesheet activity.

As noted earlier, there are many decision areas at which an ABM project can be targeted. As an example, consider the effects arising from an ABM review of customer profitability. By assigning activity costs to customers, management can gain a solid understanding of the respective profitability levels associated with each one. There are several uses for this information. One option is to aggregate customers (and their profits) by market segment. By doing so, management can see which segments earn the highest profits, and so may be worth the most concentrated effort to obtain additional customers. Conversely, this analysis can point out which market segments require reduced investments, or even strategic withdrawals.

A common reaction to a report on customer profitability is to terminate relationships with those on which the company is losing money. While this may be a valid option, the company may be walking away from a customer that could grow into a substantial purchaser. Also, the company may need to build its expertise within a specific market niche, which requires it to hold onto all customers. In addition, there may be high customer acquisition costs in some industries, which makes it difficult to walk away from established customers. Consequently, when dropping customers does not appear to be a valid option, an alternative is to change the manner in which the company does business with them; the intent is to reduce activity costs, which in turn increases profits at the customer level. Here are several possibilities:

- Encourage customers to place orders less frequently, but in larger volumes. By doing so, the costs associated with recording customer orders will be reduced.

- Encourage customers to place electronic orders that are routed directly into the company's computer system, thereby sidestepping all ordering costs.
- Encourage customers to shift their purchases from lower-profit to higher-profit products.
- Encourage customers to buy in standard quantities, thereby avoiding the cost of breaking down standard shipping quantities.
- Encourage customers to use an automated customer service line to check on the status of their orders, rather than talking to a customer service representative.
- Change the types of sales calls made to customers to a lower-cost form, such as switching from an in-person meeting to a phone call. A variation is to lengthen sales call frequency, or to mix in-person contacts with phone contacts.
- Strip away non-value added activities from the sales staff, so that they can make more sales calls, thereby reducing the cost per sales contact.
- Impose penalties for cancelling or changing orders, so that the related costs can be avoided.
- Impose fees for expedited orders, since expediting disrupts the production process and imposes numerous costs on the company.
- Impose fees for the use of technical support, to minimize support costs.
- Impose fees for nonstandard handling of products, to minimize these costs.
- Offer special pricing during periods when customer-related activities are fully staffed, but customer order volumes have a history of being low.

When it simply makes no sense to retain customers that generate no profits, a reasonable solution is to let them go. By doing so, a competitor with a less refined costing system will probably take on the business, which will interfere with their profitability. Thus, dropping selected customers can represent a strategic advantage.

## Summary

Direct costing is an excellent analysis tool. It is used to extract pertinent information from a variety of sources and aggregate the information to assist management with any number of tactical decisions. It is most useful for short-term decisions, and least useful when a longer-term time frame is involved - especially in situations where a company must generate sufficient margins to pay for a large amount of overhead. Though useful, direct costing information is problematic in situations where incremental costs may change significantly, or where indirect costs may be pertinent to the decision.

This chapter has also shown the significant uses to which activity-based costing can be put. These advantages are all related to cost analyses that can be used to pare away at the cost structure of a business. The primary problem with ABC is that it requires a data collection system that is different from the one used by any accounting system, so it requires a company to create an entirely new system that runs in conjunction with the main accounting system – and that requires both money and employee time to create and maintain. Because of the significant investment in time and money, it is best to carefully define the mission of an ABC system before implementing it, so that management can spend the minimum amount in exchange for receiving a precisely defined set of actionable information.

Activity-based management can be used to enhance the performance of a business and support better decision-making. The result is usually reduced costs while maintaining stable revenues, but ABM can also support the more rapid development of products by stripping out non-value added activities, which in turn can increase sales. Yet another benefit is the acceleration of the speed with which processes are completed, which can enhance the service level provided to customers. And finally, management can decide which activities it wants to enhance, giving it the ability to construct a competitive advantage to offer customers. Given these benefits, ABM can be a valuable management tool.

# Chapter 12
# Target Costing

## Introduction

A fundamental flaw in the role of the accountant is the focus on reporting costs that *are* – the costs that are already in existence. Costs tend to continue in the same proportions into the future, so managers using this information cannot do a great deal to improve a company's profitability based on its existing cost structure.

The primary management concept that can change this situation is *target costing*, under which a company plans in advance for the product price points, product costs, and margins that it wants to achieve. If it cannot manufacture a product at these planned levels, it cancels the product entirely. With target costing, a management team has a powerful tool for continually monitoring products from the moment they enter the design phase and onward throughout their product life cycles. This chapter describes how target costing works.

**Related Podcast Episode:** Episode 57 of the Accounting Best Practices Podcast discusses target costing. It is available at: **accountingtools.com/podcasts** or **iTunes**

## The Basic Steps of Target Costing

Target costing has been in existence for a number of years and is used by many companies, so the primary steps in the process are well defined. They are:

1. *Conduct research.* The first step is to review the marketplace in which the company wants to sell products. The product design team needs to determine the set of product features that customers are most likely to buy, and the amount they will pay for those features. The team learns about the perceived value of individual features, in case they later need to determine what impact there will be on the product price if they drop one or more features. It may be necessary to later drop a product feature if the team decides that it cannot provide the feature while still meeting its target cost. At the end of this process, the team has a good idea of the target price at which it can sell the proposed product with a certain set of features, and how it must alter the price if it drops some features from the product.
2. *Calculate maximum cost.* The company provides the design team with a mandated gross margin that the proposed product must earn. By subtracting the mandated gross margin from the projected product price, the team can easily determine the maximum target cost that the product must achieve before it can be allowed into production.

3. *Engineer the product.* The engineers and procurement personnel on the team now take the leading role in creating the product. The procurement staff is particularly important if the product has a high proportion of purchased parts; they must determine component pricing based on the necessary quality, delivery, and quantity levels expected for the product. They may also be involved in outsourcing parts, if this results in lower costs. The engineers design the product to meet the cost target, which will likely include a number of design iterations to see which combination of revised features and design considerations results in the lowest cost.
4. *Ongoing activities.* Once a product design is finalized and approved, the team is reconstituted to include fewer designers and more industrial engineers. The team now enters into a new phase of reducing production costs, which continues for the life of the product. For example, cost reductions may come from waste reductions in production (known as kaizen costing), or from planned supplier cost reductions. Kaizen costing is the process of continual cost reduction that occurs after a product design has been completed and is now in production. Cost reduction techniques can include working with suppliers to reduce the costs in their processes, or implementing less costly re-designs of the product, or reducing waste costs. These ongoing cost reductions yield enough additional gross margin for the company to further reduce the price of the product over time in response to increases in the level of competition. Kaizen costing does not generate the size of cost reductions that can be achieved through initial design changes, but it can have a cumulatively significant impact over time.

---

**EXAMPLE**

SkiPS is a maker of global positioning systems (GPS) for skiers, which they use to log how many vertical feet they ski each day. SkiPS conducts a marketing survey to decide upon the features it needs to include in its next generation of GPS device, and finds that skiers want a device they can strap to their arm or leg, and which does not require recharging during a multi-day vacation.

The survey indicates that skiers are willing to pay no more than $150 for the device, while the first review of costs indicates that it will cost $160 to manufacture. At a mandated gross margin percentage of 40%, this means that the device must attain a target cost of $90 ($150 price × (1 – 40% gross margin). Thus, the design team must reduce costs from $160 to $90.

The team decides that the GPS unit requires no display screen at all, since users can plug the device into a computer to download information. This eliminates the LCD display and one computer chip. It also prolongs the battery life, since the unit no longer has to provide power to the display. The team also finds that a new microprocessor requires less power; given these reduced power requirements, the team can now use a smaller battery.

Finally, the team finds that the high-impact plastic case is over-engineered, and can withstand a hard impact with a much thinner shell. After the team incorporates all of these changes, it has reached the $90 cost target. SkiPS can now market a new device at a price point that allows it to earn a generous gross profit.

---

## Value Engineering Considerations

The product engineering process noted above in step three involves many considerations. Here are examples of ways to reduce the cost of a product in order to meet a target cost:

- *Revise the manufacturing process.* The industrial engineering staff may be called upon to create an entirely new manufacturing process that uses less labor or less expensive machinery. It is entirely possible that multiple processes will be entirely eliminated from the production process. In particular, there may be an opportunity to eliminate various quality reviews from the process if product quality can be ensured by other means.
- *Reduce durability.* It is possible that the preliminary product design incorporates a product durability level that is actually *too* robust, thereby creating an opportunity to carefully decrease the level of product durability in order to cut costs. The typical result of this change is to completely eliminate some types of structural reinforcement from the product, or to at least downgrade to a less durable material in some parts of the product.
- *Reduce product features.* It may turn out to be quite expensive to offer certain features in a product. If so, the team needs to decide if it can delete one or more of these features while accepting a lower projected product price for which the net effect is an improved product margin. This type of value engineering must be weighed against the problem of eliminating so many key features that the product will no longer be attractive to customers.
- *Reduce the number of parts.* It may be possible to simplify the design by using fewer parts, especially if doing so reduces the cost of assembling the final product. However, this concept can be taken too far, especially when many standard parts are replaced by a smaller number of customized (and therefore more expensive) parts.
- *Replace components.* It is possible that slightly different components are available at a substantially reduced cost; if so, the design engineers can modify the product to accommodate the different components. This is an especially common avenue when a product is initially designed to include components that have a high per-unit cost, and which can be replaced with components on which the company already earns significant volume discounts by using them across multiple product lines.
- *Design for easier manufacture.* To avoid time-consuming mistakes in the manufacturing process, consider designing the product so that it can only be assembled in a single way – all other attempts to assemble the product in an incorrect manner will fail. By doing so, there will be fewer product failures

or recalls, which reduces the total cost of the product. It may be necessary to *increase* the cost of a product in order to create the optimum design for manufacturing, thereby reducing the total cost of the product over its full life span.

- *Ask suppliers*. Suppliers may have significant insights into how to reduce the costs of the various components they are contributing to the final product design, particularly in regard to altering material content or changing the manufacturing process. Suppliers may be willing to serve on design teams and contribute their expertise in exchange for being the sole source of selected components.

If the project team finds that it can comfortably meet the target cost without engaging in all of the preceding steps, it should work through the activity list anyways. By doing so, it can generate sufficient room between the actual and target gross margins that management now has the option to reduce the product price below the target level, which may attract additional sales.

## The Cost Reduction Program

The methods used by the design team are more sophisticated than simply saying, "folks, we need to cut $150 in costs – anyone have any ideas?" Instead, the team uses one of two approaches to more tightly focus its cost reduction efforts:

- *Tied to components*. The design team allocates the cost reduction goal among the various product components. This approach tends to result in incremental cost reductions to the same components that were used in the last iteration of the product. This approach is commonly used when a company is simply trying to refresh an existing product with a new version, and wants to retain the same underlying product structure. The cost reductions achieved through this approach tend to be relatively low, but also result in a high rate of product success, as well as a fairly short design period.
- *Tied to features*. The product team allocates the cost reduction goal among various product features, which focuses attention away from any product designs that may have been inherited from the preceding model. This approach tends to achieve more radical cost reductions (and design changes), but also requires more time to design, and also runs a greater risk of product failure or at least greater warranty costs.

Of the two methods noted here, companies are more likely to use the first approach if they are looking for a routine upgrade to an existing product, and the second approach if they want to achieve a significant cost reduction or break away from the existing design.

## The Milestone Review Process

What if the project team simply cannot meet the target cost? Rather than completing the design process and creating a product with a substandard profit margin, the correct response is to stop the development process and move on to other projects instead. This does not mean that management allows its project teams to struggle on for months or years before finally giving up. Instead, they must come within a set percentage of the cost target on various milestone dates, with each successive milestone requirement coming closer to the final target cost. Milestones may occur on specific dates, or when key completion steps are reached in the design process, such as at the end of each design iteration.

---

**EXAMPLE**

Milagro Corporation is developing a new espresso machine that only works with its specially-developed strain of coffee bean. Milagro conducts market research and concludes that the product cannot sell for more than $200. At the company's required gross margin of 40%, this means that the target cost of the product is $120. Management sets a maximum design duration of six months, with milestone reviews at one-month intervals. The results of the month-end milestone reviews are:

| Review Date | Cost Goal | Actual Cost Estimate | Actual Cost Variance from Goal | Allowed Variance From Cost Goal |
|---|---|---|---|---|
| Jan. 31 | $120 | $150 | 25% | 30% |
| Feb. 28 | 120 | 143 | 19% | 20% |
| Mar. 31 | 120 | 138 | 15% | 15% |
| Apr. 30 | 120 | 134 | 12% | 10% |
| May 31 | 120 | Cancelled | -- | 5% |
| June 30 | 120 | Cancelled | -- | 0% |

As the table reveals, the Milagro project team was able to stay ahead of the cost target at the end of the first two months, but then was barely able to meet the allowable variance in the third month, and finally fell behind in the fourth month. Management then cancelled the project, saving itself the cost of continuing the project team for several more months when it was becoming obvious that the team would not be able to achieve the target cost.

---

Though management may cancel a design project that cannot meet its cost goals, this does not mean that the project will be permanently shelved; far from it. Instead, management should review old projects at least once a year to see if the circumstances have changed sufficiently for them to possibly become viable again. A more precise review approach is to have each project team formulate a set of variables that should initiate a product review if a trigger point is reached (such as a decline in the price of a commodity that is used in the product design). If any of these trigger points are reached, the projects are immediately brought to the attention of management to see if they can be revived.

## Problems with Target Costing

Target costing is difficult to initiate, because of the uncertainty surrounding the eventual release of a product. A company that allows its engineering department sole responsibility for creating products will achieve product releases on a fairly consistent schedule, even though some of the products may not be overly profitable. Under target costing, it is quite possible that a company may cancel a series of projects before they reach fruition, resulting in a frantic marketing department that sees no new products entering the pipeline. The solution is a combination of firm support by senior management and ongoing questioning of whether the target gross margin is too high to be achievable. It is entirely possible that an overly enthusiastic management team sets an excessively high gross margin standard for its new target costing process, and then sees no products survive the process. Consequently, it may take some time before management understands what gross margin levels will result in a target costing process that can churn out an acceptable number of products.

Another problem with target costing is the unwillingness of management to cancel a project. They do not want to see their investment in a project thrown away, and so they keep funding it for "just one more month," hoping that the team will find a way to achieve the target cost. The end result is a very long design process that absorbs more design costs than expected, and which still does not achieve the target cost. The only way to resolve this issue is an iron resolve to terminate projects in a timely manner.

Finally, a design team needs a strong leader to keep control of the opinions of the various departments that are represented on the team. For example, the marketing department may hold out for certain product features, while the design engineers claim that those same features introduce too many costs into the product. The best team leader is not one who unilaterally decides on the product direction, but rather one who can craft a group decision, and if necessary weed out those who are unwilling to work with the rest of the group.

## The Members of a Design Team

The members of the design team are drawn from multiple disciplines, and their contributions are all essential to the success of a product launch. These positions are:

- *Design engineering.* The design engineers play the most prominent role on the team, since they must create a series of product iterations that incorporate the cost reductions needed to achieve the target cost.
- *Industrial engineering.* A significant part of a product's cost arises during the production process, so industrial engineers must become involved in order to give feedback to the design engineers regarding which design elements should be used that require the lowest production costs.

- *Accounting*. A cost accountant should be with the team at all times, constantly compiling the expected cost of a design as it goes through a series of iterations. The cost accountant also compares the expected cost to the target cost, and communicates the status of the product cost situation to both the team members and management on a periodic basis.
- *Procurement*. The purchasing department is a valuable contributor to the team, since many components will likely be sourced to third parties, and an experienced procurement person can have a significant positive impact on the cost of purchased components.
- *Marketing*. The marketing department is particularly useful during the initial stages of target costing, where it investigates the prices of competing products and conducts polls to determine the value of specific product features.

## The Role of Accounting in Target Costing

The accounting role on a design team is to continually compile the projected cost of the product as it moves forward through the design process. This job is assigned to a cost accountant, who compares the projected cost to the total target cost, and communicates the variance between the two figures to management, along with qualitative information about where projected costs are expected to decline further, what design changes are most likely to achieve further cost declines, and how these design changes will affect the value proposition of the final product. Management uses this information to periodically monitor the progress of the design project, and to cancel the project if it appears likely that the product cannot be designed within the cost and value parameters of the project.

It may be necessary to purchase new manufacturing equipment to create a new product. If so, the cost accountant is the best person to create purchase requests for this equipment, since part of his normal responsibilities are to review capital expenditure proposals. Also, since he obviously has a working relationship with the accounting department, he is the best intermediary for relaying any accounting questions about capital proposals.

A key part of the cost accountant's role is to obtain cost information from suppliers, which in turn is predicated on the assumption of a certain amount of purchasing volume, which may not ultimately prove to be correct. If there are significant cost differences at varying purchase volume levels, it may be necessary for the cost accountant to present several possible product costs, one for each volume level.

---

**EXAMPLE**

Active Exercise Machines is designing a new treadmill for the home exercise market, and is having trouble pricing the laminated rubber conveyor belt. Since Active is creating a treadmill in a non-standard length, the conveyor belt supplier will incur a setup cost, and must spread this cost over the projected number of treadmills to be produced. Since the setup cost is significant, the cost per unit will decline dramatically if Active orders more conveyor belts. The cost is $95 per unit if Active only orders 5,000 belts, and drops to $50 if Active orders 10,000 belts. Since the total cost of the treadmill is projected to be $500, this difference represents 9% of the total cost, which is significant enough to bring to the attention of management. Consequently, the cost accountant presents management with two projected costs for the treadmill – one at a unit volume of 5,000, and another at a unit volume of 10,000.

---

The cost accountant's cost information is likely to be vague when the project is initiated, since he is working with general design concepts and rough estimates of production volumes. Consequently, the initial cost reports are likely to be within a range of possible costs, which gradually tighten up as the team generates more precise designs and better sales estimates.

A final task is for the cost accountant to continue monitoring the cost of the product after its release, and throughout its product life. This is a key role, because management needs to know immediately if the initial cost structure that the design team worked so hard to create is no longer valid, and why the cost has increased.

The tasks ascribed to a cost accountant in his role as a member of a design team are not minor. For a larger design project, it is entirely possible that he will be released for special duty to the project, so that no other routine tasks will interfere with his work on the team. In a larger company where product design is the lifeblood of the entity, the cost accountant may find himself permanently assigned to a series of project teams.

## Data Sources for Target Costing

A target costing team may have a difficult time obtaining data from which to develop the cost of a new product design. Here are some of the data sources needed for a target costing project:

- *New components*. The design team may be creating entirely new components from scratch, so there is no cost information available. In this case, the team needs to locate roughly comparable components and extrapolate from them what the new components might cost, including tooling costs.
- *Materials sourcing*. Some materials that the design team wants to include in a product may be difficult to obtain, or be subject to significant price swings. These issues should be highlighted, particularly by using outside sources of historical commodity prices to note the range of price swings that have occurred in the recent past. It is dangerous to only report to management the current market price of these materials, since management may

decide to continue product development when it might otherwise drop the project in the face of large potential cost increases.

- *Competitor costs*. It is extremely useful to disassemble competing products to determine what they cost to produce. The cost accountant can assemble this information into a database, which is useful for not only calculating the likely gross margins that competing products are earning, but also for comparing the design team's choice of components to those used by competitors. In many instances, the design team can copy some aspects of a competing design in order to quickly achieve a lower cost.
- *Production costs*. If a company has engaged in product design for a number of years, it may have developed a table that contains the cost to produce specific components or the cost of the production functions used to create those components. This type of information is difficult to obtain, and requires a great deal of analysis to compile, so having the information available from previous design projects is a significant advantage in the design of new products.
- *Downstream costs*. When the design team modifies a product design, there is a good chance that it will cause modifications in other parts of the design, in a ripple effect. The only source of information for what these changes may be is the design team itself, which the cost accountant must regularly interview for clues about the cost effects of these changes.
- *Supplier performance data*. Suppliers are likely going to provide a significant proportion of the components of a new product, so the team needs access to the company's database of supplier performance to see if key suppliers are capable of supplying goods within the performance constraints required by the new design. This is less of a cost issue than a qualitative review of the ability of a supplier to perform within the company's specifications.

Clearly, there must be access to a broad array of data sources in order to compile a quality set of cost information. These data sources frequently do not contain the high degree of data accuracy needed, so the result is likely to be a significant degree of uncertainty in costing information, especially during the initial stages of product design.

## The Product Life Cycle and Target Costing

Target costing generates a significant and immediate cost reduction at the beginning of a product's life cycle. Kaizen costing then generates an ongoing series of smaller cost reductions that gradually decline as cost reduction opportunities are eliminated. A company that wants to stay competitive with its product offerings should carefully track the gradual decline in product costs, and replace the original product with a new one when there are minimal cost reductions still to be garnered from the old product. The new product is subjected to the same target costing approach in order to create a new value proposition for the consumer, to be followed by another round of kaizen costing.

In order to remain competitive over the long term, it is clear that a company must be aware of where its products stand within their product cycles, and be willing to replace them when there are minimal costs to be eliminated from the old designs.

## Summary

Target costing is most applicable to companies that compete by continually issuing a stream of new or upgraded products into the marketplace (such as consumer goods). For them, target costing is a key survival tool. Conversely, target costing is less necessary for those companies that have a small number of legacy products that require minimal updates, and for which long-term profitability is more closely associated with market penetration and geographical coverage (such as soft drinks).

Target costing is an excellent tool for planning a suite of products that have high levels of profitability. This is opposed to the much more common approach of creating a product that is based on the engineering department's view of what the product should be like, and then struggling with costs that are too high in comparison to the market price. Given the extremely cooperative nature of target costing across multiple departments, it can be quite a difficult change for the engineering manager to accept.

The accounting function plays a key role in target costing, since a cost accountant is the key compiler of information for the project team, keeping both them and management continually informed of progress toward the cost goals that a product must reach.

# Chapter 13
# Constraint Analysis

## Introduction

When reaching a decision, the mindset is usually that the decision should be based on a specific item or activity. The decision does not take into account the greater corporate structure within which it takes place. For example, a manager may be called upon to judge whether a product should be cancelled because of an excessively low margin, or to choose between two possible capital investments based on their cash flows. However, the impacts of these decisions are rarely considered in relation to a company's *entire* capability, as an integrated unit, to earn a profit.

Constraint analysis does the reverse – its starting point is determining which company operation is constraining the entire company from earning a greater profit, and then focuses all decision-making upon how they impact this constraint (or "bottleneck"). To use the previous two examples, it may not be judicious to cancel a product that generates *any* amount of profit, since that profit helps to pay for the overhead cost of the entire system. Further, it may not be necessary to invest in any fixed assets unless it improves the capacity of the bottleneck operation.

This chapter gives an overview of constraint analysis, and then delves into a number of management decisions where using it can alter one's perception of how to manage various aspects of a company.

**Related Podcast Episodes:** Episodes 43 through 47 of the Accounting Best Practices Podcast discuss many aspects of constraint analysis. It is available at: **accountingtools.com/podcasts** or **iTunes**

## Constraint Analysis Operational Terminology

Constraint analysis makes use of several unique terms, so we will begin with a set of definitions before proceeding to an overview of constraint analysis. The key operational terms are:

- *Drum*. This is a third variation of the *constraint* term, along with *bottleneck*. It is the operation, person, or (occasionally) the materials within a company that prevent the business from generating additional sales. Since the ultimate profitability of the company depends on this one item, it sets the pace for how the company operates. Picture the drum beating on a rowed galley, and you can see why it is called a *drum*.
- *Buffer*. The drum operation should operate at as close to 100% of capacity as possible, but this is impossible when the flow of materials from upstream

operations is unreliable. The buffer is inventory that is positioned in front of the drum operation, and which protects the drum from any stoppage in materials coming from upstream operations. The buffer may need to be quite large if there is considerable variability in the inflow of materials, or it may be of more modest proportions if the inflow is more stable.

- *Rope*. The rope represents the date and time when jobs must be released into the production process in order to have inventory arrive at the buffer just when it is needed by the drum; thus, it is really the total time duration needed to bring work-in-process to the drum.

These three terms are sometimes strung together in a single phrase, and are called the *drum-buffer-rope* system. As a group, they describe the essential operational components of constraint analysis.

## Overview of Constraint Analysis

The key points in understanding constraint analysis are the following two concepts:

1. A company is an integrated set of processes that function together to generate a profit; and
2. There is a chokepoint somewhere in a company that absolutely controls its ability to earn a profit.

The chokepoint is also known as the drum operation (as defined previously, or the bottleneck, or the constrained resource). We will refer to it as bottleneck, since the word most clearly describes its impact on an organization.

The first concept, that of a company being an integrated set of processes, applies very strongly at the product line level, but less so at the corporate parent level. At the product line level, there is almost certainly a bottleneck that restricts the ability to generate more profit. At the corporate parent level, there may be multiple subsidiaries, each with a multitude of product lines. Thus, from the perspective of the corporate parent, there are still bottlenecks, but there may be a number of them scattered throughout the operations of the subsidiaries.

The second concept, that of the bottleneck, is most typically characterized by a machine that can only process a certain number of units per day. To improve profits, a company must focus all of its attention on that machine by taking such steps as:

- Adding supplemental staff to cover any employee breaks or downtime during shift changes
- Reviewing the quality of work-in-process going into the operation, so that it does not waste any time processing items that are already defective
- Positioning extra maintenance personnel near it to ensure that service intervals are short
- Reducing the amount of processing time per unit, so that more units can be run through the machine

- Adding more capacity to the machine
- Outsourcing work to suppliers

It is also possible that the bottleneck is not in the production area at all. It may be caused by a materials shortage, or by a lack of sales staff. In those rare cases where there is simply no bottleneck to be found, the company has excess capacity, and can choose to either reduce its capacity (and the related cost) or try to sell more volume, possibly at a lower price.

---

**EXAMPLE**

Hammer Industries produces construction equipment. Its products are large, complex, and mostly sold through a request for proposals process. Its financial analyst has reviewed all production operations in detail and concluded that there is no bottleneck operation to be found. Instead, the real chokepoint appears to be in the sales department.

Hammer has a multi-tiered sales process, where one group makes initial contacts with prospective customers, another group of technical writers responds to requests for proposal (RFP), yet another group conducts sales presentations, and a fourth group conducts final contract negotiations. A brief analysis shows that the technical writers are completely overwhelmed with writing RFP responses, and have missed several RFP filing deadlines. The sales staff positioned ahead of them in the process flow, those making contacts with prospective customers, are aware of the problem and have scaled back their activities to meet with new customers, since they know the company is not capable of making timely RFP responses. Thus, it is evident that the sales department is the true company bottleneck.

The analyst reports this issue to management, and recommends a combination of additional technical writer hiring and the purchase of RFP response software to simplify the writing task.

---

It is usually not difficult to tell where a bottleneck is located, because it has a large amount of work piled up in front of it, while the work operation immediately downstream from it is starved for work.

A major part of the management of the bottleneck operation is the inventory buffer located immediately in front of it. Constraint analysis holds that there will always be flaws in the production process that result in variability in the flow of materials to the bottleneck, so build up a buffer to insulate the bottleneck from these issues. The buffer is quite large if there are lots of upstream production problems, or much smaller if the production flow is relatively placid.

If production problems start to eat into the size of the inventory buffer, the bottleneck is in danger of having a stock-out condition, which may cause it to run out of work. To avoid this, there should be a large *sprint capacity* in selected upstream production operations. Sprint capacity is essentially excess production capacity. There should be a sufficient amount of this capacity available to rapidly rebuild the inventory buffer. If a company has invested in significant sprint capacity, there is less need for a large inventory buffer.

Finally, there is the concept of the *rope* that was mentioned earlier as a key definition. It is very important to only release new jobs into the production queue so that they arrive at the inventory buffer just in time to be used. The natural inclination of a production scheduler is to release jobs too soon, to ensure that there is always a healthy flow of jobs arriving at the inventory buffer. However, doing so represents an excessive inventory investment, and also confuses the production staff, which does not know which of the plethora of jobs to process next. Thus, the rope concept represents a fine balance between overloading the system and starving it of work.

In summary, the bottleneck operation is the most important operation in a company. The management team needs to know where it is located, and spend a great deal of time figuring out how to maximize its operation so that it hardly ever stops.

## The Cost of the Bottleneck

How expensive is it when a bottleneck operation is not running? The traditional financial analysis approach would be to calculate the foregone gross margin on any products that would otherwise have been produced if it had been operational. Under constraint analysis, the calculation is the entire operating cost of the facility, divided by the bottleneck's operating hours. We use the entire cost of the facility, because the bottleneck drives the profitability of the entire facility.

For example, a bottleneck operation is running 160 hours a week, which is three shifts, less eight hours for maintenance downtime. The facility has operating expenses of $1,600,000 per week. Therefore, the cost of *not* running the bottleneck operation is $10,000 per hour. When viewed from this perspective, it very expensive indeed to stop a bottleneck operation.

---

**EXAMPLE**

Mole Industries incurs $250,000 of operational expenses per week for its Digger equipment line. The bottleneck work center is operational 150 hours per week, with the remaining 18 hours of the week being used for necessary maintenance. Thus, the cost of not running the bottleneck is $1,667 per hour ($250,000 operational expenses ÷ 150 hours per week).

The shift supervisor has received a demand from the union to give a one-hour lunch break to the three people working in the bottleneck operation, in each of the three shifts. The shift supervisor has the choice of shutting down the operation for 21 hours per week to accede to this request (7 days × 3 shifts × 1 hour per shift), or of bringing in additional staff at an astronomical $100 per hour per person to run the operation in their absence. Which is the better alternative?

*Option 1, Stop the Bottleneck:* The cost of not running the bottleneck is $1,667 per hour, so the total cost over 21 hours would be $35,000 per week.

*Option 2, Use Supplemental Staff*: The cost of using supplemental staff is $6,300 (21 hours × 3 staff × $100 per person).

Though the use of supplemental staff initially appears excessive, the cost is still far lower than shutting down the bottleneck operation.

---

The example makes it quite clear that management should never shut down a bottleneck operation. It is always less expensive to add staff to it, or do whatever else is necessary, to ensure that it keeps running.

An ancillary question is, what is the cost of running an operation that is not the bottleneck operation? It is zero. Since company operations do not hinge on any other operation, it is usually acceptable to shut them down for short periods. The only exception is when doing so may impact the bottleneck operation.

## Local Optimization

The concept of the constraint is very much at odds with the traditional concept of local optimization, where the management team works to improve the efficiency of every operation throughout a company. In many cases, these improvements do nothing to increase overall company profits, because the primary driver of profits is still the bottleneck operation. Consequently, if investments are in local optimization projects, profits do not improve, but the investment in the company increases, so the only logical outcome is that the return on investment declines. The following exhibit contains several examples of how constraint analysis alters the view of local optimization.

**Views of Constraint Analysis**

| Situation | Local Optimization Solution | Constraint Analysis Solution |
|---|---|---|
| Overtime is 10% of payroll | Restrict all overtime | Do not restrict overtime if it is being spent on the bottleneck operation, or on any operations feeding the bottleneck |
| A machine is not being utilized | Sell the machine | Keep the machine if it provides sprint capacity for the bottleneck operation |
| A product can be redesigned | Only do so if the product is at the end of its normal life cycle | Do so if the redesign reduces the product processing time at the bottleneck operation |
| The production staff is not fully utilized | Cut back on operations and lay off staff | If there is no bottleneck operation, lower prices to attract more sales |
| A machine is reaching its maximum utilization | Buy an additional machine | Only buy an additional unit if it will provide more sprint capacity. Do not buy if it is located downstream from the bottleneck operation |
| A supplier is asking us to outsource production | Do so if it passes a cost-benefit analysis | Do so if it reduces the load on the bottleneck operation |

In all of the cases noted in the table, one should step back from the individual decision and see what the impact will be on the entire company before determining the correct course of action. In particular, be aware of two problems that are caused by local optimization:

1. *Excess inventory*. If a production operation is optimized that is not the bottleneck operation, all you have done is give it the ability to churn out even more inventory than was previously the case, and which the bottleneck will be unable to process. Thus, there has not only been a needless investment in the operation, but also a needless investment in additional inventory that must now wait to be processed.
2. *Overly efficient labor*. When a good manufacturing process was considered to be one with very long production runs, there was a considerable emphasis on highly efficient labor. If there is instead a focus on maximizing the amount of production passing through the bottleneck – and nowhere else – then grossly overstaff the bottleneck operation to make sure that it is always operating, and pay much less attention to labor efficiency elsewhere. Employees should only work if inventory is actually needed. In short, it is better to have employees be underutilized and produce less inventory than to be more efficient and produce inventory that is not needed.

In summary, a company does not even have to be especially efficient in production areas located away from the bottleneck operation. Instead, the one and only focus is on maximizing the efficiency of the bottleneck. This change in focus alters most of the decisions that the manager would reach by only focusing on local optimization.

## Constraint Analysis Financial Terminology

By now it should be apparent that constraint analysis is quite a valuable tool from an operational perspective. But what about from a financial perspective? How is the concept used to make decisions? There is a model for using constraint analysis in this role, but first we need to define the terms in the model. They are:

- *Throughput*. This is the margin left after subtracting totally variable costs from revenue. This tends to be a large proportion of revenues, since all overhead costs are excluded from the calculation.
- *Totally variable costs*. This is usually just the cost of materials, since it is only those costs that vary when a company manufactures one incremental unit of a product. This does not normally include the cost of labor, since employees are not usually paid based on one incremental unit of output. There are a few other possible costs that may be totally variable, such as commissions, subcontractor fees, customs duties, and freight costs.
- *Operating expenses*. This is all company expenses other than totally variable costs. There is no differentiation between overhead costs, administrative costs or financing costs – quite simply, *all* other company expenses are lumped into this category.
- *Investment*. This is the amount invested in assets. "Investment" includes changes in the level of working capital resulting from a management decision.
- *Net profit*. This is throughput, less operating expenses.

## Constraint Analysis from a Financial Perspective

When a company is examined from the perspective of constraints, it no longer makes sense to evaluate individual products, because overhead costs do not vary at the individual product level. In reality, most companies spend a great deal of money to maintain a production infrastructure, and that infrastructure is what really generates a profit – the trick is making that infrastructure produce the maximum profit with the best mix of products having the highest possible throughput. Under the constraint analysis model, there are three ways to improve the financial position of the entire production infrastructure. They are:

- *Increase throughput*. This is by either increasing revenues or reducing the amount of totally variable costs.
- *Reduce operating expenses*. This is by reducing some element of overhead expenses.
- *Improve the return on investment*. This is by either improving profits in conjunction with the lowest possible investment, or by reducing profits slightly along with a correspondingly larger decline in investment.

Note that only the increase in throughput is related in any way to decisions made at the product level. The other two improvement methods may be concerned with changes anywhere in the production system.

## The Constraint Analysis Model

An excellent constraint analysis model was developed by Thomas Corbett, which is outlined here. The basic thrust of the model is to give priority in the bottleneck operation to those products that generate the highest throughput per minute of bottleneck time. After these products are manufactured, give priority to the product having the next highest throughput per minute, and so on. Eventually, the production queue is filled, and the operation can accept no additional work.

The key element in the model is the use of throughput per minute, because the key limiting factor in a bottleneck operation is time – hence, maximizing throughput within the shortest possible time frame is paramount. Note that throughput *per minute* is much more important than total throughput *per unit*. The following example illustrates the point.

---

**EXAMPLE**

Mole Industries manufacturers trench digging equipment. It has two products with different amounts of throughput and processing times at the bottleneck operation. The key information about these products is:

| Product | Total Throughput | Bottleneck Processing Time | Throughput per Minute |
|---|---|---|---|
| Mole Hole Digger | $400 | 2 minutes | $200 |
| Mole Driver Deluxe | 800 | 8 minutes | 100 |

Of the two products, the Mole Driver Deluxe creates the most overall throughput, but the Mole Hole Digger creates more throughput per minute of bottleneck processing time. To determine which one is more valuable to Mole Industries, consider what would happen if the company had an unlimited order quantity of each product, and could run the bottleneck operation nonstop, all day (which equates to 1,440 minutes). The operating results would be:

| Product | Throughput per Minute | | Total Processing Time Available | | Total Throughput |
|---|---|---|---|---|---|
| Mole Hole Digger | $200 | × | 1,440 minutes | = | $288,000 |
| Mole Driver Deluxe | 100 | × | 1,440 minutes | = | 144,000 |

Clearly, the Mole Hole Digger, with its higher throughput per minute, is much more valuable to Mole Industries than its Mole Driver Deluxe product. Consequently, the company should push sales of the Mole Hole Digger product whenever possible.

---

The constraint analysis model is essentially a production plan that itemizes the amount of throughput that can be generated, as well as the total amount of operating expenses and investment. In the model, we use four different products, each requiring some processing time in the bottleneck operation. The columns in the model are as follows:

- *Throughput per minute.* This is the total amount of throughput that a product generates, divided by the amount of processing time at the bottleneck operation.
- *Bottleneck usage.* This is the number of minutes of processing time required by a product at the bottleneck operation.
- *Units scheduled.* This is the number of units scheduled to be processed at the bottleneck operation.
- *Total bottleneck time.* This is the total number of minutes of processing time required by a product, multiplied by the number of units to be processed.
- *Total throughput.* This is the throughput per minute multiplied by the number of units processed at the bottleneck operation.

This grid produces a total amount of throughput to be generated if production proceeds according to plan. Below the grid of planned production, there is a subtotal of the total amount of throughput, from which the total amount of operating expenses are subtracted to arrive at the amount of profit. Finally, the total amount of investment in assets is divided into the profit to calculate the return on investment. Thus, the model provides a complete analysis of all three ways in which one can improve the results of a company – increase throughput, decrease operating expenses, or increase the return on investment. An example of the model follows:

**Sample Constraint Analysis Model**

| Product | Throughput per Minute | Bottleneck Usage (minutes) | Units Scheduled | Total Bottleneck Time | Total Throughput |
|---|---|---|---|---|---|
| 1. Hedgehog Deluxe | $80 | 14 | 1,000 | 14,000 | $1,120,000 |
| 2. Hedgehog Mini | 70 | 20 | 500 | 10,000 | 700,000 |
| 3. Hedgehog Classic | 65 | 40 | 200 | 8,000 | 520,000 |
| 4. Hedgehog Digger | 42 | 10 | 688 | 6,880 | 288,960 |
| | | Total bottleneck scheduled time | | 38,880 | |
| | | Total bottleneck time available* | | 38,880 | |
| | | | | | |
| | | | | Total throughput | $2,628,960 |
| | | | | Total operating expenses | 2,400,000 |
| | | | | Profit | $228,960 |
| | | | | Profit percentage | 8.7% |
| | | | | Investment | $23,000,000 |
| | | | | Annualized return on investment | 11.9% |

* Minutes per month (30 days × 24 hours × 60 minutes × (1 – 0.10 maintenance time)

In the example, the Hedgehog Deluxe product has the largest throughput per minute, and so is scheduled to be first priority for production. The Hedgehog Digger has the lowest throughput per minute, so it is given last priority in the production schedule. If there is less time available on the bottleneck operation, the company should reduce the number of the Hedgehog Digger product manufactured in order to maximize overall profits.

In the middle of the model, the "Total bottleneck scheduled time" row contains the total number of minutes of scheduled production. The row below it, labeled "Total bottleneck time available," represents the total estimate of time that the bottleneck should have available for production purposes during the scheduling period. Since the time scheduled and available are identical, this means that the production schedule has completely maximized the availability of the bottleneck operation.

One calculation anomaly in the model is that the profit percentage is normally calculated as profit divided by revenues. However, since revenues are not included in the model, we instead use profits divided by throughput. Since throughput is less than revenue, we are overstating the profit percentage as compared to the traditional profit percentage calculation.

One can use the constraint analysis model in a before-and-after mode, to see what effect a proposed change will have on profitability or the return on investment. If the model improves as a result of a change, then implement the change. In the next few sections, we will examine how the constraint analysis model is used to arrive at several management decisions.

## The Decision to Sell at a Lower Price

A common scenario is for a customer to promise a large order, but only if the company agrees to a substantial price drop. The sales department may favor such deals, because they bolster the company backlog, earn commissions, and increase market share. The trouble is that these deals also elbow out other jobs that may have higher throughput per minute. If so, the special deal drops overall throughput and may lead to a loss. The following example, which uses the basic constraint model as a baseline, illustrates the problem.

**EXAMPLE**

Mole Industries has received an offer from a customer to buy 2,000 units of its highly profitable Hedgehog Deluxe, but only if the company reduces the price. The new price will shrink the Deluxe's throughput per minute to $60. The analysis is:

| Product | Throughput per Minute | Bottleneck Usage (minutes) | Units Scheduled | Total Bottleneck Time | Total Throughput |
|---|---|---|---|---|---|
| 1. Hedgehog Deluxe | $60 | 14 | 2,000 | 28,000 | $1,680,000 |
| 2. Hedgehog Mini | 70 | 20 | 500 | 10,000 | 700,000 |
| 3. Hedgehog Classic | 65 | 40 | 22 | 880 | 57,200 |
| 4. Hedgehog Digger | 42 | 10 | 0 | 0 | 0 |
| | | Total bottleneck scheduled time | | 38,880 | |
| | | Total bottleneck time available* | | 38,880 | |
| | | | | Total throughput | $2,437,200 |
| | | | | Total operating expenses | 2,400,000 |
| | | | | Profit | $37,200 |
| | | | | Profit percentage | 1.5% |
| | | | | Investment | $23,000,000 |
| | | | | Annualized return on investment | 1.9% |

* Minutes per month (30 days × 24 hours × 60 minutes × (1 – 0.10 maintenance time)

The baseline production configuration generated a profit of $228,960, while this new situation creates a profit of only $37,200. The profit decline was caused by a combination of lower throughput per minute for the Hedgehog Deluxe and the increased production capacity assigned to this lower-throughput product, which displaced other, more profitable products. Note that there was no production capacity available at all for the Hedgehog Digger product. Clearly, the company should reject the customer's offer.

## The Decision to Outsource Production

One way to manage the bottleneck operation is to outsource work to keep some of the production burden away from the bottleneck. This option is always acceptable if the throughput generated by the outsourced products exceed the price charged to the company by the supplier, *and* the company can replace the throughput per minute that was taken away from the bottleneck operation. The following example, which uses the basic constraint model as a baseline, illustrates the concept.

**EXAMPLE**

Mole Industries receives an offer from a supplier to outsource the Hedgehog Classic to it. The supplier will even drop ship the product to customers, so the product would no longer impact Mole's production process in any way. The downside of the offer is that the supplier's price is higher than the cost at which Mole can produce the Classic internally, so the total monthly throughput attributable to the Classic would decline by $300,000, from $520,000 to $220,000. However, there is a large customer order backlog for the Hedgehog Digger, so Mole could give increased production priority to the Digger instead. The analysis is:

| Product | Throughput per Minute | Bottleneck Usage (minutes) | Units Scheduled | Total Bottleneck Time | Total Throughput |
|---|---|---|---|---|---|
| 1. Hedgehog Deluxe | $80 | 14 | 1,000 | 14,000 | $1,120,000 |
| 2. Hedgehog Mini | 70 | 20 | 500 | 10,000 | 700,000 |
| 3. Hedgehog Classic | 65 | 40 | 200 | N/A | 220,000 |
| 4. Hedgehog Digger | 42 | 10 | 1,488 | 14,880 | 624,960 |
| | | Total bottleneck scheduled time | | 38,880 | |
| | | Total bottleneck time available* | | 38,880 | |
| | | | | | |
| | | | | Total throughput | $2,664,960 |
| | | | | Total operating expenses | 2,400,000 |
| | | | | Profit | $264,960 |
| | | | | Profit percentage | 9.9% |
| | | | | Investment | $23,000,000 |
| | | | | Annualized return on investment | 13.8% |

* Minutes per month (30 days × 24 hours × 60 minutes × (1 – 0.10 maintenance time)

Despite a large decline in throughput caused by the outsourcing deal, the company actually earns $36,000 more profit overall, because the Hedgehog Classic uses more of the bottleneck time per unit (40 minutes) than any other product; this allows the company to fill the available bottleneck time with 800 more Hedgehog Digger products, which require the smallest amount of bottleneck time per unit (10 minutes), and which generate sufficient additional throughput to easily offset the throughput decline caused by outsourcing. Mole Industries should accept the supplier's offer to outsource.

## The Capital Investment Decision

In a large production environment, there are constant requests to invest more funds in various areas in order to increase efficiencies. However, it rarely makes sense to invest in areas that do not favorably impact the bottleneck operation in some way. In particular, investments in the capacity of operations located downstream from the bottleneck operation rarely yield a return, since improving them does nothing for the overall profitability of the entire system. The issue is addressed in the following example, which uses the basic constraint model as a baseline.

---

**EXAMPLE**

The industrial engineering manager of Mole Industries examines the entire production line, and concludes that he can double the speed of the paint shop for an investment of $250,000. This operation is located at the very end of the production line, and so is located downstream from the bottleneck operation. The analysis is:

| Product | Throughput per Minute | Bottleneck Usage (minutes) | Units Scheduled | Total Bottleneck Time | Total Throughput |
|---|---|---|---|---|---|
| 1. Hedgehog Deluxe | $80 | 14 | 1,000 | 14,000 | $1,120,000 |
| 2. Hedgehog Mini | 70 | 20 | 500 | 10,000 | 700,000 |
| 3. Hedgehog Classic | 65 | 40 | 200 | 8,000 | 520,000 |
| 4. Hedgehog Digger | 42 | 10 | 688 | 6,880 | 288,960 |
| | | Total bottleneck scheduled time | | 38,880 | |
| | | Total bottleneck time available* | | 38,880 | |
| | | | | | |
| | | | | Total throughput | $2,628,960 |
| | | | | Total operating expenses | 2,400,000 |
| | | | | Profit | $228,960 |
| | | | | Profit percentage | 8.7% |
| | | | | Investment | $23,250,000 |
| | | | | Annualized return on investment | 11.8% |

* Minutes per month (30 days × 24 hours × 60 minutes × (1 – 0.10 maintenance time)

The only item that changes in the analysis is the amount of the investment, which increases by $250,000 and results in a reduced return on investment. Improving the capacity of the paint shop has no effect on throughput, since the entire production line can still only run at the maximum pace of the bottleneck operation.

---

There are some types of investment that can make sense, even if they are not associated with the bottleneck operation. In particular, if an investment can reduce the cost of an operation, the investment is acceptable, as long as the return on investment percentage increases as a result of the change. The concept is illustrated in the following example.

**EXAMPLE**

Rather than proposing a capacity increase in the paint shop (as was the case in the last example), the industrial engineering manager of Mole Industries proposes to invest $250,000 in the paint shop, but only to add sufficient automation to reduce operating expenses by $5,000 per month. The analysis is:

| Product | Throughput per Minute | Bottleneck Usage (minutes) | Units Scheduled | Total Bottleneck Time | Total Throughput |
|---|---|---|---|---|---|
| 1. Hedgehog Deluxe | $80 | 14 | 1,000 | 14,000 | $1,120,000 |
| 2. Hedgehog Mini | 70 | 20 | 500 | 10,000 | 700,000 |
| 3. Hedgehog Classic | 65 | 40 | 200 | 8,000 | 520,000 |
| 4. Hedgehog Digger | 42 | 10 | 688 | 6,880 | 288,960 |
| | | Total bottleneck scheduled time | | 38,880 | |
| | | Total bottleneck time available* | | 38,880 | |
| | | | | Total throughput | $2,628,960 |
| | | | | Total operating expenses | 2,395,000 |
| | | | | Profit | $233,960 |
| | | | | Profit percentage | 8.7% |
| | | | | Investment | $23,250,000 |
| | | | | Annualized return on investment | 12.1% |

* Minutes per month (30 days × 24 hours × 60 minutes × (1 – 0.10 maintenance time)

The investment creates a sufficient decline in total operating expenses to yield an increase in the annualized rate of return, to 12.1%. Consequently, this is a worthwhile investment opportunity.

## The Decision to Cancel a Product

A common practice is to review all products issued by a company, carefully allocating costs to each one, to see if any are losing money. If so, management may agree to cancel them. However, when products are reviewed from the perspective of constraint analysis, they are almost never cancelled. The reason is that the basis of measurement should be throughput, which is revenues minus totally variable expenses, and since the cost of materials is really the only variable expense, there is *always* throughput. A company rarely prices its products at or below the cost of its materials, since that would result in catastrophic losses.

Since all products are likely to have throughput, the real question is not which products have the lowest throughput, but rather which ones have the highest throughput. By focusing on these high-throughput products, management can readily see which items to bring most forcibly to the attention of customers. If the result is an increased volume of production of products having high throughput, the low throughput products may be forced out of the production mix, simply because there is no production capacity left to manufacture them.

If the management team were to follow the more traditional approach of assigning overhead to products and then deciding if they are unprofitable, the result would be the ongoing elimination of products, as overhead costs are gradually shifted to fewer and fewer remaining products, driving up the cost of each one in turn and forcing management to conclude that each one should be cancelled. The following example illustrates the concept.

---

**EXAMPLE**

Mole Industries has three versions of a trench digging tool. The company has $4,000,000 of overhead that it allocates to the three products. The company allocates the overhead based on revenue. The cost characteristics of the products are:

| Product | Revenue | Variable Costs | Overhead Costs | Margin |
|---|---|---|---|---|
| Hedgehog Classic | $2,000,000 | $1,300,000 | $800,000 | -$100,000 |
| Hedgehog Mini | 3,000,000 | 1,600,000 | 1,200,000 | 200,000 |
| Hedgehog Deluxe | 5,000,000 | 2,400,000 | 2,000,000 | 600,000 |
| Totals | $10,000,000 | $5,300,000 | $4,000,000 | $700,000 |

Hedgehog's president decides that, since the full cost of the Hedgehog Classic results in a loss, he should cancel that product. This results in the next table, where the same overhead is now being allocated (based on revenue) between the two remaining products.

| Product | Revenue | Variable Costs | Overhead Costs | Margin |
|---|---|---|---|---|
| Hedgehog Mini | $3,000,000 | $1,600,000 | $1,500,000 | -$100,000 |
| Hedgehog Deluxe | 5,000,000 | 2,400,000 | 2,500,000 | 100,000 |
| Totals | $8,000,000 | $4,000,000 | $4,000,000 | $0 |

Hedgehog's president now sees that the Hedgehog mini is losing money! Not knowing what else to do, he cancels that product, too. The result is shown in the next table:

| Product | Revenue | Variable Costs | Overhead Costs | Margin |
|---|---|---|---|---|
| Hedgehog Deluxe | 5,000,000 | 2,400,000 | 4,000,000 | -$1,400,000 |
| Totals | $5,000,000 | $2,400,000 | $4,000,000 | -$1,400,000 |

Hedgehog's president gives up, closes down the company, and takes a cost accounting class to figure out what happened. He later learns that all three products were contributing toward the pool of overhead that needed to be paid for. As he successively stripped away each product, that left the remaining products to shoulder more of the overhead load. Eventually, the Hedgehog Deluxe was left, and it did not generate enough of a margin to pay for all of the overhead.

---

## Summary

Constraint analysis is one of the primary tools available for the financial analysis of operational decisions. It makes quite clear where the bottleneck operation is located, the extreme expense associated with not maximizing it, and how to manage operations to maximize profits.

However, constraint analysis can be a foreign concept to many managers, who have spent their careers working on local optimization issues, allocating overhead, and improving the efficiency of labor – all of which are concepts that constraint analysis teaches do not improve overall profitability. Accordingly, we suggest management training in constraint analysis for anyone who has a say in the design of operations.

# Chapter 14
# Budgeting Concepts

## Introduction

A budget is a document that forecasts the financial results and financial position of a business for one or more future periods. At a minimum, a budget contains an estimated income statement that describes anticipated financial results. A more complex budget also contains an estimated balance sheet, which contains the entity's anticipated assets, liabilities, and equity positions at various points in time in the future.

A budget can be of considerable use to management, since it can be used to develop alternative financial scenarios for a business, test assumptions, and plan for future cash flows. Given the importance and prevalent use of budgets, we provide a detailed review of how a comprehensive budget is derived, tested for reasonableness, and assembled into a set of budgeted financial statements.

**Related Podcast Episodes:** Episodes 71, 76, 130, and 131 of the Accounting Best Practices Podcast discuss budget model improvement, budgeting controls, the problems with budgets, and operating without a budget, respectively. They are available at: **accountingtools.com/podcasts** or **iTunes**

## The System of Budgets

The key driver of any budget is the amount of revenue that is expected during the budget period. Revenue is usually compiled in a separate revenue budget. The information in this budget is derived from estimates of which products or services will sell, and the prices at which they can be sold. Forecasted revenue for this budget cannot be derived just from the sales staff, since this would limit the information to the extrapolation of historical sales figures into the future. The chief executive officer provides additional strategic information, while the marketing manager addresses new-product introductions and the purchasing staff provides input on the availability of raw materials that may restrict sales. Thus, a group effort from many parts of a company is needed to create the revenue budget.

Once the revenue budget is in place, a number of additional budgets are derived from it that relate to the production capabilities of the company. The following components are included in this cluster of budgets:

- *Ending inventory budget.* As its name implies, this budget sets the inventory level as of the end of each accounting period listed in the budget. Management uses this budget to force changes in the inventory level, which is usually driven by a policy to have more or less finished goods inventory on hand. Having more inventory presumably improves the speed with which a company can ship goods to customers, at the cost of an increased investment in working capital. A forced reduction in inventory may delay some shipments to customers due to stockout conditions, but requires less working capital to maintain. The ending inventory budget is used as an input to the production budget.

- *Production budget.* This budget shows expected production at an aggregated level. The production budget is based primarily on the sales estimates in the revenue budget, but it must also take into consideration existing inventory levels and the desired amount of ending inventory as stated in the ending inventory budget. If management wants to increase inventory levels in order to provide more rapid shipments to customers, the required increase in production may trigger a need for more production equipment and direct labor staff. The production budget is needed in order to derive the direct labor budget, manufacturing overhead budget, and direct materials budget.
- *Direct labor budget.* This budget calculates the amount of direct labor staffing expected during the budget period, based on the production levels itemized in the production budget. This information can only be generally estimated, given the vagaries of short-term changes in actual production scheduling. However, direct labor usually involves specific staffing levels to crew production lines, so the estimated amount of direct labor should not vary excessively over time, within certain production volume parameters. This budget should incorporate any planned changes in the cost of labor, which may be easy to do if there is a union contract that specifies pay increases as of specific dates. It provides rough estimates of the number of employees needed, and is of particular interest to the human resources staff in developing hiring plans. It is a key source document for the cost of goods sold budget.
- *Manufacturing overhead budget.* This budget includes all of the overhead costs expected to be incurred in the manufacturing area during the budget period. It is usually based on historical cost information, but can be adjusted for step cost situations, where a change in the structure or capacity level of a production facility strips away or adds large amounts of expenses at one time. Even if there are no changes in structure or capacity, the manufacturing overhead budget may change somewhat in the maintenance cost area if management plans to alter these expenditures as machines age or are replaced. This budget is a source document for the cost of goods sold budget.
- *Direct materials budget.* This budget is derived from a combination of the manufacturing unit totals in the production budget and the bills of material for those units, and is used in the cost of goods sold budget. If a company produces a large variety of products, this can become an excessively detailed and burdensome budget to create and maintain. Consequently, it is customary to estimate material costs in aggregate, such as at the product line level.

- *Cost of goods sold budget.* This budget contains a summarization of the expenses detailed in the direct material budget, manufacturing overhead budget, and direct materials budget. This budget usually contains such additional information as line items for revenue, the gross margin, and key production statistics. It is heavily used during budget iterations, since management can consult it to view the impact of various assumptions on gross margins and other aspects of the production process.

Once the revenue and production-related budgets have been completed, there are still several other budgets to assemble that relate to other functions of the company. They are:

- *Sales and marketing budget.* This budget is comprised of the compensation of the sales and marketing staff, sales travel costs, and expenditures related to various marketing programs. It is closely linked to the revenue budget, since the number of sales staff (in some industries) is the prime determinant of additional sales. Further, marketing campaigns can impact the timing of the sales shown in the revenue budget.
- *Administration budget.* This budget includes the expenses of the executive, accounting, treasury, human resources, and other administrative staff. These expenses are primarily comprised of compensation, followed by office expenses. A large proportion of these expenses are fixed, with some headcount changes driven by total revenues or other types of activity elsewhere in the company.

A budget that is not directly impacted by the revenue budget is the research and development budget. This budget is authorized by senior management, and is set at an amount that is deemed appropriate, given the projected level of new product introductions that management wants to achieve, and the company's competitive posture within the industry. The size of this budget is also influenced by the amount of available funding and an estimate of how many potentially profitable projects can be pursued.

Once these budgets have been completed, it is possible to determine the capital budgeting requirements of the company, as well as its financing needs. These two topics are addressed in the capital budget and the financing budget:

- *Capital budget.* This budget shows the cash flows associated with the acquisition of fixed assets during the budget period. Larger fixed assets are noted individually, while smaller purchases are noted in aggregate. The information in this budget is used to develop the budgeted balance sheet, depreciation expense, and the cash requirements needed for the financing budget. Capital budgeting issues are addressed in the Investment Decisions chapter.
- *Financing budget.* This budget is the last of the component budgets developed, because it needs the cash inflow and outflow information from the other budgets. With this information in hand, the financing budget ad-

dresses how funds will be invested (if there are excess cash inflows) or obtained through debt or equity financing (if there is a need for additional cash). This budget also incorporates any additional cash usage information that is typically addressed by the board of directors, including dividends, stock repurchases, and repositioning of the company's debt to equity ratio. The interest expense or interest income resulting from this budget is incorporated into the budgeted income statement.

Once the capital budget and financing budget have been created, the information in all of the budgets is summarized into a master budget. This master budget is essentially an income statement. A more complex budget also includes a balance sheet that itemizes the major categories of assets, liabilities, and equity. There may also be a statement of cash flows that itemizes the sources and uses of funds.

The complete system of budgets is shown in the following exhibit.

**Exhibit: The System of Budgets**

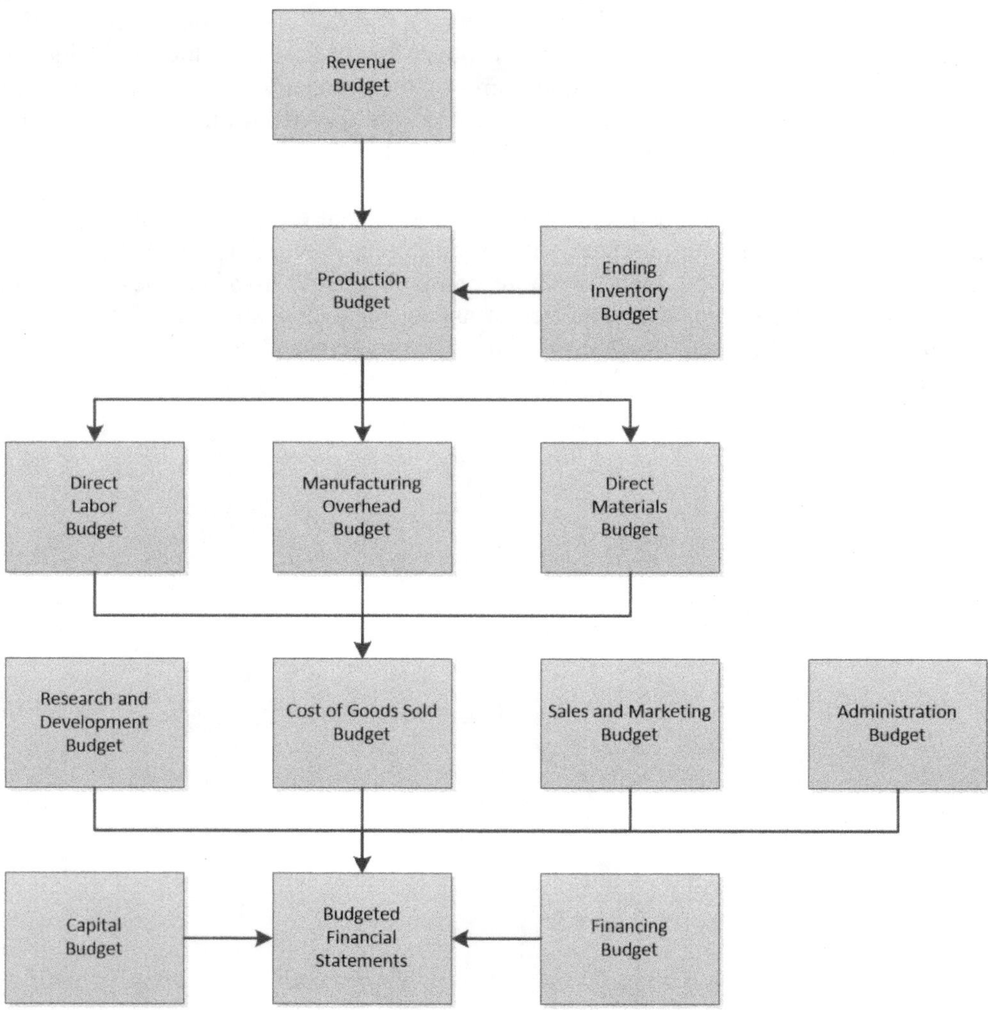


It may be useful to append a ratios page to the budget. These ratios are most useful when compared to historical trends, to see if the results generated by the budget model appear reasonable. Typical ratios to consider for this page are revenue per person, inventory turnover, accounts receivable turnover, and working capital as a percentage of sales.

In summary, the system of budgets ultimately depends upon the revenue budget and the amount of planned ending inventory. These two budgets directly or indirectly influence the amounts budgeted in many other parts of the corporate budget.

## The Reasons for Budget Iterations

There are several very good reasons why the first version of a corporate budget is sent back for additional work. These issues are:

- *Constraints*. If there are bottlenecks within the company that interfere with its ability to generate additional sales, does the budget provide sufficient funding to impact these bottlenecks? If not, the company can budget whatever results it wants, but it has virtually no chance of achieving them. For example, a machine in the production area may be a bottleneck that keeps a company from producing any more products – if the bottleneck is not dealt with, sales will not increase, irrespective of improvements anywhere else in the company.
- *Pacing*. If a company intends to expand operations in new geographical areas, or to open new distribution channels, or to offer entirely new products, it should build into the budget an adequate amount of time to ramp up each operation. This issue of pacing should include consideration of the sales cycle of customers, which may be extremely long. For example, expanding the customer base to include municipal governments may be an excellent idea, but may require a sales cycle of greater than a year, given the advance notice needed by governments to budget for purchases.
- *Financing*. If a company has a hard cap on the amount of funding that it will have available during the budget period, the requirements of the budget must not exceed that funding limitation. This is one of the more common reasons for budget iterations, especially in small companies, where it may be difficult to obtain new funding.
- *Historical metrics*. If a company has been unable to achieve certain performance benchmarks in the past, what has changed to allow it to do so now? The chances are good that the company will still have trouble improving beyond its historical ability to do so, which means that the budget should be adjusted to meet its historical metrics. For example, if a business has historically been unable to generate more than $1 million of sales per salesperson, the preliminary budget should continue to support a similar proportion of sales to salespeople. Similarly, a historical tendency for accounts receivable to be an average of 45 days old prior to payment should probably be reflected in the preliminary budget, rather than a more aggressive collection assumption.

This section has highlighted the need to conduct a close examination of preliminary versions of a budget to see if it meets a number of reasonableness criteria. This usually calls for a number of adjustments to the budget, which typically begins with excessively optimistic assumptions, followed by a certain amount of retrenching.

We now turn to an examination of the various components of the corporate budget.

## Overview of the Revenue Budget

The basic revenue budget contains an itemization of a company's sales expectations for the budget period, which may be in both units and dollars. If a company has a large number of products, it usually aggregates its expected sales into a smaller number of product categories; otherwise, the revenue budget becomes too unwieldy.

The projected unit sales information in the sales budget feeds directly into the production budget, from which the direct materials and direct labor budgets are created. The revenue budget is also used to give managers a general sense of the scale of operations, for when they create the manufacturing overhead budget, the sales and marketing budget, and the administration budget. The total net sales dollars listed in the revenue budget are carried forward into the revenue line item in the master budget.

Most companies sell a large number of products and services, and must find a way to aggregate them into a revenue budget that strikes a balance between revealing a reasonable level of detail and not overwhelming the reader with a massive list of line-item projections. There are several ways to aggregate information to meet this goal.

One approach is to summarize revenue information by sales territory, as shown below. This approach is most useful when the primary source of information for the revenue budget is the sales managers of the various territories, and is particularly important if the company is planning to close down or open up new sales territories; changes at the territory level may be the primary drivers of changes in sales. In the example, the Central Plains sales territory is expected to be launched midway through the budget year and to contribute modestly to total sales volume by year end.

**Sample Revenue Budget by Territory**

| Territory | Quarter 1 | Quarter 2 | Quarter 3 | Quarter 4 | Total |
|---|---|---|---|---|---|
| Northeast | $135,000 | $141,000 | $145,000 | $132,000 | $553,000 |
| Mid-Atlantic | 200,000 | 210,000 | 208,000 | 195,000 | 813,000 |
| Southeast | 400,000 | 425,000 | 425,000 | 395,000 | $1,645,000 |
| Central Plains | 0 | 0 | 100,000 | 175,000 | 275,000 |
| Rocky mountain | 225,000 | 235,000 | 242,000 | 230,000 | 932,000 |
| West coast | 500,000 | 560,000 | 585,000 | 525,000 | 2,170,000 |
| Totals | $1,460,000 | $1,571,000 | $1,705,000 | $1,652,000 | $6,388,000 |

If revenue information is aggregated by sales territory, the various territory managers are expected to maintain additional detail regarding sales in their territories, which is kept separate from the formal budget document.

Another approach is to summarize revenue information by contract, as shown below. This is realistically the only viable way to structure the revenue budget in situations where a company is heavily dependent upon a set of contracts that have definite ending dates. In this situation, divide the budget into existing and projected contracts, with subtotals for each type of contract, in order to separately show firm revenues and less-likely revenues. This type of revenue budget is commonly used when a company is engaged in services or government work.

**Sample Revenue Budget by Contract**

| Contract | Quarter 1 | Quarter 2 | Quarter 3 | Quarter 4 | Total |
|---|---|---|---|---|---|
| **Existing Contracts:** | | | | | |
| Air Force #01327 | $175,000 | $175,000 | $25,000 | $-- | $375,000 |
| Coast Guard #AC124 | 460,000 | 460,000 | 460,000 | 25,000 | 1,405,000 |
| Marines #BG0047 | 260,000 | 280,000 | 280,000 | 260,000 | 1,080,000 |
| Subtotal | $895,000 | $915,000 | $765,000 | $285,000 | $2,860,000 |
| | | | | | |
| **Projected Contracts:** | | | | | |
| Air Force resupply | $-- | $-- | $150,000 | $300,000 | $450,000 |
| Army training | -- | 210,000 | 600,000 | 550,000 | 1,360,000 |
| Marines software | 10,000 | 80,000 | 80,000 | 100,000 | 270,000 |
| Subtotal | $10,000 | $290,000 | $830,000 | $950,000 | $2,080,000 |
| | | | | | |
| Totals | $905,000 | $1,205,000 | $1,595,000 | $1,235,000 | $4,940,000 |

Yet another approach for a company having a large number of products is to aggregate them into product lines, and then create a summary-level budget at the product line level. This approach is shown below. However, if a revenue budget is created for product lines, consider creating a supporting schedule of projected sales for each of the products within that product line, in order to properly account for the timing and revenue volumes associated with the ongoing introduction of new products and cancellation of old ones. An example of such a supporting schedule is also shown below, itemizing the "Alpha" line item in the product line revenue budget. Note that this schedule provides detail about the launch of a new product (the Alpha Windmill) and the termination of another product (the Alpha Methane Converter) that are crucial to the formulation of the total revenue figure for the product line.

**Sample Revenue Budget by Product Line**

| Product Line | Quarter 1 | Quarter 2 | Quarter 3 | Quarter 4 | Total |
|---|---|---|---|---|---|
| Product line alpha | $450,000 | $500,000 | $625,000 | $525,000 | $2,100,000 |
| Product line beta | 100,000 | 110,000 | 150,000 | 125,000 | 485,000 |
| Product line charlie | 250,000 | 250,000 | 300,000 | 300,000 | 1,100,000 |
| Product line delta | 80,000 | 60,000 | 40,000 | 20,000 | 200,000 |
| Totals | $880,000 | $920,000 | $1,115,000 | $970,000 | $3,885,000 |

**Sample Supporting Schedule for the Revenue Budget by Product Line**

| | Quarter 1 | Quarter 2 | Quarter 3 | Quarter 4 | Total |
|---|---|---|---|---|---|
| **Alpha product line detail:** | | | | | |
| Alpha flywheel | $25,000 | $35,000 | $40,000 | $20,000 | $120,000 |
| Alpha generator | 175,000 | 225,000 | 210,000 | 180,000 | 790,000 |
| Alpha windmill | -- | -- | 200,000 | 250,000 | 450,000 |
| Alpha methane converter | 150,000 | 140,000 | 25,000 | -- | 315,000 |
| Alpha nuclear converter | 100,000 | 100,000 | 150,000 | 75,000 | 425,000 |
| Totals | $450,000 | $500,000 | $625,000 | $525,000 | $2,100,000 |

A danger in constructing a supporting schedule for a product line revenue budget is that one can delve too deeply into all of the various manifestations of a product, resulting in an inordinately large and detailed schedule. This situation might arise when a product comes in many colors or options. In such cases, engage in as much aggregation at the individual product level as necessary to yield a schedule that is not *excessively* detailed. Also, it is nearly impossible to forecast sales at the level of the color or specific option mix associated with a product, so it makes little sense to create a schedule at that level of detail.

In summary, the layout of the revenue budget is highly dependent upon the type of revenue that a company generates. We have described different formats for companies that are structured around products, contract-based services, and sales territories. If a company engages in more than one of these activities, you should still create the revenue-specific formats shown in this section in order to provide insights into the sources of revenues, and then carry forward the totals of those schedules to a master revenue budget that lists the totals in separate line items. Users of this master revenue budget can then drill down to the underlying revenue budget schedules to obtain additional information. An example of a master revenue budget that is derived from the last two example revenue budgets is shown in the following exhibit.

**Sample Master Revenue Budget**

| | Quarter 1 | Quarter 2 | Quarter 3 | Quarter 4 | Total |
|---|---|---|---|---|---|
| Contract revenue | $905,000 | $1,205,000 | $1,595,000 | $1,235,000 | $4,940,000 |
| Product revenue | 880,000 | 920,000 | 1,115,000 | 970,000 | 3,885,000 |
| Totals | $1,785,000 | $2,125,000 | $2,710,000 | $2,205,000 | $8,825,000 |

## The Ending Finished Goods Inventory Budget

The ending finished goods inventory budget states the number of units of finished goods inventory at the end of each budget period. It also calculates the cost of finished goods inventory. The amount of this inventory tends to be similar from period to period, assuming that the production department manufactures to meet demand levels in each budget period. However, there are a variety of reasons why it may be necessary to alter the amount of ending finished goods inventory, such as:

- *Customer service.* If management wants to improve customer service, one way to do so is to increase the amount of ending inventory, which allows the company to fulfill customer orders more quickly and avoid backorder situations.
- *Inventory record accuracy.* If the inventory record keeping system is inaccurate, it is necessary to maintain additional amounts of inventory on hand, both of raw materials and finished goods, to ensure that customer orders are fulfilled on time.
- *Manufacturing planning.* If there is a manufacturing resources planning (MRP) system in use, the company is producing in accordance with a sales and production plan, which requires a certain amount of both raw materials and finished goods inventory. If there is a change to the just-in-time (JIT) manufacturing planning system, the company is only producing as required by customers, which tends to reduce the need for inventory.
- *Product life cycles.* If there are certain products or even entire product lines that a company is planning to terminate, factor the related inventory reductions into the amount of planned ending inventory.
- *Product versions.* If the sales and marketing staff want to offer a product in a number of versions, the company may need to keep a certain amount of each type of inventory in stock. Thus, an increase in the number of product versions equates to an increase in ending inventory.
- *Supply chain duration.* If there is a plan to switch to a supplier located far away from the company, be aware that this calls for having a larger safety stock of finished goods on hand, so that deliveries to customers will not be impacted if there is a problem in receiving goods on time from the supplier.
- *Working capital reduction.* If management wants to increase the amount of inventory turnover, this reduces the amount of cash invested in working capital, but also has the offsetting effect of leaving less inventory in reserve to cover sudden surges in customer orders.

If there is a plan to alter the ending amount of inventory, it is useful to create separate layers of ending inventory in the budget that reflect each of the decisions made, so that readers of the budget can see the numerical impact of operational decisions.

In the following example, we assume that changes made in the immediately preceding budget period will continue to have the same impact on inventory in the *next* budget period, so that the adjusted ending inventory in the last period will be the starting point for our adjustments in the next period. We can then make the following adjustments to the unadjusted ending inventory level to arrive at an adjusted ending inventory:

- *Internal systems changes*. Shows the impact of altering the manufacturing system, such as changing from an MRP to a JIT system.
- *Financing changes*. Shows the impact of altering inventory levels in order to influence the amount of working capital used.
- *Product changes*. Shows the impact of product withdrawals and product introductions.
- *Seasonal changes*. Shows the impact of building inventory for seasonal sales, followed by a decline after the selling season has concluded.
- *Service changes*. Shows the impact of changing inventory levels in order to alter order fulfillment rates.

If management is attempting to reduce the company's investment in inventory, it may mandate such a large drop in ending inventory that the company will not realistically be able to operate without significant production and shipping interruptions. These situations can be spotted by including the budgeted inventory turnover level in each budget period, as well as the actual amount of turnover in the corresponding period in the preceding year. This is shown in the following example as the historical actual days of inventory, followed by the planned days of inventory for the budget period. Comparing the two measurements may reveal large period-to-period changes, which management should examine to see if it is really possible to reduce inventory levels to such an extent.

---

**EXAMPLE**

Milagro Corporation has a division that sells portable coffee machines for campers. Milagro wants to incorporate the following changes into its calculation of the ending finished goods inventory:

1. Switch from the MRP to the JIT manufacturing system in the second quarter, which will decrease inventory by 250 units.
2. Reduce inventory by 500 units in the first quarter to reduce working capital requirements.
3. Add 500 units to inventory in the third quarter as part of the rollout of a new product.
4. Build inventory in the first three quarters by 100 units per quarter in anticipation of seasonal sales in the fourth quarter.

5. Increase on-hand inventory by 400 units in the second quarter to improve the speed of customer order fulfillment for a specific product.

The ending finished goods inventory unit and cost calculation follows:

| (units) | Quarter 1 | Quarter 2 | Quarter 3 | Quarter 4 |
|---|---|---|---|---|
| Unadjusted ending inventory level | 2,000 | 1,600 | 1,850 | 2,450 |
| +/- Internal system changes | 0 | -250 | 0 | 0 |
| +/- Financing changes | -500 | 0 | 0 | 0 |
| +/- Product changes | 0 | 0 | 500 | 0 |
| +/- Seasonal changes | 100 | 100 | 100 | -300 |
| +/- Service changes | 0 | 400 | 0 | 0 |
| Adjusted ending inventory | 1,600 | 1,850 | 2,450 | 2,150 |
| | | | | |
| × Standard cost per unit | $45 | $45 | $45 | $45 |
| Total ending inventory cost | $72,000 | $83,250 | $110,250 | $96,750 |
| | | | | |
| Historical actual days of inventory | 100 | 108 | 135 | 127 |
| Planned days of inventory | 92 | 106 | 130 | 114 |

The days of inventory calculation at the bottom of the table shows few differences from actual experience in the second and third quarters, but the differences are greater in the first and fourth quarters. Management should review its ability to achieve the indicated inventory reductions in those quarters.

---

The ending finished goods inventory budget shown in the preceding example is quite simplistic, for it assumes that the same inventory policies and systems will be applied to a company's *entire* inventory. For example, this means that management may want to increase inventory levels for all types of inventory in order to increase customer order fulfillment speeds, when in fact it only wants to do so for a relatively small part of the inventory.

If inventory levels will be adjusted at a finer level of detail, consider creating a budget that sets inventory levels by business unit or product line. It is generally too time-consuming to set inventory levels at the individual product level, especially if demand at this level is difficult to predict.

## The Production Budget

The production budget calculates the number of units of products that must be manufactured, and is derived from a combination of the sales forecast and the planned amount of finished goods inventory to have on hand. The production budget is typically presented in either a monthly or quarterly format. The basic calculation used by the production budget is:

+ Forecasted unit sales
+ Planned finished goods ending inventory balance
= Total production required

- Beginning finished goods inventory
= Units to be manufactured

It can be very difficult to create a comprehensive production budget that incorporates a forecast for every variation on a product that a company sells, so it is customary to aggregate the forecast information into broad categories of products that have similar characteristics. The calculation of the production budget is illustrated in the following example.

---

**EXAMPLE**

Milagro Corporation plans to produce an array of plastic coffee cups for the upcoming budget year. Its production needs are as follows:

| | Quarter 1 | Quarter 2 | Quarter 3 | Quarter 4 |
|---|---|---|---|---|
| Forecast unit sales | 5,500 | 6,000 | 7,000 | 8,000 |
| + Planned ending inventory units | 500 | 500 | 500 | 500 |
| = Total production required | 6,000 | 6,500 | 7,500 | 8,500 |
| | | | | |
| - Beginning finished goods inventory | -1,000 | -500 | -500 | -500 |
| = Units to be manufactured | 5,000 | 6,000 | 7,000 | 8,000 |

The planned ending finished goods inventory at the end of each quarter declines from an initial 1,000 units to 500 units, since the materials manager believes that the company is maintaining too much finished goods inventory. Consequently, the plan calls for a decline from 1,000 units of ending finished goods inventory at the end of the first quarter to 500 units by the end of the second quarter, despite a projection for rising sales. This may be a risky forecast, since the amount of safety stock on hand is being cut while production volume increases by over 30 percent. Given the size of the projected inventory decline, there is a fair chance that Milagro will be forced to increase the amount of ending finished goods inventory later in the year.

---

The production budget deals entirely with unit volumes; it does not translate its production requirements into dollars. Instead, the unit requirements of the budget are shifted into other parts of the budget, such as the direct labor budget and the direct materials budget, which are then translated into dollars.

When formulating the production budget, it is useful to consider the impact of proposed production on the capacity of any bottleneck operations in the production area. It is entirely possible that some production requirements will not be possible given the production constraints, so management will either have to scale back on production requirements, invest in more fixed assets, or outsource the work. The following example illustrates the issue.

---

**EXAMPLE**

Milagro Corporation revises the production budget described in the preceding example to incorporate the usage of a bottleneck machine in its manufacturing area. The revised format follows, beginning with the last row of information from the preceding example:

| | Quarter 1 | Quarter 2 | Quarter 3 | Quarter 4 |
|---|---|---|---|---|
| Units to be manufactured | 5,000 | 6,000 | 7,000 | 8,000 |
| × Minutes of bottleneck time/unit | 15 | 15 | 15 | 15 |
| = Planned bottleneck usage (minutes) | 75,000 | 90,000 | 105,000 | 120,000 |
| | | | | |
| - Available bottleneck time (minutes)* | 110,160 | 110,160 | 110,160 | 110,160 |
| = Remaining available time (minutes) | 35,160 | 20,160 | 5,160 | -9,840 |

* Calculated as 90 days × 24 hours × 60 minutes × 85% up time = 110,160 minutes

The table reveals that there is not enough bottleneck time available to meet the planned production level in the fourth quarter. However, Milagro can increase production in earlier quarters to make up the shortfall, since there is adequate capacity available at the bottleneck in the earlier periods.

---

Note in the preceding example that the amount of available bottleneck time was set at 85 percent of the maximum possible amount of time available. We make such assumptions because of the inevitable amount of downtime associated with equipment maintenance, unavailable raw materials, scrapped production, and so forth. The 85 percent figure is only an example – the real amount may be somewhat higher or substantially lower.

Another issue impacting the production budget is the need to incur step costs when production exceeds a certain volume level. For example, a company may need to open a new production facility, production line, or work shift to accommodate any additional increase in production past a certain amount of volume. It may be possible to adjust the production schedule to accelerate production in slow periods in order to stockpile inventory and avoid such step costs in later periods.

## Production Budgeting for Multiple Products

The production budget shown thus far has centered on the manufacture of a single product. How is a production budget created when there are multiple products? The worst solution is to attempt to re-create in the budget a variation on the production schedule for the entire budget period – the level of detail required to do so would be inordinately high. Instead, consider one of the following alternatives:

- *Bottleneck focus*. Rather than focusing on the production of a variety of products, only budget for the amount of time that they require at the bottleneck operation. For example, rather than focusing on the need to manufacture every aspect of 20 different products, focus on the time that each product needs at a single production operation. If there are multiple production lines or facilities, only budget for usage of the bottleneck at each location.
- *Product line focus*. In many cases, there are only modest differences in the production activities needed to create any product within a product line. If there are such production commonalities, consider treating the entire production line as a single product with common production requirements.
- *80/20 rule*. It is likely that only a small number of products comprise most of a company's production volume. If this is the case, consider detailed budgeting for the production of the 20 percent of all products that typically comprise 80 percent of all sales, and a vastly reduced (and aggregated) amount of budgeting for the remaining products.
- *MRP II planning*. If a company uses a manufacturing requirements planning (MRP II) system, the software may contain a planning module that allows for the inputting of estimated production requirements, and the generation of detailed requirements for machine usage, direct labor, and direct materials. If so, the accountant can input the totals from this module into the budget without also copying in all of the supporting details.

## The Direct Materials Budget (Roll up Method)

The direct materials budget calculates the materials that must be purchased, by time period, in order to fulfill the requirements of the production budget. The basic calculation for the roll up method is to multiply the estimated amount of sales (in units) in each reporting period by the standard cost of each item to arrive at the standard amount of direct materials cost expected for each product. Standard costs are derived from the bill of materials for each product. A bill of materials is the record of the materials used to construct a product. A sample calculation appears in the following exhibit.

**Sample Calculation of the Cost of Direct Materials**

| | Quarter 1 | Quarter 2 | Quarter 3 | Quarter 4 |
|---|---|---|---|---|
| **Product A** | | | | |
| Units | 100 | 120 | 110 | 90 |
| Standard cost/each | $14.25 | $14.25 | $14.25 | $14.25 |
| Total cost | $1,425 | $1,710 | $1,568 | $1,283 |
| | | | | |
| **Product B** | | | | |
| Units | 300 | 350 | 375 | 360 |
| Standard cost/each | $8.40 | $8.40 | $8.40 | $8.40 |
| Total cost | $2,520 | $2,940 | $3,150 | $3,024 |
| | | | | |
| Grand total cost | $3,945 | $4,650 | $4,718 | $4,307 |

Note that the preceding example only addressed the direct materials *expense* during the budget period. It did not address the amount of materials that should be purchased during the period; doing so requires that you also factor in the planned amounts of beginning and ending inventory. The calculation used for direct material purchases is:

+ Raw materials required for production
+ Planned ending inventory balance
= Total raw materials required

\- Beginning raw materials inventory
= Raw materials to be purchased

The presence or absence of a beginning inventory can have a major impact on the amount of direct materials needed during a budget period – in some cases, there may be so much inventory already on hand that a company does not need to purchase *any* additional direct materials. In other cases, and especially where management wants to build the amount of ending inventory (as arises when a company is preparing for a seasonal sales surge), it may be necessary to purchase far more direct materials than are indicated by sales requirements in just a single budget period. The following example illustrates how beginning and ending inventory levels can alter direct material requirements.

---

**EXAMPLE**

Milagro Corporation plans to produce a variety of large-capacity coffee dispensers for camping, and 98% of the raw materials required for this production involve plastic resin. Thus, there is only one key commodity to be concerned with. The production needs of Milagro for the resin commodity are shown in the following direct materials budget:

| | Quarter 1 | Quarter 2 | Quarter 3 | Quarter 4 |
|---|---|---|---|---|
| Product A (units to produce) | 5,000 | 6,000 | 7,000 | 8,000 |
| × Resin/unit (lbs) | 2 | 2 | 2 | 2 |
| = Total resin needed (lbs) | 10,000 | 12,000 | 14,000 | 16,000 |
| + Planned ending inventory | 2,000 | 2,400 | 2,800 | 3,200 |
| = Total resin required | 12,000 | 14,400 | 16,800 | 19,200 |
| | | | | |
| - Beginning inventory | 1,600 | 2,000 | 2,400 | 2,800 |
| = Resin to be purchased | 10,400 | 12,400 | 14,400 | 16,400 |
| | | | | |
| Resin cost per pound | $0.50 | $0.50 | $0.55 | $0.55 |
| Total resin cost to purchase | $5,200 | $6,200 | $7,920 | $9,020 |

The planned ending inventory at the end of each quarter is planned to be 20% of the amount of resin used during that month, so the ending inventory varies over time, gradually increasing as production requirements increase. The reason for the planned increase is that Milagro has some difficulty receiving resin in a timely manner from its supplier, so it maintains a safety stock of inventory on hand.

The purchasing department expects that global demand will drive up the price of resin, so it incorporates a slight price increase into the third quarter, which carries forward into the fourth quarter.

---

If a company uses the roll up method, it is basing the unit volume of materials on the quantities listed in the bill of materials for each item. It is essential that the information in bills of material be as accurate as possible, since the materials management department relies on this information to purchase materials and schedule production. However, what if the bill of materials information is incorrect, even if only by a small amount? Then, under the roll up method, that incorrect amount will be multiplied by the number of units to be produced in the budget period, which can result in quite a large error in the amount of materials used in the budget.

## The Direct Materials Budget (Historical Method)

In a typical business environment, there may be a multitude of factors that impact the amount of direct materials as a percentage of sales, including scrap, spoilage, rework, purchasing quantities, and volatility in commodity prices. Many companies are unable to accurately capture these factors in their bills of material, which makes it nearly impossible for them to create a reliable direct materials budget using the roll up method that was just described.

In such cases, an alternative budget calculation is the historical method, under which it is assumed that the historical amount of direct materials, as a percentage of revenues, will continue to be the case during the budget period. This approach means that the historical percentage of direct material costs is copied forward, with additional line items to account for any budgeted changes in key assumptions.

Under the historical method, adjust the projected amount of sales for any increase or decrease in production that is required for planned changes in the amount of ending inventory, and express the result as adjusted revenue. Then multiply the adjusted revenue figure by the historical percentage of direct materials to arrive at the total direct materials cost required to achieve the production budget. Despite the need for these adjustments, it is much easier to create a direct materials budget using the historical method than by using the roll up method.

---

**EXAMPLE**

Milagro Corporation finds that its last direct materials budget, which was created using the roll up method, did not come anywhere near actual results. This year, Milagro wants to use the historical method instead, using the historical direct materials rate of 32% of revenues as the basis for the budget. To avoid having the company become complacent and not work toward lower direct material costs, the budget also includes adjustment factors that are expected from several improvement projects. There is also an adjustment factor that addresses a likely change in the mix of products to be sold during the budget period. The budget model is:

| | Quarter 1 | Quarter 2 | Quarter 3 | Quarter 4 |
|---|---|---|---|---|
| Projected revenue | $4,200,000 | $5,000,000 | $5,750,000 | $8,000,000 |
| +/- planned ending inventory change | -400,000 | +100,000 | +250,000 | -350,000 |
| Adjusted revenue | $3,800,000 | $5,100,000 | $6,000,000 | $7,650,000 |
| | | | | |
| Historical direct materials percentage | 27.1% | 27.1% | 27.1% | 27.1% |
| + / - Adjustment for product mix | +3.4% | +4.0% | +1.8% | -0.9% |
| - Adjustment for scrap reduction | 0.0% | 0.0% | -0.2% | -0.2% |
| - Adjustment for rework reduction | 0.0% | -0.1% | -0.1% | -0.1% |
| = Adjusted direct materials percentage | 30.5% | 31.0% | 28.6% | 25.9% |
| | | | | |
| Total direct materials cost | $1,159,000 | $1,581,000 | $1,716,000 | $1,981,350 |

---

The problem with the historical method is that it is based on a certain mix of products that were sold in the past, each possibly with a different proportion of direct materials to sales. It is unlikely that the same mix of products will continue to be sold through the budget period; thus, applying an historical percentage to a future period may yield an incorrect direct materials cost. This issue can be mitigated by including an adjustment factor in the budget (as was shown in the preceding example), which modifies the historical percentage for what is expected to be the future mix of product sales.

## The Direct Labor Budget

The cost of direct labor is rarely variable. Instead, the production manager must retain experienced employees, which calls for paying them irrespective of the vagaries of the production schedule. Also, a production operation usually calls for a certain minimum number of employees in order to crew the production lines or work cells – it is not possible to operate the equipment with fewer people. Because of this crewing requirement, a company must spend a certain minimum amount for direct labor personnel, irrespective of the actual quantity of items manufactured. The resulting direct labor budget, known as the *crewing method*, is quite simple. Just budget for the number of people needed to staff the production area, which tends to remain fixed within a certain range of production volumes. The following example illustrates the concept.

---

**EXAMPLE**

Milagro Corporation determines the fixed labor cost needed to crew an entire production line, and then makes adjustments to the budget for those periods in which they expect production volumes to require the use of staff overtime. It uses this method with its titanium coffee grinder production line. This production line is staffed by eight people, and can produce 1,000 grinders per quarter with no overtime. The company expects to require additional production during the second quarter that will require the addition of two temporary workers to the production line. There are also plans for a 6% pay raise at the beginning of the fourth quarter. The direct labor budget for this production line is:

| | Quarter 1 | Quarter 2 | Quarter 3 | Quarter 4 |
|---|---|---|---|---|
| Coffee grinder line: | | | | |
| Staffing headcount | 8 | 10 | 8 | 8 |
| × Quarterly pay per person | $10,400 | $10,400 | $10,400 | $11,024 |
| = Total direct labor cost | $83,200 | $104,000 | $83,200 | $88,192 |

---

## The Manufacturing Overhead Budget

The manufacturing overhead budget contains all manufacturing costs other than the costs of direct materials and direct labor. Expenses normally considered part of manufacturing overhead include:

- Depreciation
- Facilities maintenance
- Factory rent
- Factory utilities
- Indirect materials, such as supplies
- Insurance on the factory and inventory
- Materials management staff compensation
- Personal property taxes on manufacturing equipment
- Production employee fringe benefits
- Production employee payroll taxes
- Production supervisor compensation
- Quality assurance staff compensation

The information in the manufacturing overhead budget becomes part of the cost of goods sold line item in the master budget.

---

**EXAMPLE**

Milagro Corporation owns a division that produces coffee beanery equipment for third world countries. Milagro budgets all raw materials and direct labor in the direct materials budget and direct labor budget, respectively. Its manufacturing overhead costs are stated in the manufacturing overhead budget as follows:

| | Quarter 1 | Quarter 2 | Quarter 3 | Quarter 4 |
|---|---|---|---|---|
| Production management salaries | $142,000 | $143,000 | $144,000 | $145,000 |
| Management payroll taxes | 10,000 | 10,000 | 11,000 | 11,000 |
| Depreciation | 27,000 | 27,000 | 29,000 | 29,000 |
| Facility maintenance | 8,000 | 7,000 | 10,000 | 9,000 |
| Rent | 32,000 | 32,000 | 32,000 | 34,000 |
| Personal property taxes | 6,000 | 5,000 | 7,000 | 6,000 |
| Quality assurance expenses | 3,000 | 3,000 | 3,000 | 3,000 |
| Utilities | 10,000 | 10,000 | 10,000 | 12,000 |
| Total manufacturing overhead | $238,000 | $237,000 | $236,000 | $237,000 |

The production management salaries line item contains the wages paid to the manufacturing supervisors, the purchasing staff, and production planning staff, and gradually increases over time to reflect changes in pay rates. The depreciation expense is relatively fixed, though there is an increase in the third quarter that reflects the purchase of new equipment. Both the freight and supplies expenses are closely linked to actual production volume, and so their amounts fluctuate in conjunction with planned production levels. The rent expense is a fixed cost, but does increase in the fourth quarter to reflect a scheduled rent increase.

---

A step cost is a cost that does not change steadily, but rather at discrete points. Thus, it is a fixed cost within certain boundaries, outside of which it will change. Several of the larger expense line items in the manufacturing overhead budget are step costs, so they tend to be incurred when a certain production volume is reached, and then stay approximately the same until production volumes change to a significant extent. This means that some line items can be safely copied from the actual expenditures in the preceding year with only minor changes. For example, if the current production level requires a second shift and a production supervisor for that shift, the manufacturing overhead budget for the next year should include the salary of that supervisor as long as there is going to be a second shift. Examples of situations giving rise to step costs are:

- *Additional production line.* If an entire production line is added, expect to incur step costs for all supporting staff, including materials management, supervision, and quality assurance personnel. There will also likely be an increase in the cost of utilities.
- *Additional shift.* If the facility is to be kept open for a second or third shift, expect to incur step costs for additional supervisors, as well as for a jump in the cost of utilities needed to power the facility during the extra time period.

Other expenses in this budget will require more analysis than the step costs just described. In particular, expenditures for the maintenance of machines and buildings can vary over time, depending upon the age of the assets being maintained and the need for large maintenance overhauls from time to time. For example, the expenditure for machinery maintenance may have been $100,000 in the preceding year, but can now be dropped to $50,000 in the new budget period because the company has replaced much of the equipment that had been requiring the bulk of the maintenance.

It is very difficult to run a facility at close to 100% of capacity. In this situation, equipment tends to break down more frequently, so a high utilization level requires additional overhead expenditures for parts, supplies, and maintenance labor.

## The Sales and Marketing Budget

Selling expenses are those costs incurred to demonstrate products to customers and obtain orders from them, while marketing expenses involve the positioning, placement, and advertising of a company's products and services. More specifically, the following expenses fall within the general category of sales and marketing expenses:

- *Sales compensation.* This is the cost of paying base salaries, wages, bonuses, and commissions to the sales staff.
- *Other compensation.* This is the cost of the salaries and wages paid primarily to the marketing staff.
- *Order entry compensation.* This is the wages paid to the order entry staff and its management.
- *Advertising and promotions.* This is the set of activities managed by the marketing staff, and may include print advertising, Internet advertising, radio and television advertisements, billboards, coupons, catalogs, direct mail solicitations, one-time promotions, samples, and so forth.
- *Research.* This covers the expenses incurred by the marketing department to discover the optimal ways to promote products and services.
- *Office expenses.* These are the usual expenses incurred to run an office, including rent, utilities, and supplies.

Depending on the size of the department, it may be necessary to further subdivide the preceding expenses by functional area within the department. Specifically, consider separately tracking the performance of the following areas:

- Direct selling to customers
- Sales promotions
- Market research
- Customer service
- Customer warranties
- Selling activities by region

The most common type of sales and marketing budget is one that itemizes expenses by type. This is a simple design that shows budgeted compensation, promotions, travel, office expenses, and so forth. An example of this budget format appears in the following exhibit.

**Sales and Marketing Budget by Expense Type**

| Expense Type | Quarter 1 | Quarter 2 | Quarter 3 | Quarter 4 | Total |
|---|---|---|---|---|---|
| Salaries and wages | $270,000 | $275,000 | $320,000 | $380,000 | $1,245,000 |
| Commissions | 10,000 | 70,000 | 120,000 | 140,000 | 340,000 |
| Payroll taxes | 22,000 | 27,000 | 35,000 | 41,000 | 125,000 |
| Promotions | 0 | 50,000 | 85,000 | 42,000 | 177,000 |
| Advertising | 20,000 | 22,000 | 22,000 | 28,000 | 92,000 |
| Research | 0 | 0 | 35,000 | 0 | 35,000 |
| Travel and entertainment | 40,000 | 20,000 | 80,000 | 70,000 | 210,000 |
| Office expenses | 15,000 | 15,000 | 21,000 | 21,000 | 72,000 |
| Other | 5,000 | 5,000 | 5,000 | 5,000 | 20,000 |
| Totals | $382,000 | $484,000 | $723,000 | $727,000 | $2,316,000 |

Though the budget format by expense type is the most common, it also tends to hide what may be very important information at the sales region and customer level. Ideally, the primary sales and marketing budget should be by expense type, with additional budgeting at the territory and customer levels if you feel that the additional amount of budgeting investigation creates valuable information.

If a company is organized by sales territory, recast the sales and marketing budget to determine the projected level of expenditures by territory. This is particularly important if most of the sales staff is assigned to specific territories, since this means that most of the cost structure of the company is oriented toward the territory format. Then match territory gross margins with territory sales and marketing costs to determine earnings by territory. A typical format for such a budget appears in the following exhibit.

**Sales and Marketing Budget by Territory**

| Sales Territory | Quarter 1 | Quarter 2 | Quarter 3 | Quarter 4 | Total |
|---|---|---|---|---|---|
| Department overhead | $250,000 | $255,000 | $255,000 | $260,000 | $1,020,000 |
| | | | | | |
| Northeast region | | | | | |
| Compensation | 400,000 | 410,000 | 430,000 | 450,000 | 1,690,000 |
| Promotions | 65,000 | 0 | 75,000 | 0 | 140,000 |
| Travel | 23,000 | 23,000 | 25,000 | 25,000 | 96,000 |
| Other | 18,000 | 19,000 | 19,000 | 19,000 | 75,000 |
| Subtotal | $506,000 | $452,000 | $549,000 | $494,000 | $2,001,000 |
| | | | | | |
| North central region | | | | | |
| Compensation | 450,000 | 600,000 | 620,000 | 630,000 | 2,300,000 |
| Promotions | 75,000 | 0 | 80,000 | 0 | 155,000 |
| Travel | 31,000 | 33,000 | 35,000 | 39,000 | 138,000 |
| Other | 20,000 | 24,000 | 26,000 | 26,000 | 96,000 |
| Subtotal | $576,000 | $657,000 | $761,000 | $695,000 | $2,689,000 |
| | | | | | |
| Totals | $1,332,000 | $1,364,000 | $1,565,000 | $1,449,000 | $5,710,000 |

## Diminishing Returns Analysis

A company will find that, after it achieves a certain amount of sales volume, the cost of generating additional sales goes up. This is caused by a variety of factors, such as having to offer more product features, ship products into more distant sales regions, increase warranty coverage, and so forth. Thus, the cost of obtaining each incremental sale will eventually reach the point where there is no further profit to be gained.

The concept of diminishing returns analysis is a useful one for the sales manager, since he or she should realize that it requires a gradual proportional increase in the sales and marketing budget over time in order to continue to increase sales. It is not wise to assume that the costs incurred in the preceding year to generate a certain sales volume can be applied to the next tranche of projected sales growth.

The concept of diminishing returns is difficult to calculate precisely, since it can appear in varying degrees throughout the budget. Here are some areas to be aware of:

- *Incremental sales staff.* If a sales person is added to an existing sales territory, it is likely that the existing sales staff is already handling the easiest sales, which means that the new hire will have to work harder to gain a smaller amount of sales than the average salesperson. Estimate this reduced amount and build it into the budget.

- *Incremental advertising.* If a new advertising campaign is designed to bring in new customers, does the campaign target a smaller group than had been the case with previous campaigns, or is the targeted group one with less income to spend? Has research shown that increasing amounts of advertising result in incrementally fewer sales? If so, is there an optimal advertising expenditure level beyond which the return on funds expended declines?
- *Incremental region.* When a new geographic area is added, consider how the new region varies from the company's existing sales territories. If it has a less dense population, it may be more expensive to contact them regarding a sale. If there is entrenched competition, expect a lower market share than normal. If products must be converted for use in a different language, how does the cost of doing so alter the product profit?
- *Incremental product.* If a product is added to an existing product line, will the new addition cannibalize the sales of other products in the product line?
- *Incremental sales channel.* When a new sales channel is added, does it cannibalize the sales of an existing channel? What is the cost of the infrastructure required to maintain the new channel? Will the new channel damage the company's relations with distributors or retailers?

This discussion does not mean that the sales manager should not push for continual sales growth, only that a detailed analysis is needed to clarify the diminishing returns that will be generated from the increased sales, and to ensure that those returns are noted in the budget.

## The Research and Development Budget

The amount of funds to allocate to the research and development (R&D) budget can be an extraordinarily difficult discussion, for there is no correct answer – a small amount carefully invested can have an enormous payback, while a large investment can be frittered away among a variety of ho-hum projects. Still, there are several ways to generate a general estimate of how much funding to assign to R&D. They are:

- *Historical.* If a certain funding level has worked for the company in the past, consider using it again – adjusted for inflation.
- *Industry benchmark.* If the industry as a whole spends a certain proportion of sales on R&D, this at least gives an indication of the level of spending required to compete over the long term. Better yet, isolate the same metric for just the top-performing competitors, since their level of R&D spending is more likely to be the company's target.
- *Best in class benchmark.* Look outside of the industry for companies that do a very good job on their R&D, and match their spending level as a proportion of sales. This is a particularly important approach when the company is

in a moribund industry where R&D spending is minimal, and management wants to take a different approach.

- *Percent of cash flow.* Management may be willing to spend a certain proportion of its available cash on R&D on an ongoing basis, irrespective of what competitors are spending. This is a much better approach than apportioning a percentage of net income to R&D, since net income does not necessarily equate to cash flow, and a commitment to spend a certain proportion of net income could lead to a cash shortage.

No matter what method is used to derive the appropriate funding level, senior management should settle upon the *minimum* R&D funding level that must be maintained over the long term in order to remain competitive in the industry, and be sure never to drop below that figure.

The R&D budget is typically comprised of the following expense categories:

- *Compensation and benefits.* Compensation tends to be the largest R&D expenditure.
- *Contract services.* It is common to shift some research work to independent laboratories that specialize in particular types of work. In some cases, virtually all R&D work may be contracted out, in which case this becomes the largest R&D expenditure category.
- *Consumable supplies.* In some types of R&D, the staff may use (or destroy) a significant amount of supplies as part of its work. Depending on the situation, this can be quite a significant expense.
- *Office expenses.* These are the standard operational costs of running a department, such as utilities and office rent.
- *Depreciation on equipment.* There will be recurring depreciation charges for any fixed assets used by the R&D staff.
- *Amortization of acquired intangible assets.* If a company has acquired a patent or other intangible asset from another entity, it will likely have to amortize the asset over its useful life.

There are three general formats that can be used to construct an R&D budget. They are:

- *Integrated into engineering department.* If the amount of funds expended on R&D is minor, it is not necessary to budget for it separately. Instead, include it within the budget for the engineering department, either aggregated into a single line item or spread among the various expense line items attributable to that department.
- *Treated as a separate department.* If the expenditures associated with specific projects are relatively minor, and the R&D staff may be occupied with several projects at the same time, it may be sufficient to simply aggregate all expenses into a department-level budget for R&D, and not attempt to further assign expenses to specific projects.

- *Treated as projects within a department.* If there are significant expenditures that can be traced to individual projects, consider creating an R&D budget that clearly shows which projects are expected to consume funds.

The following two examples show the budget reporting format for treating R&D as a separate department with no further subdivision by project, and for revealing projects within the department.

**Sample R&D Budget at the Department Level**

| | Quarter 1 | Quarter 2 | Quarter 3 | Quarter 4 | Total |
|---|---|---|---|---|---|
| Compensation | $150,000 | $150,000 | $160,000 | $165,000 | $625,000 |
| Contract services | 320,000 | 180,000 | 450,000 | 250,000 | 1,200,000 |
| Consumable supplies | 25,000 | 25,000 | 25,000 | 25,000 | 100,000 |
| Office expenses | 8,000 | 8,000 | 9,000 | 9,000 | 34,000 |
| Depreciation | 10,000 | 10,000 | 10,000 | 10,000 | 40,000 |
| Amortization | 15,000 | 15,000 | 15,000 | 15,000 | 60,000 |
| Totals | $528,000 | $388,000 | $669,000 | $474,000 | $2,059,000 |

**Sample R&D Budget at the Project Level**

| | Quarter 1 | Quarter 2 | Quarter 3 | Quarter 4 | Total |
|---|---|---|---|---|---|
| Department overhead | $23,000 | $24,000 | $24,000 | $26,000 | $97,000 |
| | | | | | |
| Project Alpha | | | | | |
| Compensation | 82,000 | 82,000 | 84,000 | 84,000 | 332,000 |
| Contract services | 65,000 | 65,000 | 75,000 | 70,000 | 275,000 |
| Other | 15,000 | 18,000 | 18,000 | 20,000 | 71,000 |
| Project subtotal | 162,000 | 165,000 | 177,000 | 174,000 | 678,000 |
| | | | | | |
| Project Beta | | | | | |
| Compensation | 40,000 | 60,000 | 60,000 | 60,000 | 220,000 |
| Contract services | 35,000 | 30,000 | 30,000 | 30,000 | 125,000 |
| Other | 5,000 | 7,000 | 7,000 | 10,000 | 29,000 |
| Project subtotal | 80,000 | 97,000 | 97,000 | 100,000 | 374,000 |
| | | | | | |
| Totals | $265,000 | $286,000 | $298,000 | $300,000 | $1,149,000 |

Note in the second example that not all expenses could be assigned to a specific project, so they were instead listed separately from the projects under the "department overhead" designation.

## The Administration Budget

The administration budget contains all of the expenses that are not directly involved in the provision of products or services to customers, or their sale to customers. This usually means that the following departments are included in the administration budget:

| | | |
|---|---|---|
| Accounting | Human resources | Public relations |
| Corporate | Information technology | Risk management (insurance) |
| Facilities | Internal auditing | Treasury |
| | Legal | |

In a larger company, there may be individual budgets for each of these departments, rather than an administration department.

The expense line items included in the administration budget generally include the following:

| | | |
|---|---|---|
| Audit fees | Director fees | Payroll taxes |
| Bank fees | Dues and subscriptions | Property taxes |
| Charitable contributions | Employee benefits | Rent |
| Compensation | Insurance | Supplies |
| Consulting fees | Legal fees | Travel and entertainment |
| Depreciation | | Utilities |

The information in the administration budget is not directly derived from any other budgets. Instead, managers use the general level of corporate activity to determine the appropriate amount of expenditure. When creating this budget, consider the following issues:

- *Compensation*. The largest item in this budget is usually employee compensation, so pay particular attention to the formulation of this amount and test it for reasonableness.
- *Historical basis*. The amounts in this budget are frequently carried forward from actual results in the preceding year. This may be reasonable, but some costs may disappear due to the termination of a contract, or increase due to contractually scheduled price increases.
- *Step costs*. Determine when any step costs may be incurred, such as additional staff to support reporting requirements when a company goes public, and incorporate them into the budget.

- *Zero base analysis*. It may be useful to occasionally re-create the administration budget from the ground up, justifying the need for each expense. This is a time-consuming process, but may uncover a few expense items that can be eliminated.

The following example illustrates the basic layout of an administration budget.

---

**EXAMPLE**

Milagro Corporation compiles the following administration budget, which is organized by expense line item:

| | Quarter 1 | Quarter 2 | Quarter 3 | Quarter 4 |
|---|---|---|---|---|
| Audit fees | $35,000 | $0 | $0 | $0 |
| Bank fees | 500 | 500 | 500 | 500 |
| Insurance | 5,000 | 5,500 | 6,000 | 6,000 |
| Payroll taxes | 10,000 | 10,500 | 10,500 | 11,000 |
| Property taxes | 0 | 25,000 | 0 | 0 |
| Rent | 11,000 | 11,000 | 11,000 | 14,000 |
| Salaries | 140,000 | 142,000 | 144,000 | 146,000 |
| Supplies | 2,000 | 2,000 | 2,000 | 2,000 |
| Travel and entertainment | 4,500 | 8,000 | 4,000 | 4,000 |
| Utilities | 2,500 | 3,000 | 3,000 | 4,000 |
| Other expenses | 1,500 | 1,500 | 1,500 | 2,000 |
| Total expenses | $212,000 | $209,000 | $182,500 | $189,500 |

The CEO of Milagro likes to restate the administration budget by department, so that he can assign responsibility for expenditures to the managers of those departments. This results in the following variation on the same budget:

| | Quarter 1 | Quarter 2 | Quarter 3 | Quarter 4 |
|---|---|---|---|---|
| Accounting department | $130,500 | $102,500 | $102,000 | $108,000 |
| Corporate department | 30,000 | 30,000 | 30,000 | 30,000 |
| Human resources department | 19,500 | 19,500 | 18,000 | 19,000 |
| IT department | 25,000 | 25,000 | 25,000 | 25,000 |
| Treasury department | 7,000 | 7,000 | 7,500 | 7,500 |
| Unassigned expenses | 0 | 25,000 | 0 | 0 |
| Total expenses | $212,000 | $209,000 | $182,500 | $189,500 |

The reconfigured administration budget contains an "unassigned expenses" line item for property taxes, since management does not believe that expense is specifically controllable by any of the administrative departments.

---

The preceding example reveals a common characteristic of many line items in the administration budget, which is that most costs are fixed over the short term, and so only vary slightly from period to period. The exceptions are pay increases and scheduled events, such as audits. Otherwise, the main reason for a sudden change in an administrative expense is a step cost, such as increasing the headcount. This type of minimal cost variability is typical for the administration budget.

## The Compensation Budget

The key goals of a compensation budget are to itemize the pay rates of all employees, the dates on which their pay will be altered, and all associated payroll taxes. This budget is usually contained within the various departmental budgets. We describe it separately here, because it involves several unique budgeting issues.

The compensation budget in the following example separates the calculation of compensation, social security taxes, Medicare taxes, and federal unemployment taxes. The separate calculation of these items is the only way to achieve a reasonable level of accuracy in the calculation of payroll taxes, since there are different tax rates and wage caps associated with each of the taxes. The pertinent information related to each of the indicated payroll taxes is noted in the following exhibit.

**Payroll Tax Information**

| Tax Type | Tax Rate | 2019 Wage Cap |
|---|---|---|
| Social security | 6.20% | $132,900 |
| Medicare | 1.45% | No cap |
| Federal unemployment | 0.80% | $7,000 |

In a lower-wage environment, there may be few employees whose pay exceeds the social security wage cap, which makes the social security tax budget quite simple to calculate. However, in situations where compensation levels are quite high, expect to meet social security wage caps within the first two or three quarters of the year. Given the size of the social security match paid by employers, it is especially important to budget for the correct amount of tax; otherwise, the compensation budget could be inaccurate by a significant amount.

The simplest of the tax calculations is for the Medicare tax, since there is no wage cap for it. We have presented its calculation in the example as a table in which we calculate it for each individual employee. However, given the lack of a wage cap, you can more easily create a budget for it with a single line item that multiplies total compensation in every budget period by the Medicare tax rate.

Given the size of the social security and Medicare expenses, the paltry amount of the federal unemployment tax may seem like an afterthought. However, since it is based on a very low wage cap, nearly all of the expense is incurred in the first calendar quarter of each year, where it represents a modest expense bump. Some companies create a separate budget schedule for this expense, just to ensure that the correct amount is included in the first quarter of each year. Others find the cost to be so insignificant that they do not track it.

These concepts are noted in the following example, where we present separate budgets for base pay, social security, Medicare, and federal unemployment taxes, and then aggregate them into a master compensation budget.

---

**EXAMPLE**

Milagro Corporation is starting up a small group that will deal with research concerning the flavor of Kenyan and Ethiopian coffee beans. The company decides to create a separate compensation budget for the group, which includes five employees. The compensation budget is as follows, with quarters in which pay raises are scheduled being highlighted. Note that the annual salary is stated in each calendar quarter.

**Base Pay Budget**

| | Quarter 1 | Quarter 2 | Quarter 3 | Quarter 4 |
|---|---|---|---|---|
| Erskin, Donald | $75,000 | $75,000 | $79,500 | $79,500 |
| Fells, Arnold | 45,000 | 46,250 | 46,250 | 46,250 |
| Gainsborough, Amy | 88,000 | 88,000 | 88,000 | 91,500 |
| Harmon, Debra | 68,500 | 68,500 | 70,000 | 70,000 |
| Illescu, Adriana | 125,000 | 125,000 | 125,000 | 125,000 |
| Annual compensation | $401,500 | $402,750 | $408,750 | $412,250 |
| Quarterly compensation | $100,375 | $100,688 | $102,188 | $103,063 |

**Social Security Budget (6.2% tax, $132,900 wage cap)**

| | Quarter 1 | Quarter 2 | Quarter 3 | Quarter 4 |
|---|---|---|---|---|
| Erskin, Donald | $1,163 | $1,163 | $1,232 | $1,232 |
| Fells, Arnold | 698 | 717 | 717 | 717 |
| Gaisborough, Amy | 1,364 | 1,364 | 1,364 | 1,418 |
| Harmon, Debra | 1,062 | 1,062 | 1,085 | 1,085 |
| Illescu, Adriana | 1,938 | 1,938 | 1,938 | 1,938 |
| Totals | $6,225 | $6,244 | $6,336 | $6,390 |

**Medicare Budget (1.45% tax, no wage cap)**

| | Quarter 1 | Quarter 2 | Quarter 3 | Quarter 4 |
|---|---|---|---|---|
| Erskin, Donald | $272 | $272 | $288 | $288 |
| Fells, Arnold | 163 | 168 | 168 | 168 |
| Gaisborough, Amy | 319 | 319 | 319 | 332 |
| Harmon, Debra | 248 | 248 | 254 | 254 |
| Illescu, Adriana | 453 | 453 | 453 | 453 |
| Totals | $1,455 | $1,460 | $1,482 | $1,495 |

**Federal Unemployment Tax Budget (0.8% tax, $7,000 wage cap)**

| | Quarter 1 | Quarter 2 | Quarter 3 | Quarter 4 |
|---|---|---|---|---|
| Erskin, Donald | $56 | $0 | $0 | $0 |
| Fells, Arnold | 56 | 0 | 0 | 0 |
| Gaisborough, Amy | 56 | 0 | 0 | 0 |
| Harmon, Debra | 56 | 0 | 0 | 0 |
| Illescu, Adriana | 56 | 0 | 0 | 0 |
| Totals | $280 | $0 | $0 | $0 |

Milagro then shifts the summary totals from each of the preceding tables into a master compensation budget, as follows:

**Master Compensation Budget**

| | Quarter 1 | Quarter 2 | Quarter 3 | Quarter 4 |
|---|---|---|---|---|
| Total base pay | $100,375 | $100,688 | $102,188 | $103,063 |
| Total social security | 6,225 | 6,244 | 6,336 | 6,390 |
| Total Medicare | 1,455 | 1,460 | 1,482 | 1,495 |
| Total unemployment | 280 | 0 | 0 | 0 |
| Grand totals | $108,335 | $108,392 | $110,006 | $110,948 |

---

In the preceding example, compensation is shown in each quarter on an annualized basis, since it is easier to review the budget for errors when the information is presented in this manner. The information is then stepped down to a quarterly basis, which is used to calculate payroll taxes.

Overtime is difficult to predict at the level of an individual employee, but can be estimated at a more aggregated level. It is easiest to use the historical proportion of overtime hours, adjusted for expectations in the budget period. This means that an overtime percentage can be multiplied by the aggregate amount of employee compensation to derive the amount of budgeted overtime pay. The following example illustrates the concept.

**EXAMPLE**

Milagro Corporation operates a production line for which the sales season is November through January. Milagro prefers to deactivate the production line for the first half of the calendar year and then run it with substantial employee overtime during the third quarter and a portion of the fourth quarter of the year. Doing so results in the following overtime budget, which also assumes that a production crew is still working during the first half of the year – they just happen to be working on other production lines.

| | Quarter 1 | Quarter 2 | Quarter 3 | Quarter 4 |
|---|---|---|---|---|
| Total wage expense | $250,000 | $255,000 | $270,000 | $240,000 |
| Overtime percentage | 0% | 2% | 28% | 12% |
| Overtime pay | $0 | $5,100 | $75,600 | $28,800 |
| | | | | |
| Social security for overtime pay | $0 | $316 | $4,687 | $1,786 |
| Medicare for overtime pay | 0 | $74 | $1,096 | $418 |
| | | | | |
| Total overtime compensation | $0 | $390 | $5,783 | $2,204 |

There is no calculation of the federal unemployment tax in the overtime budget, since that amount has such a low wage cap that the maximum amount would already have been included in the compensation budget.

The trouble with the overtime calculation format just presented is that it does not account for the social security wage cap, which is calculated at the level of the individual employee. It is easiest to simply assume that the wage cap is never reached, which may result in some excess amount of social security tax being budgeted. Realistically, few employees who are paid on an hourly basis will exceed the wage cap, so this should be a minor issue for most companies.

## The Budgeted Income Statement

The core of the master budget is the budgeted income statement. It is derived from nearly all of the budgets that we have already discussed, and looks quite a bit like a standard income statement. This is a sufficient summarization of the budget for many companies, because they are primarily concerned with *financial performance.* However, some companies may still have an interest in their projected *financial position* (especially cash), which is contained in the balance sheet. Since the balance sheet is more difficult to derive than the income statement, they may be content to use a rough calculation of ending cash position whose components are mostly derived from information already in the budget. The following sample income statement contains this rough estimation of the ending cash balance in each period.

**Sample Budgeted Income Statement**

| | Quarter 1 | Quarter 2 | Quarter 3 | Quarter 4 |
|---|---|---|---|---|
| Revenue | $2,200,000 | $2,425,000 | $2,500,000 | $2,545,000 |
| | | | | |
| Cost of goods sold: | | | | |
| Direct labor expense | 220,000 | 253,000 | 253,000 | 253,000 |
| Direct materials expense | 767,000 | 838,000 | 831,000 | 840,000 |
| Manufacturing overhead | 293,000 | 293,000 | 309,000 | 310,000 |
| Total cost of goods sold | 1,280,000 | 1,384,000 | 1,393,000 | 1,403,000 |
| Gross margin | $920,000 | $1,041,000 | $1,107,000 | $1,142,000 |
| | | | | |
| Sales and marketing | 315,000 | 351,000 | 374,000 | 339,000 |
| Administration | 453,500 | 452,500 | 435,000 | 447,000 |
| Research and development | 50,000 | 52,000 | 54,000 | 55,500 |
| Profits before taxes | $101,500 | $185,500 | $244,000 | $300,500 |
| Income taxes | 35,500 | 65,000 | 85,500 | 105,000 |
| Profits after taxes | $66,000 | $120,500 | $158,500 | $195,500 |
| | | | | |
| Cash flow: | | | | |
| Beginning cash | $50,000 | -$52,500 | $77,500 | $7,000 |
| + Net profit | 66,000 | 120,500 | 158,500 | 195,500 |
| + Depreciation | 19,500 | 17,500 | 18,000 | 18,000 |
| - Capital purchases | -38,000 | -8,000 | -47,000 | -28,000 |
| - Dividends | -150,000 | 0 | -200,000 | 0 |
| Ending cash | -$52,500 | $77,500 | $7,000 | $192,500 |

The calculation of ending cash is appended to the budgeted income statement because it is partly derived from the net income figure located directly above it in the budget. Also, if a company does not intend to create a balance sheet, it is practical to include a cash calculation on the same page as the income statement.

The trouble with the ending cash measurement presented in the sample is that it is not complete. It does not incorporate any timing delays for when cash may be received or issued, and it also does not factor in the impact of changes in working capital. Thus, it can present inaccurate estimates of cash flow. For a more detailed derivation of ending cash, we need a balance sheet. The compilation of that document is discussed in the next section.

## The Budgeted Balance Sheet

The balance sheet is difficult to derive as part of the budgeting process, because little of the information derived through the budgeting process is designed for it. Instead, a variety of estimates are needed to approximate the amounts of certain asset and liability line items as of the end of each budgeted reporting period. The key elements of the balance sheet that require estimation are accounts receivable, inventory, fixed assets, and accounts payable. We will address the derivation of these items next.

### Accounts Receivable

Accounts receivable is the amount of sales made on credit that have not yet been paid by customers. It is closely correlated with sales, with a delay measured using days sales outstanding (DSO). DSO is calculated as:

$$\frac{\text{Accounts receivable}}{\text{Annual sales} \div 365 \text{ days}}$$

Then apply the DSO figure to projected credit sales during the budget period to determine the amount of accounts receivable outstanding at any given time.

---

**EXAMPLE**

Milagro Corporation has a division whose annual sales are $10 million. Its accounts receivable balance at the end of the most recent month was $1,400,000. Its DSO is calculated as:

$$\frac{\$1{,}400{,}000 \text{ accounts receivable}}{\$10{,}000{,}000 \text{ annual sales} \div 365 \text{ days}}$$

$$= 51 \text{ days sales outstanding}$$

Thus, it takes an average of 51 days for Milagro to collect an account receivable. In its balance sheet budget, Milagro would record as accounts receivable the current month's sales plus 21/30ths of the sales budgeted in the immediately preceding month. Thus, Milagro's budgeted receivables would be calculated as follows for a four-month sample period:

| | December* | January | February | March |
|---|---|---|---|---|
| Credit sales | $790,000 | $810,000 | $815,000 | $840,000 |
| | | | | |
| Receivables for month | -- | 810,000 | 815,000 | 840,000 |
| Receivables from prior month | -- | 553,000 | 567,000 | 571,000 |
| Total receivables in balance sheet | -- | $1,363,000 | $1,382,000 | $1,411,000 |

* Prior year

An alternative approach for calculating the amount of accounts receivable is to determine the percentage of credit sales that are collected within the month of sales and within each of the next 30-day time buckets, and apply these layers of collections to a calculation of the ending accounts receivable in each budget period. The following example illustrates the concept.

---

**EXAMPLE**

The controller of Milagro Corporation decides to use an alternative method for deriving the ending accounts receivable balance for the division described in the preceding example. The controller finds that, historically, the following percentages of credit sales are paid within the stated time periods:

| | Percent Paid | Percent Unpaid |
|---|---|---|
| In month of sale | 10% | 90% |
| In following month | 65% | 25% |
| In 2nd month | 18% | 7% |
| In 3rd month | 5% | 2% |
| In 4th month | 2% | 0% |
| Total | 100% | |

The controller then uses the following table to derive the ending accounts receivable balance for the month of January, which is part of the budget period. The information from the preceding three months is needed to derive the ending accounts receivable balance in January.

| | October (prior year) | November (prior year) | December (prior year) | January |
|---|---|---|---|---|
| Credit sales | $815,000 | $820,000 | $790,000 | $810,000 |
| | | | | |
| 90% of January sales | | | | 729,000 |
| 25% of December sales | | | | 198,000 |
| 7% of November sales | | | | 57,000 |
| 2% of October sales | | | | 16,000 |
| Total ending accounts receivable | | | | $1,000,000 |

---

A truly detailed model would assume an even longer collection period for some receivables, which may extend for twice the number of months shown in the model. If this method is chosen, the increased accuracy from adding more months to the model does not appreciably improve the accuracy of the ending accounts receivable figure. Thus, restrict the accounts receivable layering to no more than three or four months.

The receivables layering method is clearly more labor intensive than the DSO method, though it may result in slightly more accurate results. In the interests of modeling efficiency, we prefer the DSO method. It requires much less space in the budget model, is easy to understand, and produces reasonably accurate results.

## Inventory

There should be a relatively constant relationship between the level of sales and the amount of inventory on hand. Thus, if the historical number of days of inventory on hand is calculated and matched against the budgeted amount of cost of goods sold through the budget period, you can estimate the amount of inventory that should be on hand at the end of each budget period. The calculation of the days of inventory on hand is:

$$\frac{\text{Inventory}}{\text{Annual cost of goods sold} \div 365\text{ days}}$$

The estimation concept is shown in the following example.

---

**EXAMPLE**

Milagro Corporation has a division that manufactures industrial-grade coffee bean roasters. It maintains a substantial amount of raw materials and finished goods. The company calculates the days of inventory on hand for the preceding quarter as follows:

$$\frac{\$1{,}000{,}000\text{ ending inventory}}{\$1{,}875{,}000\text{ quarterly cost of goods sold} \div 91\text{ days}}$$

$$= 49\text{ days of inventory on hand}$$

Milagro expects that the division will continue to have roughly the same proportion of inventory to sales throughout the budget period, so it uses the same days of inventory on hand calculation to derive the ending inventory for each budget period as follows:

| | Quarter 1 | Quarter 2 | Quarter 3 | Quarter 4 |
|---|---|---|---|---|
| Cost of goods sold (quarterly) | $1,875,000 | $2,000,000 | $2,100,000 | $1,900,000 |
| Cost of goods sold (monthly) | 625,000 | 667,000 | 700,000 | 633,000 |
| | | | | |
| Days of inventory assumption | 49 days | 49 days | 49 days | 49 days |
| Ending inventory* | $1,021,000 | $1,089,000 | $1,143,000 | $1,034,000 |

* Calculated as monthly cost of goods sold × (49 days ÷ 30 days)

The calculation reduces the quarterly cost of goods sold to a monthly figure, so that it can more easily be compared to the days of inventory on hand.

---

### Fixed Assets

The amount and timing of expenditures for fixed assets come from the capital budgeting process, and are easily transferred into a fixed asset table that can be used as a source document for the budgeted balance sheet. Further, it may be useful to include in the schedule a standard amount of capital expenditures for each new employee hired; this typically includes the cost of office furniture and computer equipment. Finally, there will always be unforeseen asset purchases, so be sure to reserve some funds for them.

In addition, one can add to the table a calculation of the depreciation associated with newly-acquired assets. Also include an estimate of the depreciation associated with *existing* assets, which can be easily derived either from a fixed asset tracking spreadsheet or software. This information is used in the budgeted income statement.

The following example illustrates the concepts of scheduling fixed assets and depreciation.

---

**EXAMPLE**

Milagro Corporation plans to hire 10 administrative staff into one of its divisions during the budget year, and also plans to buy a variety of fixed assets. The following schedule itemizes the major types of fixed assets and the timing of their acquisition. It also includes a summary of the depreciation for both the existing and to-be-acquired assets.

| | Quarter 1 | Quarter 2 | Quarter 3 | Quarter 4 |
|---|---|---|---|---|
| Fixed asset purchases: | | | | |
| Furniture and fixtures | $28,000 | $0 | $0 | $32,000 |
| Office equipment | 0 | 40,000 | 0 | 0 |
| Production equipment | 100,000 | 25,000 | 80,000 | 0 |
| Vehicles | 32,000 | 0 | 32,000 | 0 |
| Unspecified purchases | 15,000 | 15,000 | 15,000 | 15,000 |
| Subtotal | $175,000 | $80,000 | $127,000 | $47,000 |
| | | | | |
| Purchases for new hires: | | | | |
| Headcount additions | 3 | 2 | 1 | 4 |
| $6,000 × New hires | $18,000 | $12,000 | $6,000 | $24,000 |
| | | | | |
| Total fixed asset purchases | $193,000 | $92,000 | $133,000 | $71,000 |

| | Quarter 1 | Quarter 2 | Quarter 3 | Quarter 4 |
|---|---|---|---|---|
| Depreciation on new purchases: | | | | |
| Furniture and fixtures (7 year) | $1,000 | $1,000 | $1,000 | $2,142 |
| Office equipment (5 year) | 0 | 2,000 | 2,000 | 2,000 |
| Production equipment (10 year) | 2,500 | 3,125 | 5,125 | 5,125 |
| Vehicles (5 year) | 1,600 | 1,600 | 3,200 | 3,200 |
| Unspecified purchases (5 year) | 750 | 1,500 | 2,250 | 3,000 |
| Subtotal | $5,850 | $9,225 | $13,575 | $15,467 |
| Depreciation on existing assets | 108,000 | 107,500 | 105,000 | 99,500 |
| Total depreciation | $113,850 | $116,725 | $118,575 | $114,967 |

---

## Accounts Payable

Accounts payable can be estimated with a reasonable amount of precision, because there is usually a constant relationship between the level of credit purchases from suppliers and the amount of unpaid accounts payable. Thus, if you can calculate the days of accounts payable that are usually on hand, it can be related to the estimated amount of credit purchases per accounting period to derive the ending accounts payable balance. The formula for accounts payable days is:

$$\frac{\text{Accounts payable}}{\text{Annual credit purchases} \div 365}$$

The estimation concept is illustrated in the following example.

---

**EXAMPLE**

Milagro Corporation has a division whose annual purchases on credit in the past year were $4,250,000. Its average accounts payable balance during that period was $410,000. The calculation of its accounts payable days is:

$$\frac{\$410{,}000 \text{ accounts payable}}{\$4{,}250{,}000 \text{ annual credit purchases} \div 365}$$

$$= 35 \text{ accounts payable days}$$

Milagro expects that the division will continue to have roughly the same proportion of credit terms with its suppliers through the budget period, so it uses the same accounts payable days amount to derive the ending accounts payable for each budget period as follows:

| | Quarter 1 | Quarter 2 | Quarter 3 | Quarter 4 |
|---|---|---|---|---|
| Purchases on credit (monthly) | $350,000 | $380,000 | $390,000 | $400,000 |
| | | | | |
| Accounts payable days assumption | 35 days | 35 days | 35 days | 35 days |
| Ending accounts payable* | $408,000 | $443,000 | $455,000 | $467,000 |

* Calculated as monthly purchases on credit × (35 days ÷ 30 days)

---

The problem with the calculation of accounts payable is where to find the information about credit purchases. To calculate the amount of credit purchases, start with the total expenses for the measurement period and subtract all payroll and payroll tax expenses, as well as depreciation and amortization. There are other adjusting factors, such as expense accruals and payments made in cash, but this simple calculation should approximate the amount of purchases on credit.

### Additional Estimation Elements

There are a few other line items in the balance sheet that require estimation for the budget period. These items are usually adjusted manually, rather than through the use of any formulas. They are:

- *Prepaid expenses*. This line item includes expenses that were paid in advance, and which therefore may be charged to expense at some point during or after the budget period. Examples of prepaid expenses are prepaid rent and insurance. These items may not change in proportion to the level of general corporate activity, so it is best to track them on a separate spreadsheet and manually determine when there will be additions to and deletions from the account.
- *Other assets*. There are likely to be a smorgasbord of stray assets on a company's books that are aggregated into this account. Examples of other assets are rent deposits, payroll advances, and accounts receivable from company officers. As was the case with prepaid expenses, these items may not change in proportion to the level of corporate activity, so track them separately and manually adjust the budget for any changes in them.
- *Income taxes payable*. If a company is earning a taxable profit, it must make estimated tax payments on the 15th days of April, June, September, and December. Either schedule these payments to equal the tax paid in the previous year, or a proportion of the actual tax liability in the budget year. Budgeting for this liability based on the tax paid in the previous year is quite simple. If you choose to instead budget for a liability equal to a proportion of the actual tax liability in the budget year, use the effective tax rate expected for the entire year.

If you are budgeting for this liability based on the net income in the budget year, it can be difficult to estimate. The budget model may be using accelerated depreciation for the calculation of taxable income, as well as other deferred tax recognition strategies that cause a difference between taxable and actual net income. If such is the case, track these differences in a supporting budget schedule.

- *Accrued liabilities*. There may be a variety of accrued liabilities, such as unpaid vacation time, unpaid wages, and unpaid property taxes. In some cases, such as property taxes, the liability is unlikely to vary unless the company alters its property ownership, and so can be safely extended through the budget period with no alterations. In other cases, such as unpaid vacation time and unpaid wages, there is a direct correlation between the general level of corporate activity (such as headcount) and the amount of the liability. In these cases, use a formula to adjust the liability based on the appropriate underlying measure of activity.
- *Notes payable*. This can encompass loans and leases. Most of these items are on fixed repayment schedules, so a simple repayment table is usually sufficient for tracking the gradual reduction of notes payable. Also, deduct the amount of each periodic debt repayment from the amount of cash on hand. Additions to the notes payable line are addressed in the financing budget.
- *Equity*. The equity section of the balance sheet is composed of a beginning balance that is rolled forward from the previous period, a retained earnings balance into which is incorporated any gains and losses as the budget period progresses over time, and various equity-related financing issues that are addressed in the financing budget.

## The Cash Line Item

After filling in all other parts of the balance sheet, the cash line item becomes the "plug" entry to make the statement balance. Just because an amount is entered in the cash line item does not mean that the company will necessarily generate that amount of cash. An early iteration of a budgeted balance sheet has a strange way of revealing an astonishing surplus of cash! Instead, once the initial version of the balance sheet has been created, test it to see if all of the line items are reasonable. Use the following techniques to do so:

- *Growth impact*. If the company is planning on substantial growth, this means that the investment in accounts receivable and inventory should grow significantly, which will consume cash. Conversely, if the company plans to shrink, it should be converting these same items into cash. Thus, if the proposed balance sheet appears to be retaining a consistent amount of working capital through the budget period, irrespective of the sales level, the working capital line items should probably be revised.
- *Historical comparison*. Compare all line items in the proposed balance sheet to the same line items in the balance sheet for various periods in the preced-

ing year. Are the numbers about the same, or are they approximately in the same proportions to each other? If not, investigate why there are differences.

- *Turnover analysis*. Compare the amount of accounts receivable, inventory, and accounts payable turnover in the proposed budget to the actual turnover ratios for these items in the preceding year. Unless significant structural changes are being made in a business, it is likely that the same turnover ratios should apply to the budget period.

If you are satisfied that the budgeted balance sheet appears reasonable after these tests, the cash line item may also be considered achievable.

## The Financing Budget

Once a first draft of the budget has been prepared and a preliminary balance sheet constructed, you will have an idea of the cash requirements of the business, and can then construct a financing budget.

This budget addresses the need of a business for *more* cash. A financing budget can be constructed that addresses this need in two ways:

- *Obtain a loan*. At a minimum, it is usually possible to obtain an asset-based loan (i.e., one that is backed by a company's accounts receivable and inventory). However, these loans are also limited to a proportion of those assets, and so may not be overly large. Other loans that are not tied to assets usually carry a substantially higher interest rate.
- *Sell stock*. If the existing shareholders are amenable, consider selling stock in the company to current or new investors. Unlike a loan, there is no obligation to pay the money back, so this addition to equity reduces the financial risk of the company. However, investors expect a high return on their investment through an increase in the value of the company or increased dividends.

In addition to these financing solutions, also consider going back into the main budget and making one or more of the following changes, thereby altering the amount of cash needed by the business:

- *Cost reduction*. There may be some parts of the business where expenses can be pruned in order to fund more activities elsewhere. Across-the-board reductions are usually a bad idea, since some parts of the business may already be running at a minimal expenditure level, and further reductions would cut into their performance.
- *Discretionary items*. If there are discretionary expenditures in the budget whose absence will not have an immediate impact on the business, consider reducing or eliminating them or changing the date on which they are purchased.

- *Dividends*. If there are dividends planned that have not yet been authorized by the board of directors, consider either reducing them or delaying the payment date.
- *Sales growth*. If the budgeted level of sales is creating a significant requirement for more working capital and capital expenditures, consider reducing the amount of planned growth to meet the amount of available financing.
- *Sell assets*. If there is a strong need for cash that is driven by an excellent business opportunity, it may be time to sell off assets in lower-performing parts of the business and invest the funds in the new opportunity.

Once management has made all of the preceding adjustments, construct the financing budget. It should contain an itemization of the cash position as stated in the budgeted balance sheet, after which are itemized the various types of financing needed to ensure that the company maintains a positive cash balance at all times. In addition, there should be a section that derives from the balance sheet the total amount that the company can potentially borrow against its assets; this establishes an upper limit on the amount of borrowing. The following example illustrates the concept of the financing budget.

---

**EXAMPLE**

Milagro Corporation has completed a first draft of its budget, and finds that there are several cash shortfalls during the budget period. The following financing budget is constructed to address the problem.

| | Quarter 1 | Quarter 2 | Quarter 3 | Quarter 4 |
|---|---|---|---|---|
| Available asset base: | | | | |
| Ending inventory | $1,200,000 | $1,280,000 | $1,310,000 | $1,350,000 |
| Ending trade receivables | 1,800,000 | 1,850,000 | 1,920,000 | 1,980,000 |
| | | | | |
| Allowable inventory (60%) | 720,000 | 768,000 | 786,000 | 810,000 |
| Allowable receivables (80%) | 1,440,000 | 1,480,000 | 1,536,000 | 1,584,000 |
| Total borrowing base | $2,160,000 | $2,248,000 | $2,322,000 | $2,394,000 |
| | | | | |
| Preliminary ending cash balance | -$320,000 | -$480,000 | -$600,000 | -$680,000 |
| | | | | |
| **Debt Funding:** | | | | |
| Beginning loan balance | $2,000,000 | | | |
| Available debt* | 160,000 | 88,000 | 74,000 | 72,000 |
| Adjusted ending cash balance | -160,000 | -$232,000 | -$278,000 | -$286,000 |
| | | | | |
| **Equity Funding:** | | | | |
| Stock issuance | $400,000 | 0 | 0 | 0 |
| Final ending cash balance | $240,000 | $168,000 | $122,000 | $114,000 |

* Calculated as the total borrowing base minus existing debt

The financing budget reveals that Milagro has already used most of the debt available under its loan agreement, and is only able to incrementally borrow in each quarter as the amount of underlying assets gradually increases. To fund the remaining cash shortfall, Milagro plans to sell $400,000 of stock to investors in the first quarter. This not only provides enough cash to cover the projected shortfall, but also leaves a small residual cash buffer.

---

If the financing budget includes a provision for more debt, include a line item in the budgeted income statement to address the associated incremental increase in interest expense. This means that there is a feedback loop between the financing budget and the balance sheet from which it draws its beginning cash balance; the company's financing solutions may impact the beginning cash balance upon which the financing budget is based, which in turn may impact the amount of financing needed.

## The Compiled Balance Sheet

The budgeted balance sheet is derived from all of the preceding discussions in this section about the components of the balance sheet. The balance sheet should be compiled in two parts: a detailed compilation that contains a variety of calculations, and a summary-level version that is indistinguishable from a normal balance sheet. The following sample of a detailed balance sheet compilation includes a discussion of each line item. The numbers in the sample are irrelevant – we are only showing how the balance sheet is constructed.

## Sample Detailed Balance Sheet Compilation

| Line Item | Source | Amount |
|---|---|---|
| **Assets** | | |
| Cash | The amount needed to equalize both sides of the balance sheet | $225,000 |
| Accounts receivable | Based on sales by period and days receivables outstanding | 450,000 |
| Inventory | Based on cost of goods sold by period and days of inventory on hand | 520,000 |
| Prepaid expenses | Based on beginning balance and adjusted for specific changes | 55,000 |
| Fixed assets | Based on beginning balance and changes in the capital budget | 1,490,000 |
| Accumulated depreciation | Based on beginning balance and changes in the capital budget | -230,000 |
| Other assets | Based on beginning balance and adjusted for specific changes | 38,000 |
| **Total assets** | | $2,548,000 |
| | | |
| **Liabilities** | | |
| Accounts payable | Based on credit purchases and days of accounts payable | $182,000 |
| Accrued liabilities | Based on schedule of specific liabilities or based on corporate activity | 99,000 |
| Income taxes payable | Based on either the tax paid in the previous year or a proportion of the actual tax liability in the current year | 75,000 |
| Notes payable | Based on the beginning balance | 720,000 |
| - Debt repayments | Based on a schedule of required repayments | -120,000 |
| + New debt | From the financing budget | 90,000 |
| **Total liabilities** | | $1,046,000 |
| | | |
| **Equity** | | |
| Retained earnings | Based on the beginning balance | 802,000 |
| - Dividends | As per management instructions | -75,000 |
| - Treasury stock purchases | As per management instructions | -50,000 |
| + Profit/loss | From the budgeted income statement | 475,000 |
| + Stock sales | From the financing budget | 350,000 |
| **Total equity** | | $1,502,000 |
| | | |
| **Total liabilities and equity** | | $2,548,000 |

## Summary

This chapter has addressed how to compile an annual budget, using a variety of supporting schedules to create a budgeted income statement and balance sheet. When creating this budget, be careful to examine how well the various elements of the budget support each other, and whether the budgeted outcome is a reasonable extension of how well the company has performed in the past. If not, conduct another iteration of the budget to correct these potential problem areas. If the management team instead elects to operate under the current budget version, it is likely that actual results will soon depart from budgeted expectations.

Thus far, we have only addressed the formulation of a budget. In the next chapter, we discuss how to use a budget as a benchmark for controlling the operations of a business.

# Chapter 15
# Budgetary Control

## Introduction

After creating a budget, it can be used as a basis of comparison to actual results so that management can see how well the business is performing in relation to their expectations. This can be done at a general level, merely reporting differences between budget and actual revenues and expenses. However, this does not show the reasons *why* variances have arisen. In this chapter, we address the various reporting formats that give management the actionable information they need to address unfavorable budget variances. When set up as a standard reporting structure that is closely monitored, the result can be a system for controlling the activities of a business.

**Related Podcast Episode:** Episode 111 of the Accounting Best Practices Podcast discusses variance analysis. It is available at: **accountingtools.com/podcasts** or **iTunes**

## General Reporting Format

There is almost always a budget versus actual reporting format available in the accounting software for the income statement and the departmental income statements. This report reveals any variances between the budgeted and actual amounts. A budget variance is the difference between the budgeted amount of expense or revenue and the actual amount. The budget variance is favorable when the actual revenue is higher than the budget or when the actual expense is less than the budget. The format of such a report is similar to the one in the following sample.

**Sample Budget versus Actual Income Statement**

| | Actual Results | Budget Results | Variance ($) | Variance (%) |
|---|---|---|---|---|
| Revenue | $1,000,000 | $1,100,000 | -$100,000 | -9% |
| | | | | |
| Cost of goods sold: | | | | |
| Direct materials | 300,000 | 330,000 | 30,000 | 9% |
| Direct labor | 100,000 | 90,000 | -10,000 | -11% |
| Manufacturing overhead | 150,000 | 155,000 | 5,000 | 3% |
| Total cost of goods sold | 550,000 | 575,000 | 25,000 | 4% |
| Gross margin | $450,000 | $525,000 | -$75,000 | -14% |
| | | | | |
| Administration expenses | 175,000 | 160,000 | -15,000 | -9% |
| Sales and marketing expenses | 225,000 | 205,000 | -20,000 | -10% |
| | | | | |
| Net profit or loss | $50,000 | $160,000 | -$110,000 | -69% |

This report format does not reveal a great deal of information by itself, since it only notifies management of the presence *of* a variance, not the reason *for* the variance. Further, the budget upon which the variance is calculated may be so far out of line with actual results that the variance is essentially meaningless.

A subtle variation on this report format is to position the largest-dollar items at the top of the report, so that the areas in which variances are likely to be largest are where management can more easily see them. The following example illustrates the concept.

**Sample Sales and Marketing Department Monthly Report**

| Expense Item | Actual | Budget | $ Variance | % Variance |
|---|---|---|---|---|
| Wages | $85,000 | $82,000 | -$3,000 | -4% |
| Commissions | 18,000 | 19,500 | 1,500 | 8% |
| Payroll taxes | 8,000 | 7,500 | -500 | -7% |
| Trade shows | 25,000 | 28,000 | 3,000 | 11% |
| Travel and entertainment | 11,000 | 7,000 | -4,000 | -57% |
| Office expenses | 6,500 | 3,500 | -3,000 | -86% |
| Promotional materials | 5,000 | 5,000 | 0 | 0% |
| Other | 1,200 | 500 | -700 | -58% |
| Totals | $159,700 | $153,000 | -$6,700 | -4% |

Note how the preceding report is structured to place wages and related expenses at the top of the report; this is because compensation costs are the largest expenditure for many departments, and so should be a center of attention.

An alternative format is one that presents a historical trend line of revenues and expenses for each line item in the income statement. Doing so eliminates the risk of comparing a completely inaccurate budget to the actual results. A sample report format follows.

**Sample Trend Line Report Format**

| | Jan. | Feb | Mar. | Apr. | May |
|---|---|---|---|---|---|
| Accounting fees | $1,000 | $1,100 | $1,050 | $1,900 | $1,150 |
| Legal | 0 | 0 | 5,000 | 0 | 250 |
| Maintenance | 550 | 575 | 400 | 600 | 3,250 |
| Office expenses | 925 | 2,800 | 890 | 790 | 850 |
| Travel and entertainment | 6,500 | 1,200 | 1,350 | 1,400 | 995 |
| Utilities | 500 | 310 | 420 | 1,600 | 375 |
| Totals | $9,475 | $5,985 | $9,110 | $6,290 | $6,870 |

The key assumption behind a trend line report is that most expenses do not vary much from period to period. If that assumption is true, the report is excellent for highlighting anomalies over time.

No matter which of the preceding report formats are used, it is rarely sufficient to simply issue financial information to managers without at least some explanation of the larger variances. Instead, the accounting staff should investigate the more material variances and issue a separate report that delves into the reasons for them. The following sample report states the amount of each expense or revenue item that requires explanation, and then spends a fair amount of time describing the situation.

**Sample Variance Discussion Report**

| Line Item | Discussion |
|---|---|
| Product Alpha revenue | Revenues were $100,000 lower than expected, due to a product recall and free replacement. The problem was a design flaw that is being investigated by Engineering. Recommend stopping sales until an engineering change order is released. |
| Direct materials expense | Freight expense was $40,000 higher than expected, due to air freight of late delivery from overseas supplier. Recommend sourcing the part locally. |
| Rent expense | Expense was $20,000 lower than expected, due to renegotiation of building lease. Note that the lease now runs an additional three years. |
| Travel and entertainment expense | Expense was $25,000 higher than expected, due to damage to rental party room during company Christmas party. |
| Utilities expense | Electricity cost was $15,000 higher than expected, due to unusually cold December temperatures. Recommend additional building insulation. |

Note that the best reports of this type very clearly quantify the issue and state the exact cause of the problem, possibly with an accompanying recommendation. The report needs to be sufficiently detailed that management can use it to resolve the underlying problem.

## Revenue Reporting

If it is necessary to report on revenue variances in more detail, the key variance calculations are the selling price variance and the selling volume variance. We describe the calculation and usage of both variances in this section.

### Selling Price Variance

The selling price variance is the difference between the actual and expected revenue that is caused by a change in the price of a product or service. The formula is:

(Actual price - Budgeted price) × Actual unit sales = Selling price variance

An unfavorable variance means that the actual price was lower than the budgeted price.

The budgeted price for each unit of product or sales is developed by the sales and marketing managers, and is based on their estimation of future demand for these products and services, which in turn is affected by general economic conditions and the actions of competitors. If the actual price is lower than the budgeted price, the result may actually be favorable to the company, as long as the price decline spurs demand to such an extent that the company generates an incremental profit as a result of the price decline.

---

**EXAMPLE**

The marketing manager of Quest Adventure Gear estimates that the company can sell a green widget for $80 per unit during the upcoming year. This estimate is based on the historical demand for green widgets.

During the first half of the new year, the price of the green widget comes under extreme pressure as a new supplier in Ireland floods the market with a lower-priced green widget. Quest must drop its price to $70 in order to compete, and sells 20,000 units during that period. Its selling price variance during the first half of the year is:

($70 Actual price - $80 Budgeted price) × 20,000 Units = $(200,000) Selling price variance

---

There are a number of possible causes of a selling price variance. For example:

- *Discounts*. The company has granted various discounts to customers to induce them to buy products.
- *Marketing allowances*. The company is allowing customers to deduct marketing allowances from their payments to reimburse them for marketing activities involving the company's products.
- *Price points*. The price points at which the company is selling are different from the price points stated in its budget.
- *Product options*. Customers are buying different product options than expected, resulting in an average price that differs from the price points stated in the company's budget.

### Sales Volume Variance

The sales volume variance is the difference between the actual and expected number of units sold, multiplied by the budgeted price per unit. The formula is:

(Actual units sold - Budgeted units sold) × Budgeted price per unit

= Sales volume variance

An unfavorable variance means that the actual number of units sold was lower than the budgeted number sold.

The budgeted number of units sold is derived by the sales and marketing managers, and is based on their estimation of how the company's product market share, features, price points, expected marketing activities, distribution channels, and sales in new regions will impact future sales. If the product's selling price is lower than the budgeted amount, this may spur sales to such an extent that the sales volume variance is favorable, even though the selling price variance is unfavorable.

---

**EXAMPLE**

The marketing manager of Quest Adventure Gear estimates that the company can sell 25,000 blue widgets for $65 per unit during the upcoming year. This estimate is based on the historical demand for blue widgets, as supported by new advertising campaigns in the first and third quarters of the year.

During the new year, Quest does not have a first quarter advertising campaign, since it is changing advertising agencies at that time. This results in sales of just 21,000 blue widgets during the year. Its sales volume variance is:

(21,000 Units sold - 25,000 Budgeted units) × $65 Budgeted price per unit

= $260,000 Unfavorable sales volume variance

---

There are a number of possible causes of a sales volume variance. For example:

- *Cannibalization.* The company may have released another product that competes with the product in question. Thus, sales of one product cannibalize sales of the other product.
- *Competition.* Competitors may have released new products that are more attractive to customers.
- *Price.* The company may have altered the product price, which in turn drives a change in unit sales volume.
- *Trade restrictions.* A foreign country may have altered its barriers to competition.

## Overview of Cost of Goods Sold Variance Reporting

A number of variances have been developed for expenses categorized within the cost of goods sold. When a budget is created, this results in a standard cost against which actual costs and usage can be compared. There are two basic types of variances from a standard that can arise, which are the rate variance and the volume variance. They are:

- *Rate variance.* A rate variance (also known as a *price variance)* is the difference between the actual price paid for something and the expected price, multiplied by the actual quantity purchased. The "rate" variance designation is most commonly applied to the labor rate variance, which involves the actual cost of direct labor in comparison to the standard cost of direct labor. The rate variance uses a different designation when applied to the purchase of materials, and may be called the *purchase price variance* or the *material price variance.*
- *Volume variance.* A volume variance is the difference between the actual quantity sold or consumed and the budgeted amount, multiplied by the standard price or cost per unit. If the variance relates to the sale of goods, it

is called the *sales volume variance*. If it relates to the use of direct materials, it is called the *material yield variance*. If the variance relates to the use of direct labor, it is called the *labor efficiency variance*. Finally, if the variance relates to the application of overhead, it is called the *overhead efficiency variance*.

Thus, variances are based on either changes in cost from the expected amount, or changes in the quantity from the expected amount. The most common variances that are reported on are subdivided within the rate and volume variance categories for direct materials, direct labor, and overhead. The primary variances are noted in the following exhibit.

**Primary Variances to be Reported**

| | Rate Variance | Volume Variance |
|---|---|---|
| Materials | Purchase price variance | Material yield variance |
| Direct labor | Labor rate variance | Labor efficiency variance |
| Fixed overhead | Fixed overhead spending variance | Not applicable |
| Variable overhead | Variable overhead spending variance | Variable overhead efficiency variance |

All of the variances noted in the preceding table are explained in the following sections, including examples to demonstrate how the variances are applied.

## The Purchase Price Variance

The purchase price variance is the difference between the actual price paid to buy an item and its standard price, multiplied by the actual number of units purchased. The formula is:

(Actual price - Standard price) × Actual quantity = Purchase price variance

A positive variance means that actual costs have increased, and a negative variance means that actual costs have declined.

The standard price is the price that the company's engineers believe the company should pay for an item, given a certain quality level, purchasing quantity, and speed of delivery. Thus, the variance is really based on a standard price that was the collective opinion of several employees based on a number of assumptions that may no longer match a company's current purchasing situation.

---

**EXAMPLE**

During the development of its annual budget, the engineers and purchasing staff of Quest Adventure Gear decide that the standard cost of a green widget should be set at $5.00, which is based on a purchasing volume of 10,000 for the upcoming year. During the subsequent year, Quest only buys 8,000 units, and so cannot take advantage of purchasing discounts, and ends up paying $5.50 per widget. This creates a purchase price variance of $0.50 per widget, and a variance of $4,000 for all of the 8,000 widgets that Quest purchased.

---

There are a number of possible causes of a purchase price variance. For example:

- *Layering issue.* The actual cost may have been taken from an inventory layering system, such as a first-in first-out system, where the actual cost may vary from the current market price by a substantial margin.
- *Materials shortage.* There is an industry shortage of a commodity item, which is driving up the cost.
- *New supplier.* The company has changed suppliers for any number of reasons, resulting in a new cost structure that is not reflected in the budget.
- *Rush basis.* The company incurred excessive shipping charges to obtain materials on short notice from suppliers.
- *Volume assumption.* The budgeted cost of an item was derived based on a different purchasing volume than the amount at which the company now buys.

In what level of detail should one investigate a purchase price variance? The key issue is not to waste time on variances so small that the management team will not take action. Instead, report on the 20 percent of issues that usually cause about 80 percent of the variance. The following sample report format should contain sufficient information for a manager to engage in corrective action.

**Sample Purchase Price Variance Report**

| Item No. | Item Description | Purchase Price | Standard Price | Variance | Reason |
|---|---|---|---|---|---|
| 123A | Widget trim | $8.00 | $7.00 | -$1.00 | Ordered below standard quantity |
| 234B | Widget blue color | 4.25 | 3.00 | -1.25 | Ordered odd size lot |
| 567Q | Widget arm | 20.00 | 16.50 | -3.50 | Incorrect specifications |
| 891D | Widget case | 15.00 | 12.00 | -3.00 | Ordered on short notice |
| 112R | Widget housing | 130.00 | 115.00 | -15.00 | Ordered below standard quantity |
| 150F | Widget lens port | 82.15 | 78.00 | -4.15 | Supplier price increase |
| 115G | Widget trigger | 4.25 | 3.75 | -0.50 | Ordered on short notice |
| 227V | Widget base | 37.50 | 32.00 | -5.50 | Supplier price increase |
| 772J | Widget packing crate | 24.00 | 21.50 | -2.50 | Ordered odd lot size |

## Material Yield Variance

The material yield variance is the difference between the actual amount of material used and the standard amount expected to be used, multiplied by the standard cost of the materials. The formula is:

(Actual unit usage - Standard unit usage) × Standard cost per unit

= Material yield variance

An unfavorable variance means that the unit usage was greater than anticipated.

The standard unit usage is developed by the engineering staff, and is based on expected scrap rates in a production process, the quality of raw materials, losses during equipment setup, and related factors.

---

**EXAMPLE**

The engineering staff of Quest Adventure Gear estimates that eight ounces of rubber will be required to produce a green widget. During the most recent month, the production process used 315,000 ounces of rubber to create 35,000 green widgets, which is nine ounces per product. Each ounce of rubber has a standard cost of $0.50. Its material yield variance for the month is:

(315,000 Actual unit usage - 280,000 Standard unit usage) × $0.50 Standard cost/unit

= $17,500 Material yield variance

---

There are a number of possible causes of a material yield variance. For example:

- *Scrap*. Unusual amounts of scrap may be generated by changes in machine setups, or because changes in acceptable tolerance levels are altering the amount of scrap produced. A change in the pattern of quality inspections can also alter the amount of scrap.
- *Material quality*. If the material quality level changes, this can alter the amount of quality rejections. If an entirely different material is substituted, this can also alter the amount of rejections.
- *Spoilage*. The amount of spoilage may change in concert with alterations in inventory handling and storage.

It can be extremely difficult to ascertain the reasons for a material yield variance, since it is caused by operational issues in the production area, rather than something easily searchable in the accounting database. The report format is similar to the purchase price variance report just described, except that it is in units, rather than dollars. A sample report follows.

**Sample Material Yield Variance Report**

| Item No. | Item Description | Actual Usage | Standard Usage | Variance | Reason |
|---|---|---|---|---|---|
| 123A | Widget trim | 540 | 500 | -40 | Incorrect standard |
| 234B | Widget blue color | 200 | 150 | -50 | Materials too old; disposed of |
| 567Q | Widget arm | 1,500 | 1,100 | -400 | Supplier shipped short |
| 891D | Widget case | 800 | -720 | -80 | Incorrect machine setup |
| 112R | Widget housing | 150 | 0 | -150 | Item declared obsolete |
| 150F | Widget lens port | 300 | 100 | -200 | Receipt counting error |
| 115G | Widget trigger | 280 | 225 | -55 | Scrap due to machinist error |
| 227V | Widget base | 460 | 300 | -160 | Item declared obsolete |
| 772J | Widget packing crate | 950 | 800 | -150 | Damaged in transit |

## Labor Rate Variance

The labor rate variance is the difference between the actual labor rate paid and the standard rate, multiplied by the number of actual hours worked. The formula is:

(Actual rate - Standard rate) × Actual hours worked = Labor rate variance

An unfavorable variance means that the cost of labor was more expensive than anticipated.

The standard labor rate is developed by the human resources and industrial engineering employees, and is based on such factors as the expected mix of pay levels among the production staff, the amount of overtime likely to be incurred, the amount of new hiring at different pay rates, the number of promotions into higher pay levels, and the outcome of contract negotiations with any unions representing the production staff.

---

**EXAMPLE**

The human resources manager of Quest Adventure Gear estimates that the average labor rate for the coming year for Quest's production staff will be $25/hour. This estimate is based on a standard mix of personnel at different pay rates, as well as a reasonable proportion of overtime hours worked.

During the first month of the new year, Quest has difficulty hiring a sufficient number of new employees, and so must have its higher-paid existing staff work overtime to complete a number of jobs. The result is an actual labor rate of $30/hour. Quest's production staff worked 10,000 hours during the month. Its labor rate variance for the month is:

($30/hr Actual rate - $25/hour Standard rate) × 10,000 Hours = $50,000 Labor rate variance

---

There are a number of possible causes of a labor rate variance. For example:

- *Incorrect standards*. The labor standard may not reflect recent changes in the rates paid to employees (which tend to occur in bulk for all staff).
- *Pay premiums*. The actual amounts paid may include extra payments for shift differentials or overtime.
- *Staffing variances*. A labor standard may assume that a certain job classification will perform a designated task, when in fact a different position with a different pay rate may be performing the work.

## Labor Efficiency Variance

The labor efficiency variance is the difference between the actual labor hours used to produce an item and the standard amount that should have been used, multiplied by the standard labor rate. The formula is:

(Actual hours - Standard hours) × Standard rate = Labor efficiency variance

An unfavorable variance means that labor efficiency has worsened, and a favorable variance means that labor efficiency has increased.

The standard number of hours represents the best estimate of the industrial engineers regarding the optimal speed at which the production staff can manufacture goods. This figure can vary considerably, based on assumptions regarding the setup time of a production run, the availability of materials and machine capacity, employee skill levels, the duration of a production run, and other factors. Thus, the multitude of variables involved makes it especially difficult to create a budget that can be meaningfully compared to actual results.

---

**EXAMPLE**

During the development of its annual budget, the industrial engineers of Quest Adventure Gear decide that the standard amount of time required to produce a green widget should be 30 minutes, which is based on certain assumptions about the efficiency of Quest's production staff, the availability of materials, capacity availability, and so forth. During the month, widget materials were in short supply, so Quest had to pay production staff even when there was no material to work on, resulting in an average production time per unit of 45 minutes. The company produced 1,000 widgets during the month. The standard cost per labor hour is $20, so the calculation of its labor efficiency variance is:

(750 Actual hours - 500 Standard hours) × $20 Standard rate

= $5,000 Labor efficiency variance

---

There are a number of possible causes of a labor efficiency variance. For example:

- *Instructions*. The employees may not have received written work instructions.
- *Mix*. The standard assumes a certain mix of employees involving different skill levels, which does not match the actual staffing.
- *Training*. The standard may be based on an assumption of a minimum amount of training that employees have not received.
- *Work station configuration*. A work center may have been reconfigured since the standard was created, so the budget is now incorrect.

## Variable Overhead Spending Variance

The variable overhead spending variance is the difference between the actual and budgeted rates of spending on variable overhead. The formula is:

Actual hours worked × (Actual overhead rate - Standard overhead rate)

= Variable overhead spending variance

A favorable variance means that the actual variable overhead expenses incurred per labor hour were less than expected.

The variable overhead spending variance is a compilation of production expense information submitted by the production department, and the projected labor hours to be worked, as estimated by the industrial engineering and production scheduling staffs, based on historical and projected efficiency and equipment capacity levels.

---

**EXAMPLE**

The accounting staff of Quest Adventure Gear calculates, based on historical and projected cost patterns, that the company should experience a variable overhead rate of $20 per labor hour worked, and builds this figure into the budget. In April, the actual variable overhead rate turns out to be $22 per labor hour. During that month, production employees work 18,000 hours. The variable overhead spending variance is:

18,000 Actual hours worked × ($22 Actual variable overhead rate - $20 Standard overhead rate)

= $36,000 Variable overhead spending variance

---

There are a number of possible causes of a variable overhead spending variance. For example:

- *Account misclassification*. The variable overhead category includes a number of accounts, some of which may have been incorrectly classified and so do not appear as part of variable overhead (or vice versa).

- *Outsourcing.* Some activities that had been sourced in-house have now been shifted to a supplier, or vice versa.
- *Supplier pricing.* Suppliers have changed their prices, which have not been reflected in the budget.

## Variable Overhead Efficiency Variance

The variable overhead efficiency variance is the difference between the actual and budgeted hours worked, which are then applied to the standard variable overhead rate per hour. The formula is:

Standard overhead rate × (Actual hours - Standard hours)

= Variable overhead efficiency variance

A favorable variance means that the actual hours worked were less than the budgeted hours, resulting in the application of the standard overhead rate across fewer hours, resulting in less expense incurred.

The variable overhead efficiency variance is a compilation of production expense information submitted by the production department, and the projected labor hours to be worked, as estimated by the industrial engineering and production scheduling staffs, based on historical and projected efficiency and equipment capacity levels.

---

**EXAMPLE**

The accounting staff of Quest Adventure Gear calculates, based on historical and projected labor patterns, that the company's production staff should work 20,000 hours per month and incur $400,000 of variable overhead costs per month, so it establishes a variable overhead rate of $20 per hour. In May, Quest installs a new materials handling system that significantly improves production efficiency and drops the hours worked during the month to 19,000. The variable overhead efficiency variance is:

$20 Standard overhead rate/hour × (19,000 Hours worked - 20,000 Standard hours)

= $20,000 Variable overhead efficiency variance

---

## Fixed Overhead Spending Variance

The fixed overhead spending variance is the difference between the actual fixed overhead expense incurred and the budgeted fixed overhead expense. An unfavorable variance means that actual overhead expenditures were greater than planned. The formula is:

Actual fixed overhead - Budgeted fixed overhead = Fixed overhead spending variance

The amount of expense related to fixed overhead should (as the name implies) be relatively fixed, and so the fixed overhead spending variance should not theoretically vary much from the budget. However, if the manufacturing process reaches a step cost trigger point where a whole new expense must be incurred, this can cause a significant unfavorable variance. Also, there may be some seasonality in fixed overhead expenditures, which may cause both favorable and unfavorable variances in individual months of a year, but which cancel each other out over the full year.

---

**EXAMPLE**

The production manager of Quest Adventure Gear estimates that fixed overhead should be $700,000 during the upcoming year. However, since a production manager left the company and was not replaced for several months, actual expenses were lower than expected, at $672,000. This created the following favorable fixed overhead spending variance:

$672,000 Actual fixed overhead - $700,000 Budgeted fixed overhead

= $(28,000) Fixed overhead spending variance

---

There are a number of possible causes of a fixed overhead spending variance. For example:

- *Account misclassification.* The fixed overhead category includes a number of accounts, some of which may have been incorrectly classified and so do not appear as part of fixed overhead (or vice versa).
- *Outsourcing.* Some activities that had been sourced in-house have now been shifted to a supplier, or vice versa.
- *Supplier pricing.* Suppliers have changed their prices, which have not been reflected in the budget.

## Problems with Variance Analysis

There are several problems with the variances described in this chapter, which are:

- *The use of standards*. A central issue is the use of standards (i.e., the budget) as the basis for calculating variances. What is the motivation for creating a standard? Standard creation can be a political process where the amount agreed upon is designed to make a department look good, rather than setting a target that will improve the company. If standards are politically created, variance analysis becomes useless from the perspective of controlling the company.
- *Feedback loop*. The accounting department does not calculate variances between actual and budgeted results until after it has closed the books and created financial statements, so there is a gap of potentially an entire month from when a variance arises and when it is reported to management. A faster feedback loop would be to eliminate variance reporting and instead create a reporting process that provides for feedback within moments of the occurrence of a triggering event.
- *Information drill down*. Many of the issues that cause variances are not stored within the accounting database. For example, the reason for excessive material usage may be a machine setup error, while excessive labor usage may be caused by the use of an excessive amount of employee overtime. In neither case will the accounting staff discover these issues by examining their transactional data. Thus, a variance report only highlights the general areas within which problems occurred, but does not necessarily tell anyone the nature of the underlying problems.

The preceding issues do not always keep the accounting staff from calculating complete sets of variances for management consumption, but they do bring the question of whether the work required to calculate variances is a good use of staff time.

## Which Variances to Report

A large number of variances have been described in this chapter. Do managers really need to see the entire set? Not necessarily. If management agrees with a reduced reporting structure, reporting can be for just those variances over which the management team has some ability to reduce costs, and which contain sufficiently large variances to be worth reporting on. The following table provides commentary on the characteristics of the presented variances.

## Commentary on Variances

| Name of Variance | Commentary |
|---|---|
| **Materials** | |
| Purchase price variance | Material costs are controllable to some extent, and comprise a large part of the cost of goods sold; possibly the most important variance |
| Material yield variance | Can contain large potential cost reductions driven by quality issues, production layouts, and process flow; a good opportunity for cost reductions |
| **Labor** | |
| Labor rate variance | Labor rates are difficult to change; do not track unless work can be shifted into lower pay grades |
| Labor efficiency variance | Can drive contrary behavior in favor of long production runs, when less labor efficiency in a just-in-time environment results in greater overall cost reductions; not recommended |
| **Overhead** | |
| Variable overhead spending variance | Caused by changes in the actual costs in the overhead cost pool, and so should be reviewed |
| Variable overhead efficiency variance | Caused by a change in the basis of allocation, which has no real impact on underlying costs; not recommended |
| Fixed overhead spending variance | Since fixed overhead costs should not vary much, a variance here is worth careful review; however, most components of fixed overhead are long-term costs that cannot be easily changed in the short term |
| **Revenue** | |
| Selling price variance | Caused by a change in the product price, which is under management control, and therefore should be brought to their attention |
| Sales volume variance | Caused by a change in the unit volume sold, which is not under direct management control, though this can be impacted by altering the product price |

The preceding table shows that the variances most worthy of management's attention are the purchase price variance, variable overhead spending variance, fixed overhead spending variance, and selling price variance.

## Summary

A great many variance calculations were discussed in this chapter. Just because they have been presented does not mean that managers need to see them. Consider instead that management usually does not have time to read a complete variance report, much less act on it. A more effective report is one that contains the specific reasons for problems, and which is packaged so that the causes of the variances are readily understandable and can be acted upon at once.

A system of budgetary control will only work if the budgeted baselines are intended to set a reasonable guideline for improved company performance. Instead, if the budget was politically derived to allow managers to always report favorable variances, there is not much point in using a budget to control company operations. Under such circumstances, it may be more effective to simply monitor revenues and expenses on a trend line, or to compare results to a short-term rolling forecast.

# Glossary

### *A*

*Accounting change.* A change in an accounting principle, accounting estimate, or reporting entity.

*Accrual basis of accounting.* A system for recording revenues when earned and expenses as incurred.

*Acquiree.* A business that an acquirer gains control of via a business combination.

*Acquirer.* An entity that gains control of an acquiree.

*Activity driver.* The most significant cause of an activity.

*Allocation base.* The basis upon which an entity allocates its overhead costs.

*Amortization.* The write-off of an intangible asset over its expected period of use.

*Available-for-sale securities.* Investments that are not classified as held-to-maturity or trading securities.

### *B*

*Bargain purchase.* A business combination in which the fair value received by the acquirer exceeds the consideration paid.

*Breakeven point.* The sales level at which a business earns a zero profit.

### *C*

*Capitalization limit.* A minimum threshold above which an expenditure is recorded as a long-term asset, and below which it is charged to expense.

*Carryback.* A tax deduction or a tax credit that cannot be used in the tax return for the current year, but which can be used in an earlier year to reduce the amount of taxable income or taxes payable.

*Carryforward.* A tax deduction or tax credit that cannot be used in the tax return for the current year, but which can be used in a future period to reduce the amount of taxable income or taxes payable.

*Carrying amount.* The recorded amount of an asset, net of any accumulated depreciation or accumulated impairment losses.

*Cash basis of accounting.* A system for recording revenues when cash is received and expenses when cash is paid out.

*Causal relationship.* A situation where one event is brought about by another. Thus, an activity causes specific changes elsewhere.

*Change in accounting estimate.* A change that adjusts the carrying amount of an asset or liability, or the subsequent accounting for it.

*Change in accounting principle*. A change from one generally accepted accounting principle to another, or a change in the method of applying it.

*Compensated absence*. An employee absence for which the employee will be paid.

*Comprehensive income*. The change in equity of a business during a period, not including investments by or distributions to owners.

*Contribution margin*. The margin that results when variable production costs are subtracted from revenue.

*Cost object*. An item for which a cost is compiled, such as a product service, project, customer, or activity.

*Cost pool*. A grouping of individual costs, typically by department or service center. Cost allocations are then made from the cost pool.

*Cross price elasticity of demand*. The percentage change in the demand for one product when the price of a different product changes.

*Current assets*. Cash and other assets that are expected to be converted into cash during the normal operating cycle of a business.

*Current liabilities*. Those liabilities whose payment is expected to require the use of current assets or their replacement with other current liabilities.

## D

*Debt*. A contractual right to receive payment that is considered an asset by the lender and a liability by the borrower.

*Deferred tax liability*. A tax whose payment is delayed due to taxable temporary differences.

*Depreciation*. The gradual charging to expense of an asset's cost over its expected useful life.

*Direct costs*. Costs that can be clearly associated with specific activities or products, such as direct materials.

*Direct method*. A format of the statement of cash flows that presents specific cash flows in the operating activities section of the report.

*Due diligence*. The investigation of the financial, operational, legal, and other aspects of a target company, prior to purchasing the business.

## F

*Fair value*. The price paid for an asset or liability in an orderly transaction between market participants.

*Fixed cost*. A cost that does not vary in the short term, irrespective of changes in activity levels.

## G

*General ledger*. The master set of accounts that summarize all financial transactions in a business. There may also be a subsidiary set of more detailed ledgers that summarize into the general ledger.

*Goodwill*. An intangible asset that represents the future benefits arising from assets acquired in a business combination that are not otherwise identified.

*Gross margin*. Revenues less the cost of goods sold.

## H

*Held-to-maturity securities*. A debt security that the holder intends to hold to maturity, and who has the ability to do so.

## I

*Impairment*. A condition that arises when the carrying amount of an asset exceeds its fair value.

*Indirect method*. A format of the statement of cash flows that uses accrual-basis accounting as part of the presentation of cash flow information.

*Inventory*. Tangible items held for routine sale, or which are being produced for sale, or which are consumed in the production of goods for sale.

## O

*Other comprehensive income*. Revenue, expense, gain, and loss items that are excluded from net income but included in comprehensive income.

*Overhead*. Those costs required to run a business, but which cannot be directly attributed to any specific business activity, product, or service.

## P

*Price elasticity of demand*. The degree to which changes in price impact the unit sales of a product or service.

## S

*Salvage value*. The estimated value of an asset at the end of its useful life.

*Subsequent event*. An event that occurs after the date of the balance sheet, but before financial statements have been issued or are available to be issued.

## T

*Tax position*. A position taken in a tax return that measures tax assets and liabilities, and which results in the permanent reduction or temporary deferral of income taxes.

*Transfer price*. The price at which one part of an entity sells a product or service to another part of the same entity.

*Trial balance*. A report listing the ending debit and credit balances in all accounts at the end of a reporting period.

## U

*Useful life*. The time period over which an asset is expected to be productive or enhance cash flows, or the number of units of production expected to be generated from it.

## V

*Variable cost.* A cost that varies in relation to changes in production or other activity volume.

*Vest*. When rights have been earned, such as when the end of a service period required for the issuance of shares has been reached.

## W

*Working capital.* The amount of an entity's current assets minus its current liabilities. The key components of working capital are cash, accounts receivable, inventory, and accounts payable.

# Index

CPSIA information can be obtained
at www.ICGtesting.com
Printed in the USA
FFHW011300300919
55323926-61045FF